Tender, originally published by kuš!, Latvia, 2015.
Discount Connection, originally published by kuš!, Latvia, 2014.

drawnandquarterly.com
pixmadeobjects.com

●

978-1-77046-385-1
First edition: June 2020.
Printed in China.
10 9 8 7 6 5 4 3 2 1

Cataloguing data available from Library and Archives Canada.

Published in the USA by Drawn & Quarterly, a client publisher of Farrar, Straus and Giroux.
Published in Canada by Drawn & Quarterly, a client publisher of Raincoast Books.
Published in the United Kingdom by Drawn & Quarterly,
    a client publisher of Publishers Group UK.

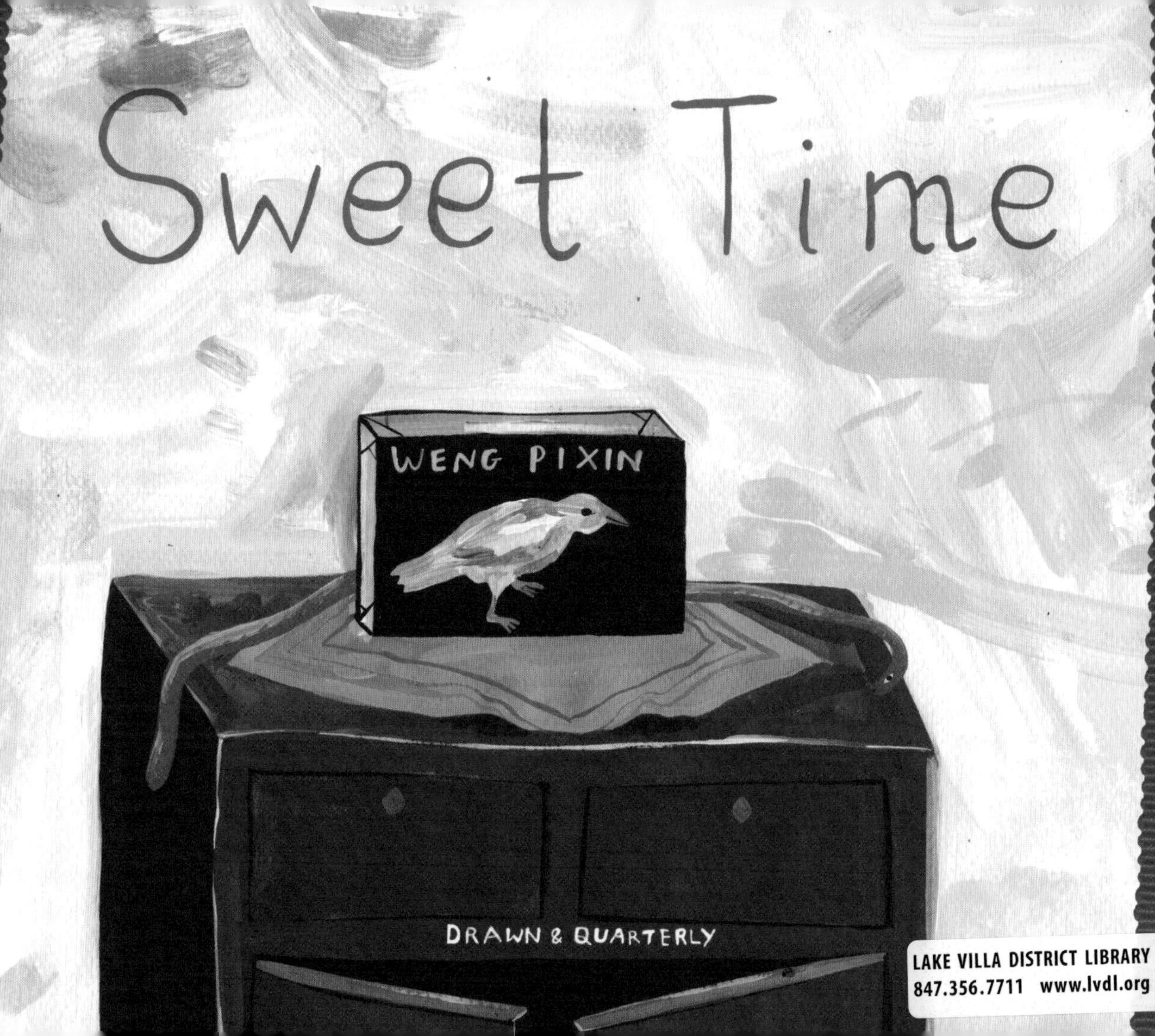
Sweet Time
WENG PIXIN
DRAWN & QUARTERLY

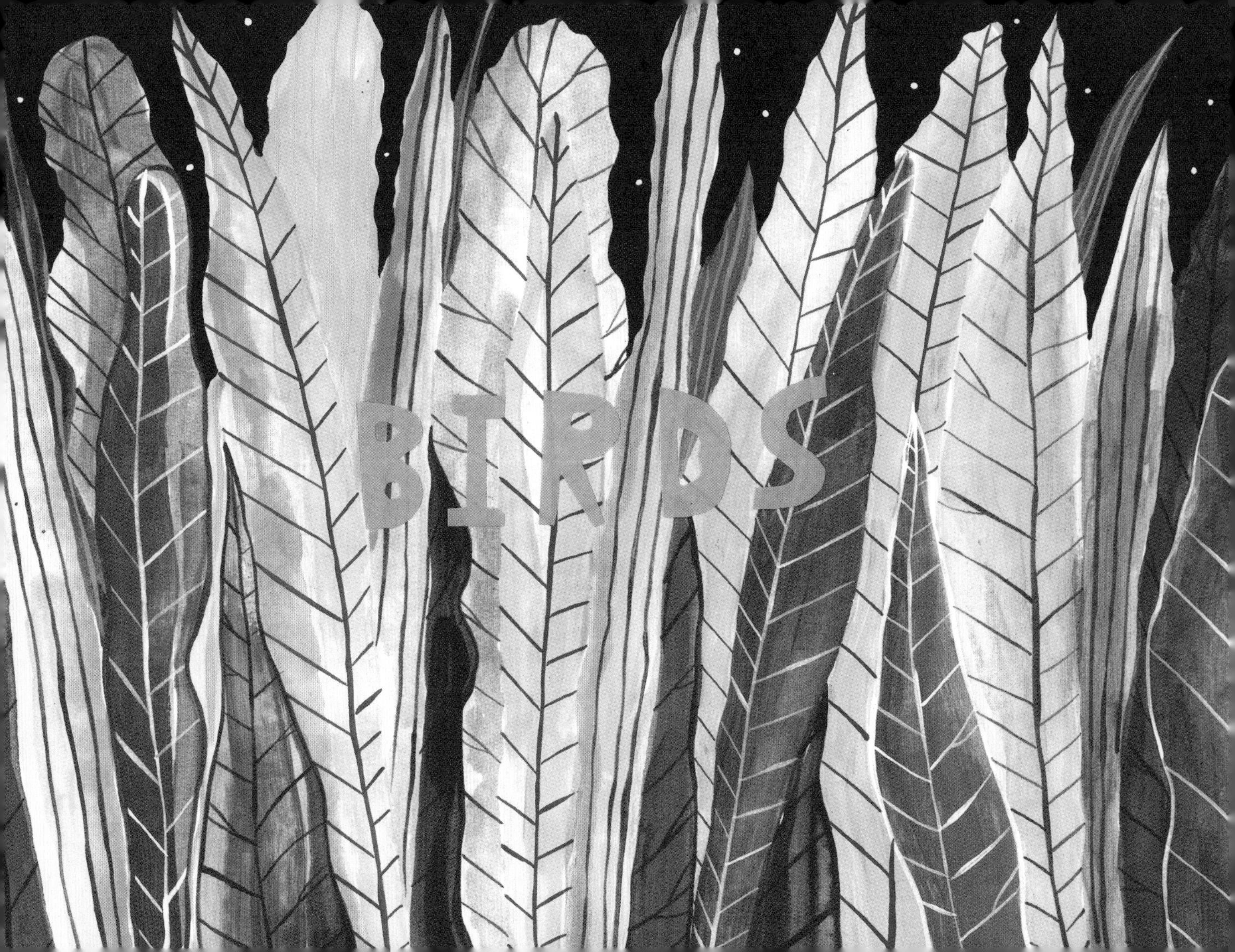
BIRDS

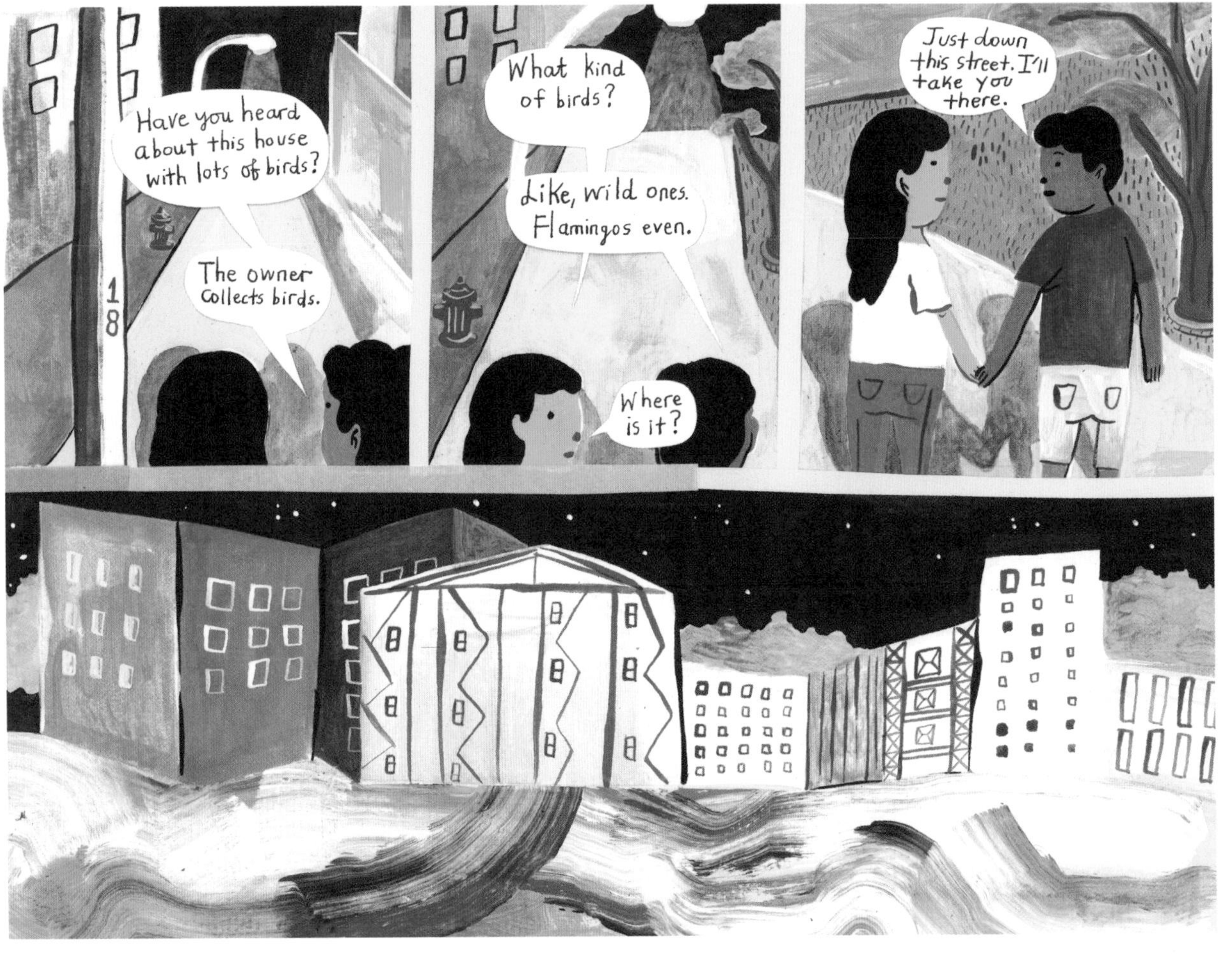
Have you heard about this house with lots of birds?
The owner collects birds.
What kind of birds?
Like, wild ones. Flamingos even.
Where is it?
Just down this street. I'll take you there.

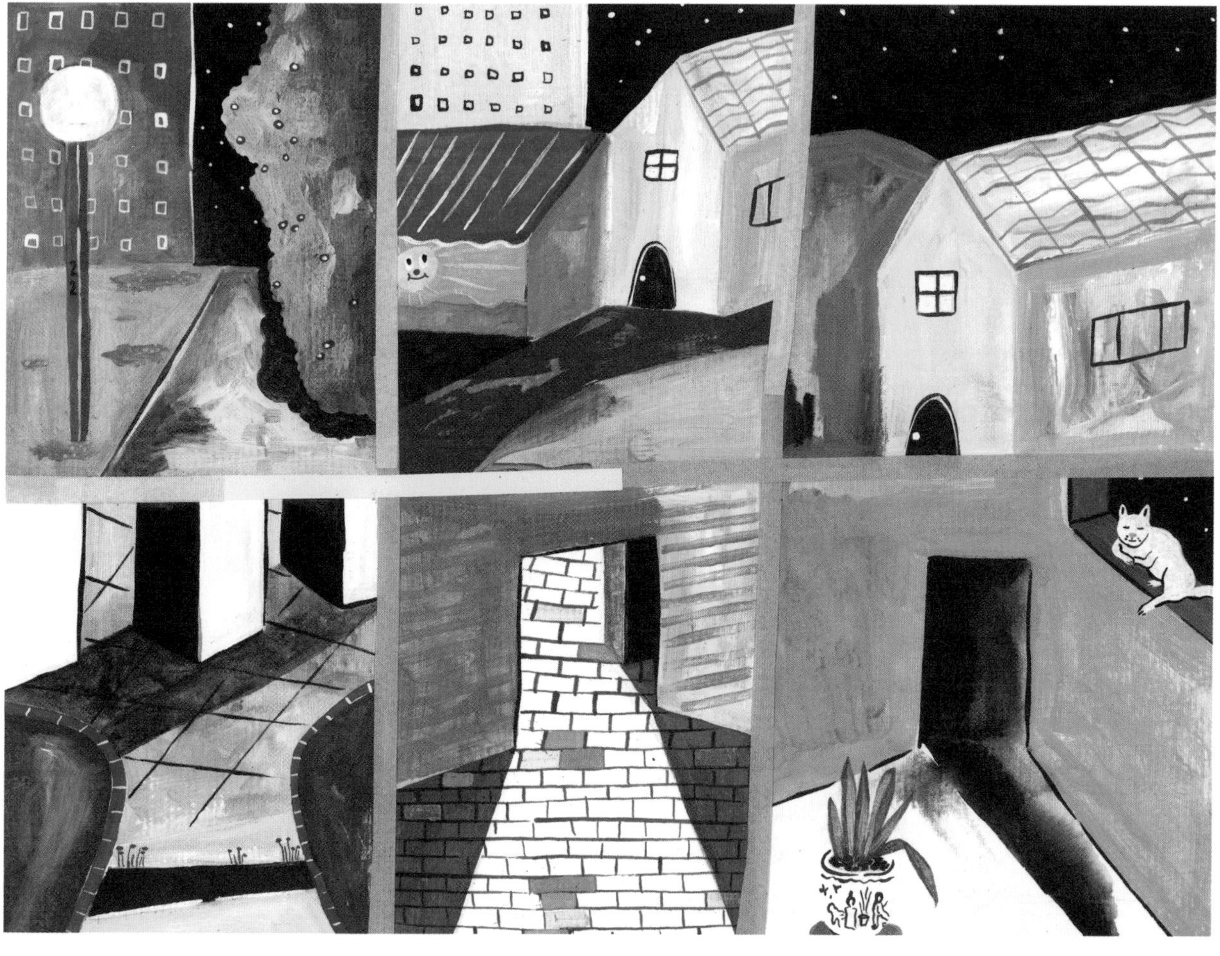

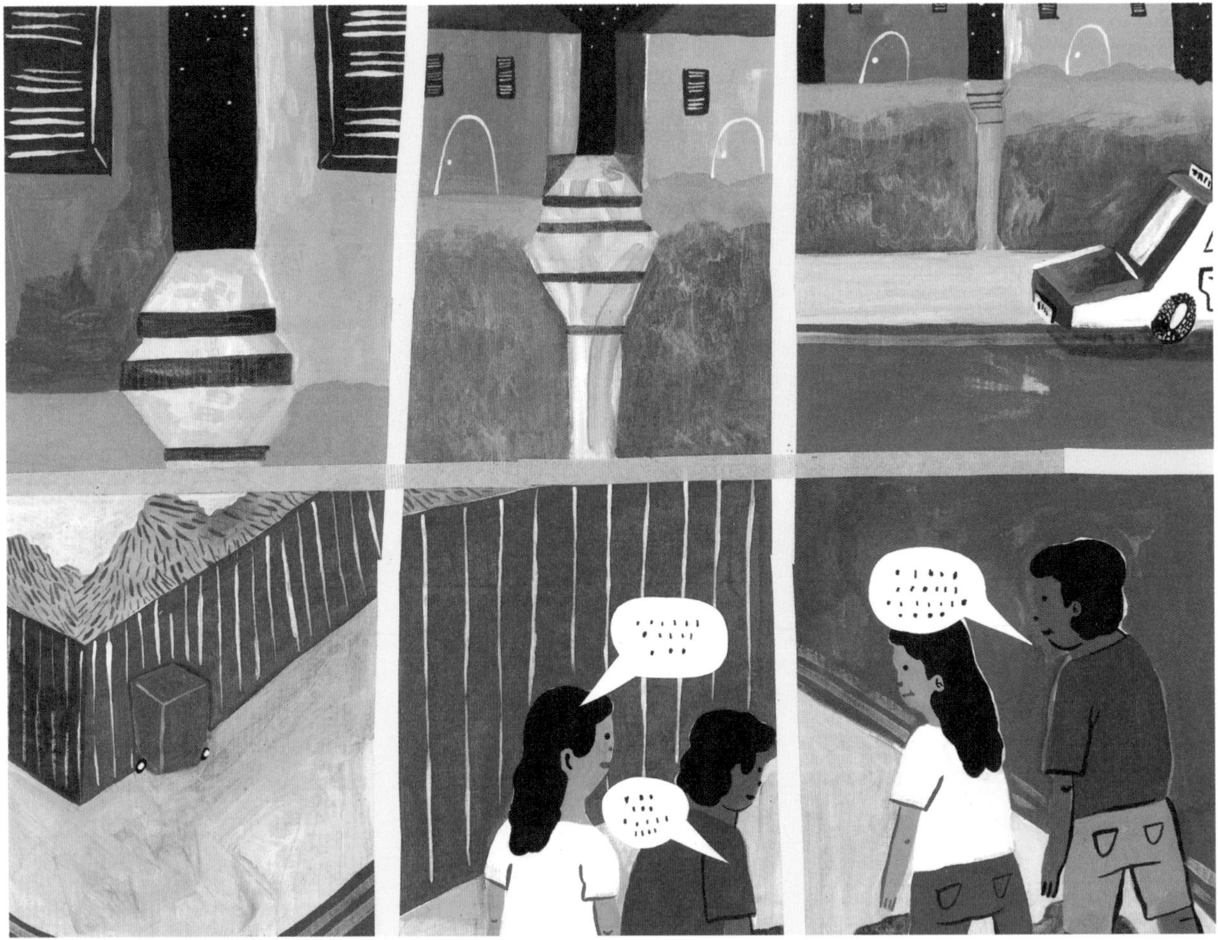

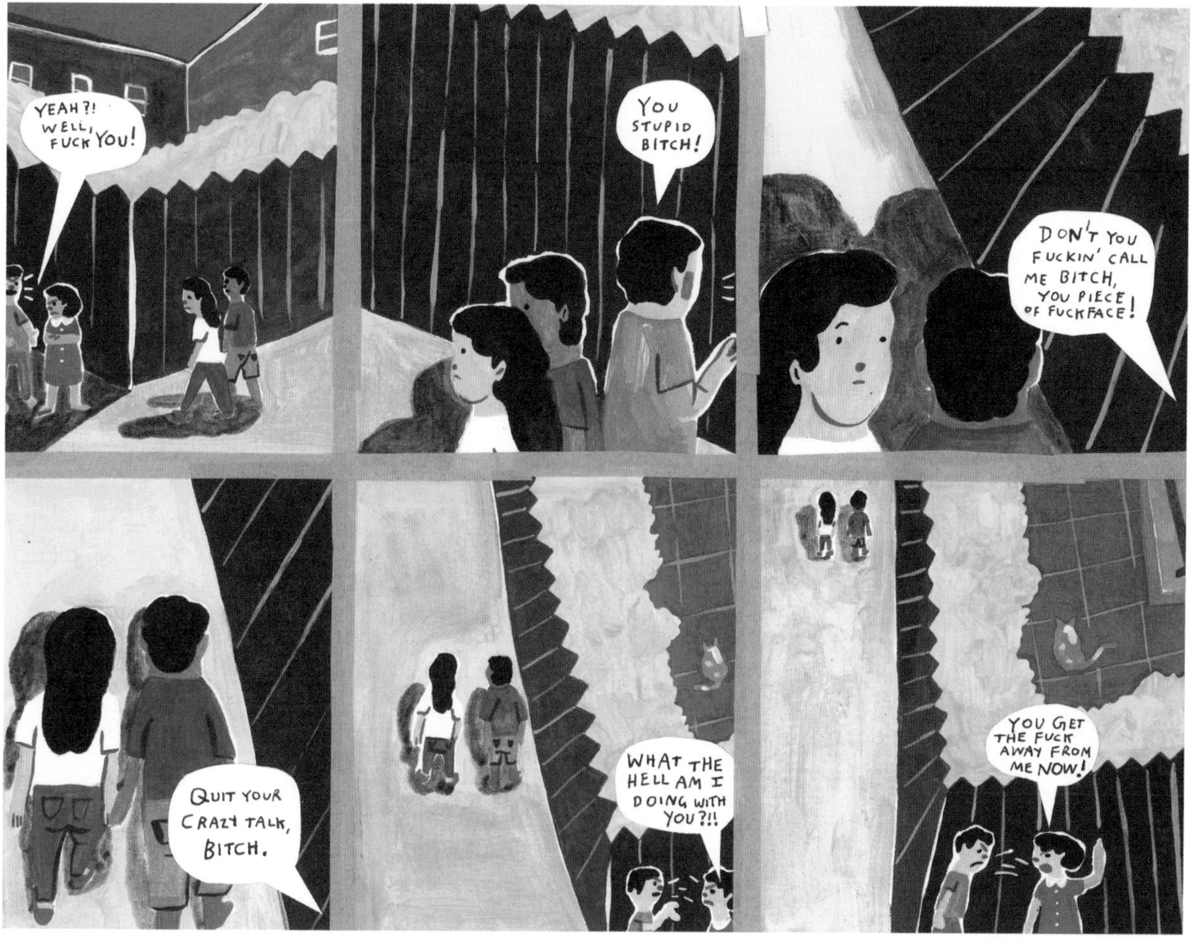
YEAH?! WELL, FUCK YOU!
YOU STUPID BITCH!
DON'T YOU FUCKIN' CALL ME BITCH, YOU PIECE OF FUCKFACE!
QUIT YOUR CRAZY TALK, BITCH.
WHAT THE HELL AM I DOING WITH YOU?!!
YOU GET THE FUCK AWAY FROM ME NOW!

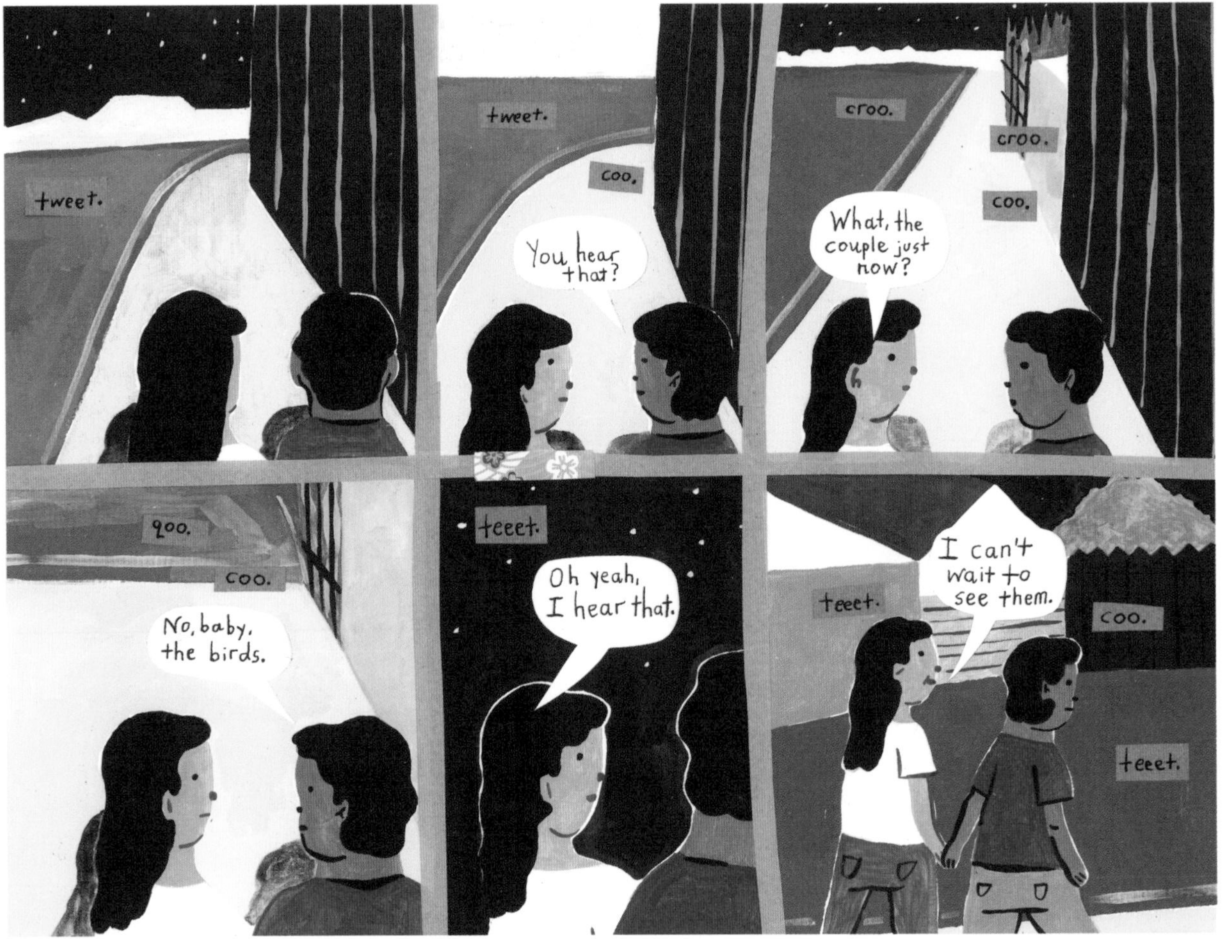
tweet.
tweet.
coo.
You hear that?
croo.
croo.
coo.
What, the couple just now?
qoo.
coo.
No, baby, the birds.
teeet.
Oh yeah, I hear that.
I can't wait to see them.
teeet.
coo.
teeet.

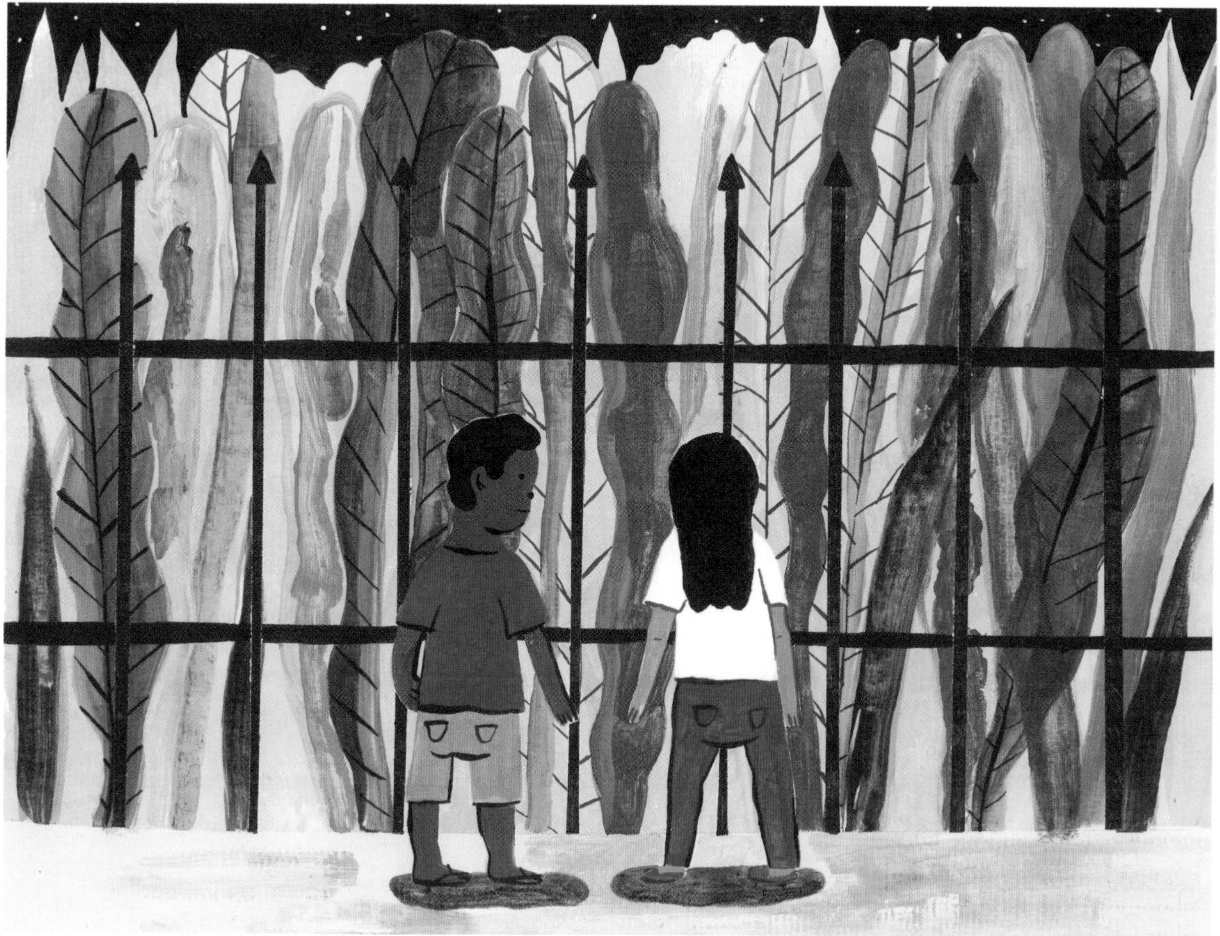

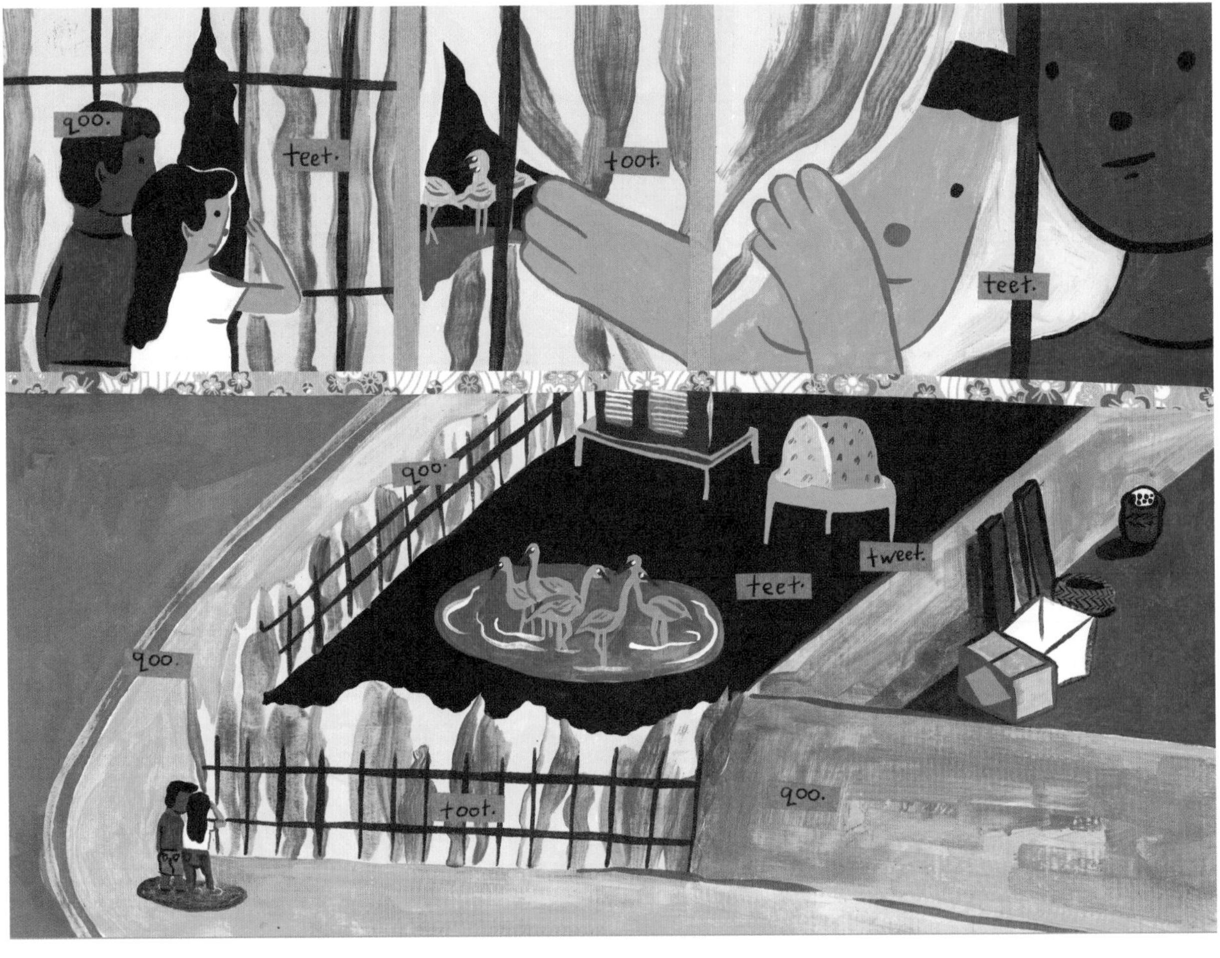

qoo.
teet.
toot.
teet.
qoo.
tweet.
teet.
qoo.
toot.
qoo.

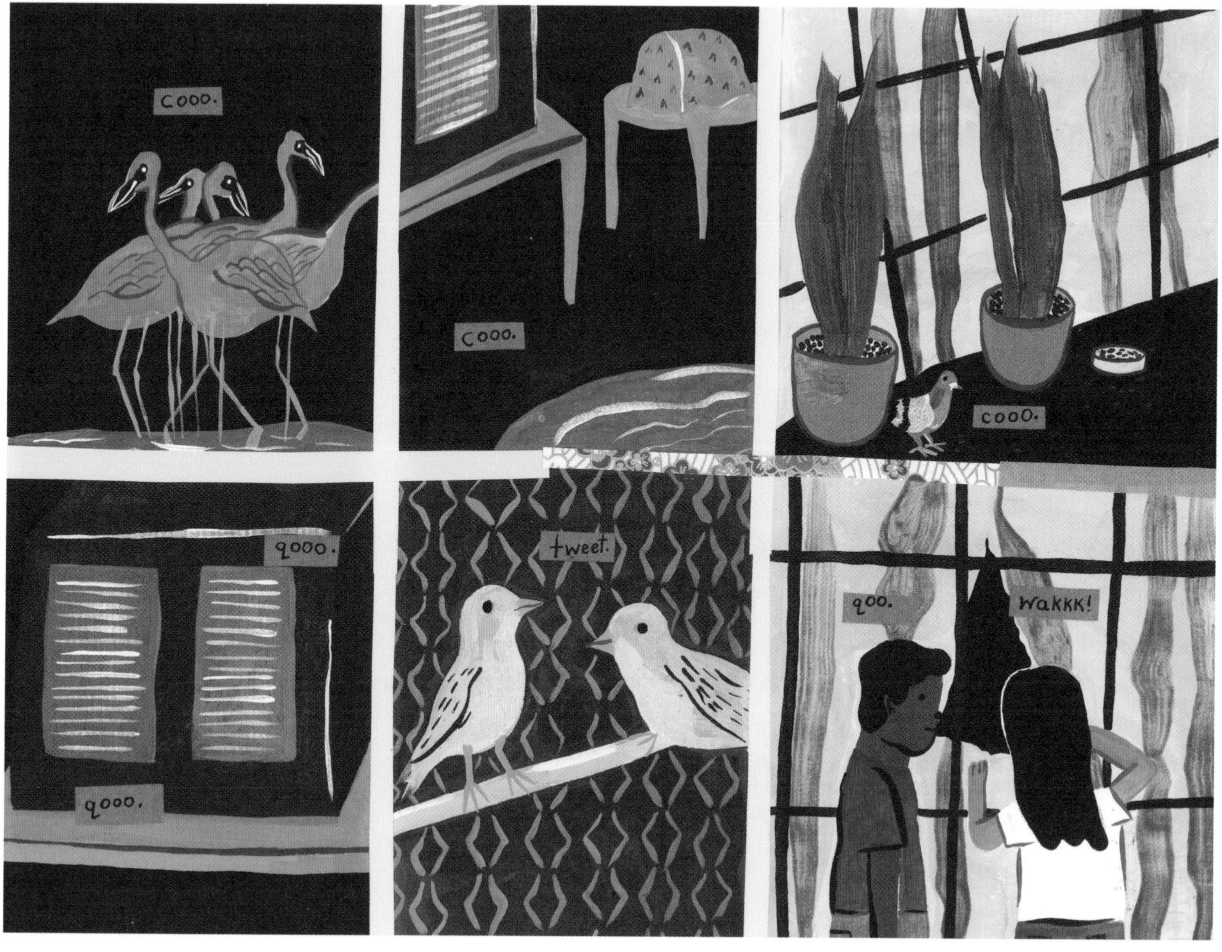
cooo.
cooo.
cooO.
qooo.
qooo.
tweet.
qoo.
wakkk!

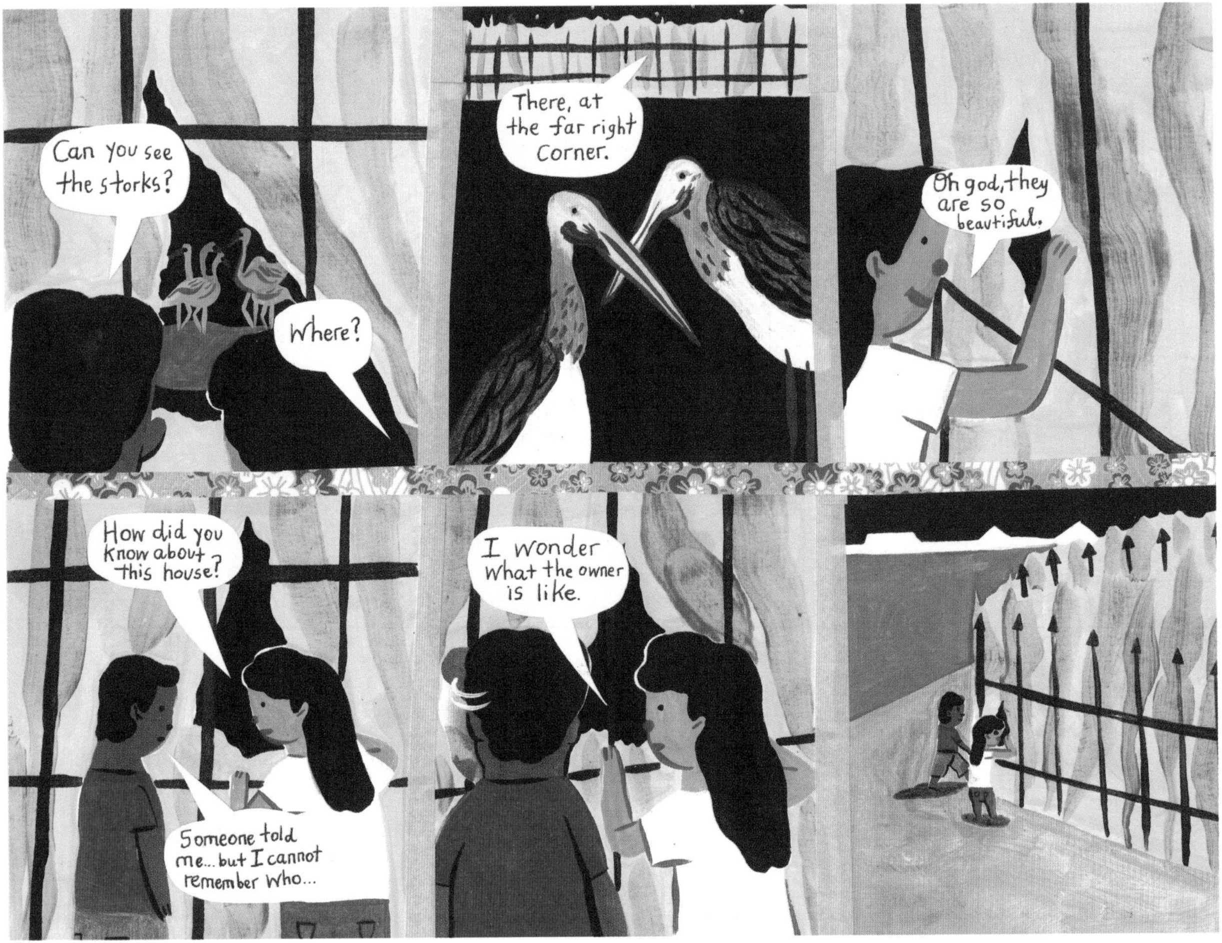
Can you see the storks?
Where?
There, at the far right corner.
Oh god, they are so beautiful.
How did you know about this house?
Someone told me... but I cannot remember who...
I wonder what the owner is like.

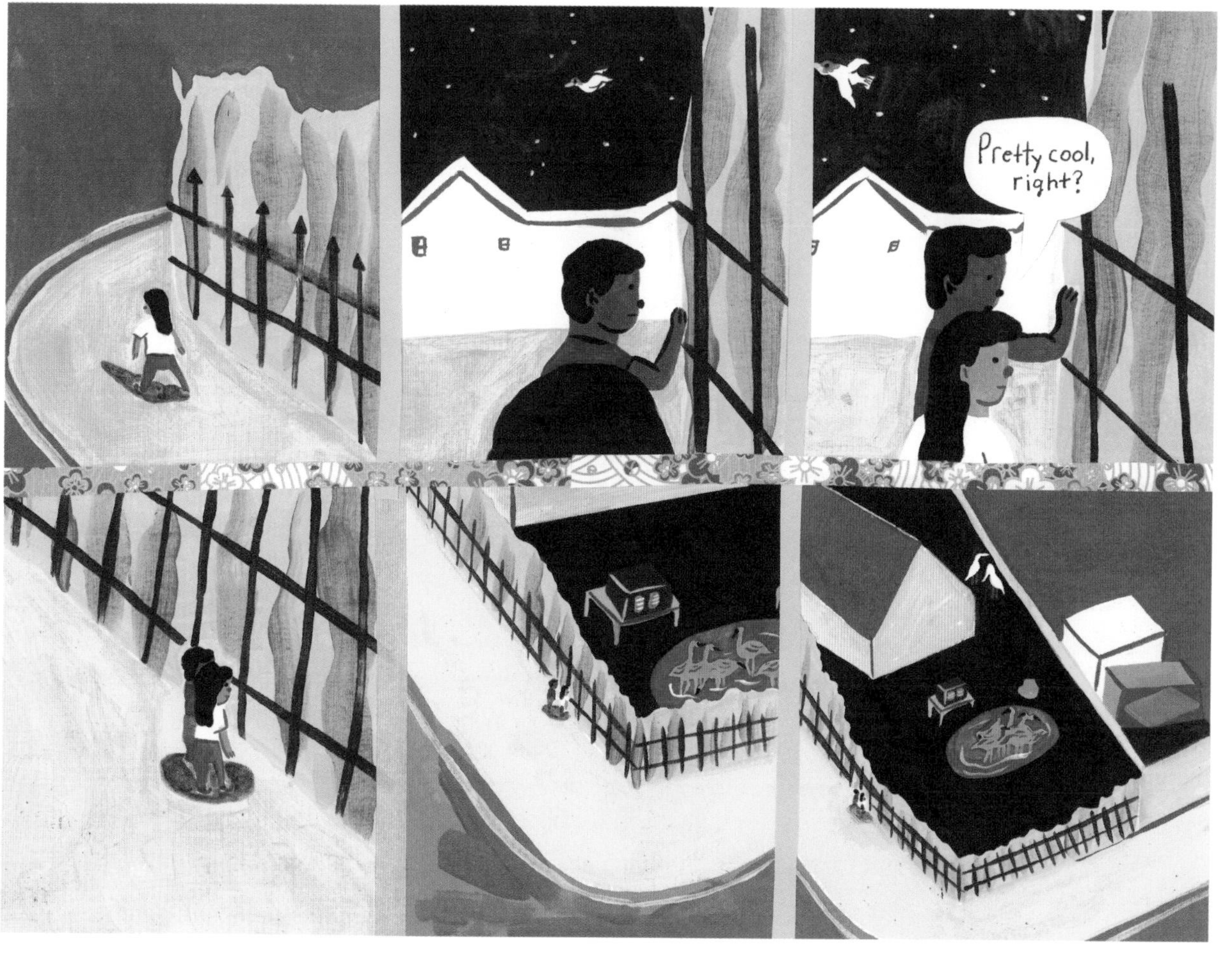
Pretty cool, right?

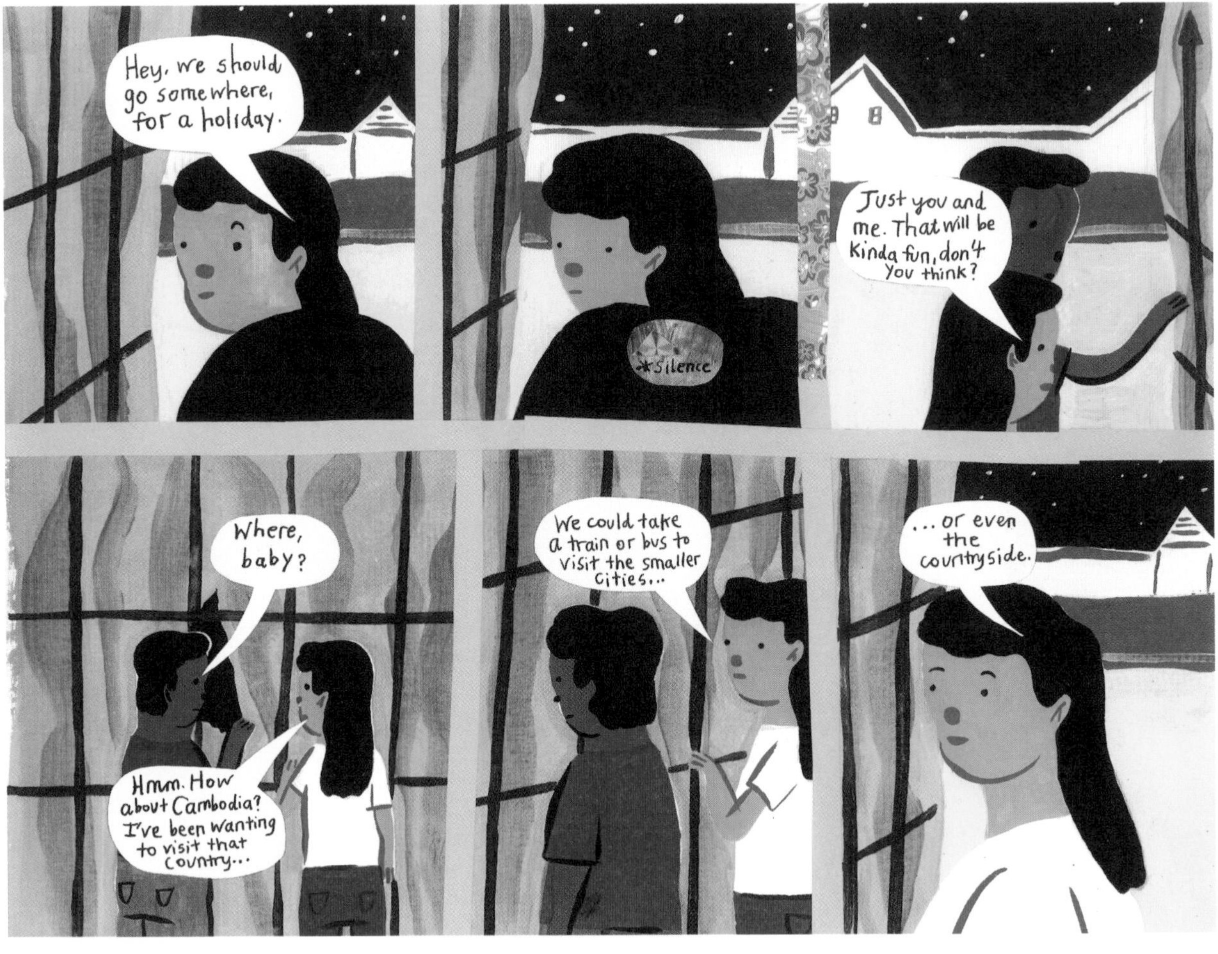
Hey, we should go somewhere, for a holiday.
*Silence
Just you and me. That will be kinda fun, don't you think?
Where, baby?
Hmm. How about Cambodia? I've been wanting to visit that country...
We could take a train or bus to visit the smaller cities...
...or even the countryside.

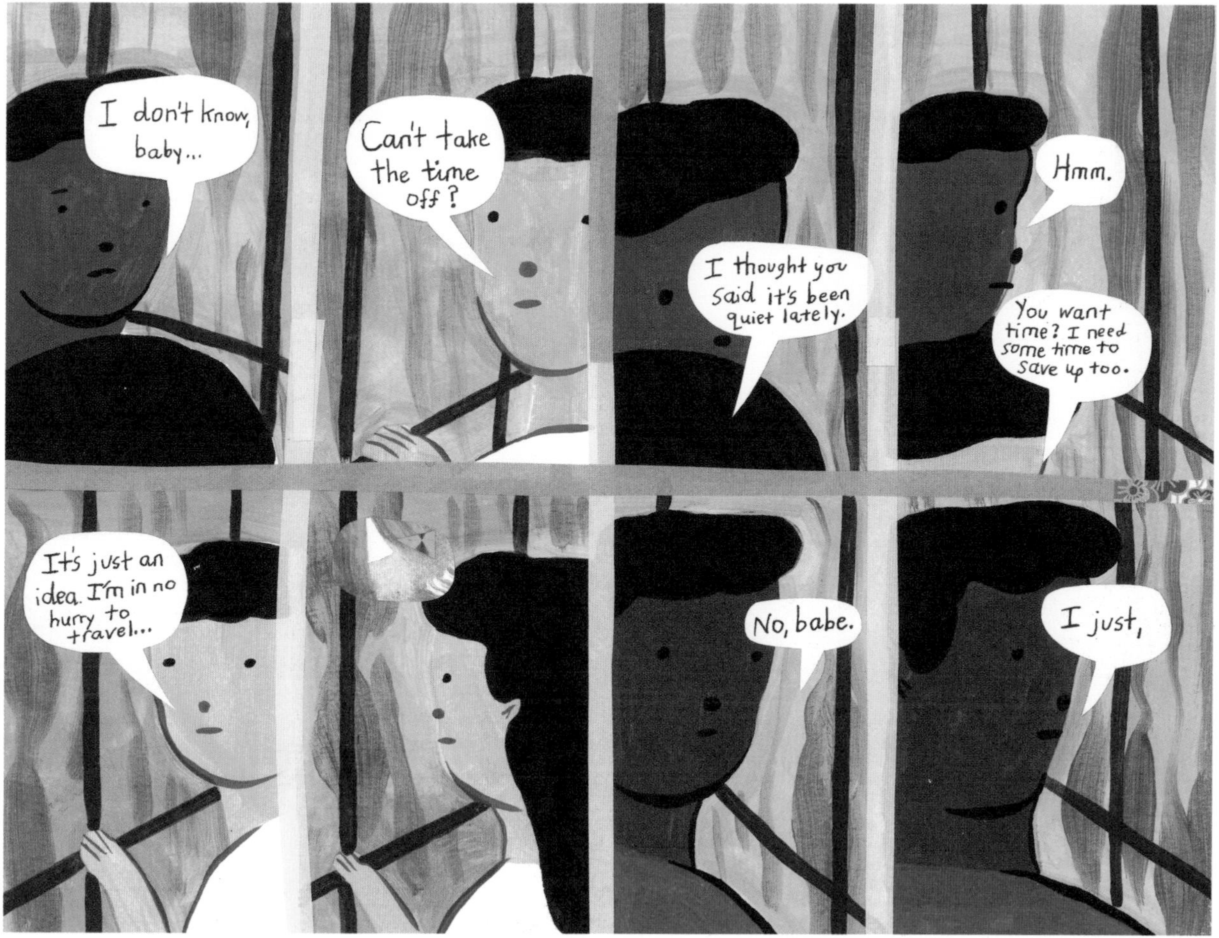
I don't know, baby...
Can't take the time off?
I thought you said it's been quiet lately.
Hmm.
You want time? I need some time to save up too.
It's just an idea. I'm in no hurry to travel...
No, babe.
I just,

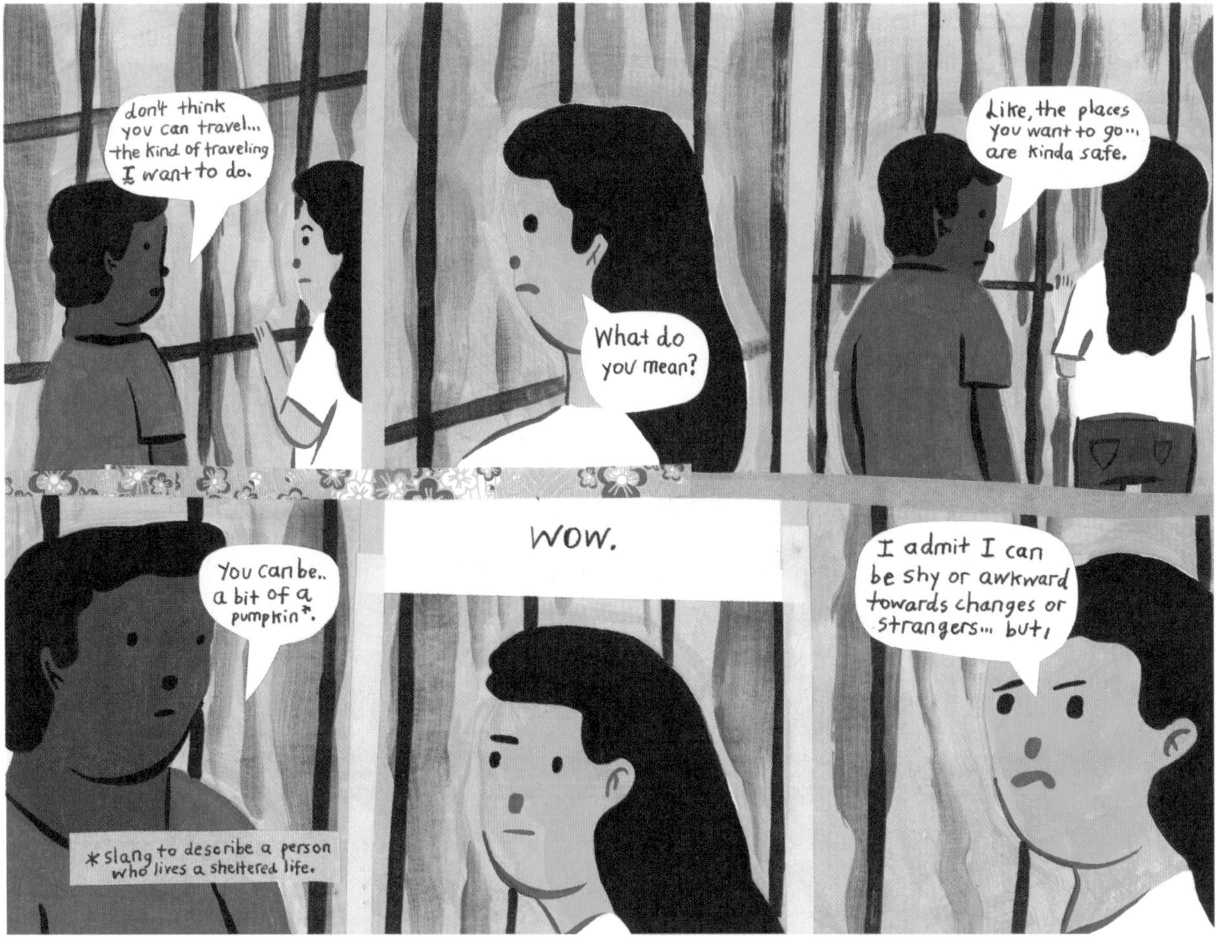
don't think you can travel... the kind of traveling I want to do.
What do you mean?
Like, the places you want to go... are kinda safe.
You can be.. a bit of a pumpkin*.
*slang to describe a person who lives a sheltered life.
WOW.
I admit I can be shy or awkward towards changes or strangers... but,

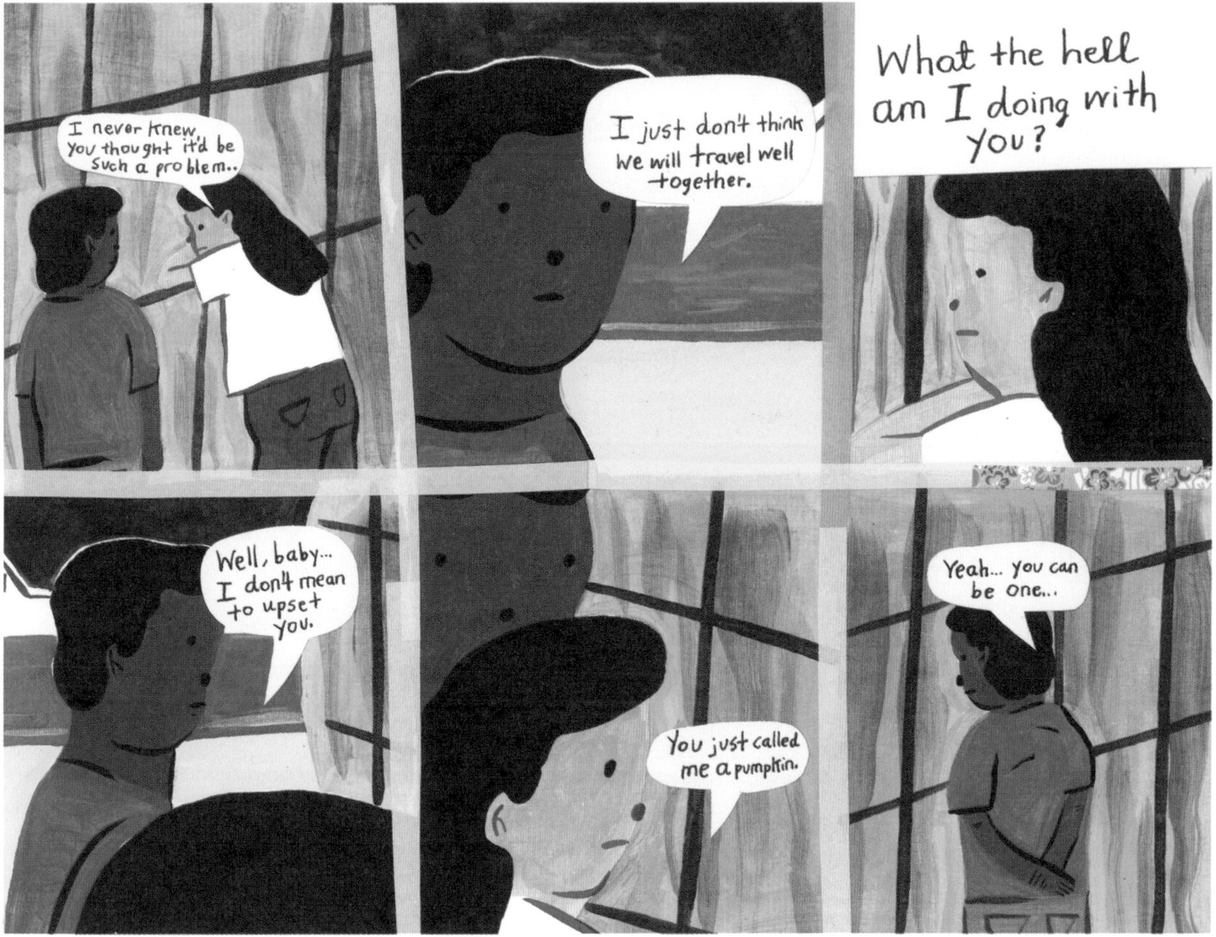
I never knew, you thought it'd be such a problem..
I just don't think we will travel well together.
What the hell am I doing with you?
Well, baby... I don't mean to upset you.
You just called me a pumpkin.
Yeah... you can be one...

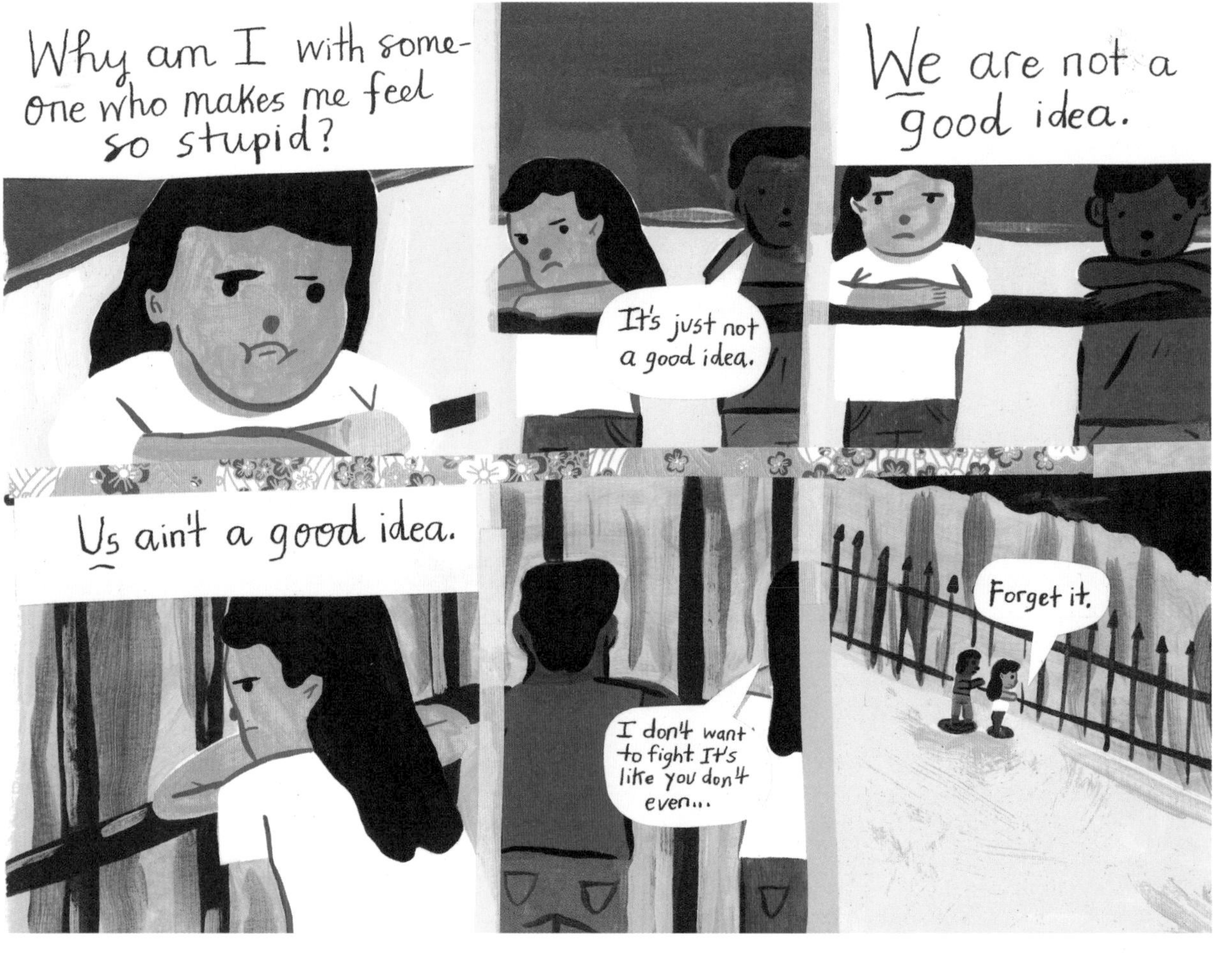
Why am I with someone who makes me feel so stupid?
It's just not a good idea.
We are not a good idea.
Us ain't a good idea.
I don't want to fight. It's like you don't even...
Forget it.

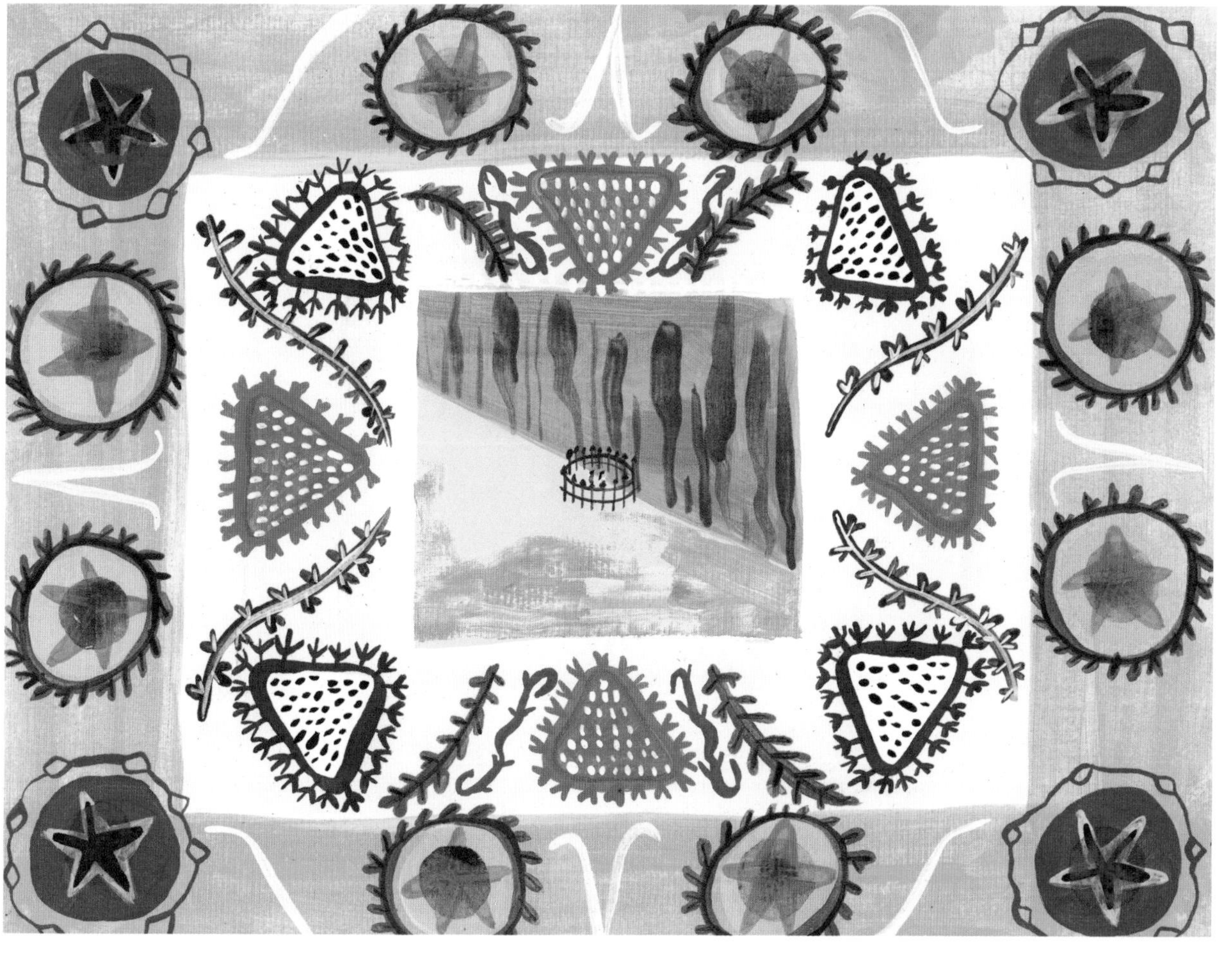

Dinner with Puss

BY PIXIN

Make him go weak in the knees, find his secret spot.

Don't worry, we don't have to take it all the way down.

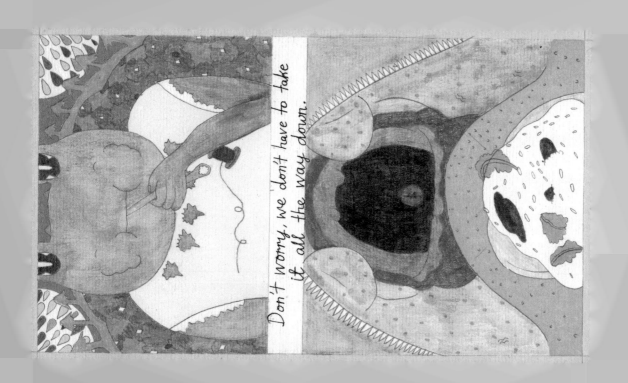

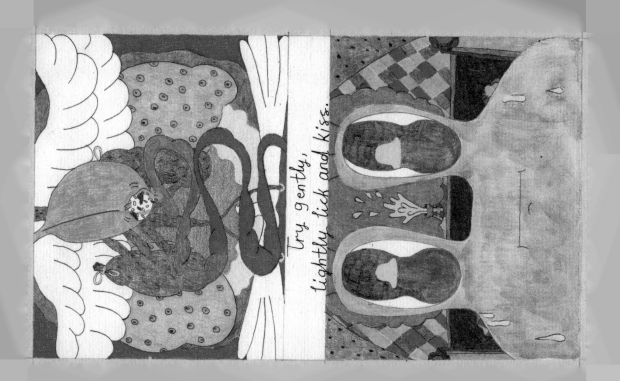

Try gently,
lightly lick and kiss.

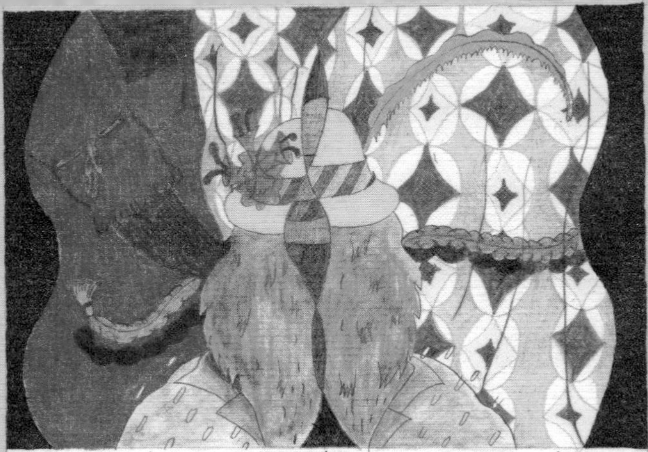

Till he's really hard, with all things going and moving.

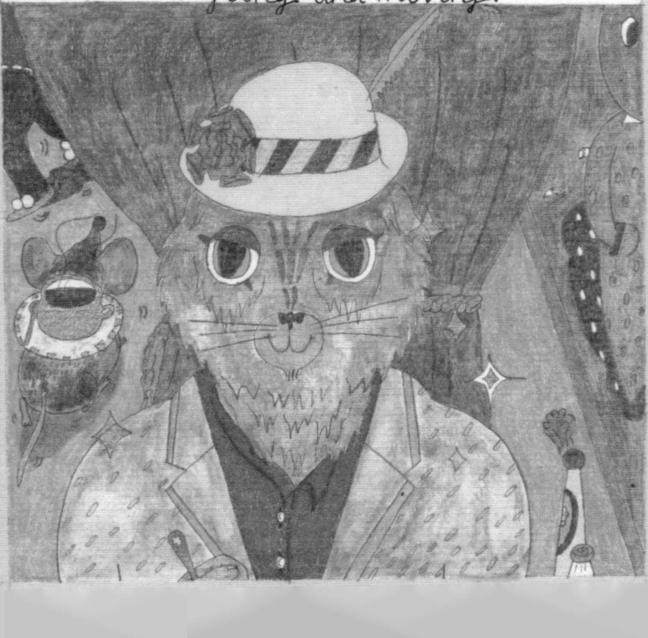

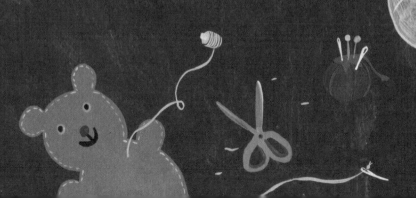

HOME DIARIES

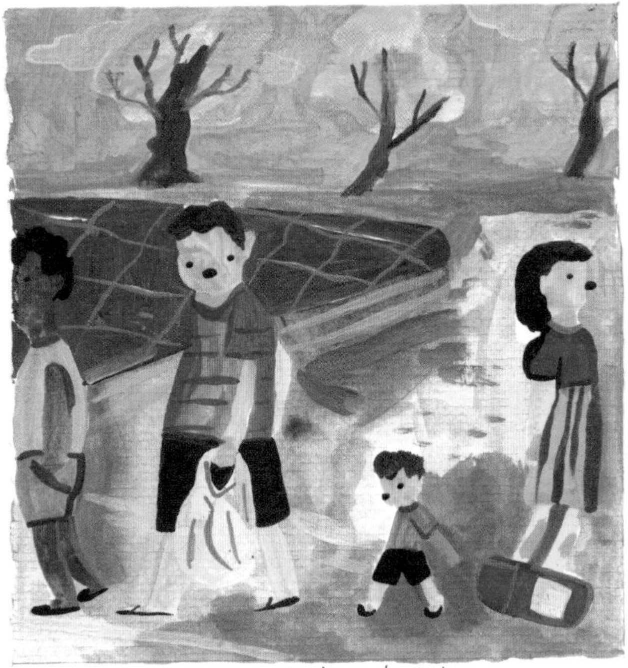

A father and his toddler son cross the street. The father carries the groceries, while his son drags a pack of diapers. It was a very funny and sweet moment.

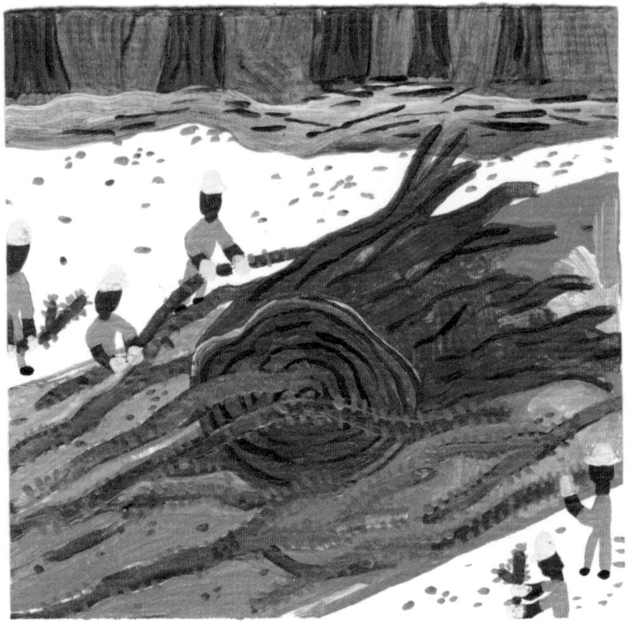

A tree had fallen. Workers placed it on a large lorry, with its branches and leaves beside it. It felt like a funeral.

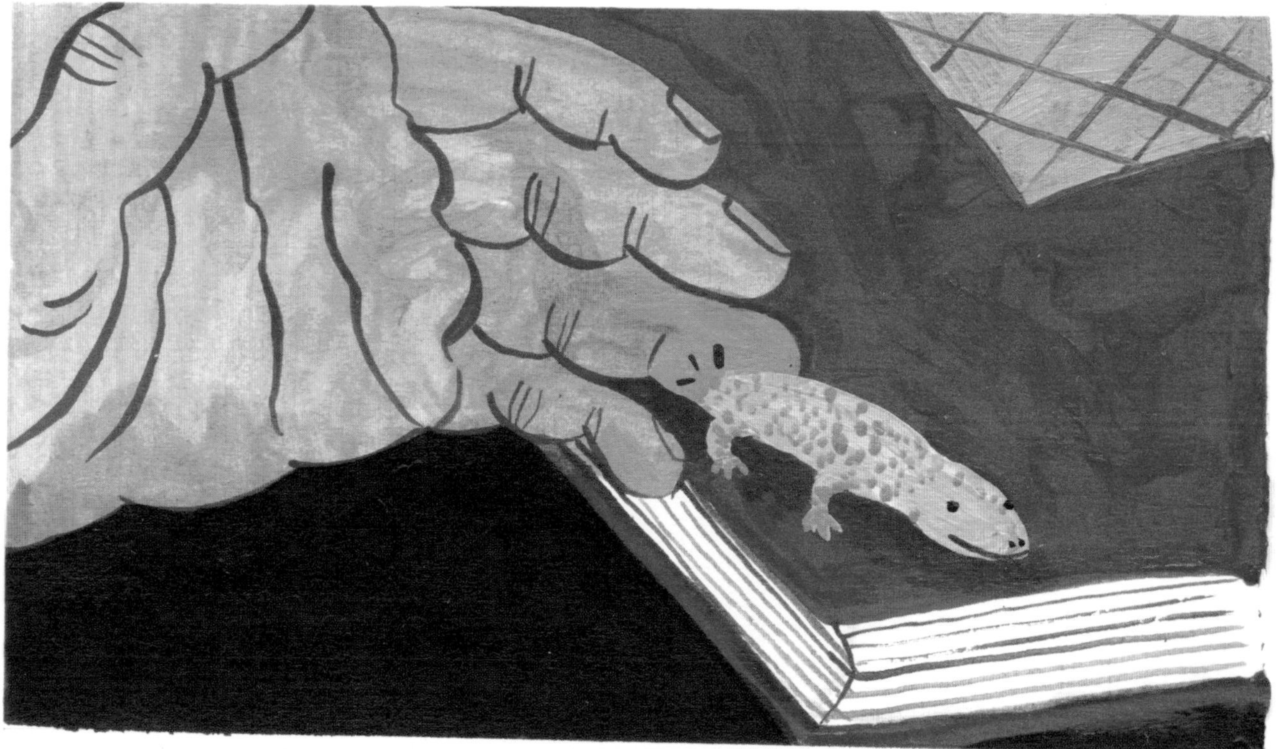

Cat chased lizard. I took lizard away. Cat gave me the you-betrayed-me look. Lizard (most likely) left happy.

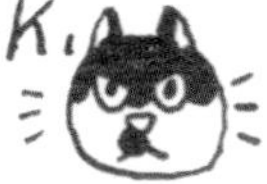

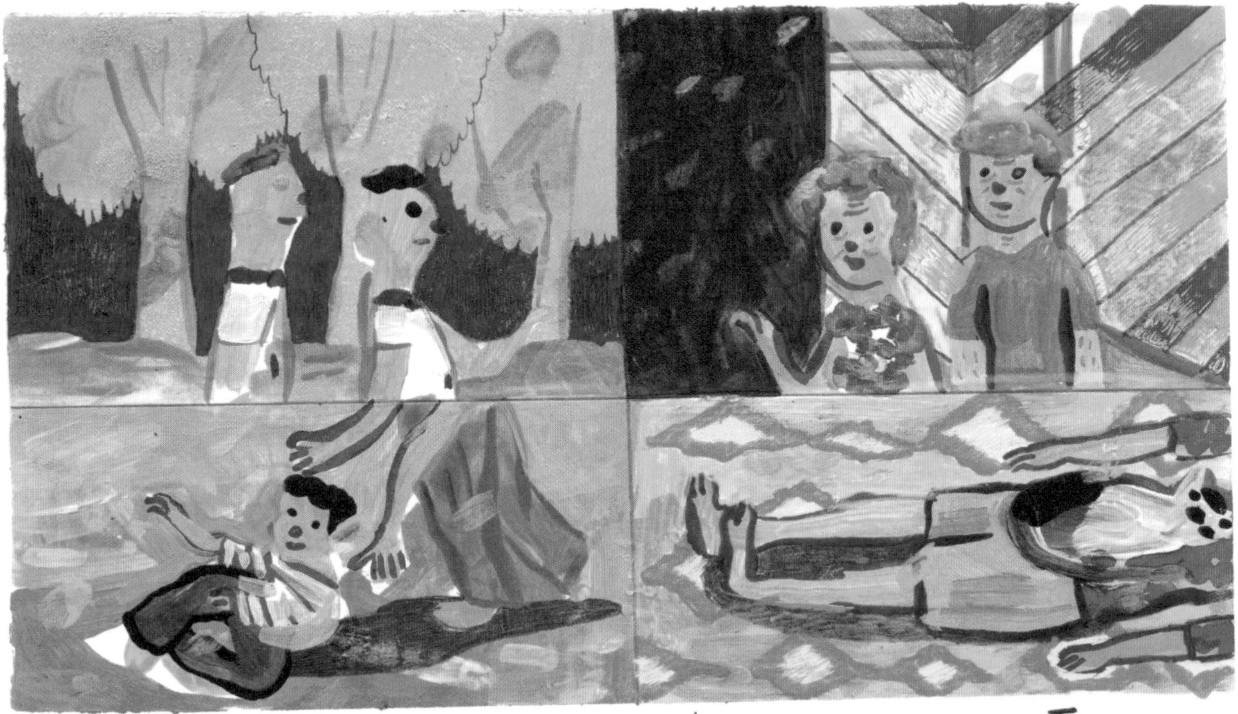

Kid-sized sailor outfits on two grown men—I wondered if it was a club's costume—elderly neighbours chatting on a hotwarm afternoon, dancing to a mental image of being inside a cold green lake, and PJ napping and purring. What an end to theday! 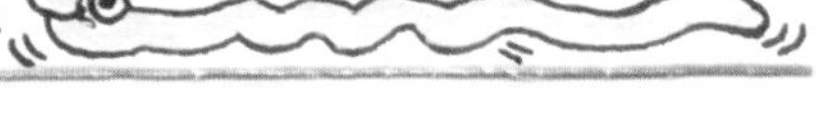

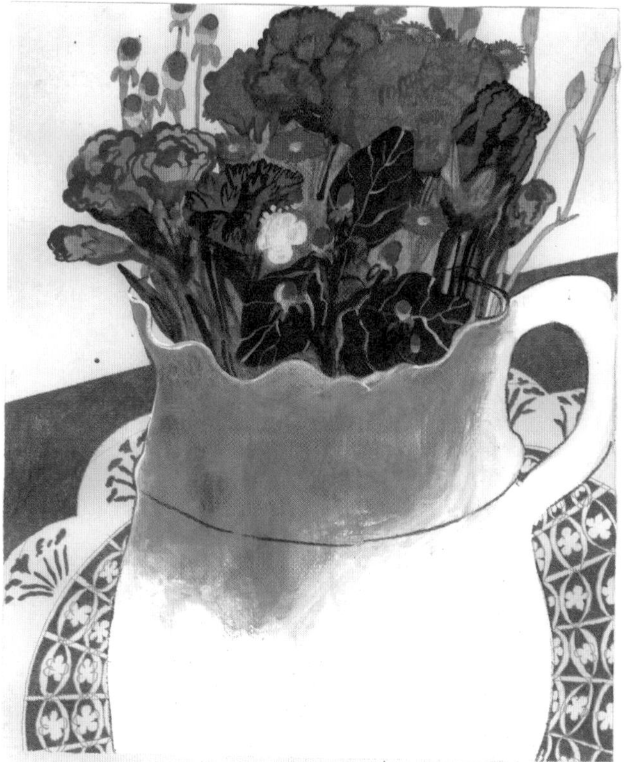

A bouquet of fresh carnations, set inside a new vase, placed on top of the house's doiley, is my mother's way of welcoming the arrival of Chinese New Year.

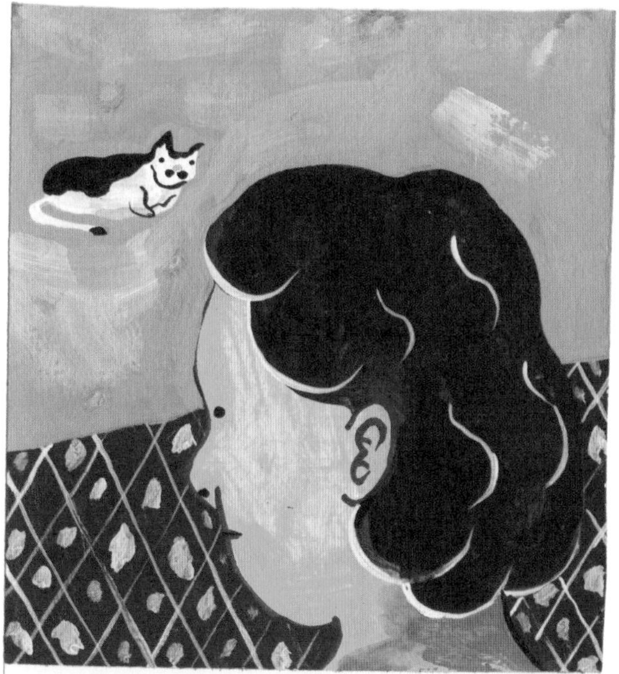

Realizing I hadn't made it easy for her to Connect to me.

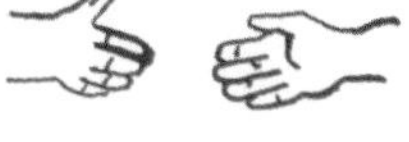

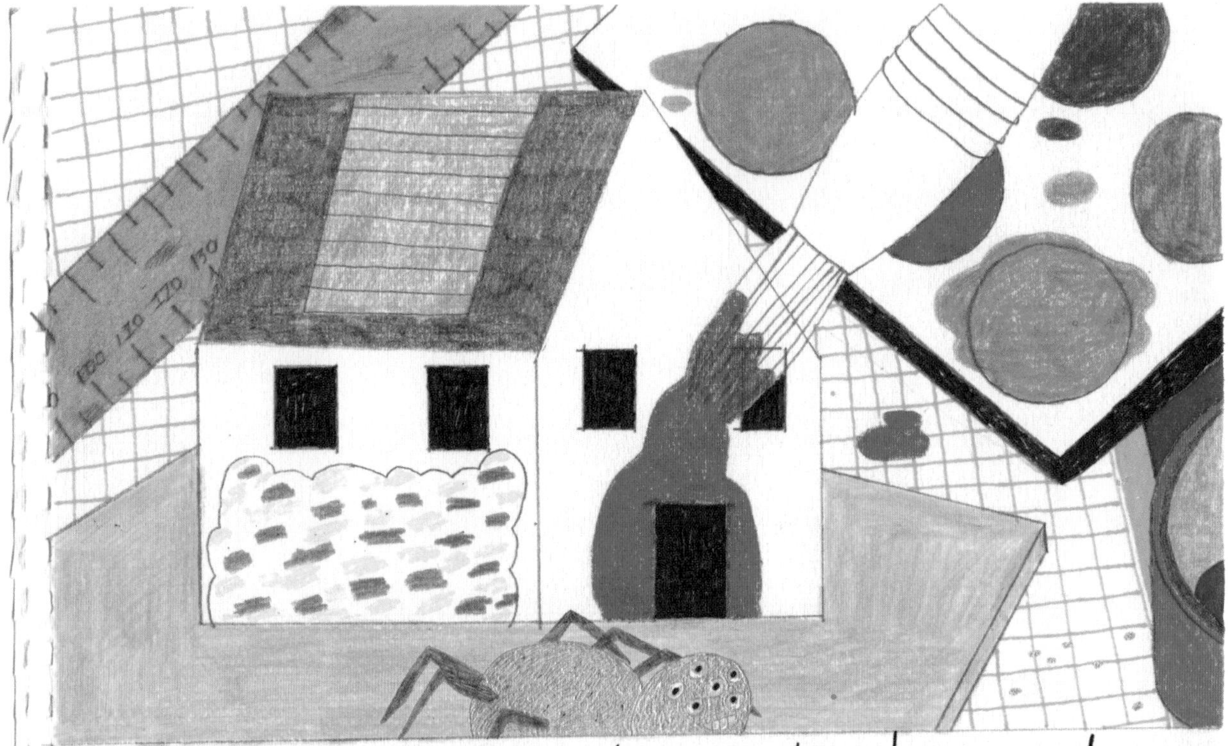

Drawing the plan to paint a house red, prior to the actual painting of a house in red (spider not included), or maybe it will be...

4

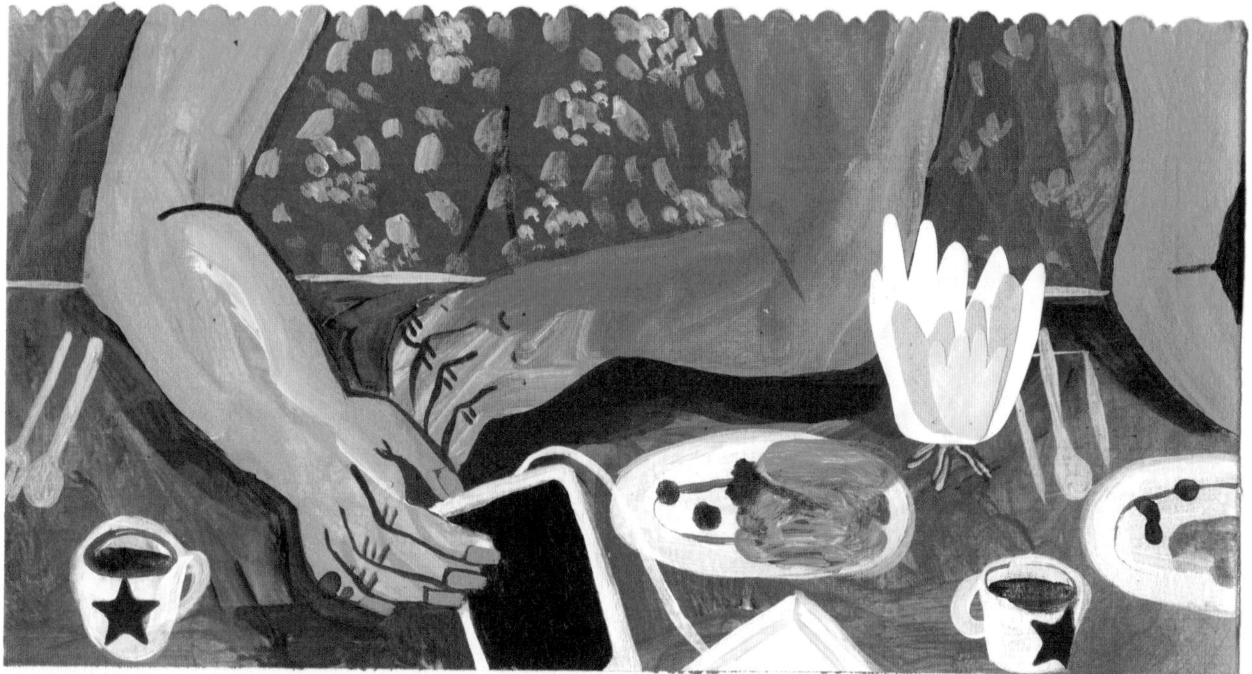

Tru Truth is, I don't love her. I'm angry with, at her. Her hypocritical, judgmental, and racist attitudes. Her fears. I hate her fears. But mostly, I hate that she affects me.

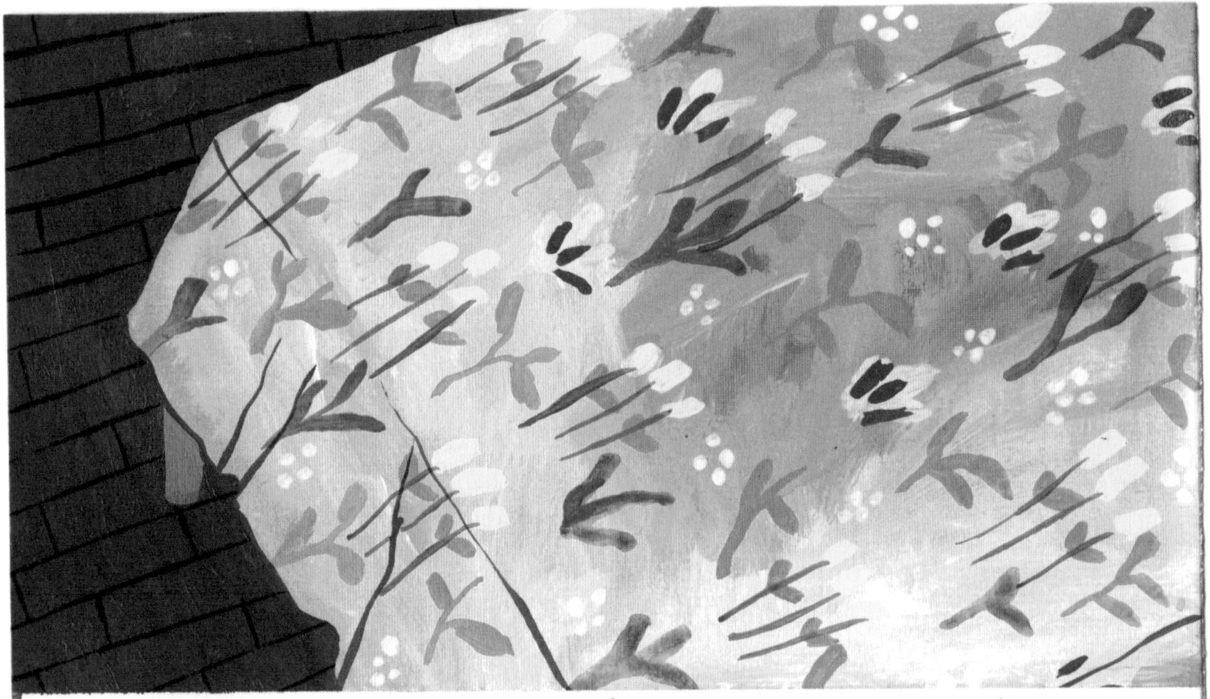

Dreaming I've completed an assignment, connecting all relevant materials together, and... waking up.

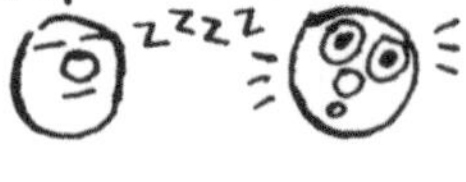
zzzz

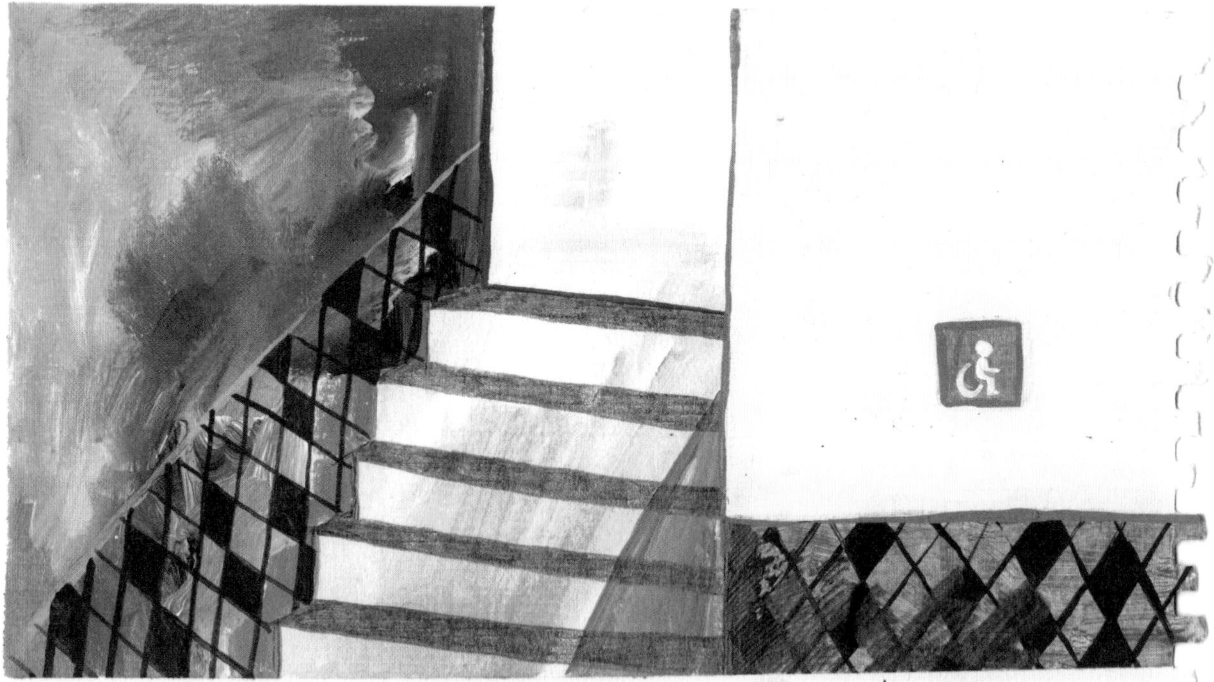

Seeing a wheelchair-user symbol near the lift, followed by steps leading up to said lift (in a newly-completed apartment).

DEADLINES WAVES
MORE CHANGES WAVES
READ THIS READ THAT WAVES
SO STRESSED! NEED SOME SUN TIMES!

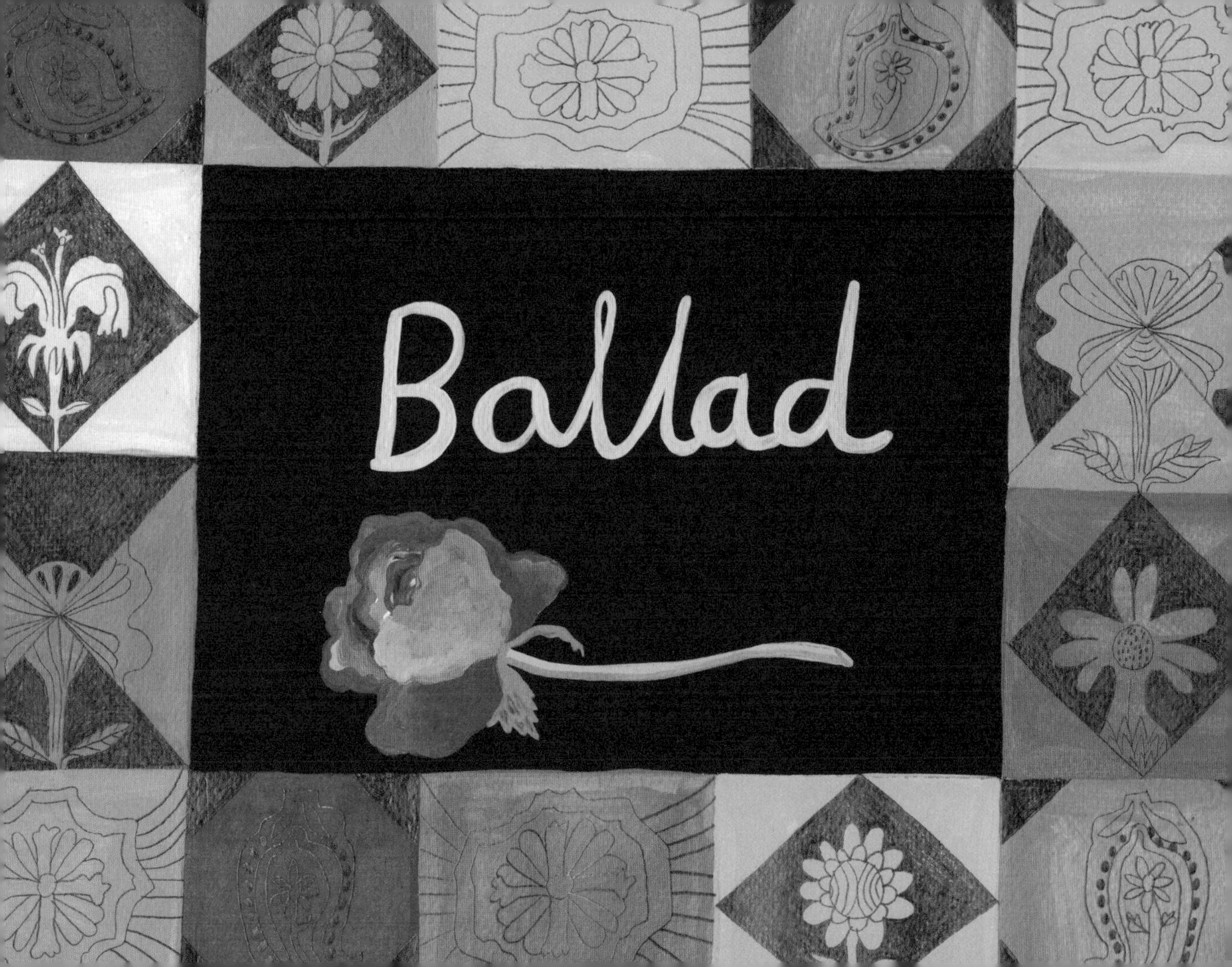
Ballad

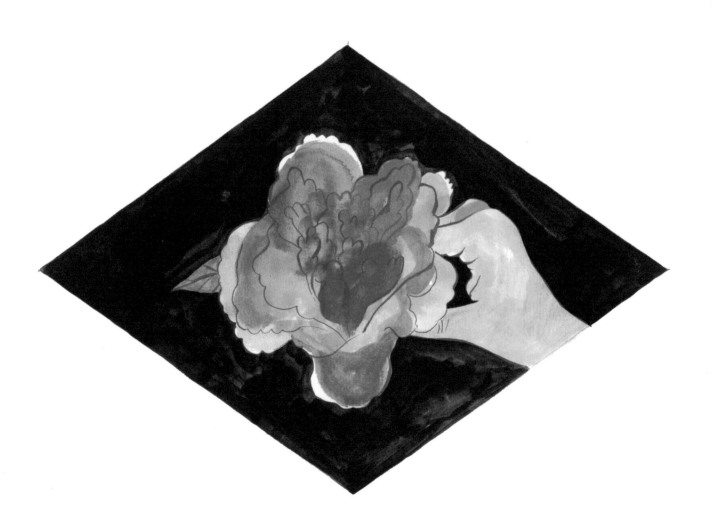

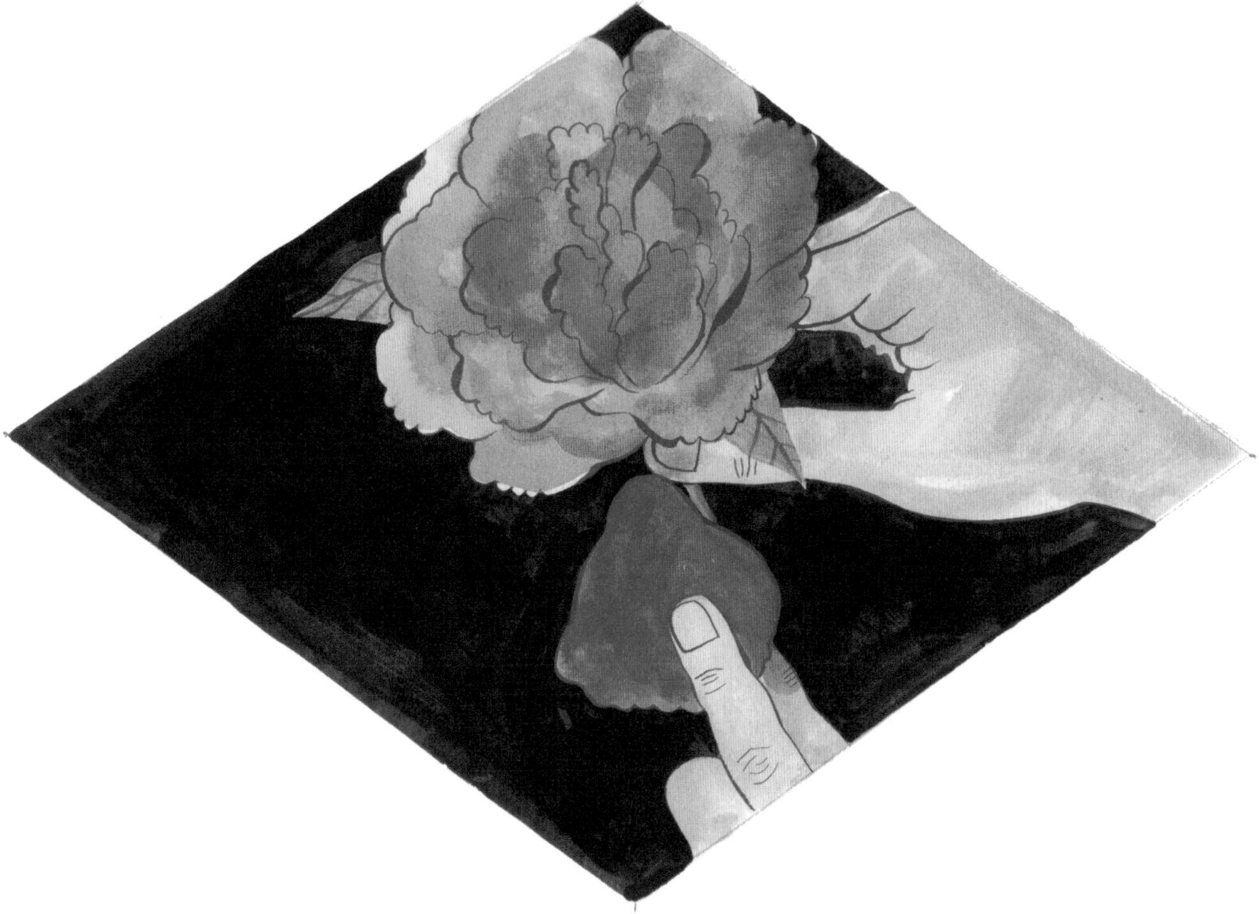

He loves me.
He mentions 'let's,'
He says 'yes'.

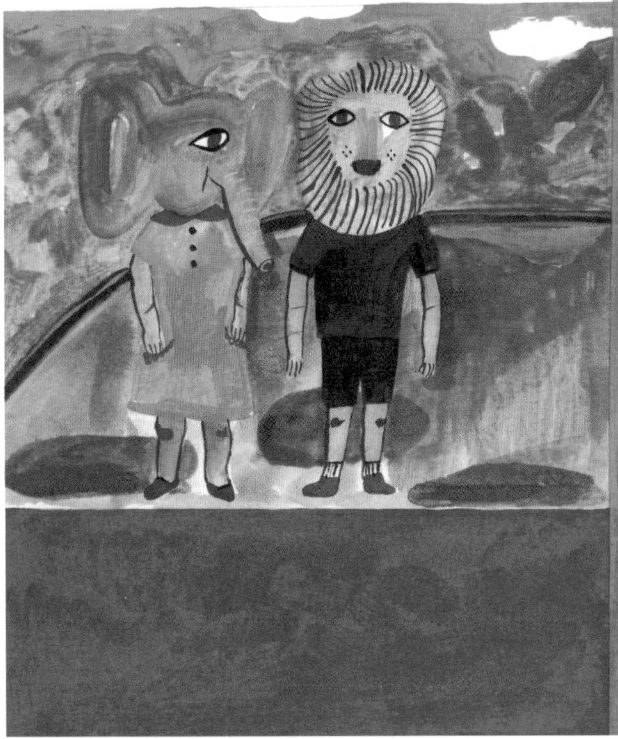

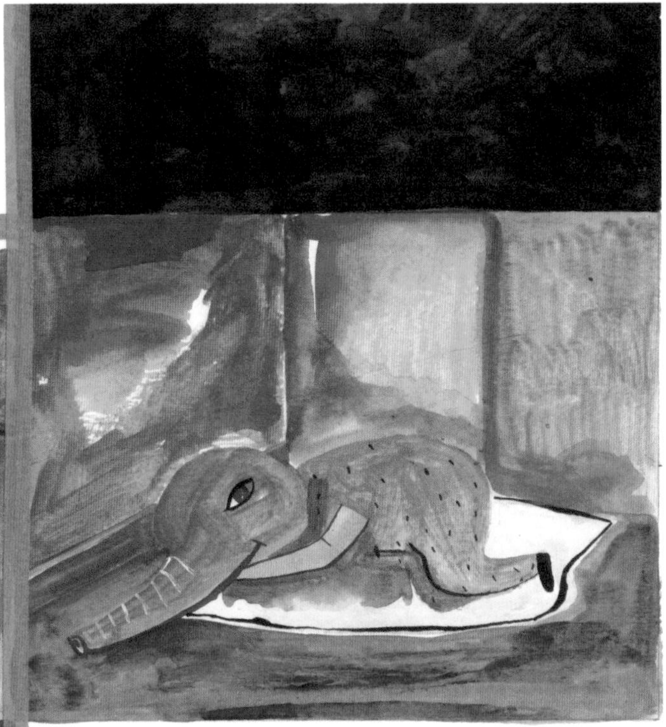

He loves me not.
He misses all this,
but is too busy for it.

He loves me.
"Take a chance," he suggests,
sensing my hesitations.

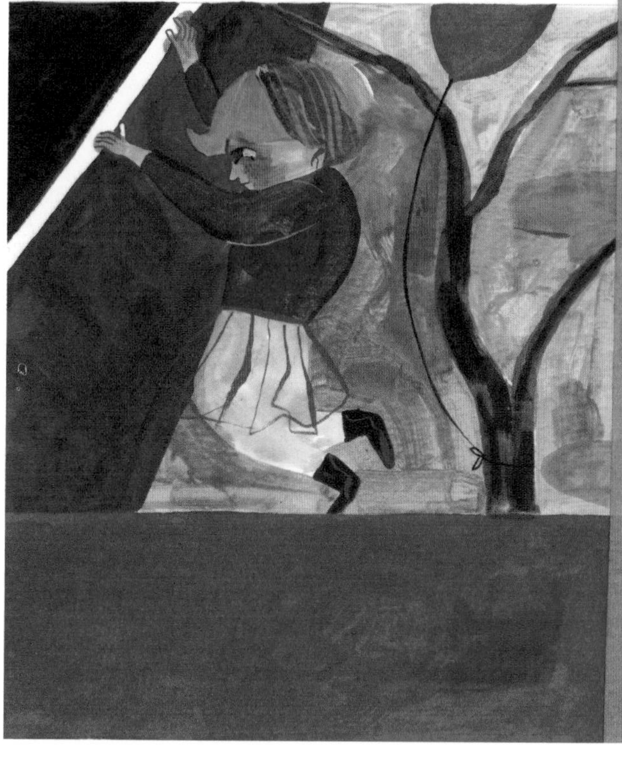

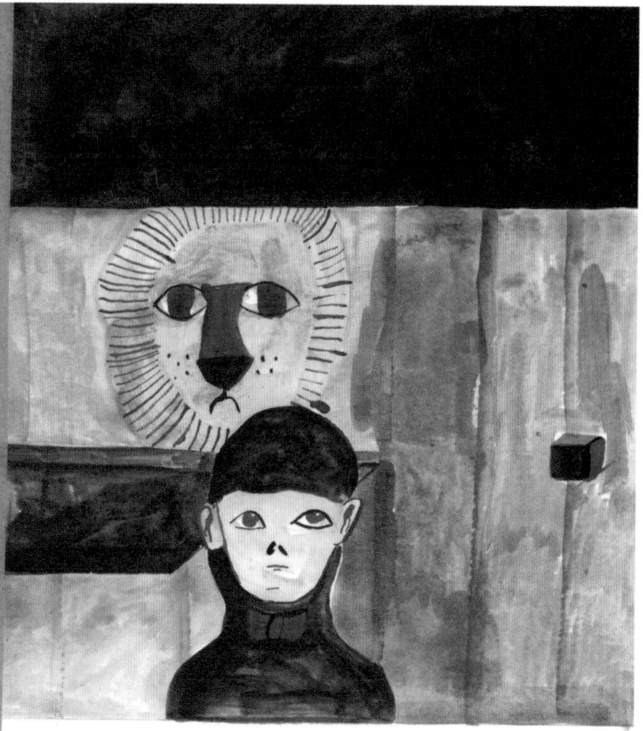

He loves me not.
He never asks.
He preaches.

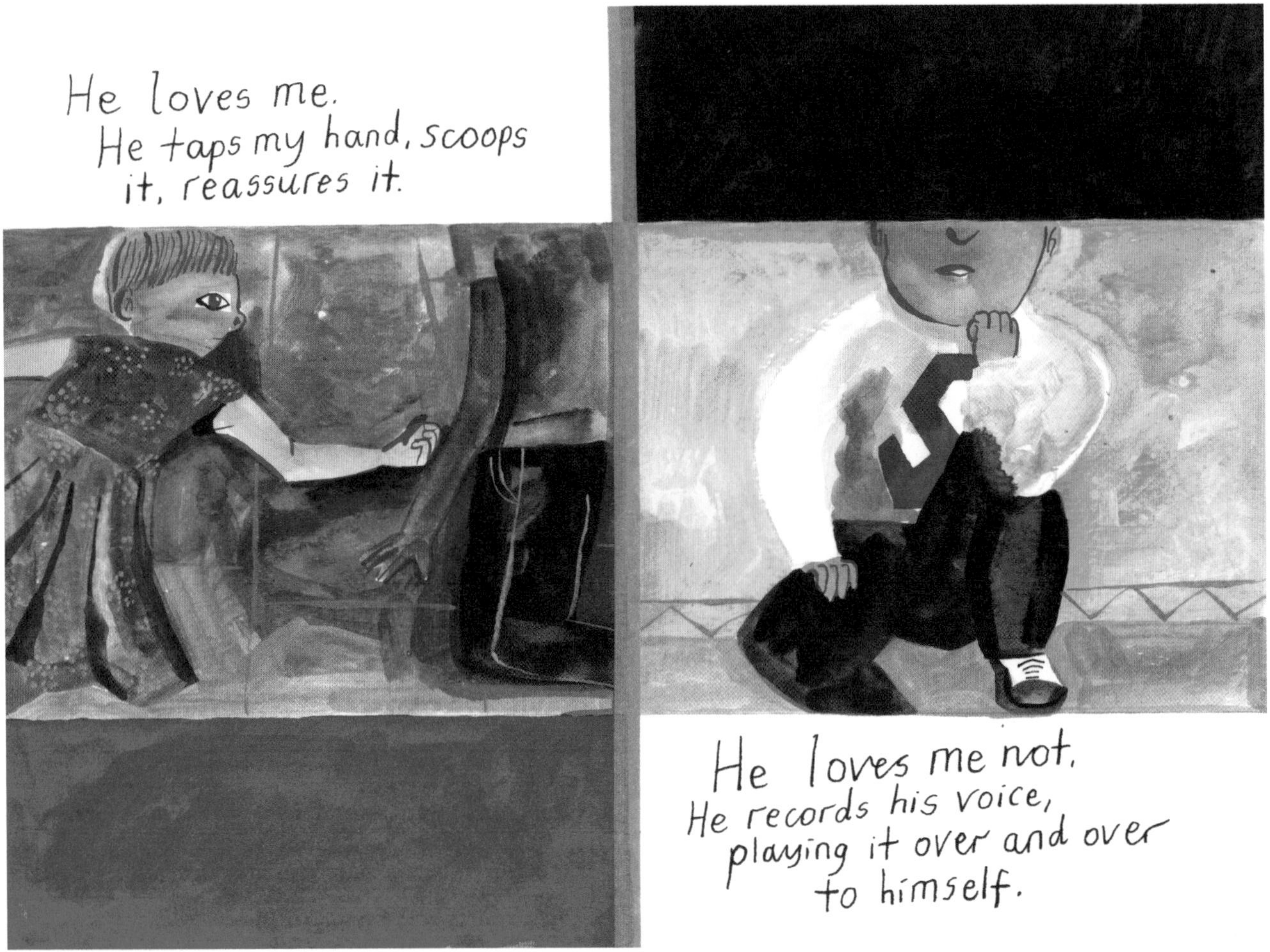
He loves me.
He taps my hand, scoops it, reassures it.
He loves me not.
He records his voice, playing it over and over to himself.

He loves me.
He doesn't steal nor
take anything away.

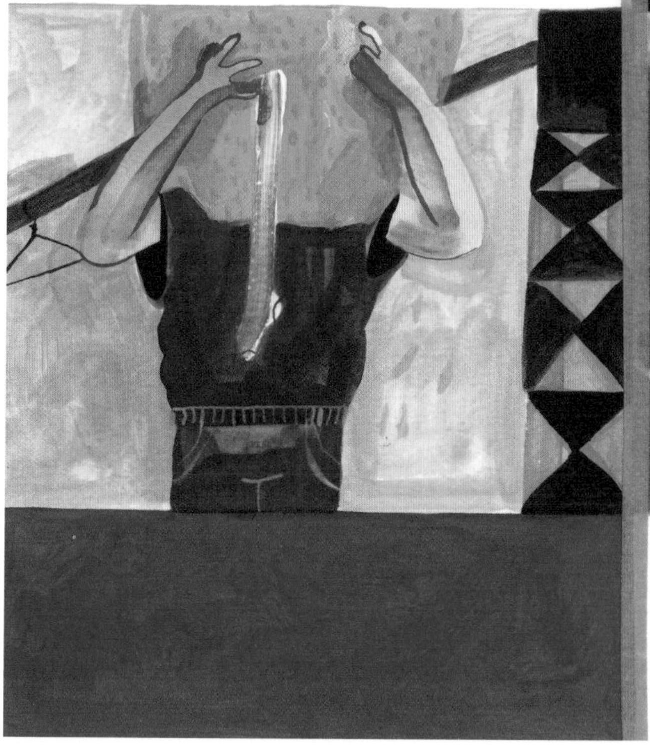

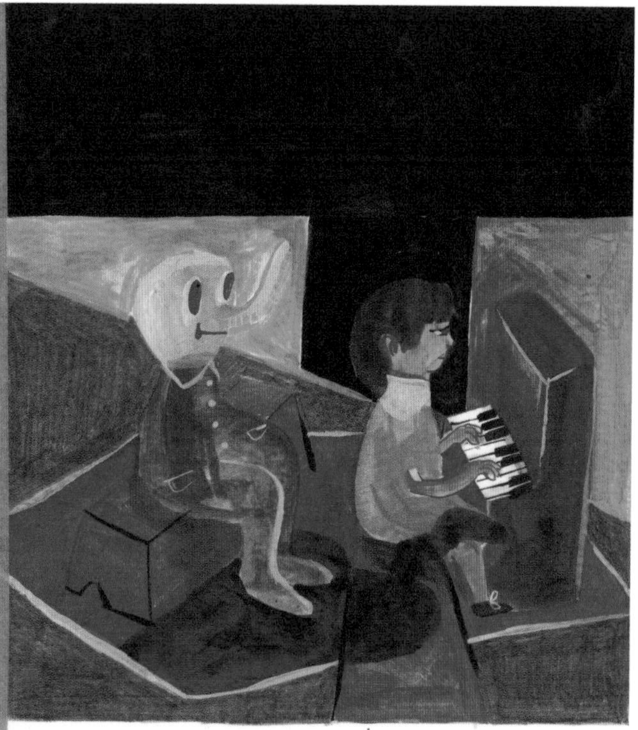

He loves me not.
He secures a shadow and
expects a performance.

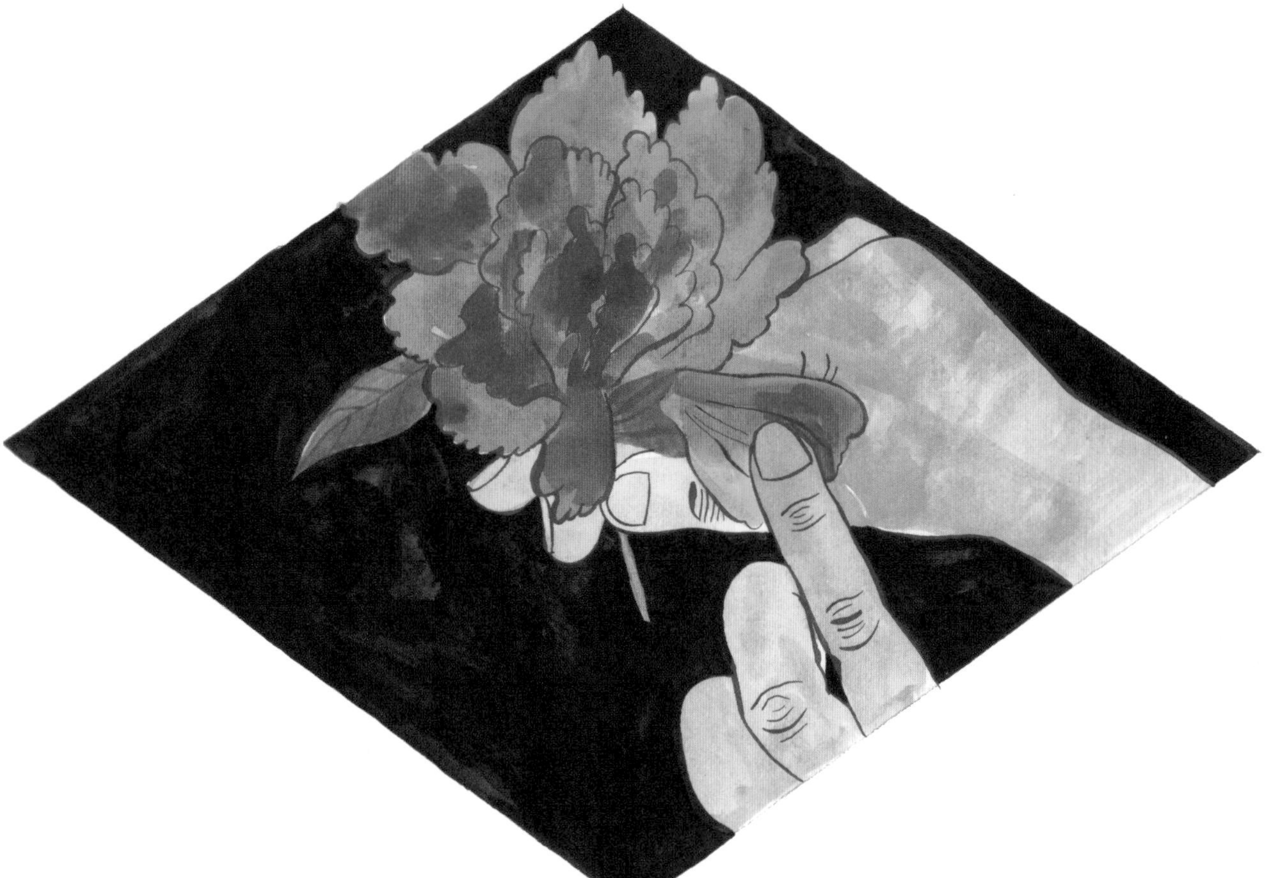

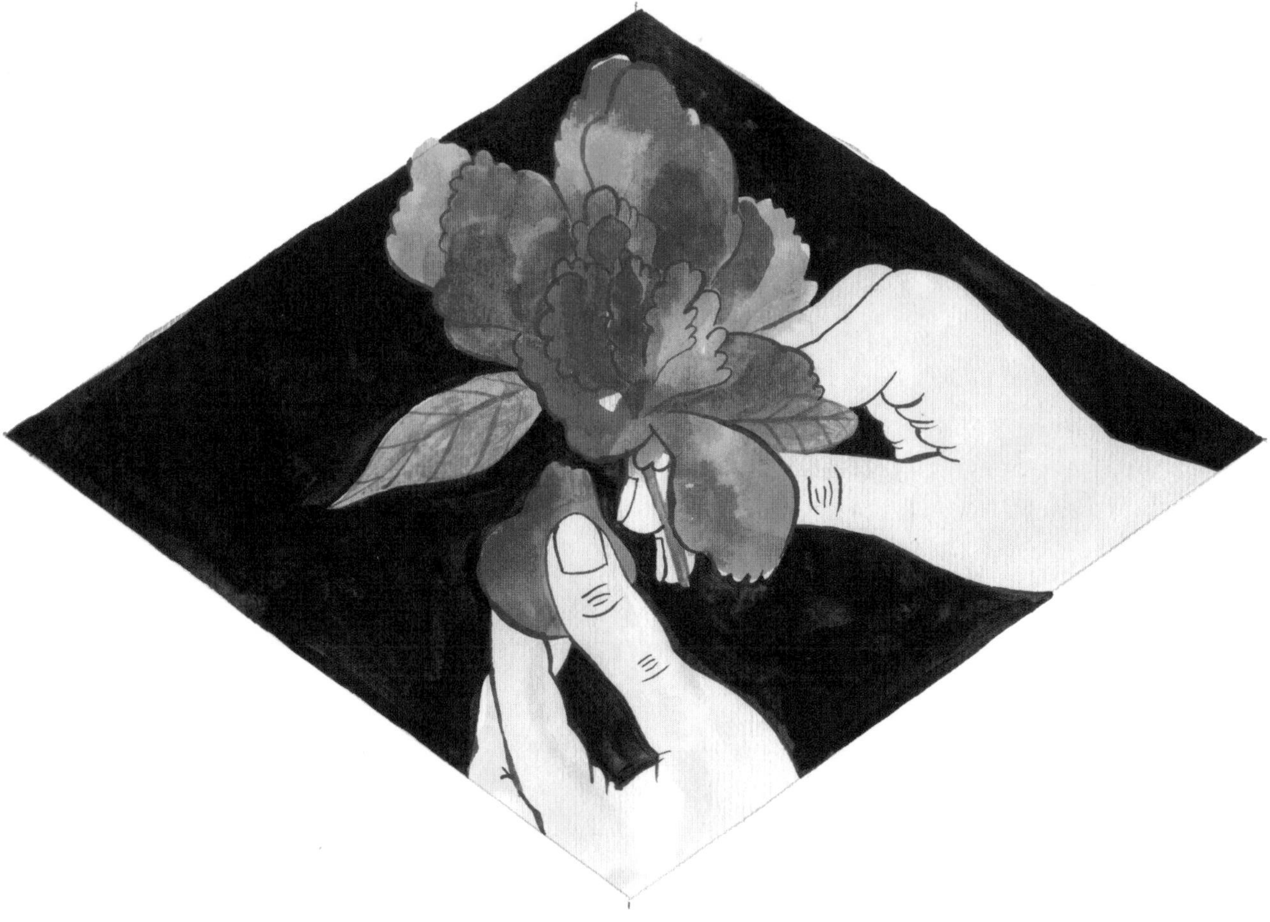

He loves me.
He shares his happiness, his time.

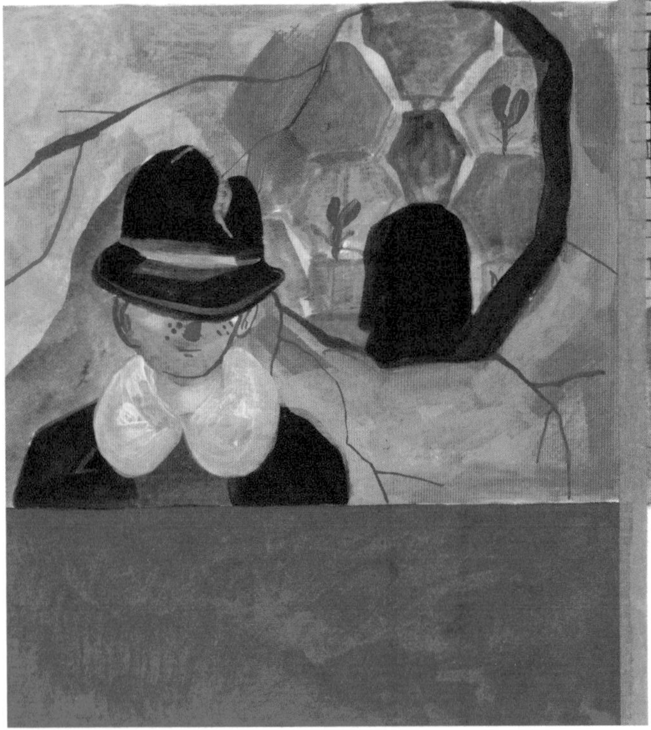

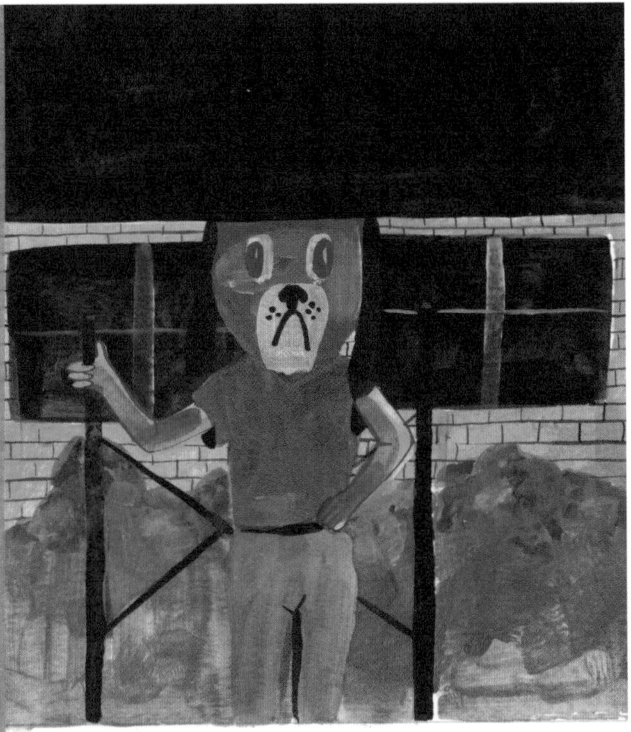

He loves me not.
He declares and demands it to be.

He loves me.
He anticipates the daily sunrises, and believes that its yellow must seem different to everyone.

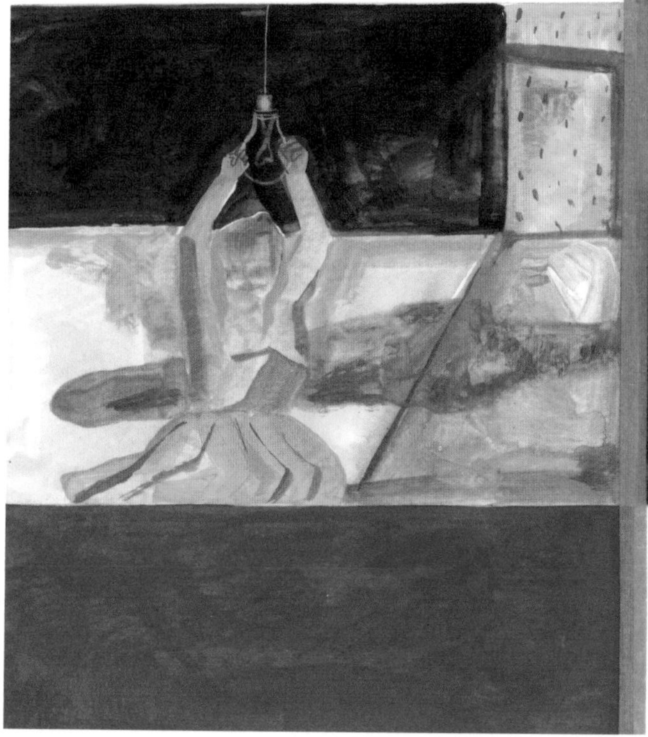

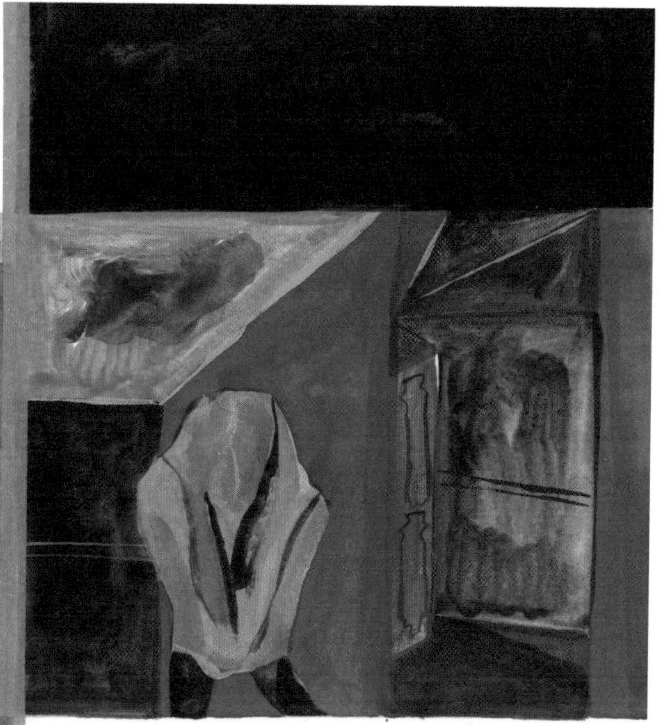

He loves me not.
He writes, he talks.
He lays, he forgets.

He loves me.
He looks up and wonders,
with a dose of necessary
doubt.

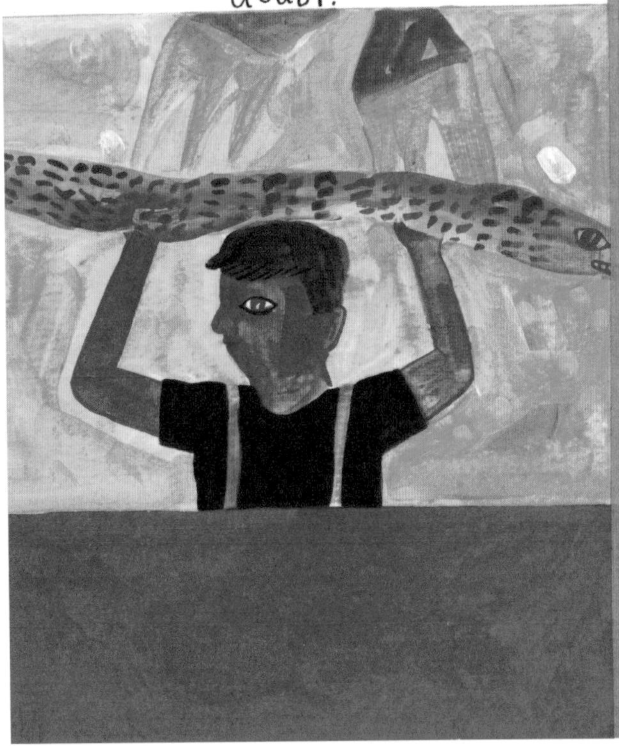

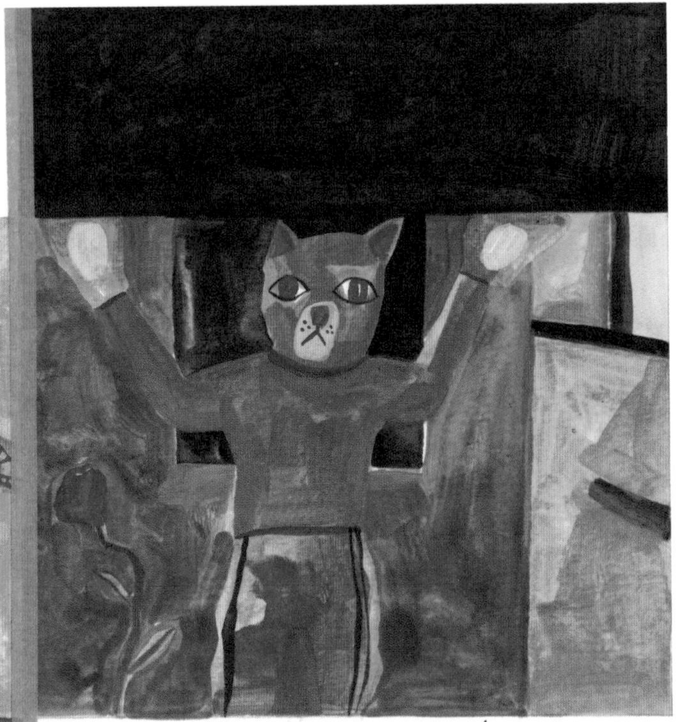

He loves me not.
He sits on his swing,
flinging away as high as he can.
All the time. Every time.

He loves me.
He paints a portrait of
his flaws.

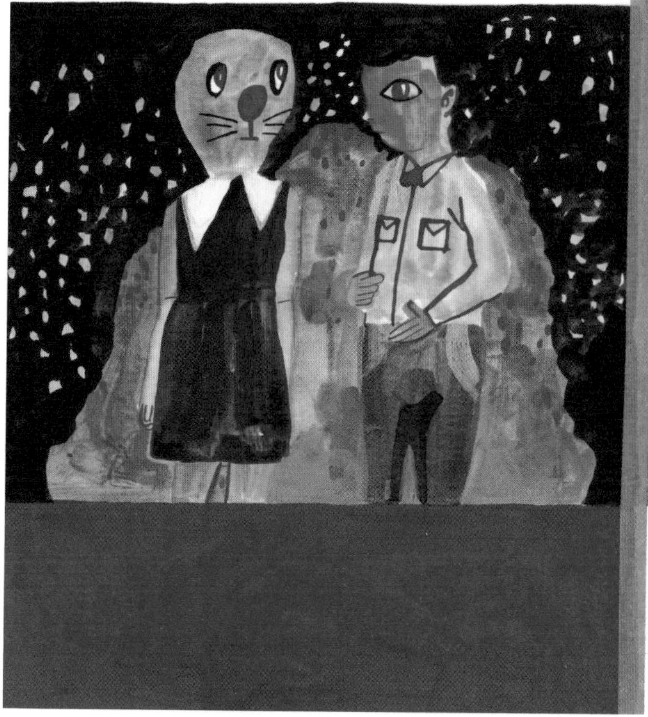

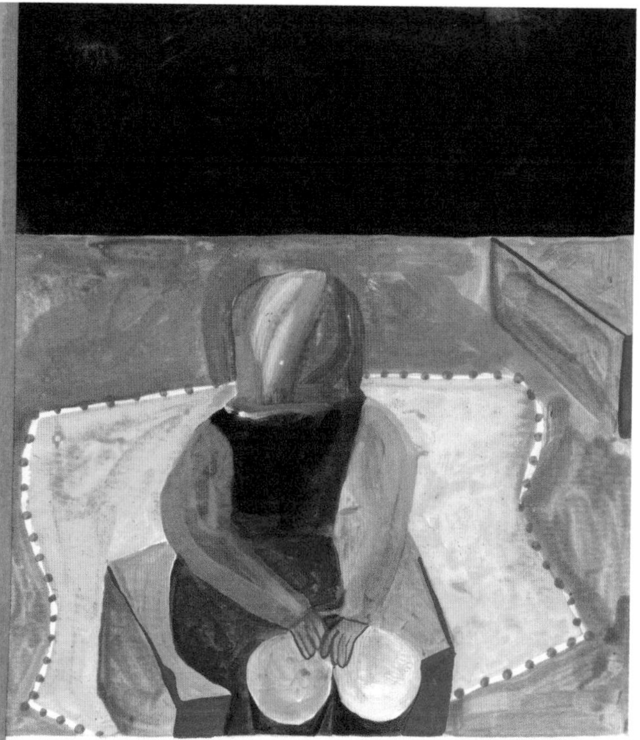

He loves me not.
He gifts his warmth so
freely to another.

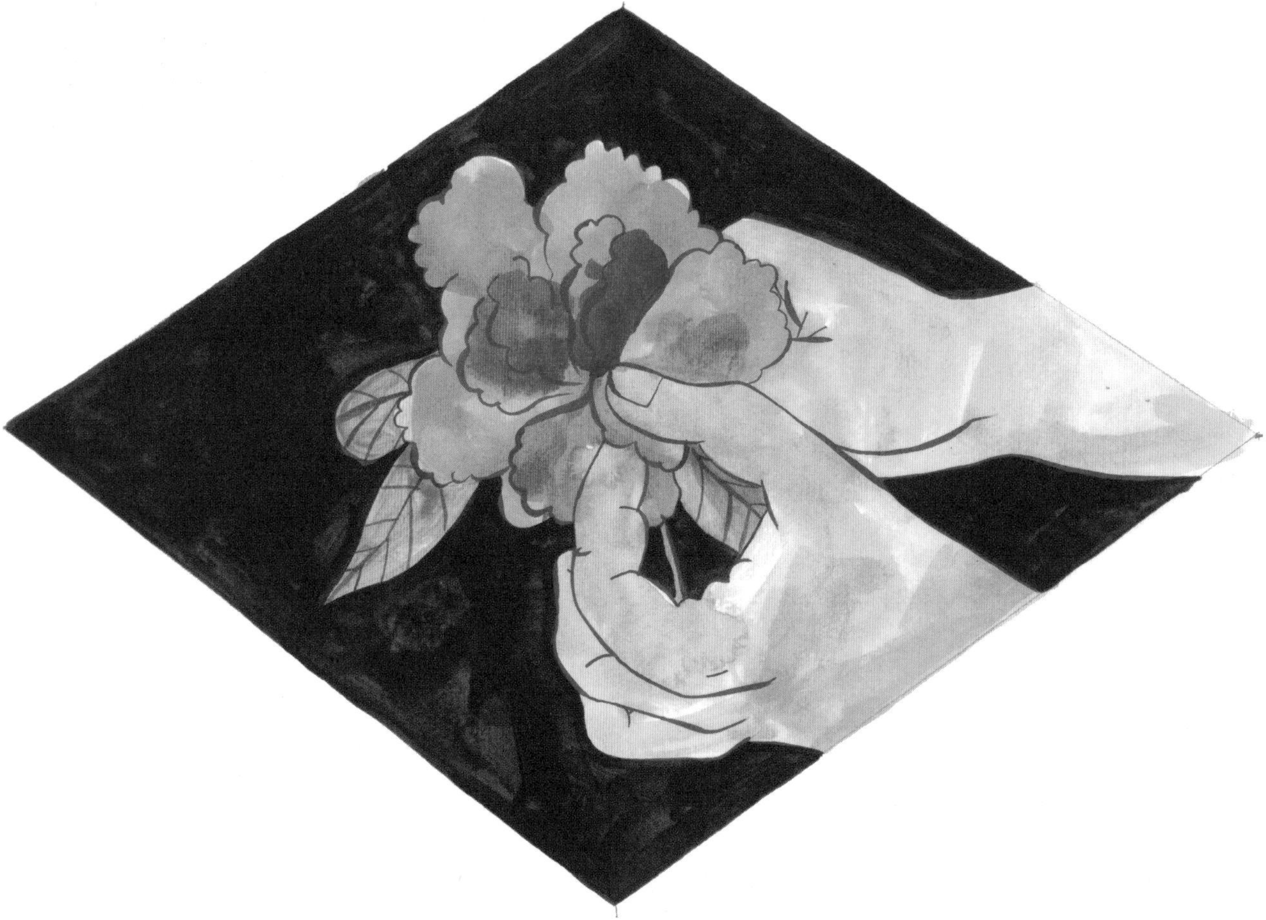

He loves me.
Encouraging butterflies
in my stomach.

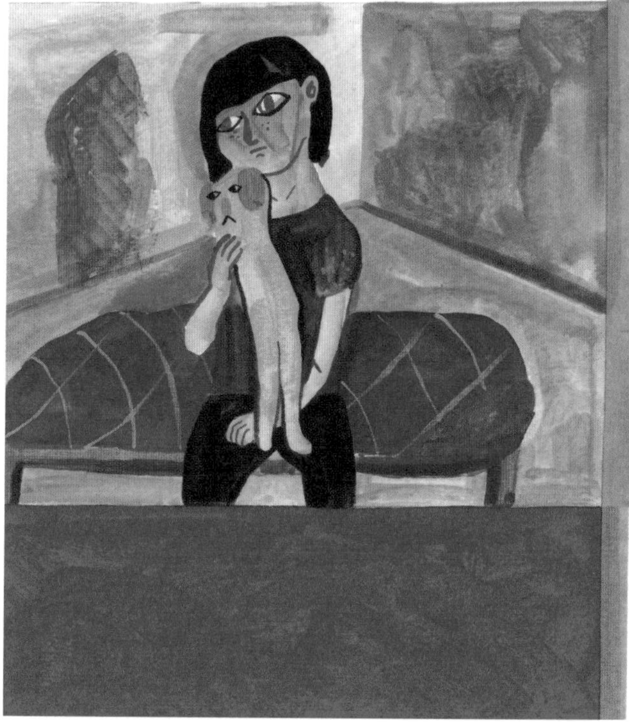

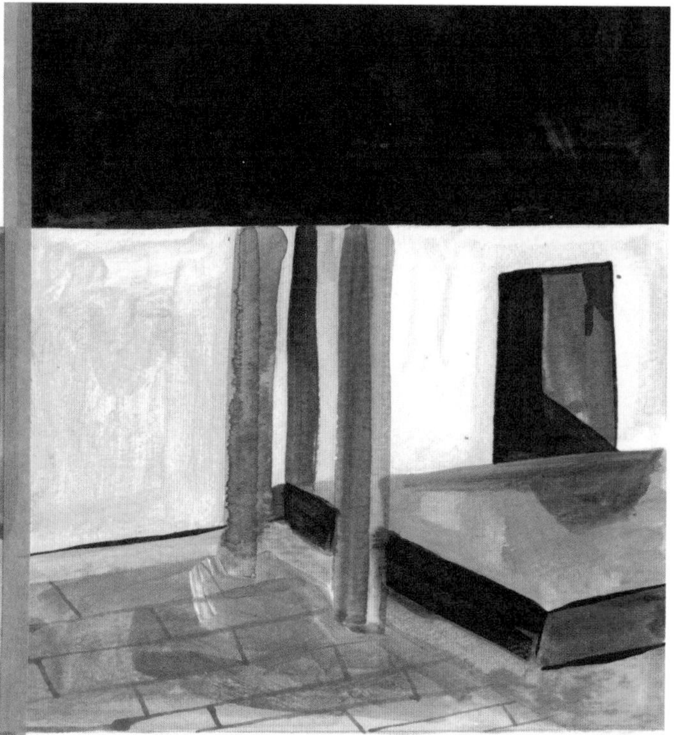

He loves me not.
Leaving no trace of
his presence.

He loves me.
He builds an elaborate
sandcastle a metre from the
rising tide.

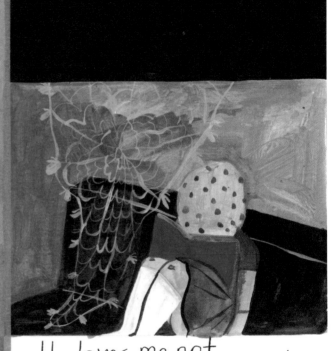

He loves me not.
I'm the carpet, the wall, the
sink. He's the air he puts his
faith in.

He loves me.
His house- just fine.
His room- a rebel.

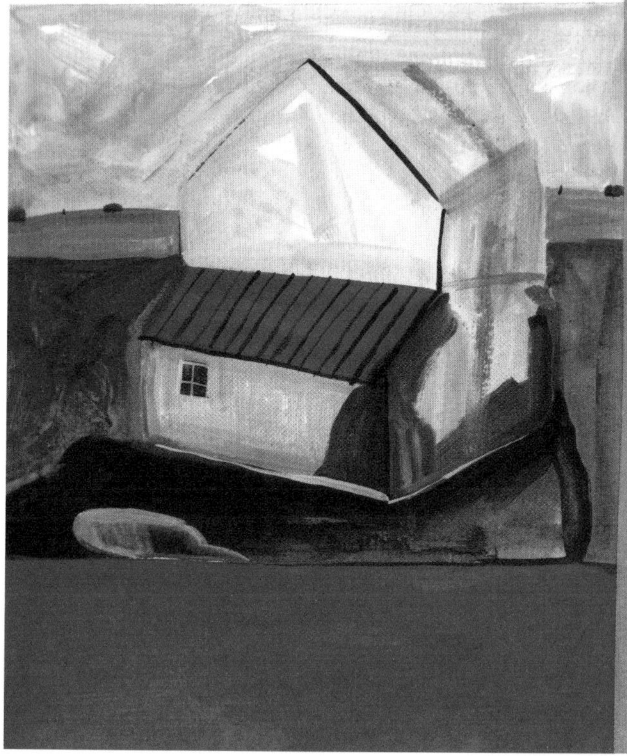

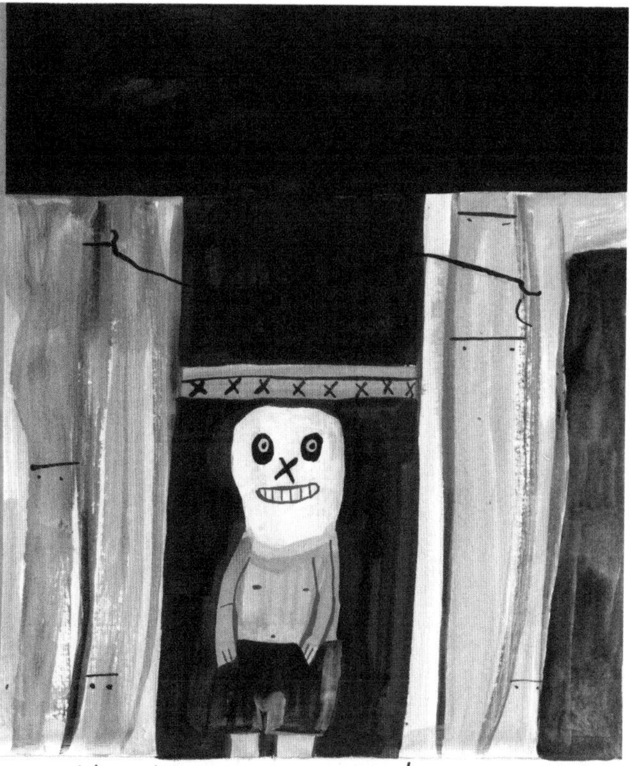

He loves me not.
Nothing completes him.
It's never enough.

He loves me.
He stays.

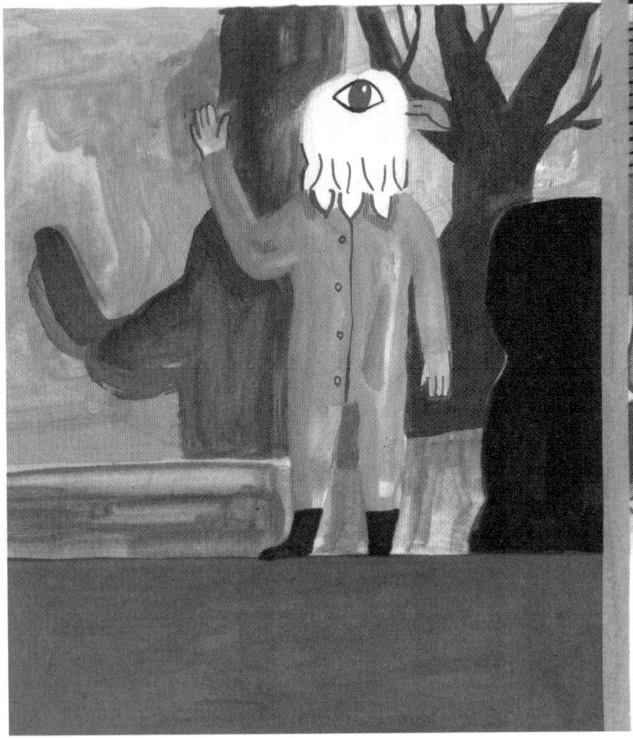

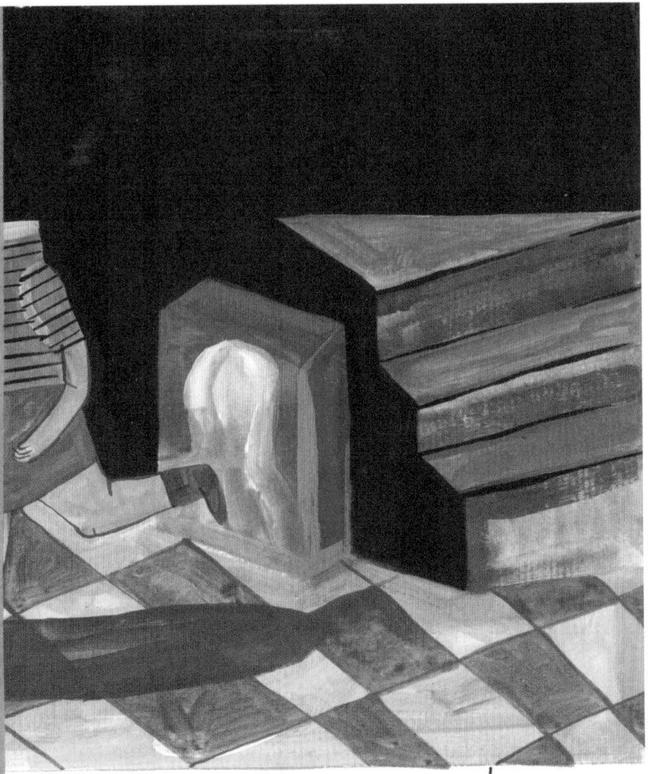

He loves me not.
He loves me not.

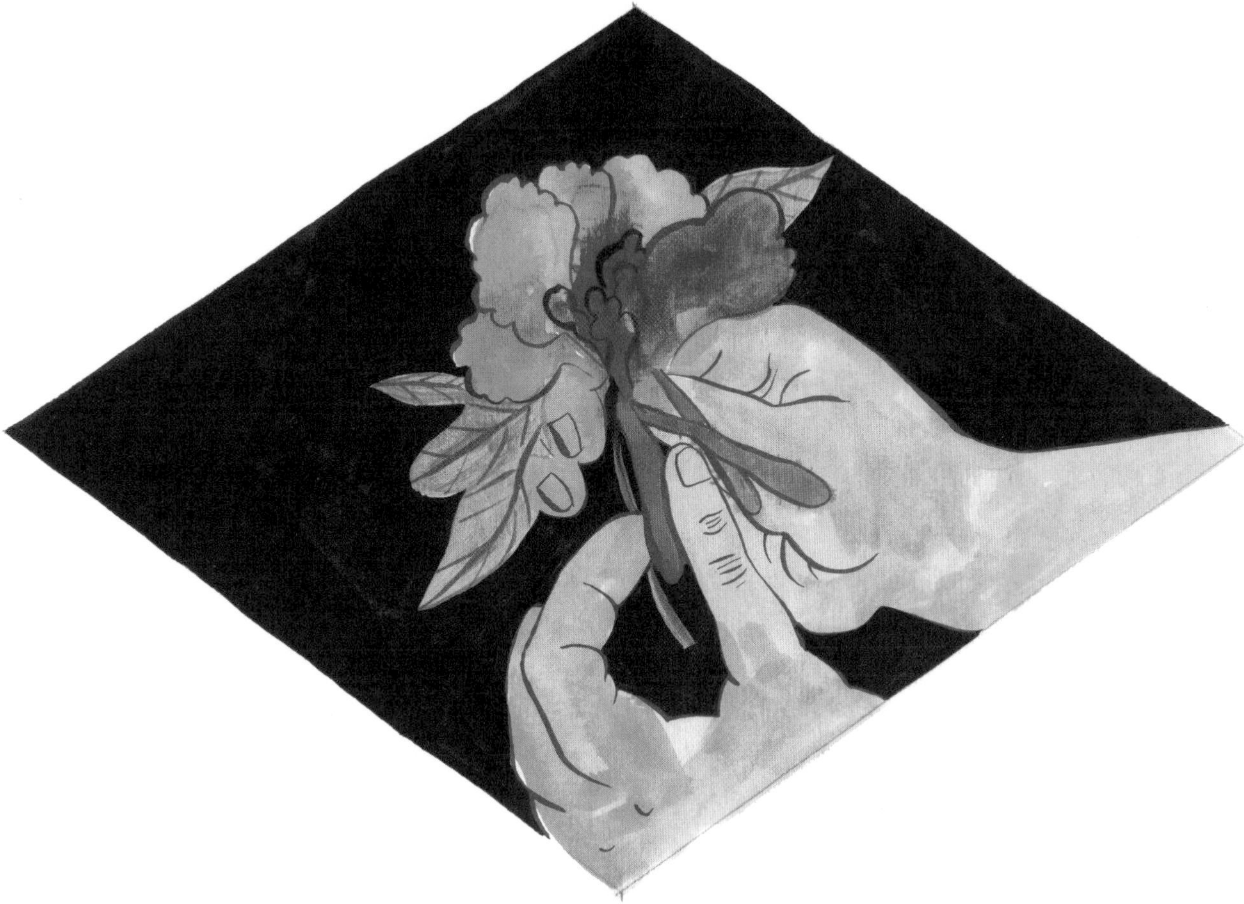

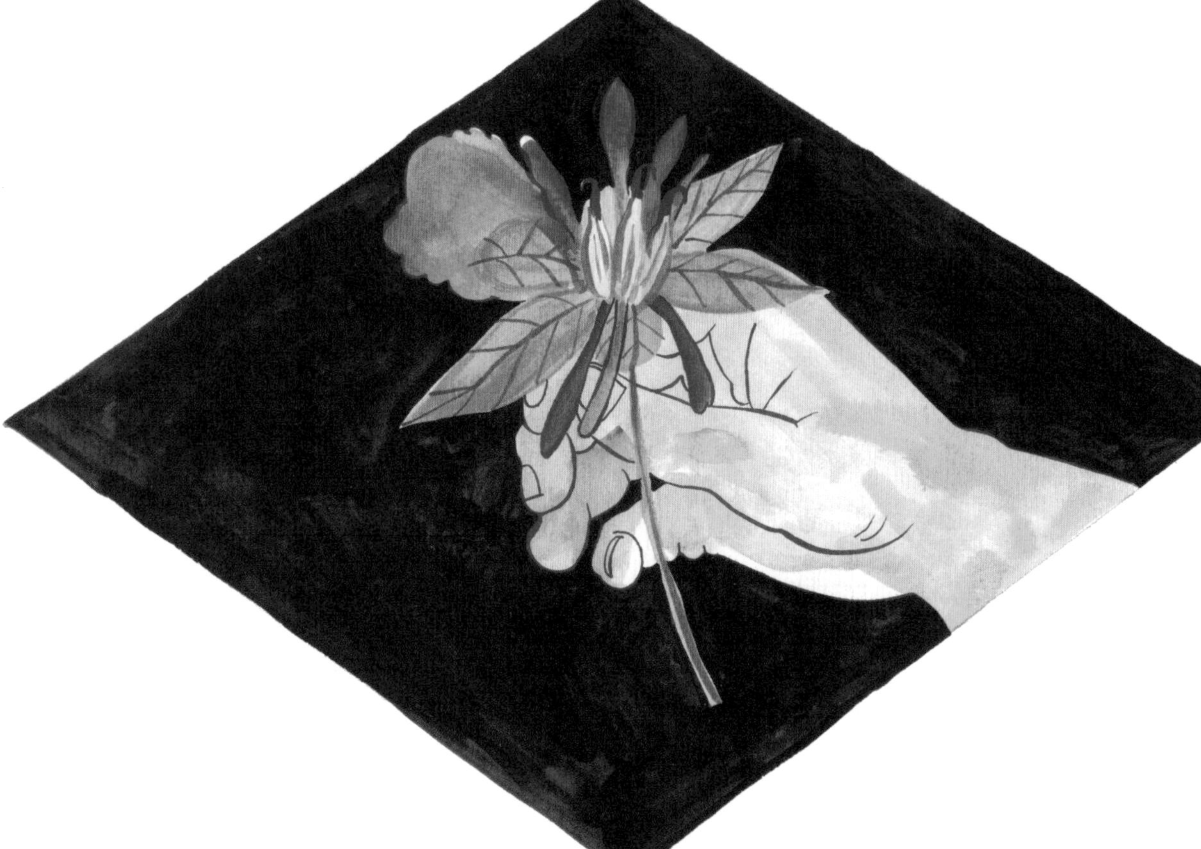

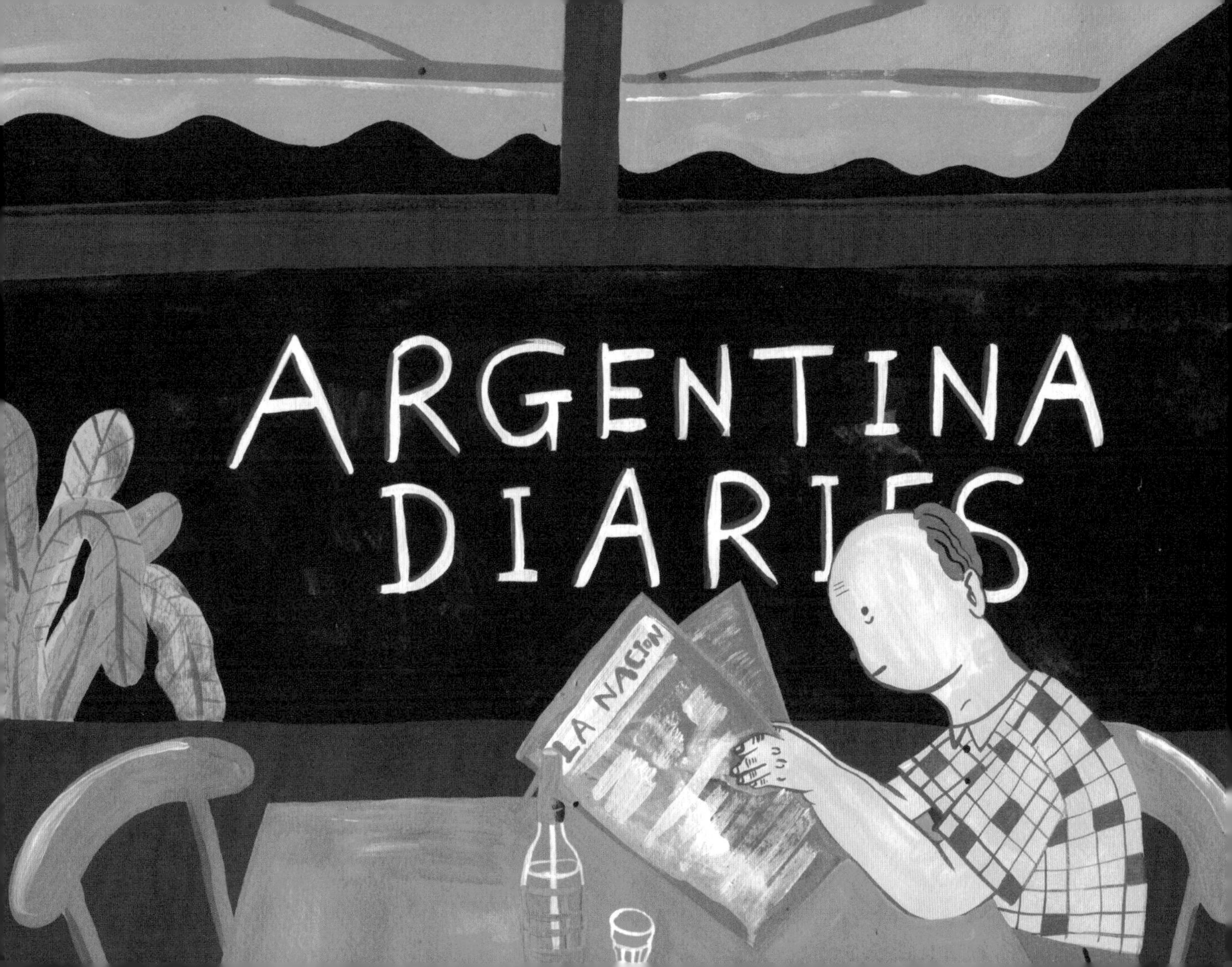
ARGENTINA
DIARIES
LA NACION

After a 26-hour flight, with bad butthurt and exhaustion, I felt happy to see Juan, Mirto, and Mirto's wife (who gives awesome hugs).

Saw a dead dog lying by the highway.
I wondered if the dog tended to the
sheeps who were close by.

A juggler performed for drivers during the brief stop-light. The bus driver watched the juggler and mumbled something under his breath.

This was a beautiful day. I met Paola, Pablo, Julia, and Mila. Ate delicious homemade pizzas.
We gathered over wine and coffee, spent the day drawing, exchanging stories and laughter.
Wonderful music, with the occasional chatter from neighbours and dogs from the streets
below.

There was a tall guy at a party, who had the blondest hair I'd ever seen, wearing a Hitler-moustache. He looked on as the others began to dance.

Saw two boys lying face down on the ground outside the supermarket. They were laughing, kicking each other playfully, and would press their faces against the ground.

Children collecting cardboards and assorted
materials left in the streets. They come in
carts drawn by horses.

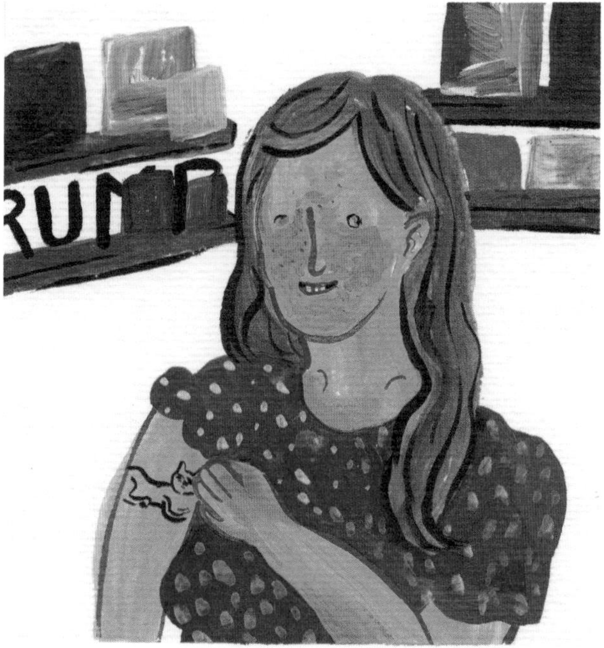

A comic shop owner showing me a tattoo she has based on Paola's art. So awesome!

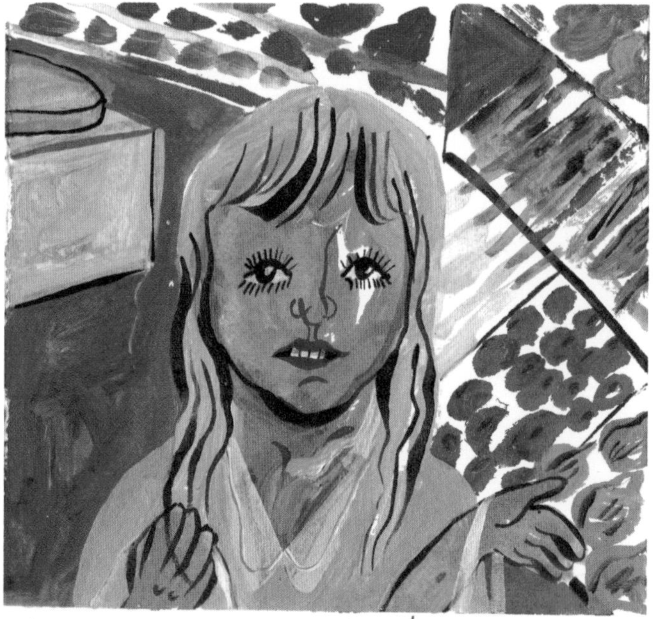

As I held a pack of strawberries, a lady came by and speaking in spanish, she spoke of something along the lines of "no, don't buy these here. There are better and cheaper ones outside". That was awfully kind of her.

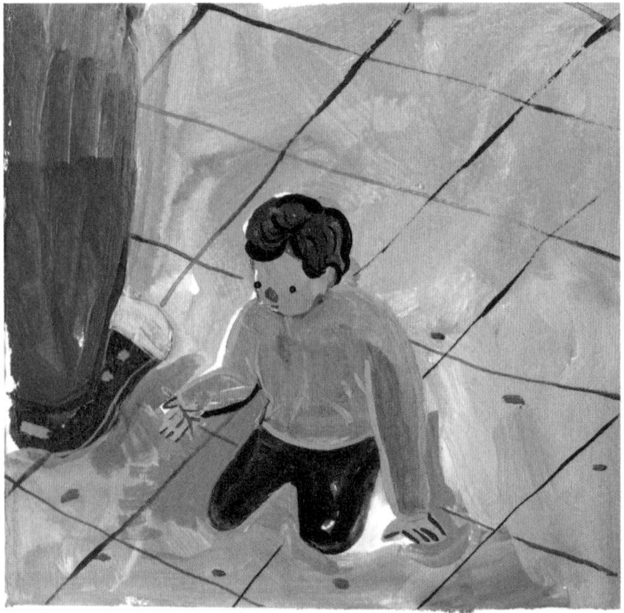

A boy held a large maple leaf. He kept looking (rather intently) at the leaf, as if he was trying to figure out how this leaf is going to fit into an imaginative play he had going on, while waiting for his dad, who's on the phone.

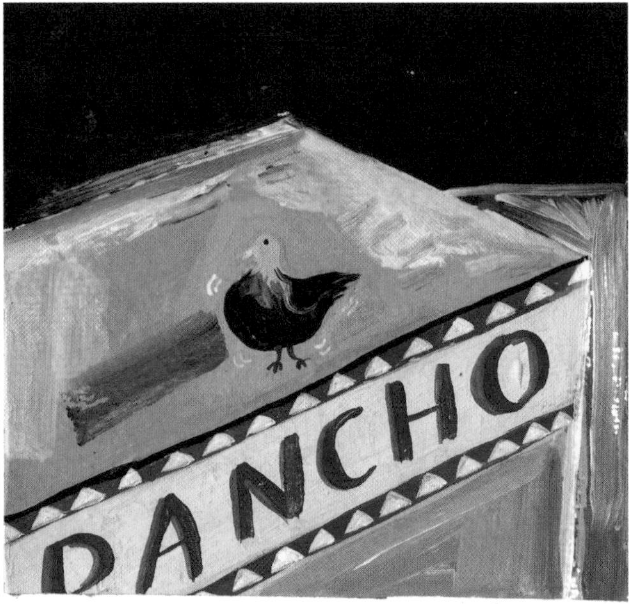
PANCHO

There was a really chubby pigeon bobbing above Pancho's snack stall at the bus interchange. I love its style. It's a cool bird.

We met at a lovely cafe for a drawing session. The place is filled with interesting (mostly) elderly folks. The man who runs the cafe is known as "the spinner" for he spins the bottles and glasses on the table when he brings you your drinks. Plus, he makes cartoons on your coffee's foam-top.
We talked about shit, vomit, falling on dance floors, peeing, being nervous, you know, what conversations are made of when you put Paola, Julia, Solá, Sofia, and myself together on a warm humid afternoon.

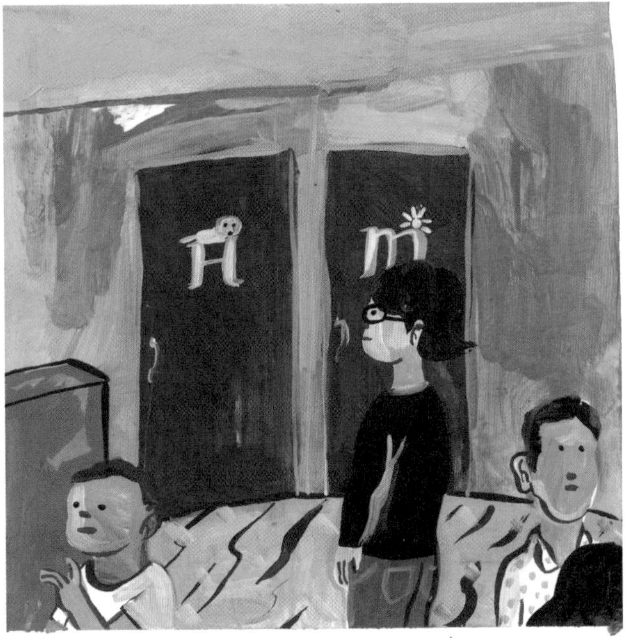
H
M

I'm in a cafe, looking for the toilet. I see a picture of a lion for the men's toilet, and a picture of a daisy for the women's toilet. Why not a picture of a lioness, perhaps?

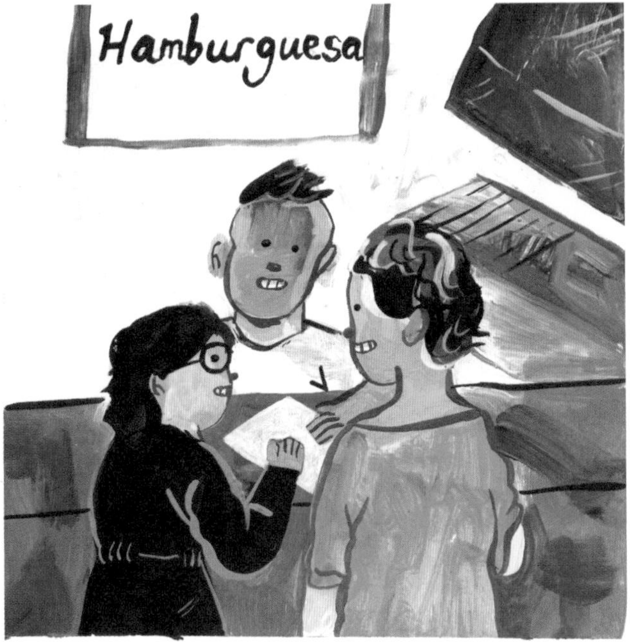
Hamburguesa

After a whole day of translating, my friend spoke to the waiter in English, and Español to me. Confusion ensues.

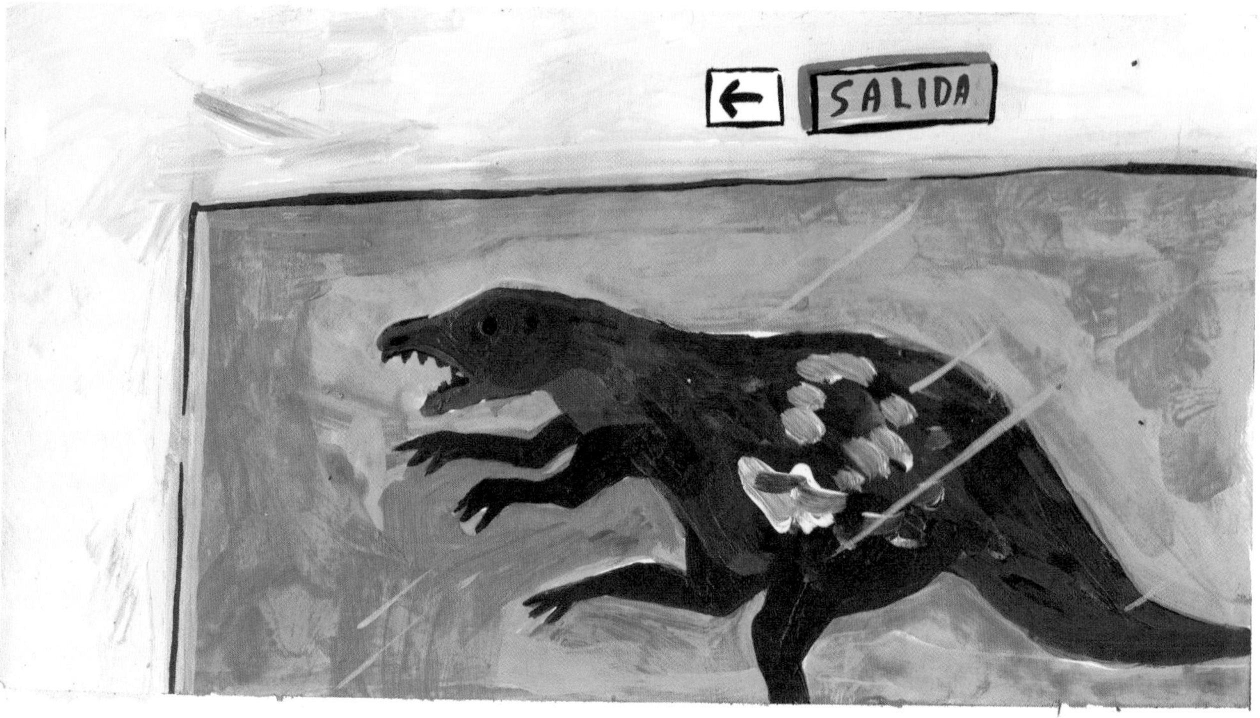
SALIDA

A dinosaur at the Museo de La Plata, heading for the exit.

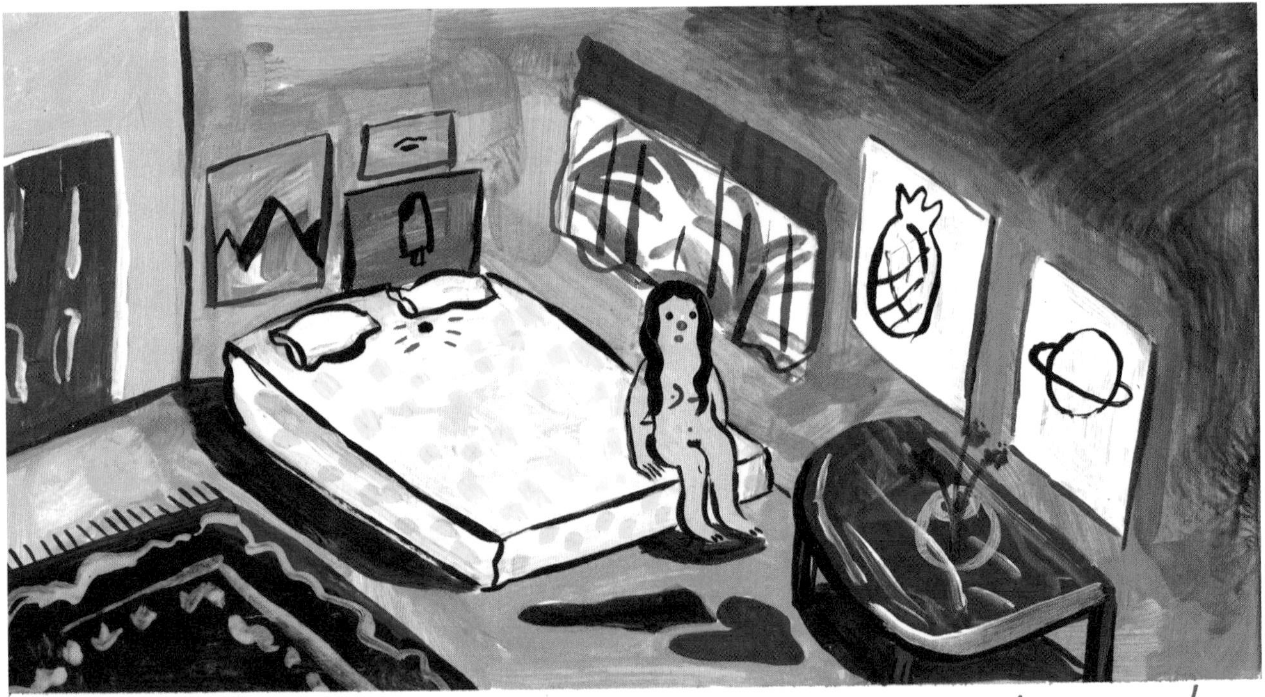

A scene from Didi's very interesting story involving a black stone left on her side of the bed, the morning after.

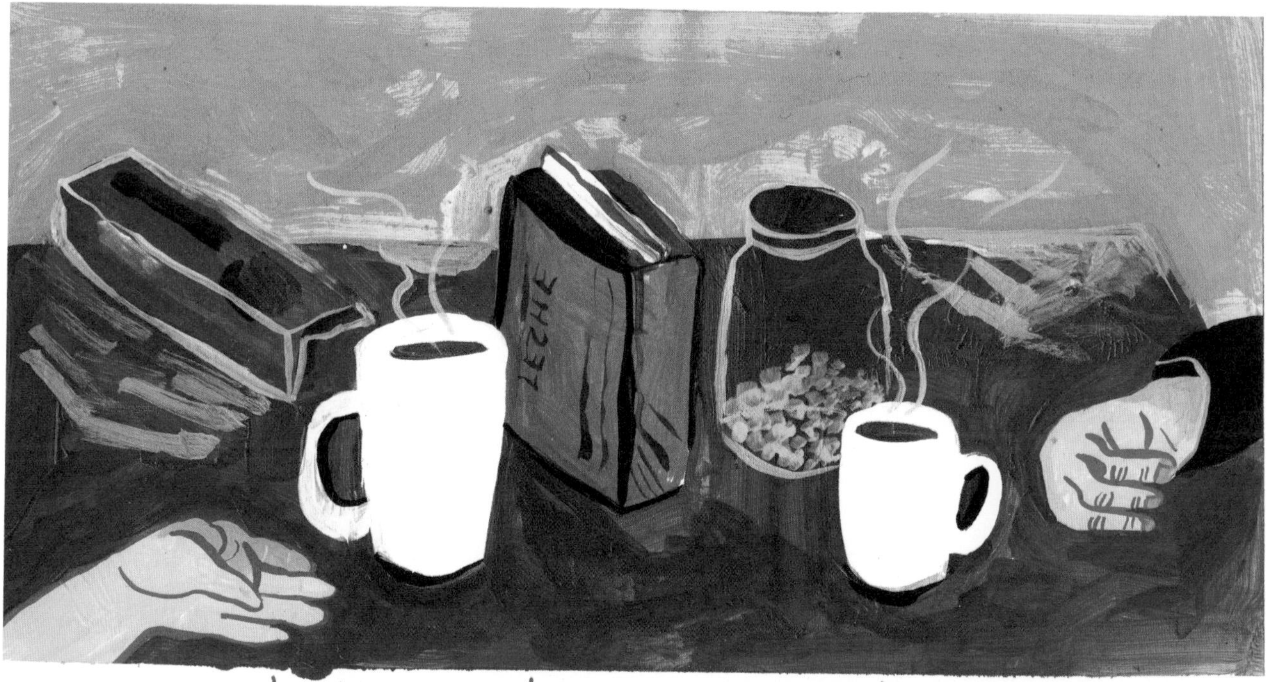
LECHE

Matters of the heart exchanged over smooth yummy coffee, biscuits, a cute milk jug, with Fragato, her neighbour's cat, strolling about between us. Muchas gracias Sofia.

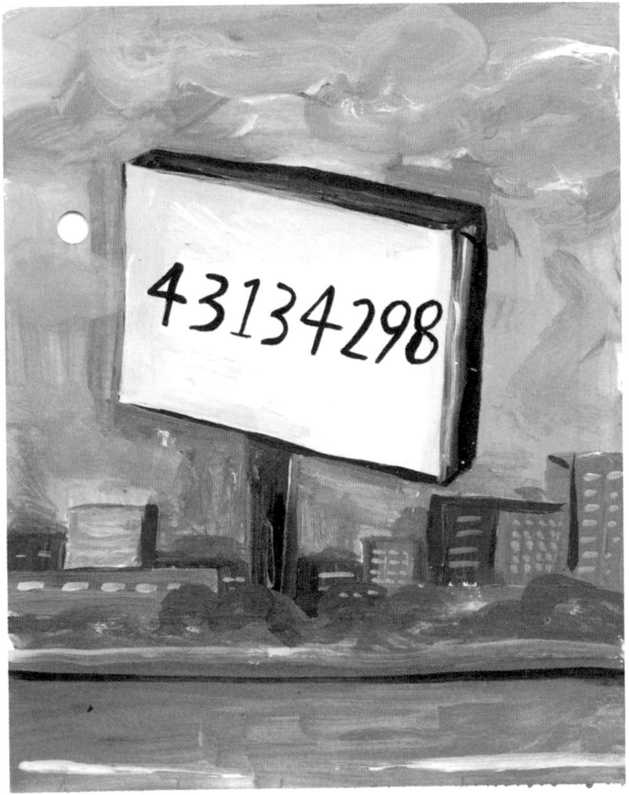
43134298

Most random advert sign goes to...

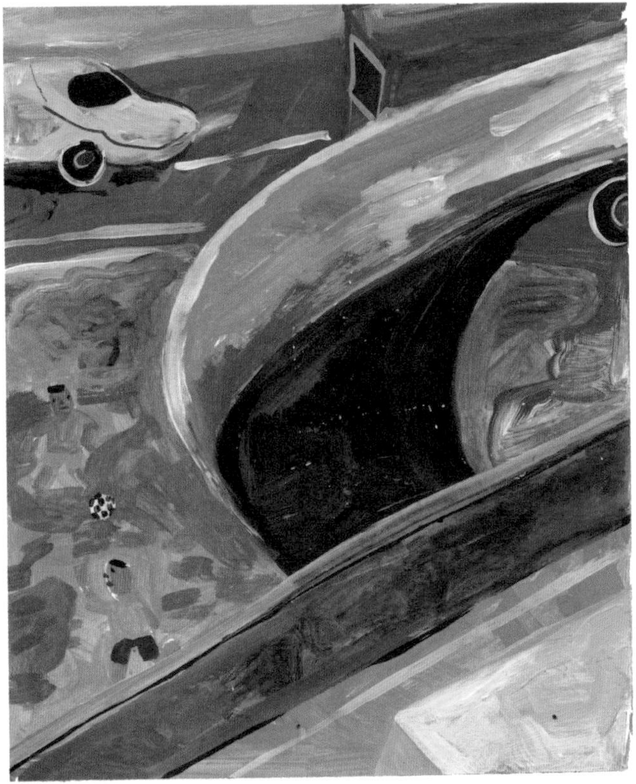

Two boys playing soccer by the highway.

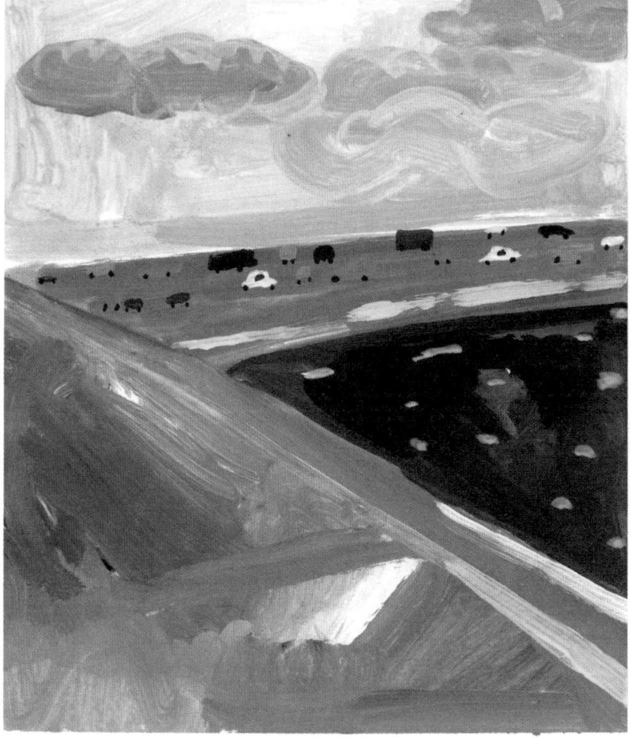

I'm lost. "Get down at this stop" my gut says. And, I found, I was exactly where I ought to be.

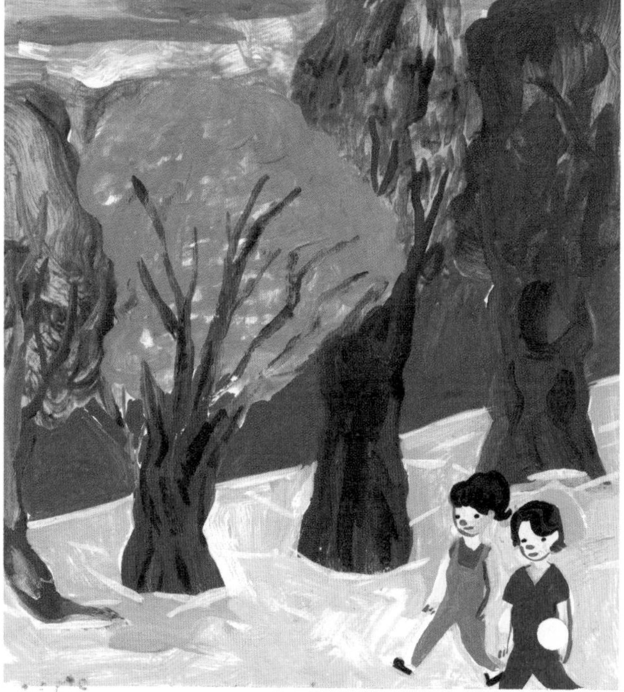

Jacarandas in bloom, Mila's shop of handcrafted beauties, and conversations of transitions and connectedness. Soon, evening arrives.

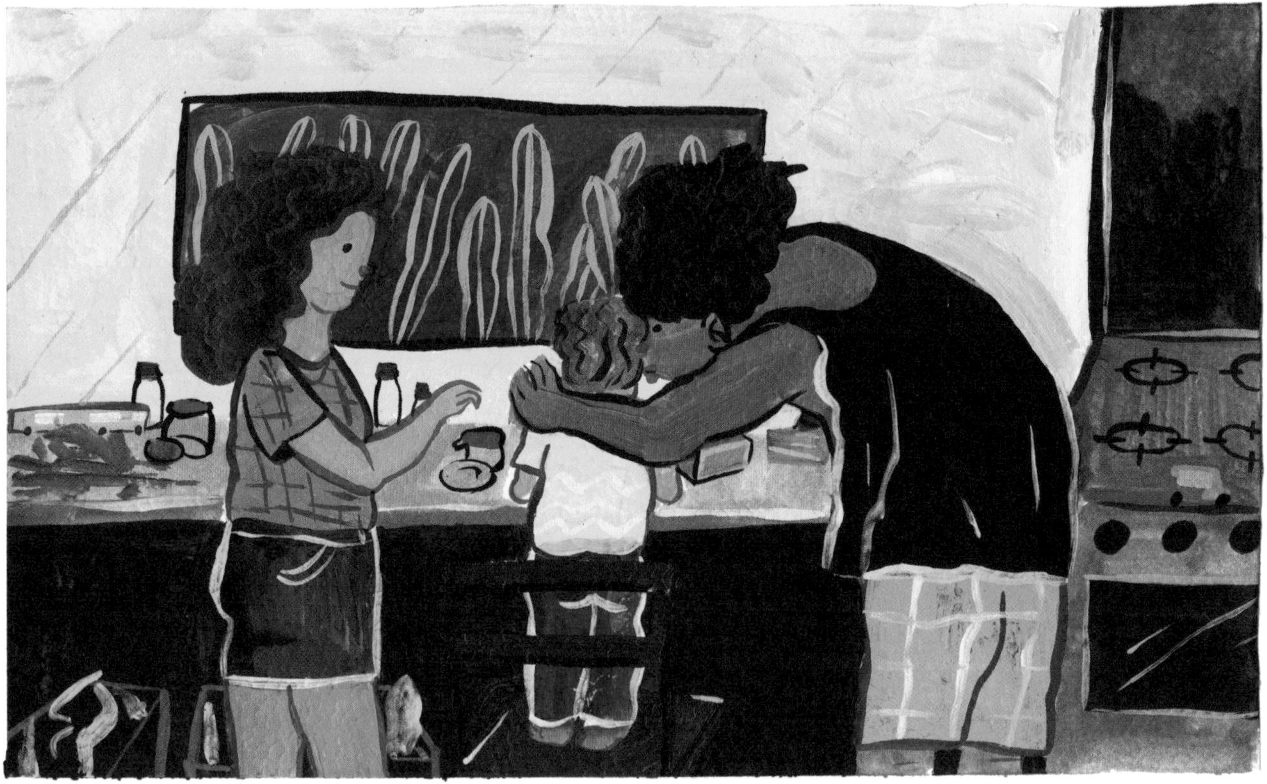

Witnessing a family making a meal together, in a house littered with little cars and trains.. photos and art... a checkered-pattern Yard. It was.. It is, a house full of bright sparks.

Infatuation

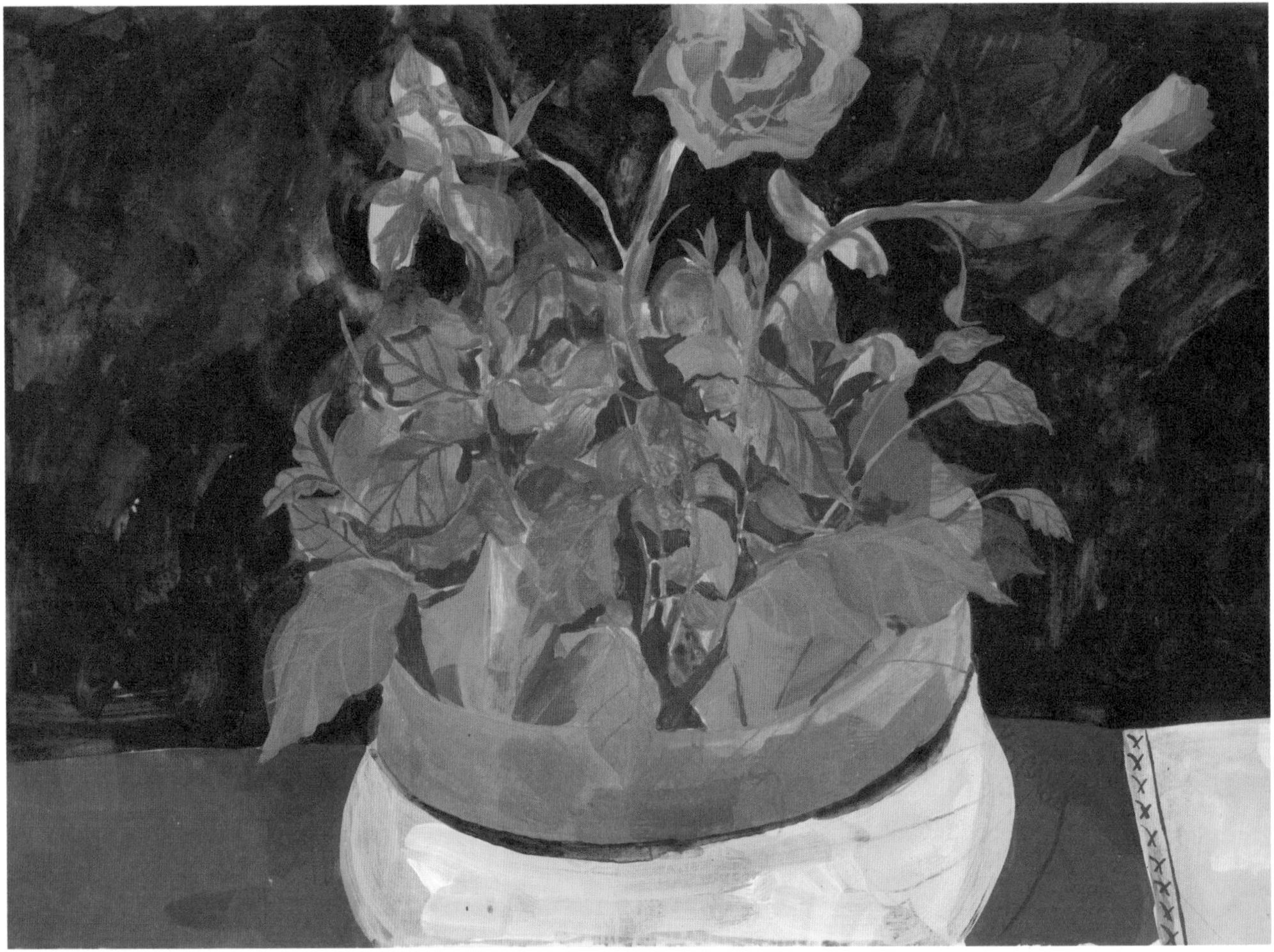

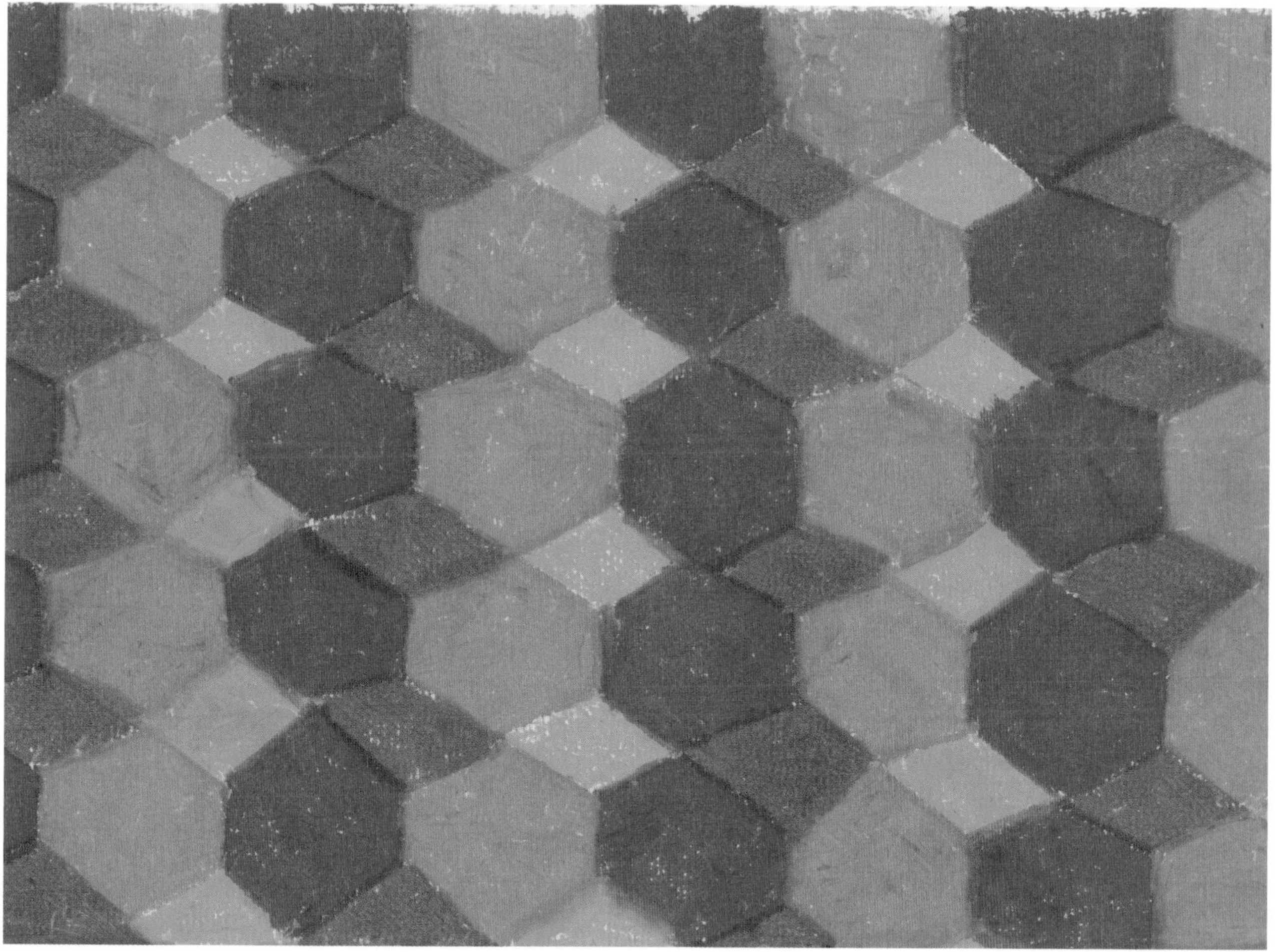

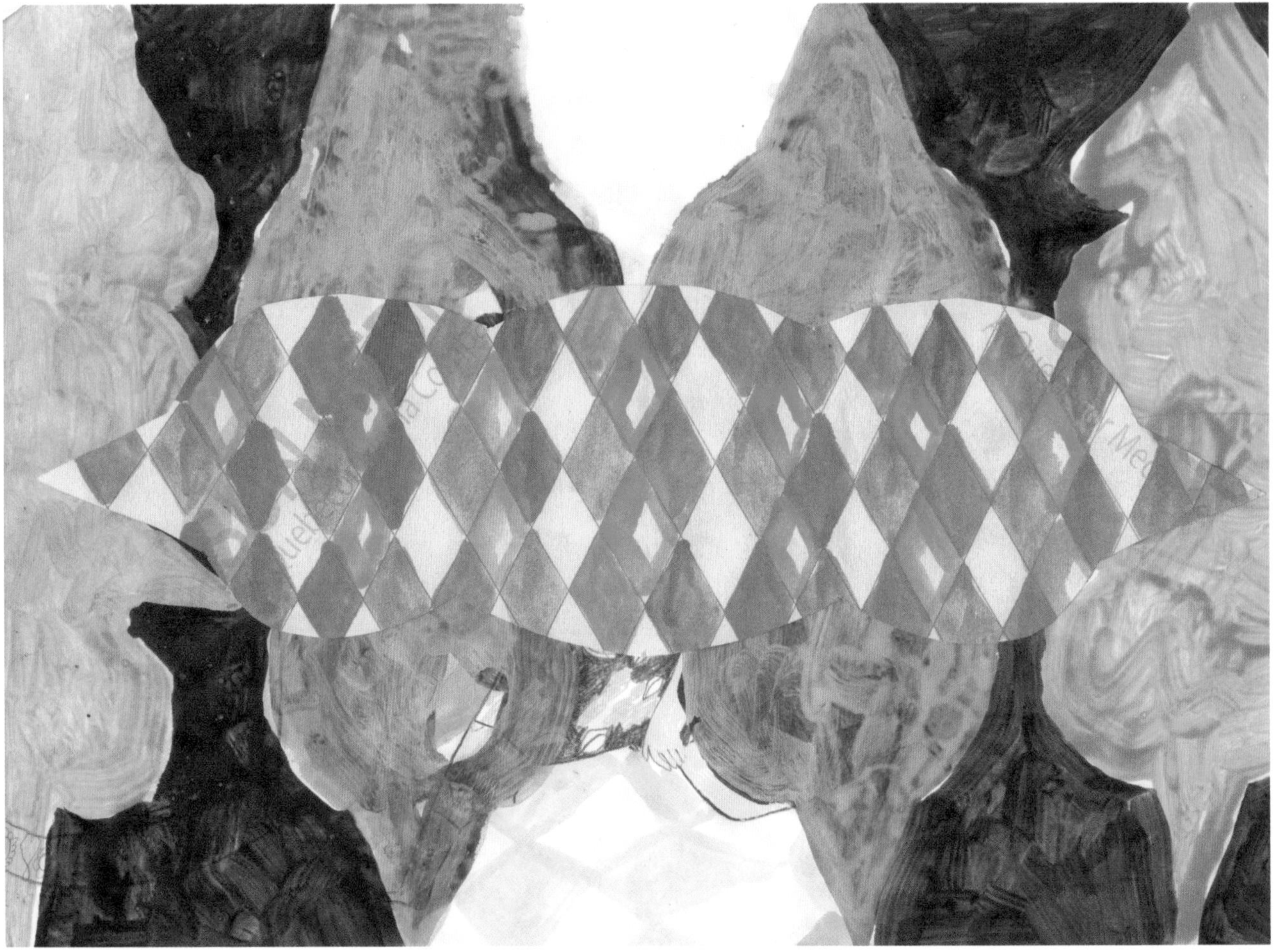

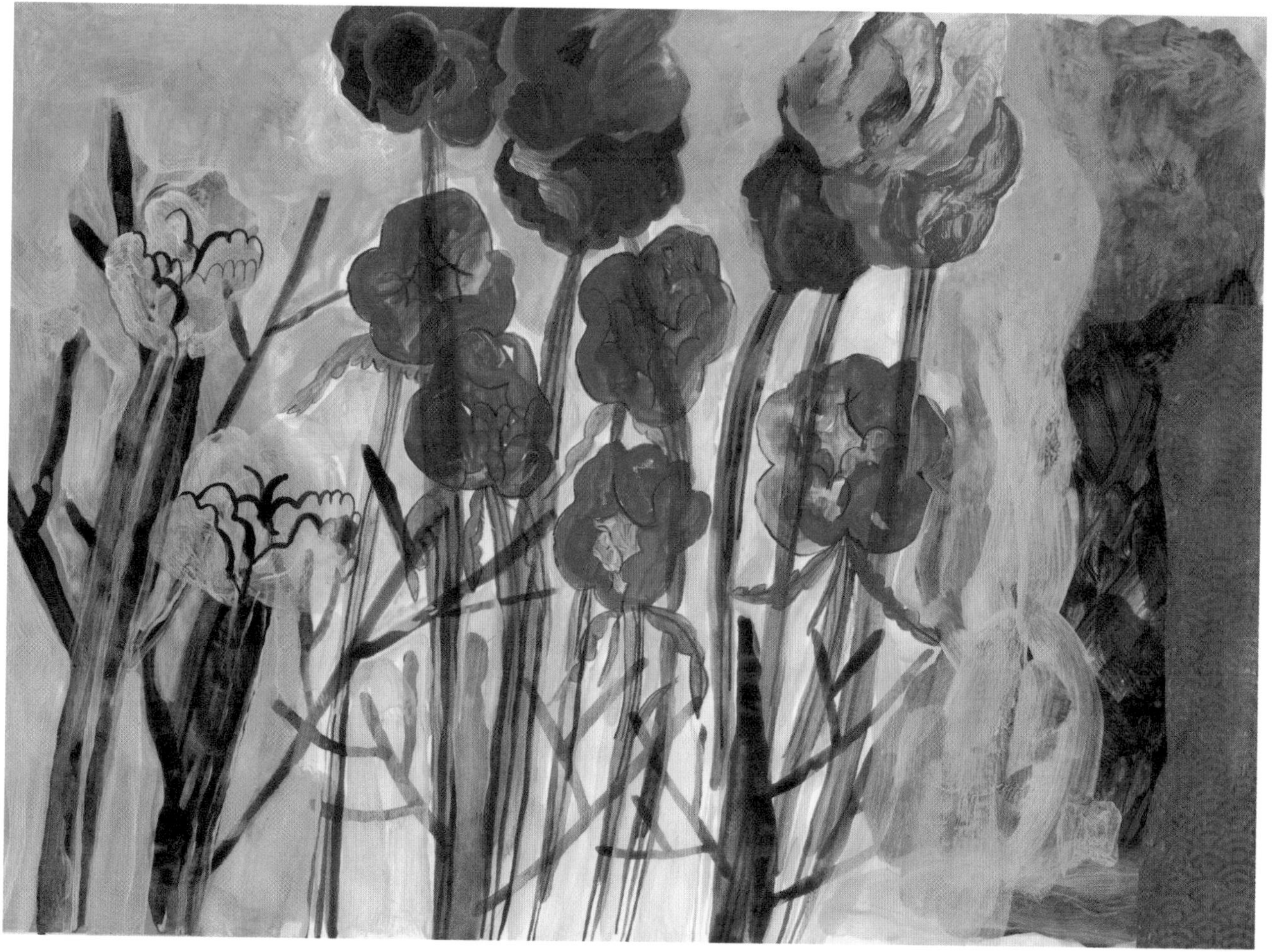

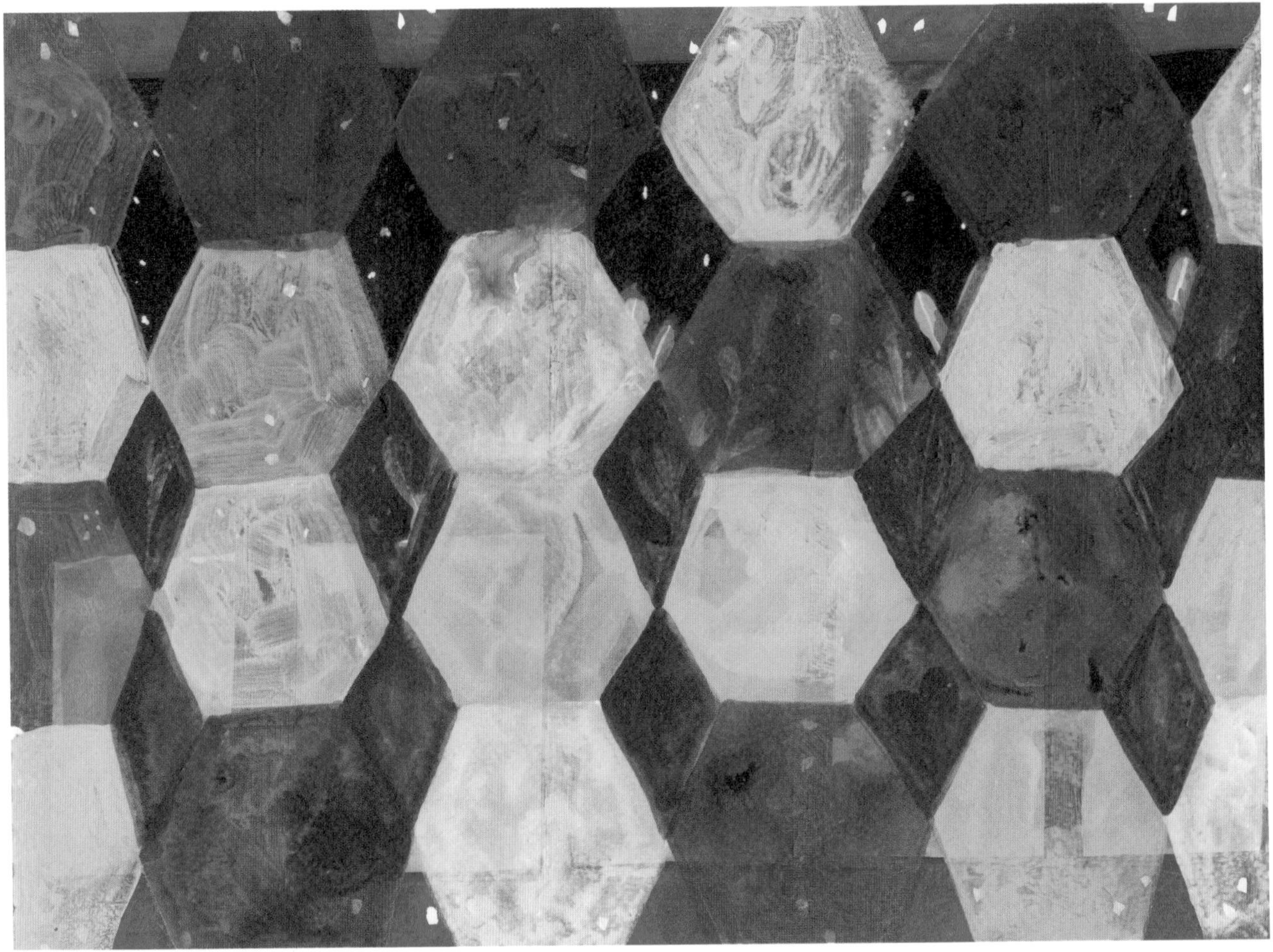

I wrote my first love letter to a boy when I was 10.

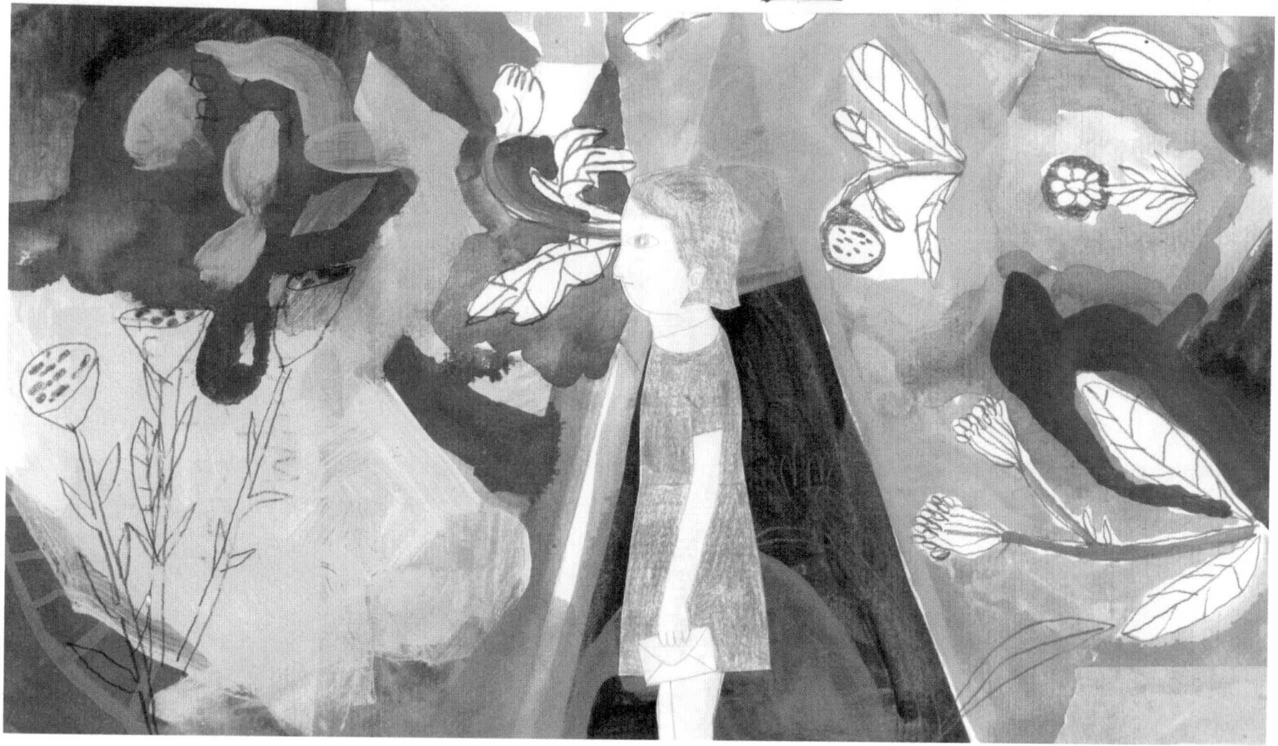

He crushed it and threw it back at me.

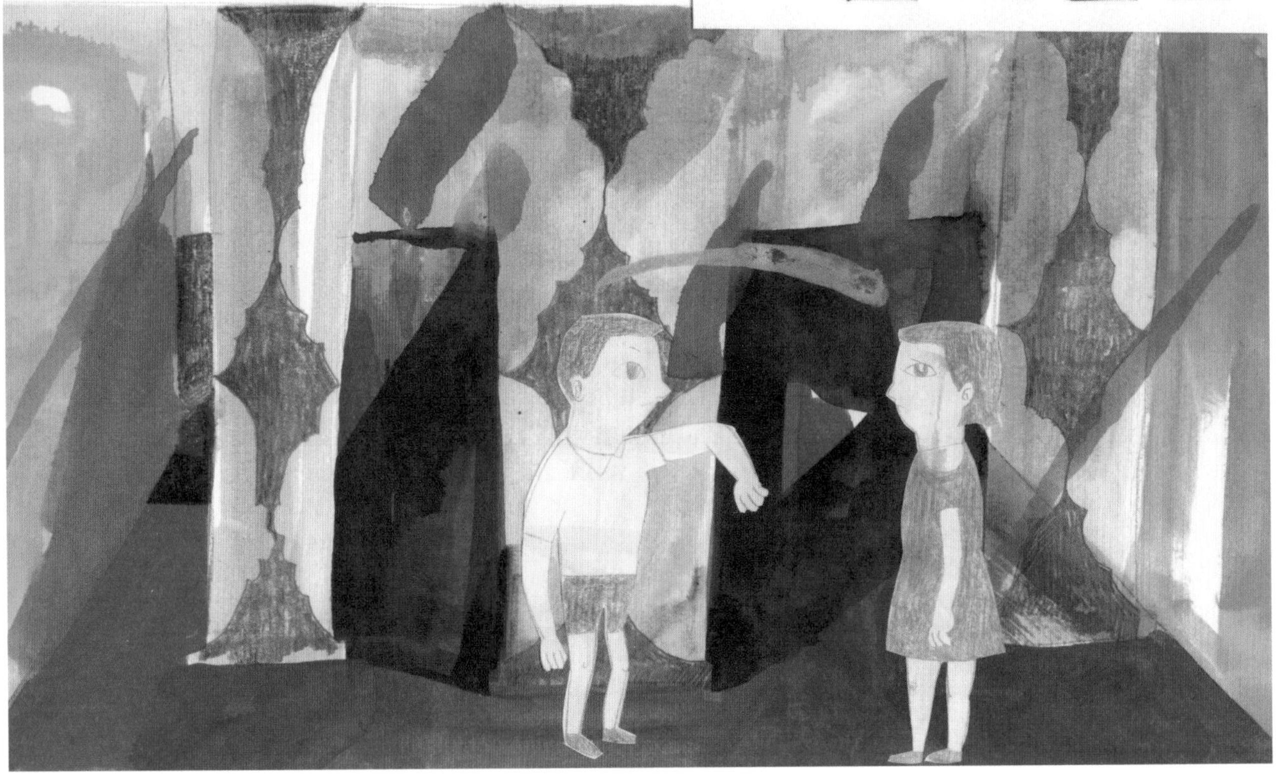

"What an asshole."

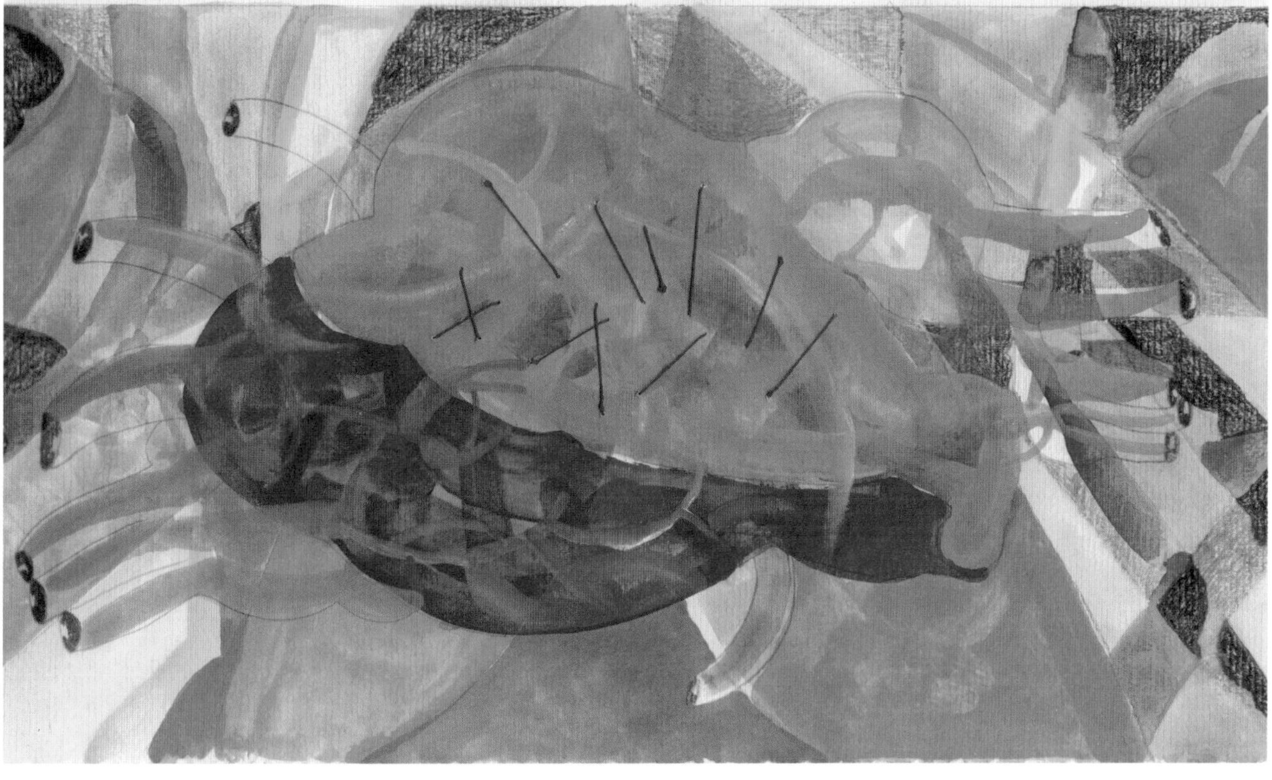

I wished that was the first thing that came to my mind, but... nope.

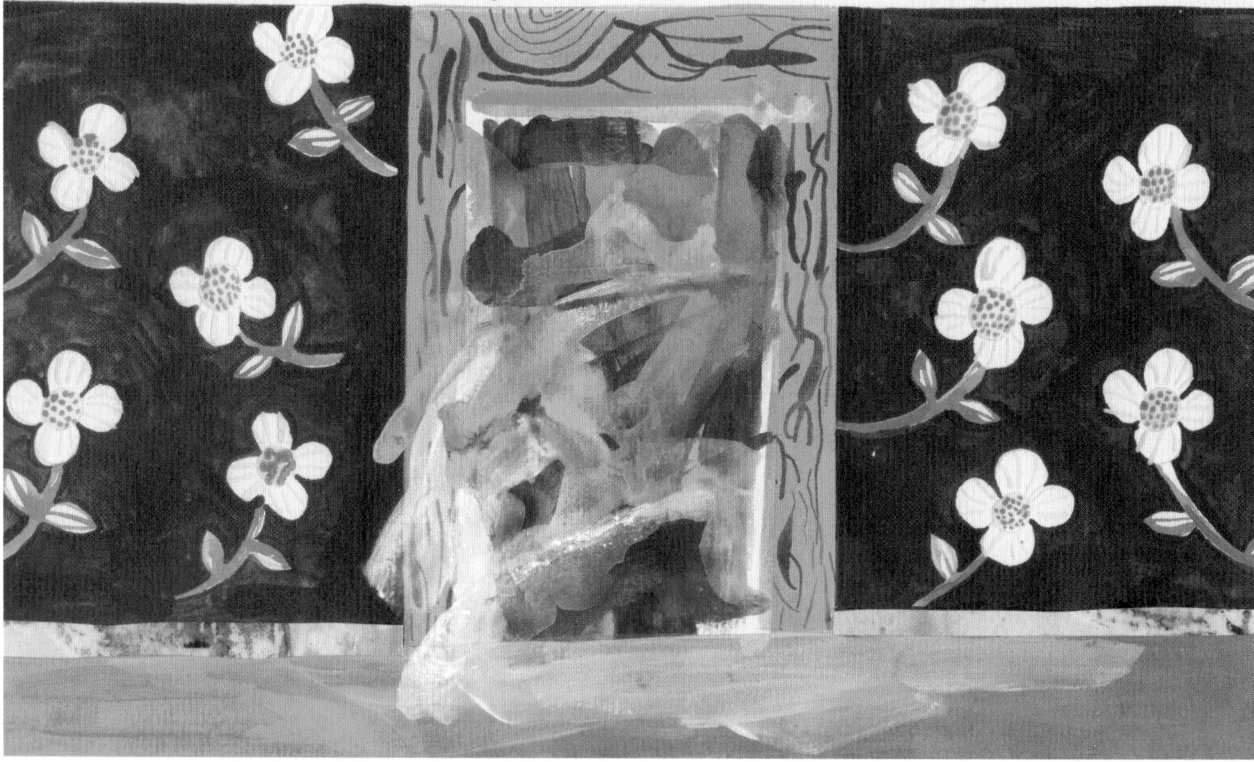

"What did I do wrong?" was my first response.

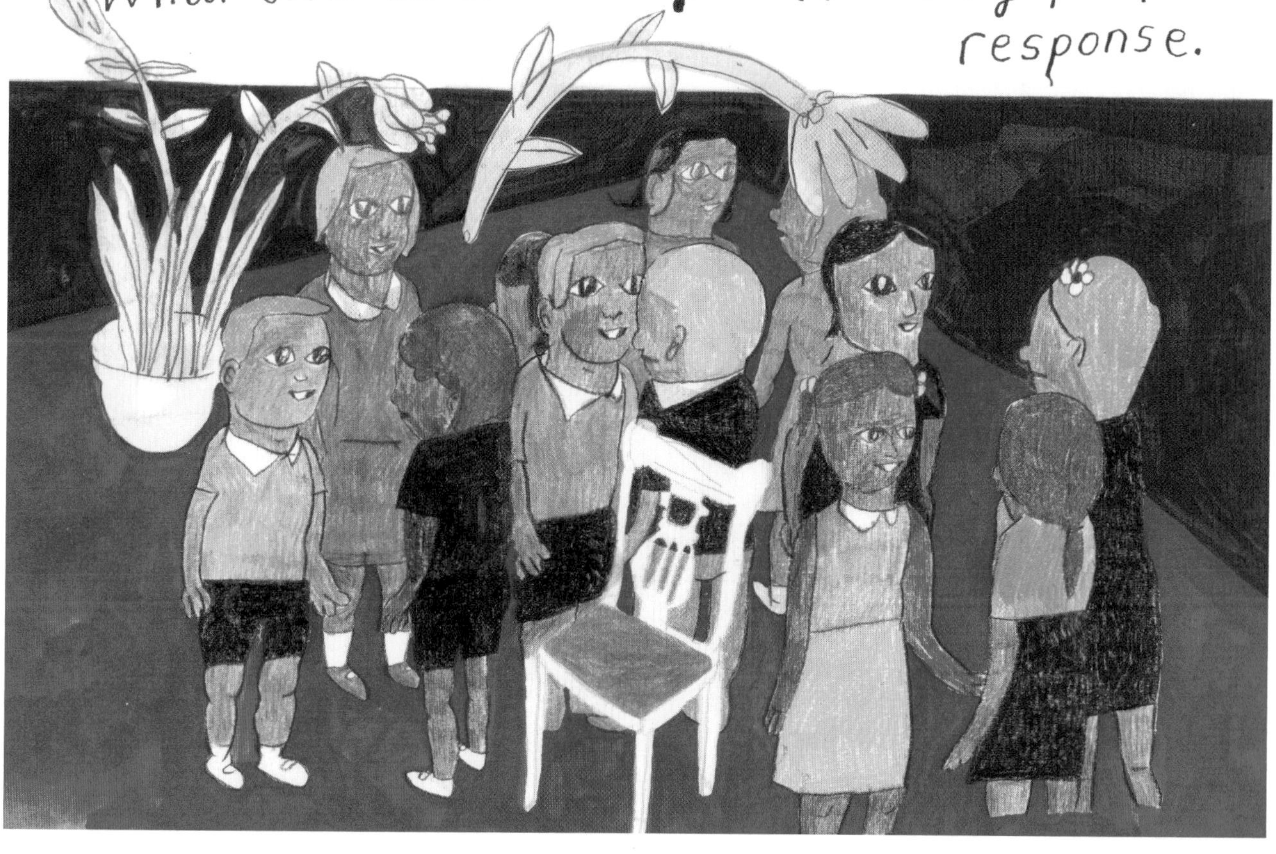

It all happened during a school assembly. We, us kids, standing in lines, facing the portraits of our president and his wife.

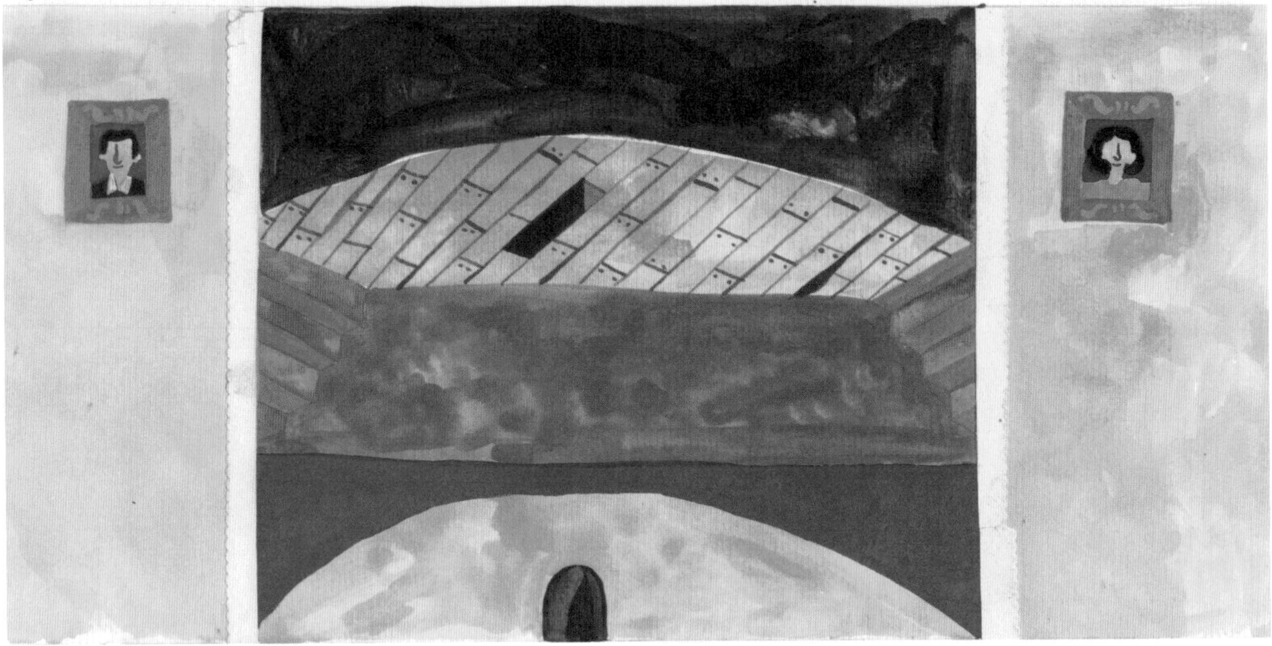

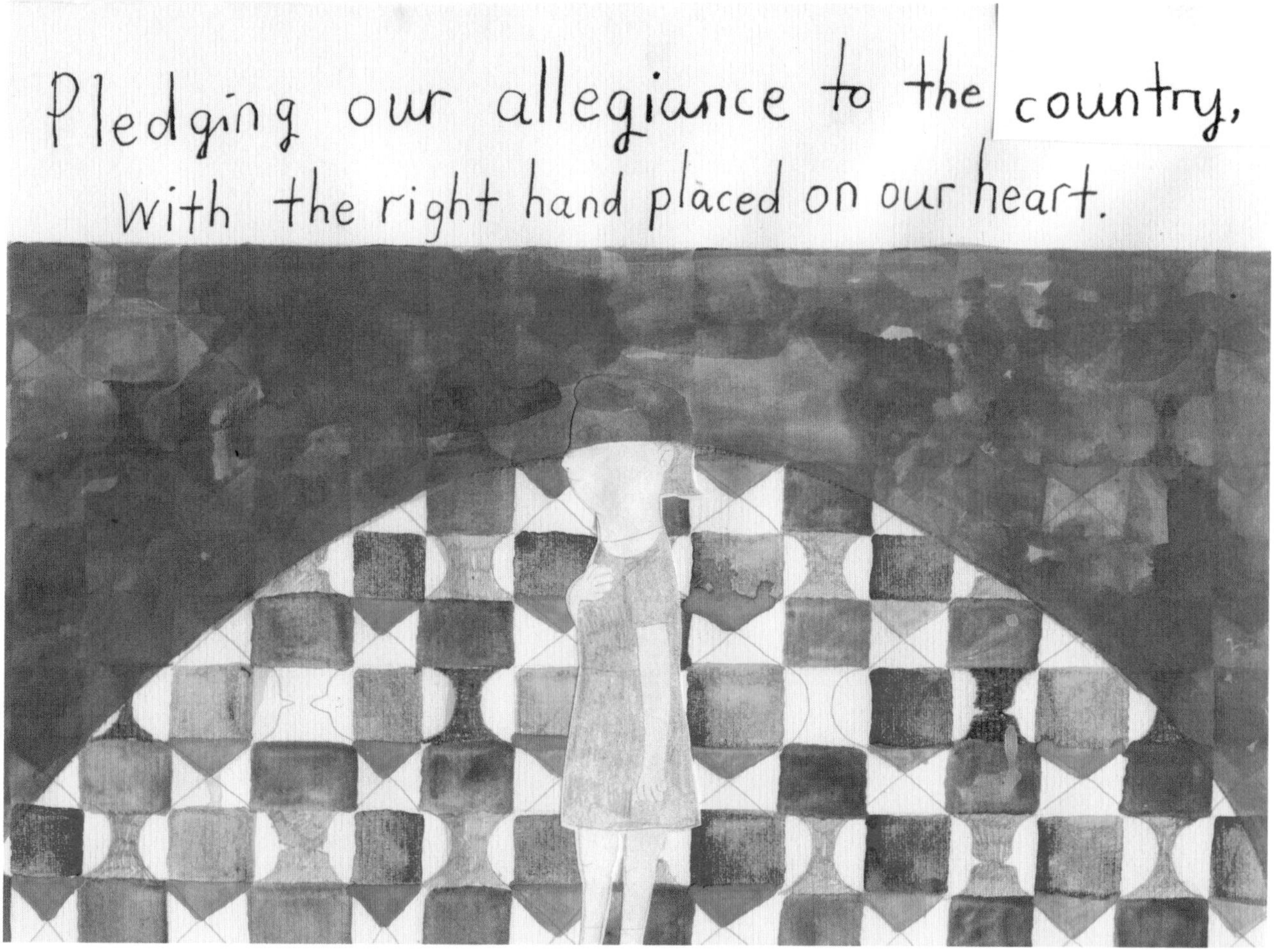
Pledging our allegiance to the country,
with the right hand placed on our heart.

Only this time, I held my rejection over my heart.

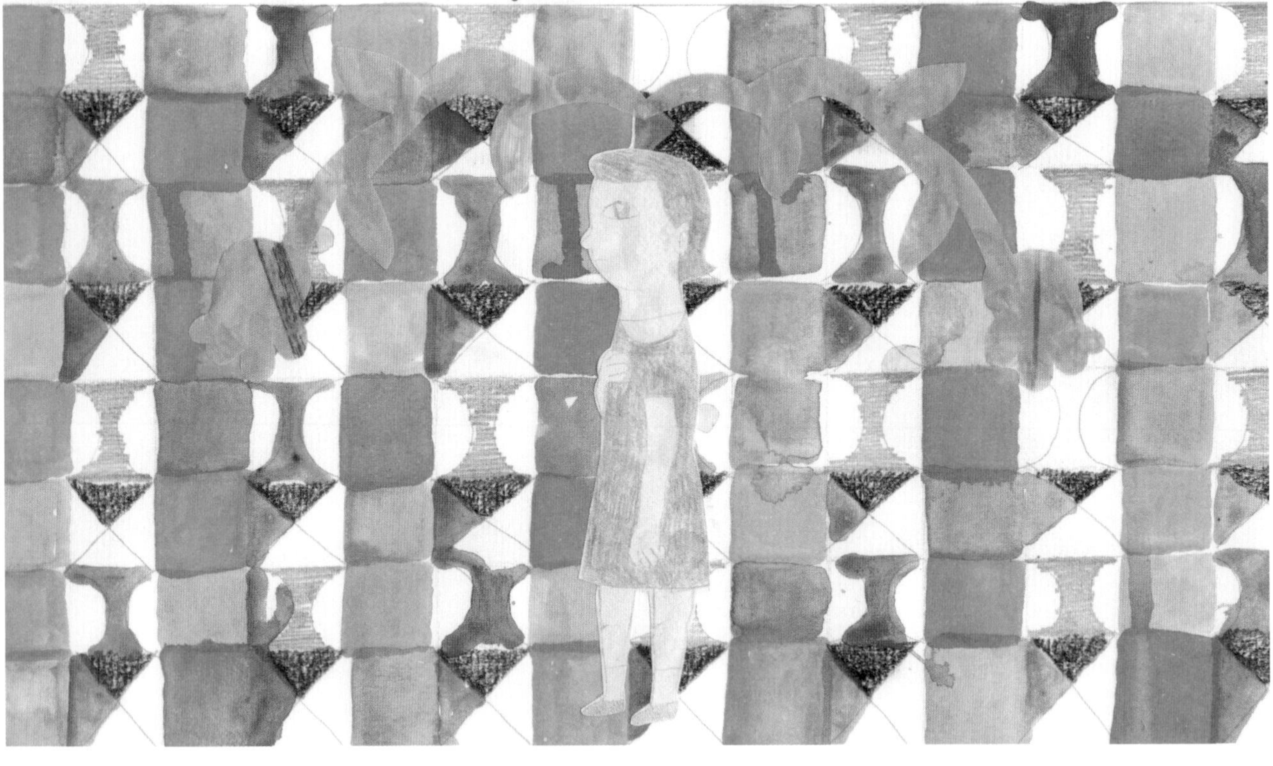

I held back my tears, 'cause feeling sad over some silly [redacted] crushed infatuation felt equivalent to being a weak wuss.

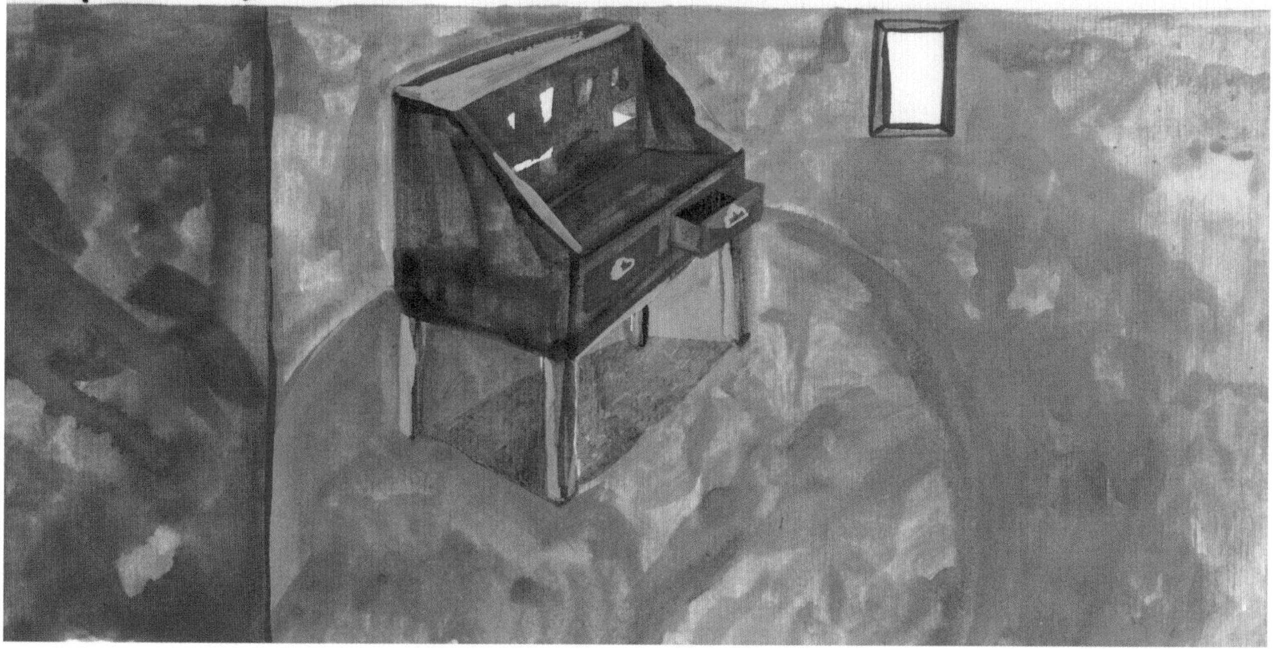

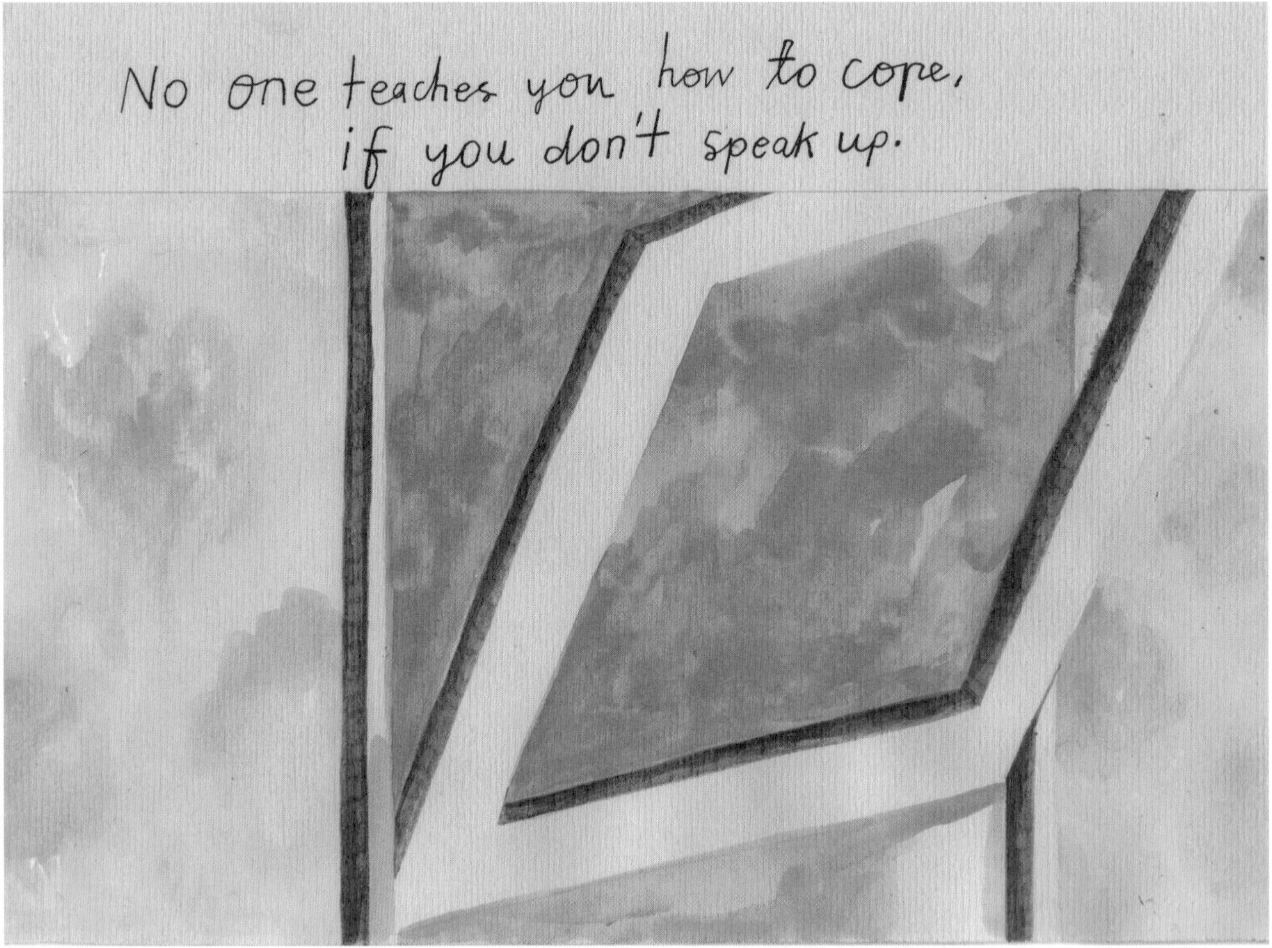
No one teaches you how to cope,
if you don't speak up.

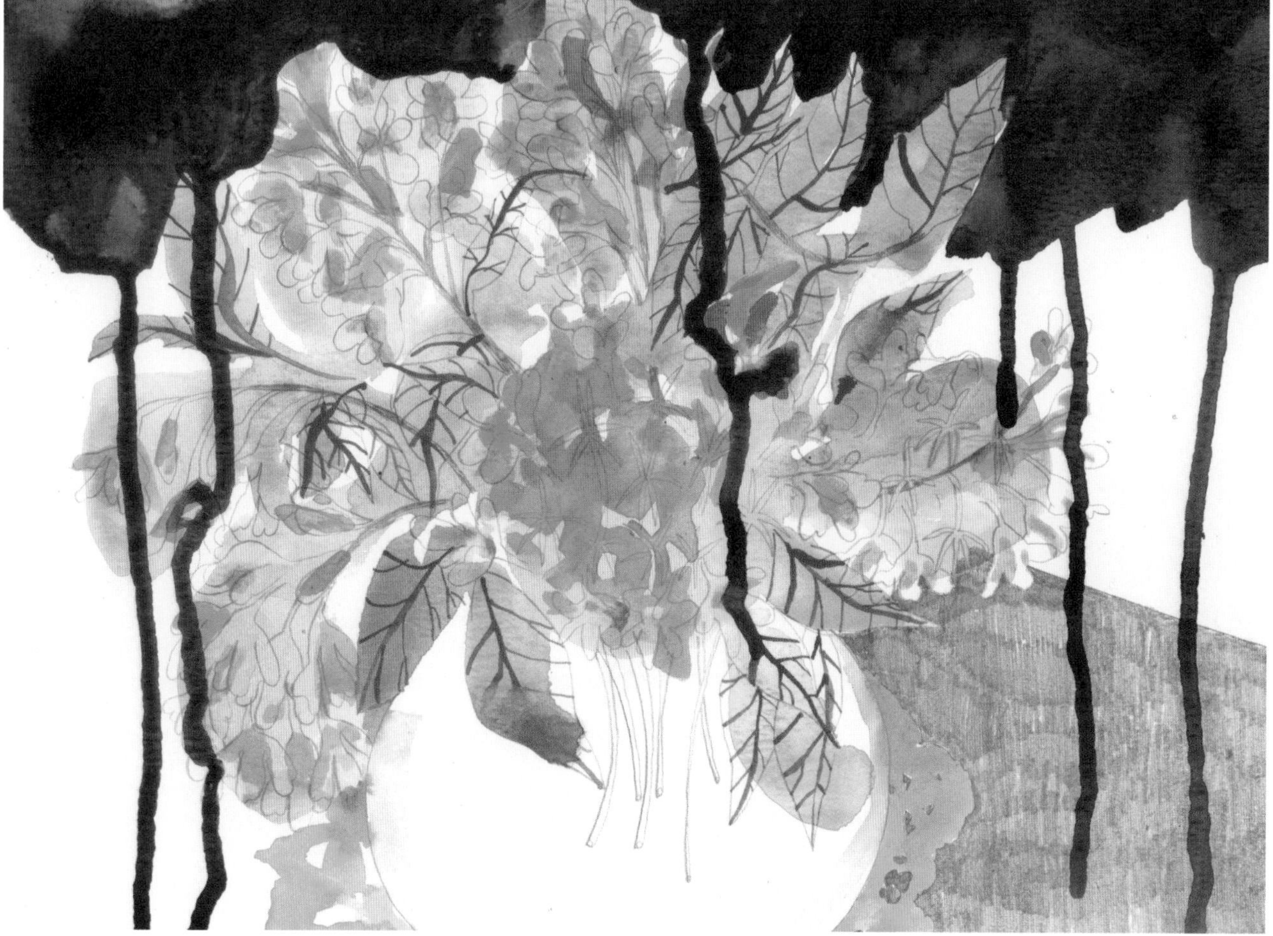

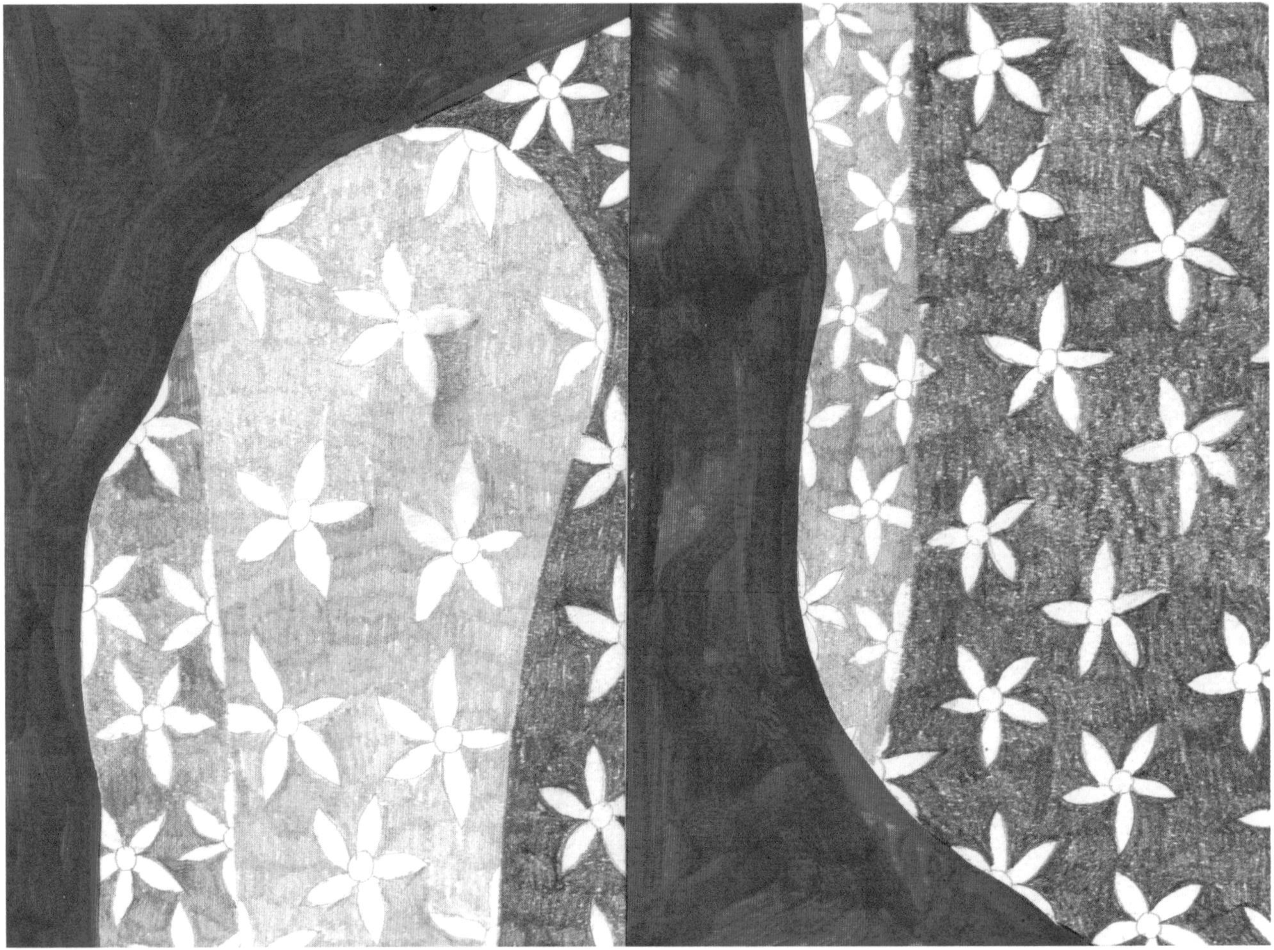

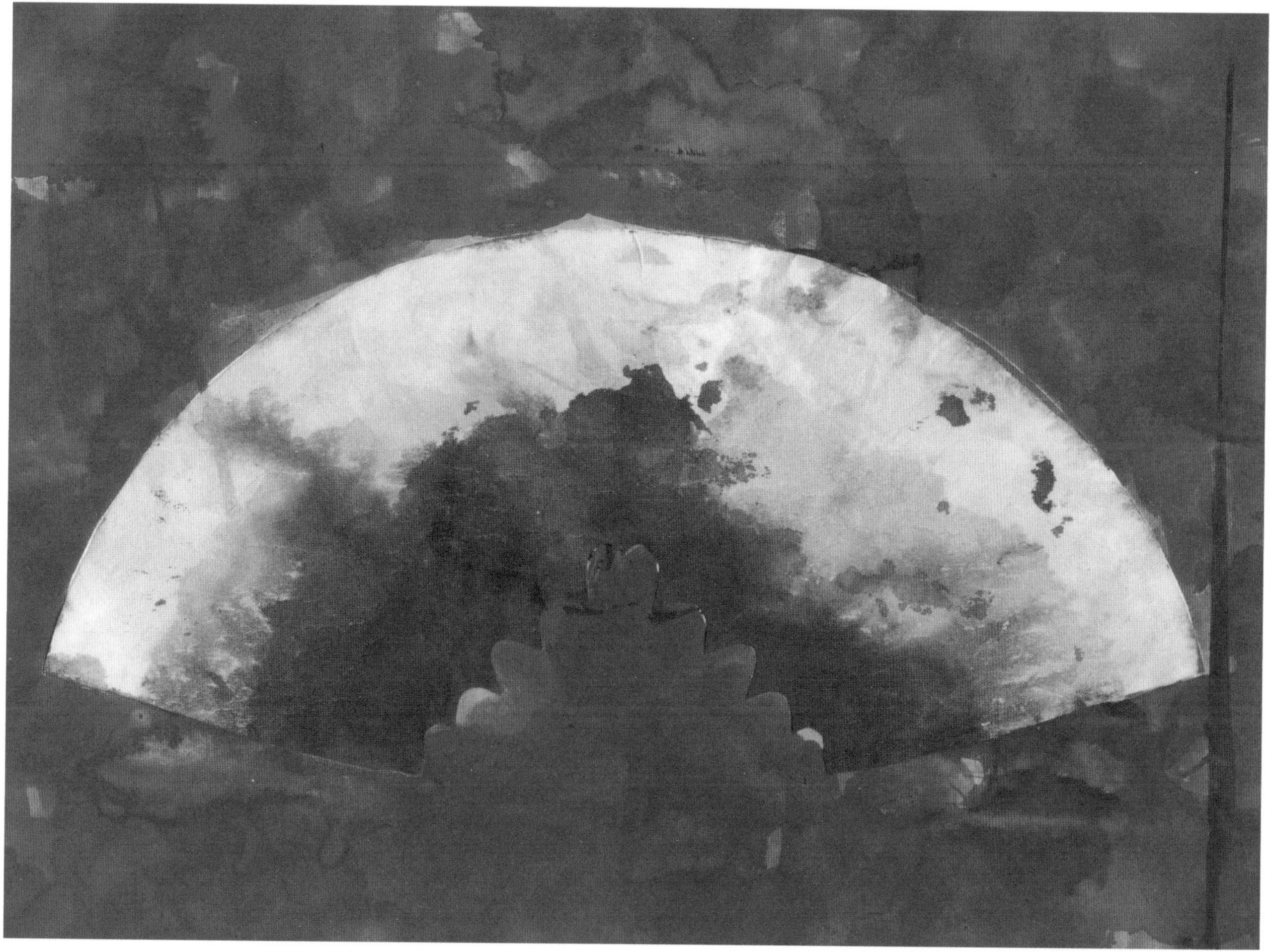

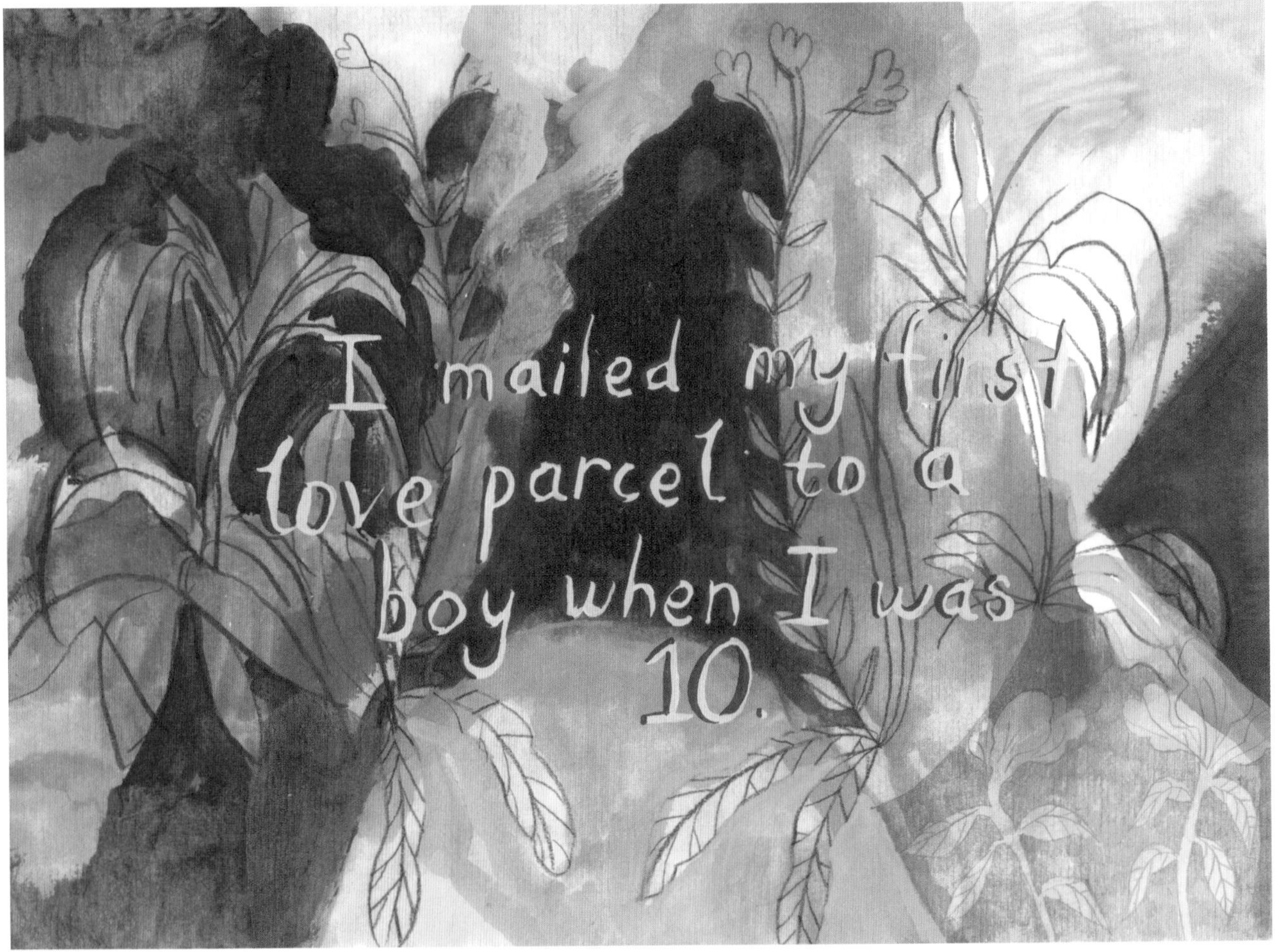
I mailed my first
love parcel to a
boy when I was
10.

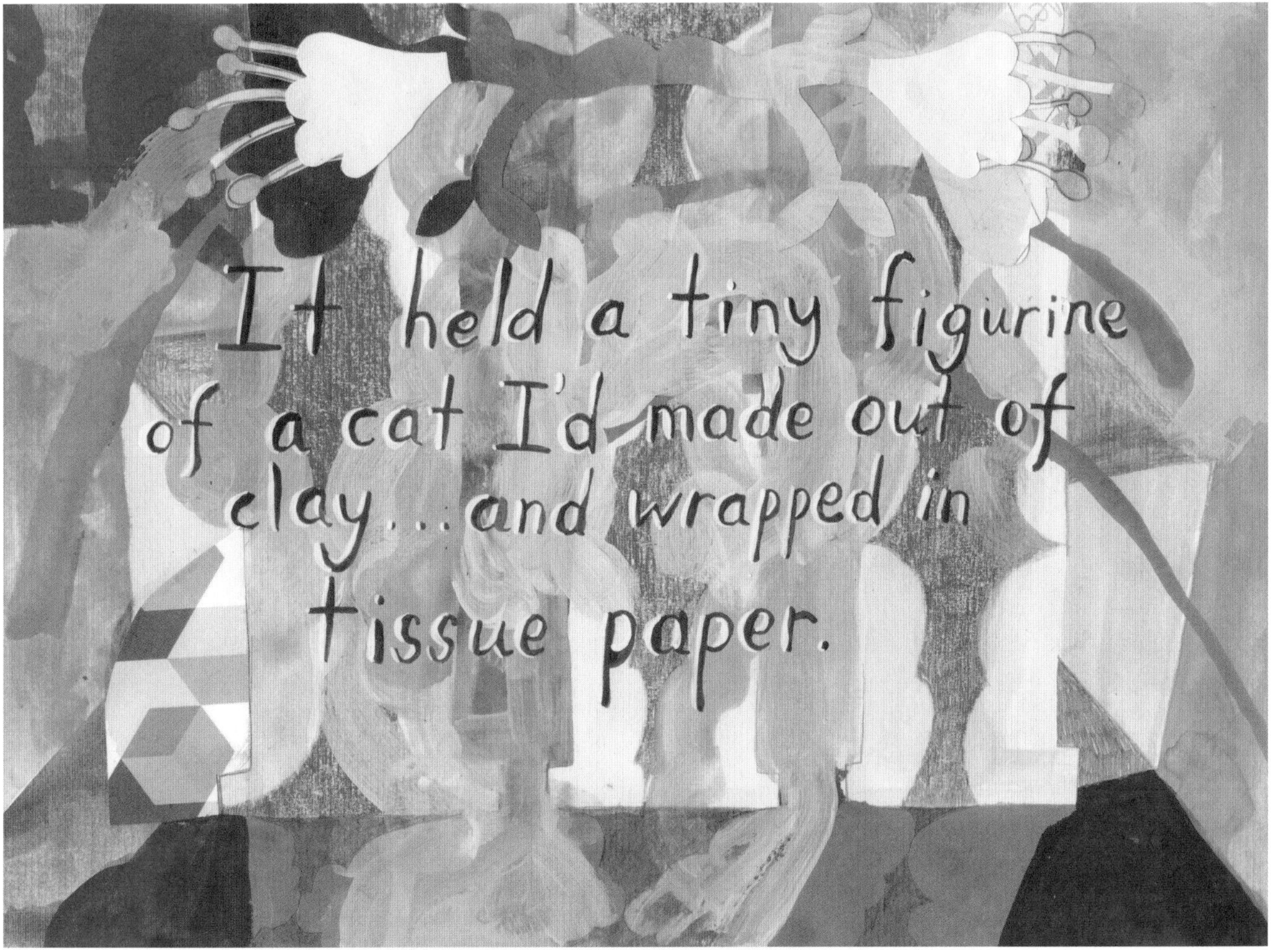
It held a tiny figurine
of a cat I'd made out of
clay...and wrapped in
tissue paper.

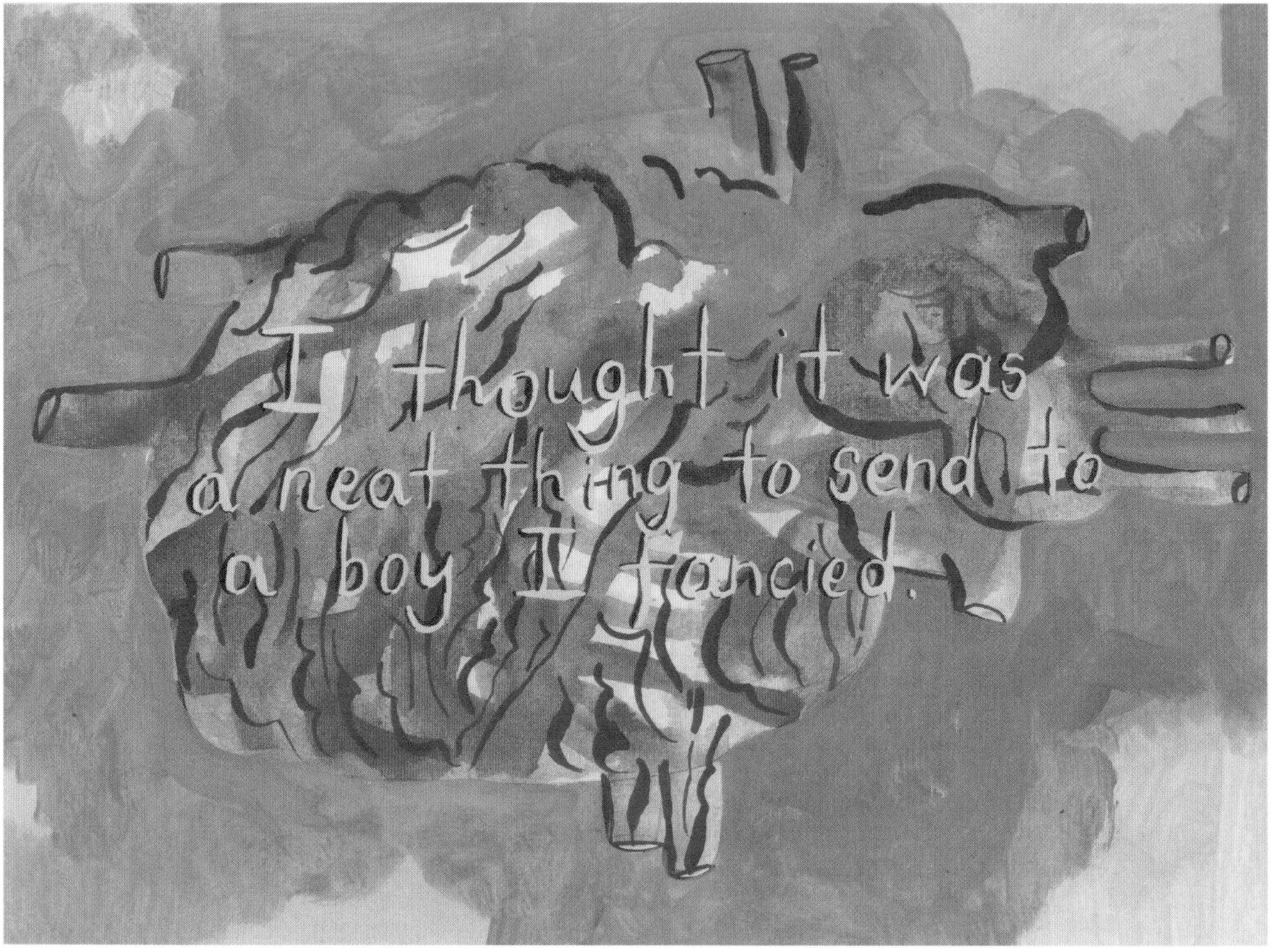
I thought it was
a neat thing to send to
a boy I fancied.

I tied the box with
a pink ribbon I'd salvaged
from an old cake box.

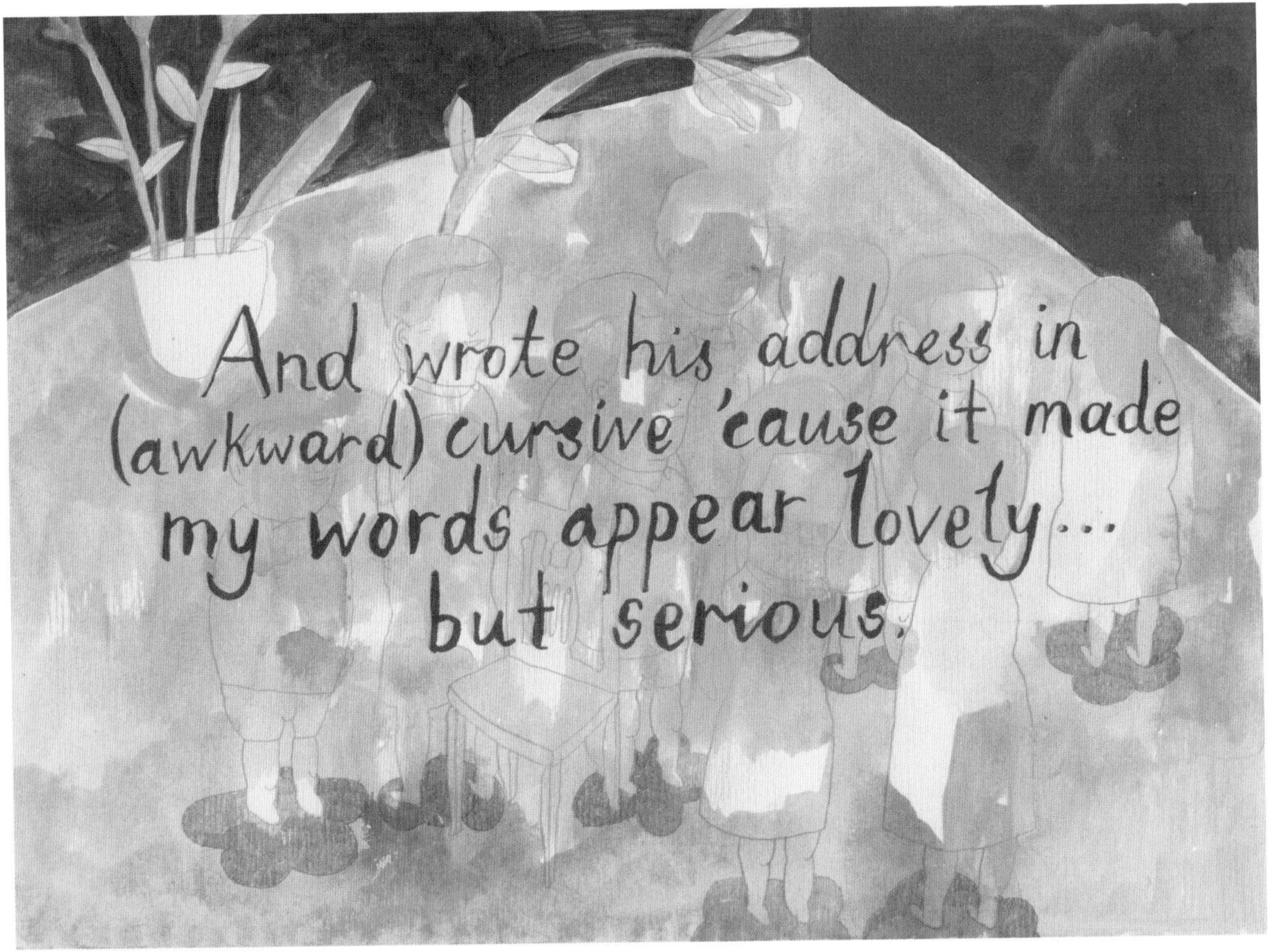
And wrote his address in
(awkward) cursive 'cause it made
my words appear lovely...
but serious.

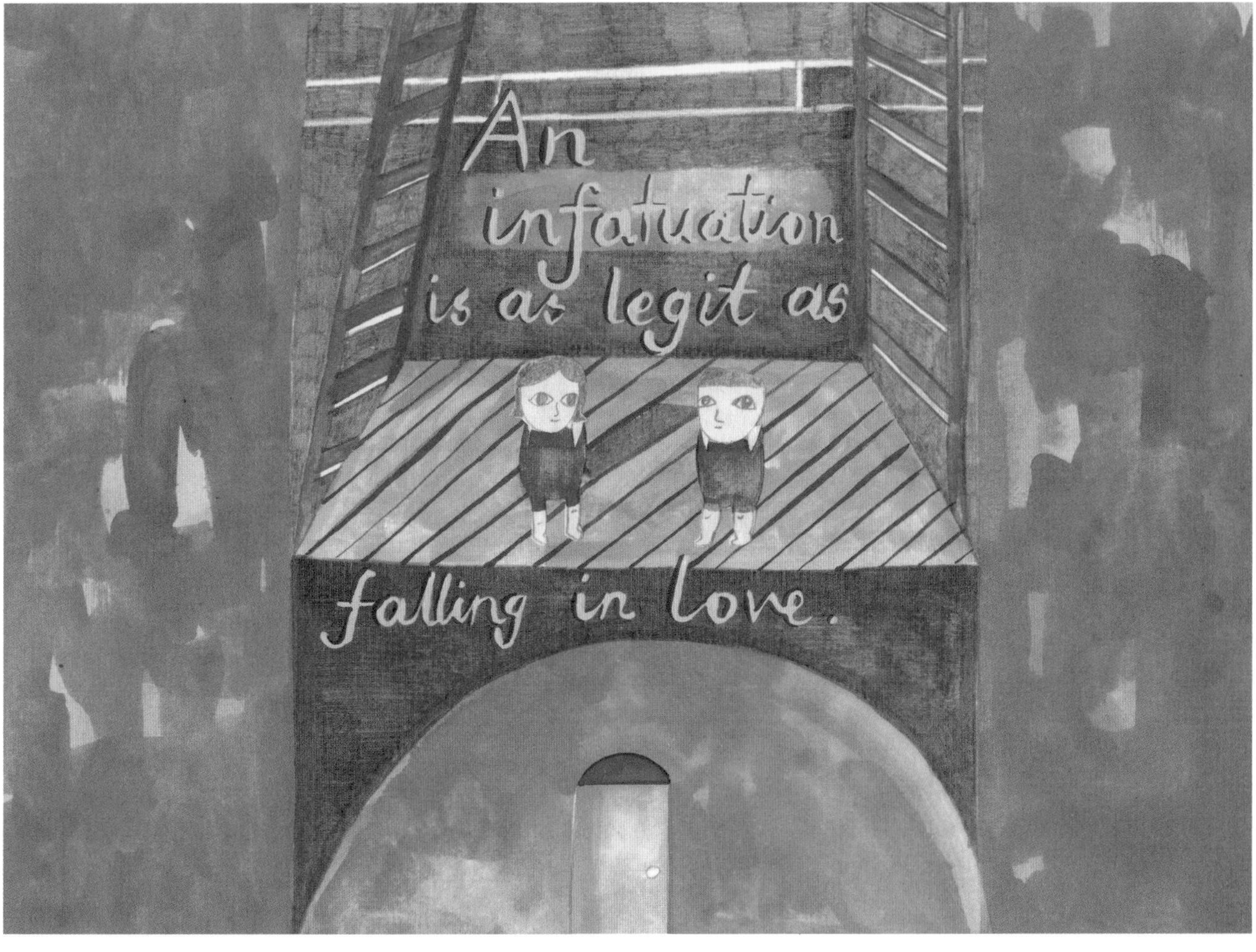
An infatuation is as legit as
falling in love.

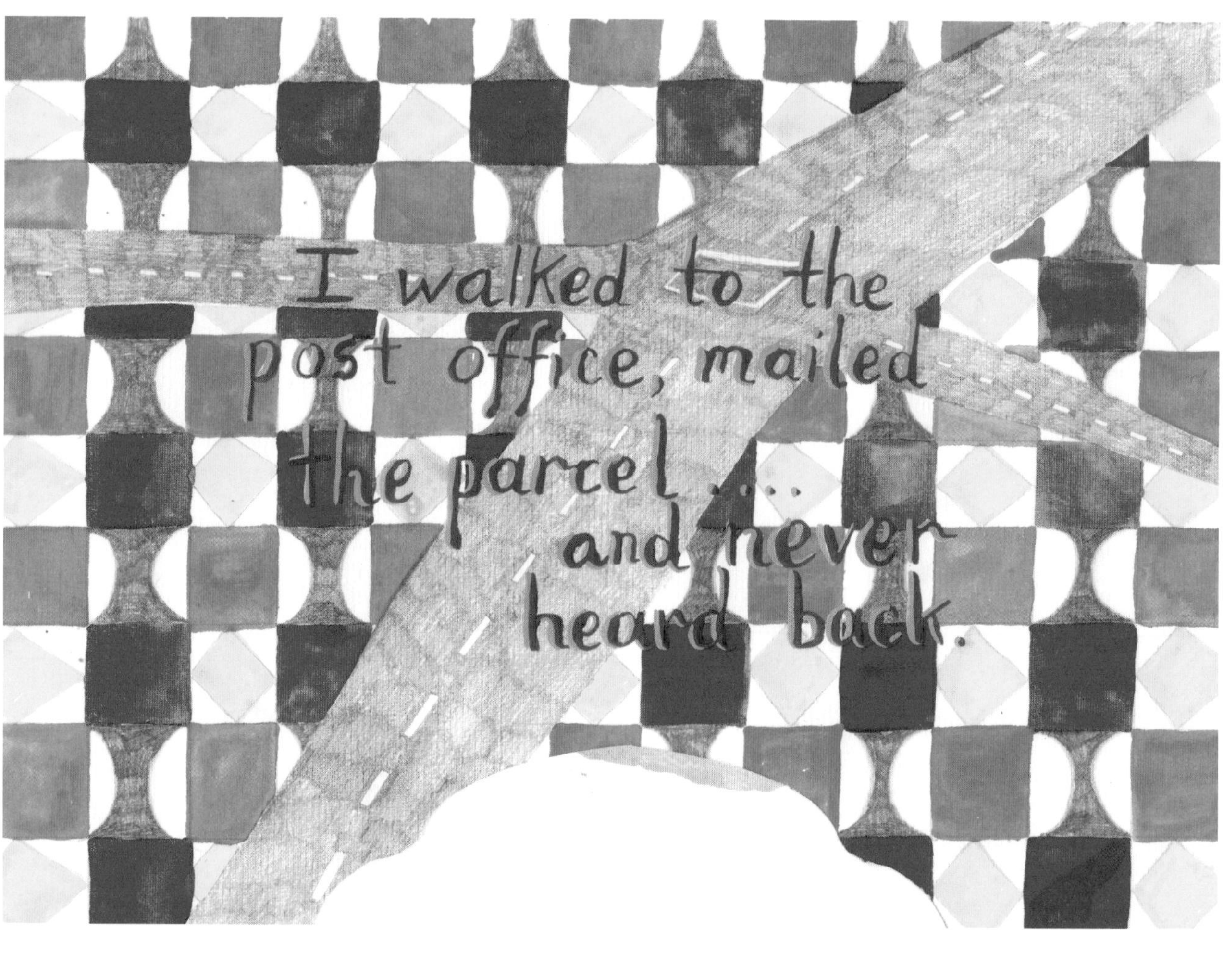
I walked to the
post office, mailed
the parcel ...
and never
heard back.

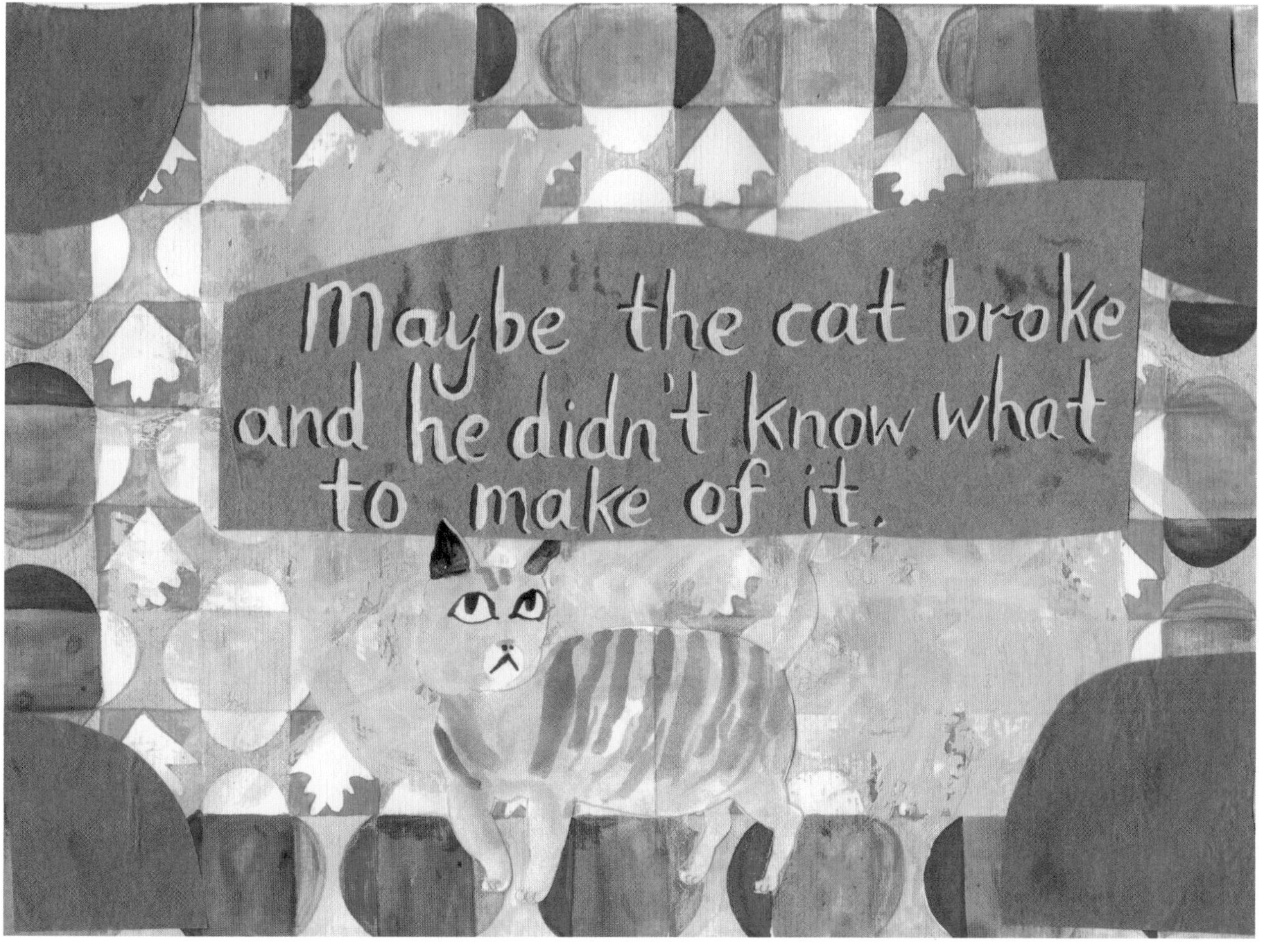
Maybe the cat broke
and he didn't know what
to make of it.

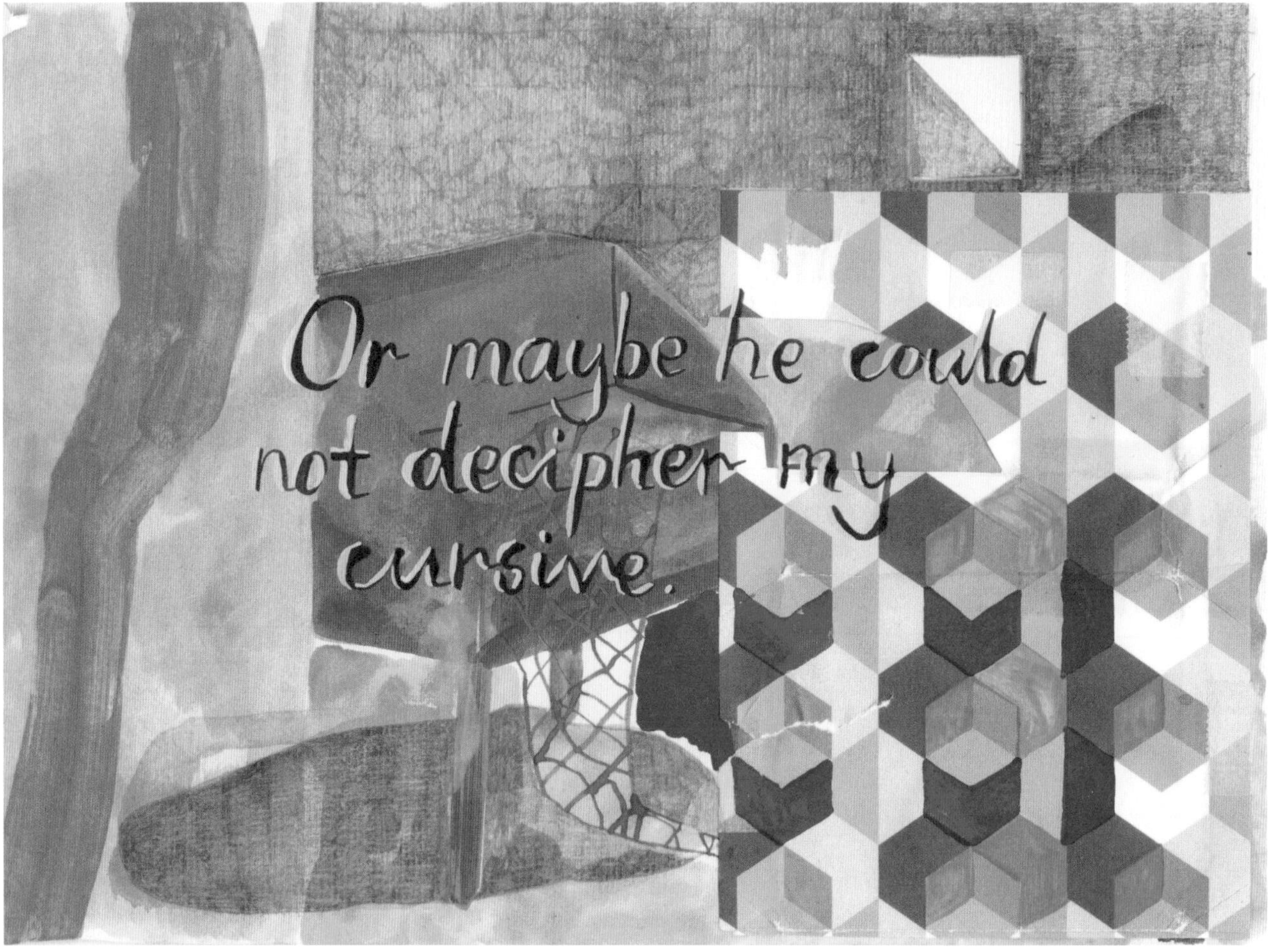
Or maybe he could
not decipher my
cursive.

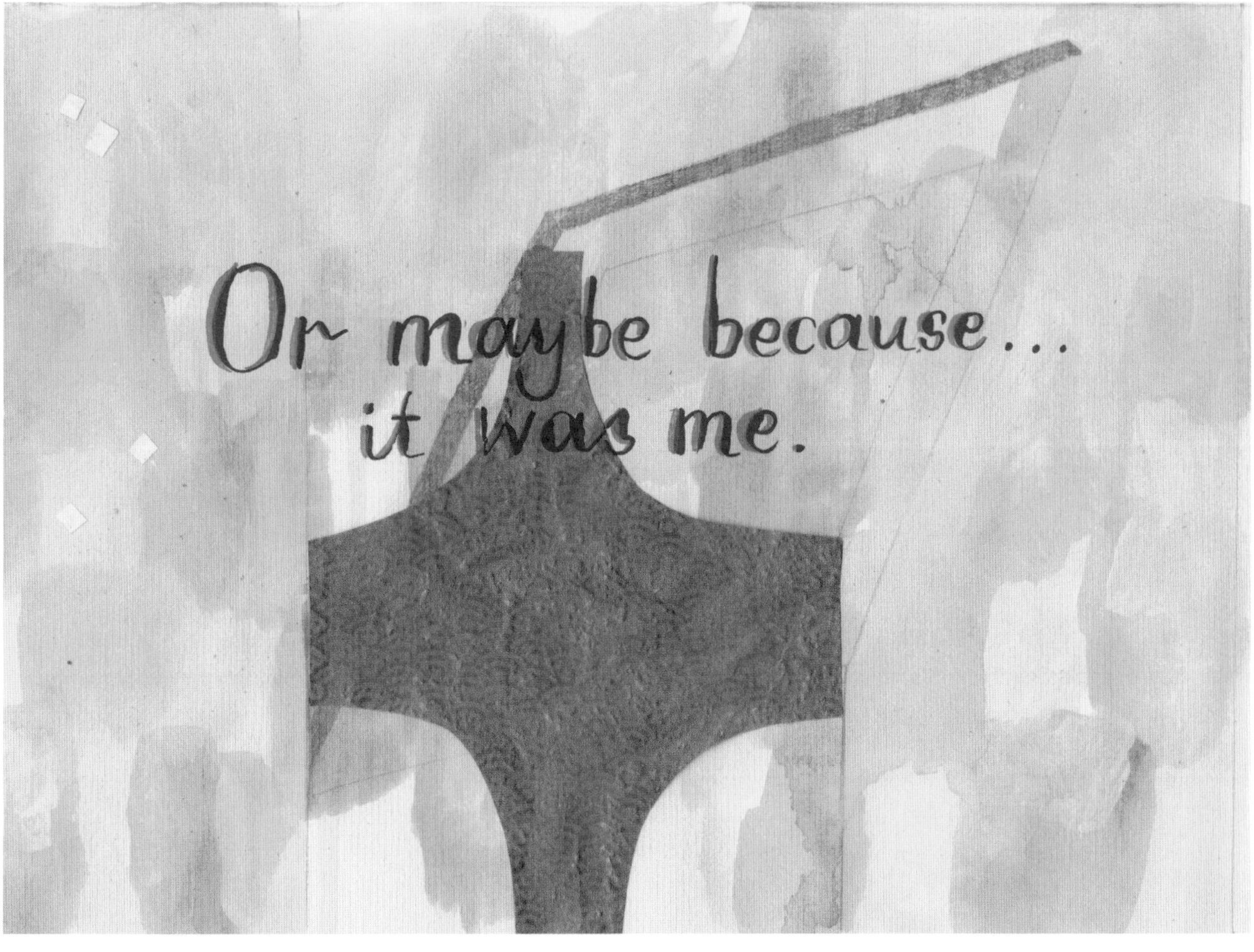
Or maybe because...
it was me.

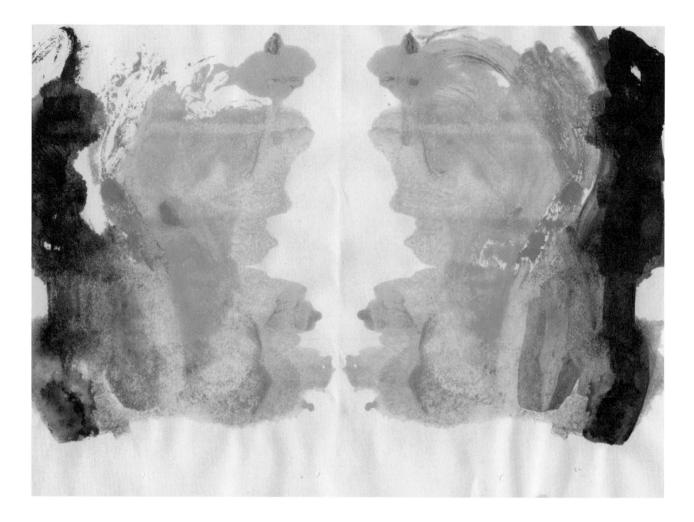

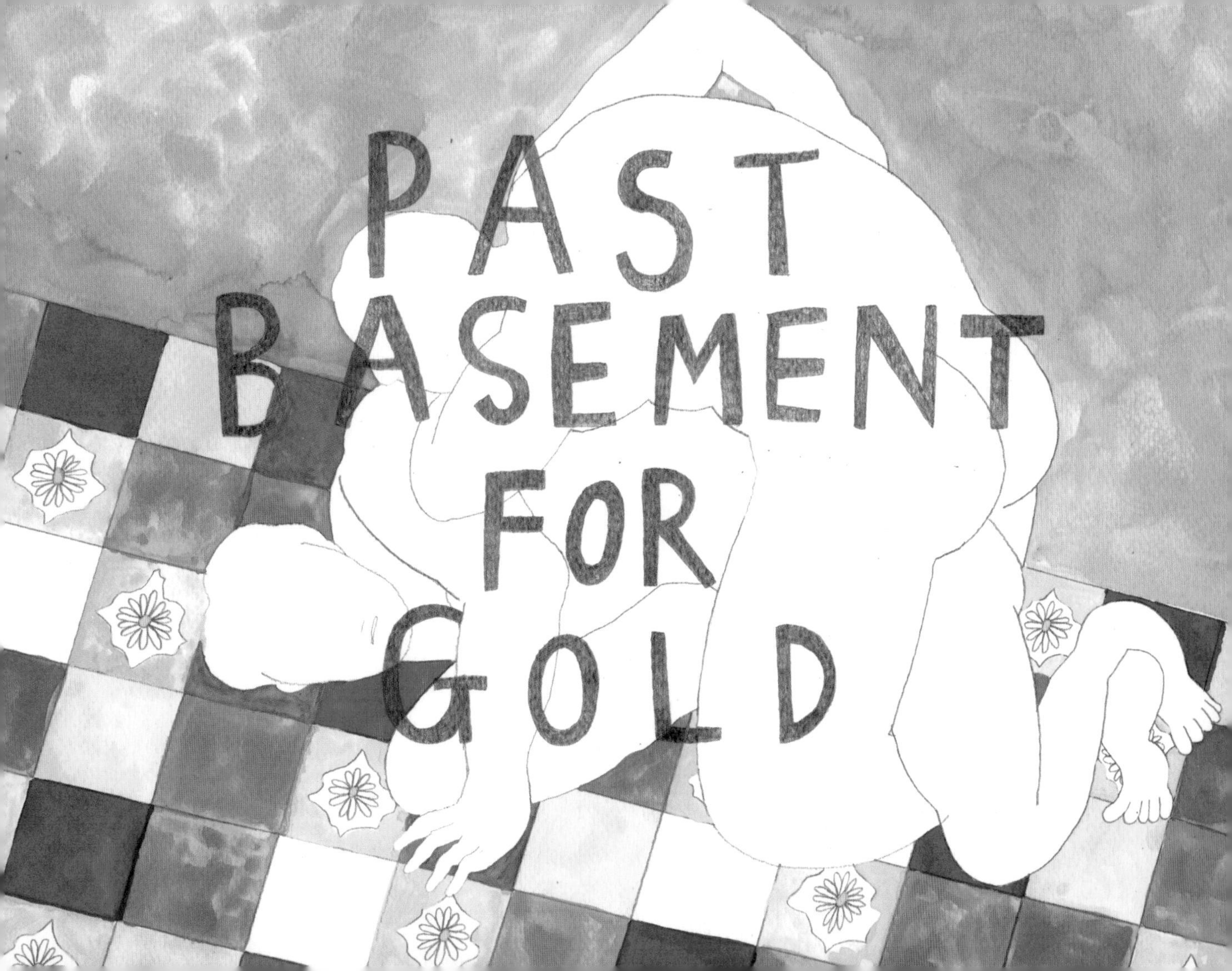
PAST
BASEMENT
FOR
GOLD

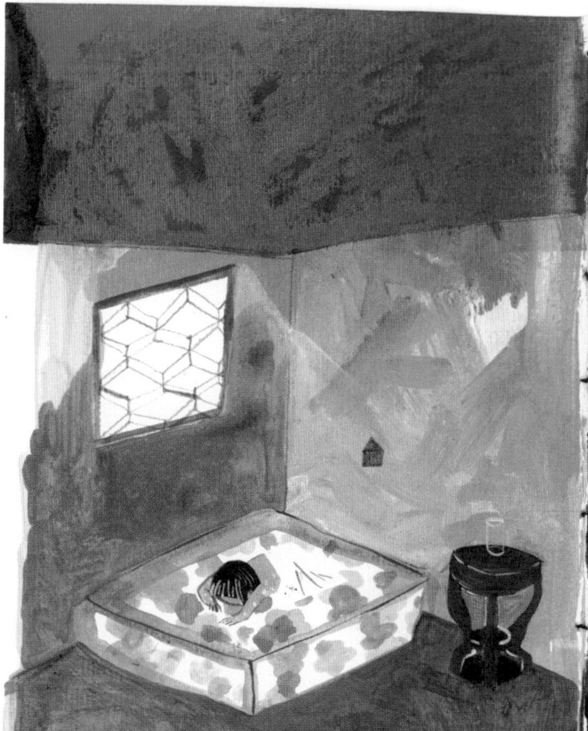

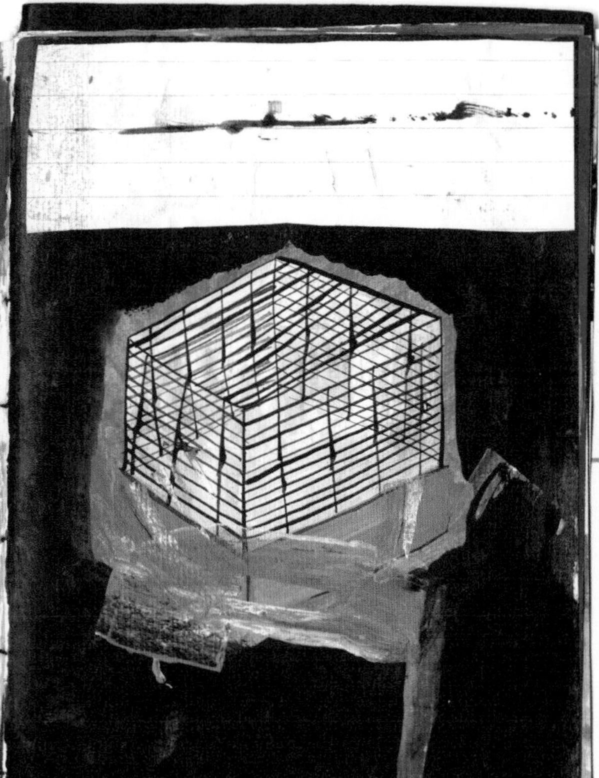

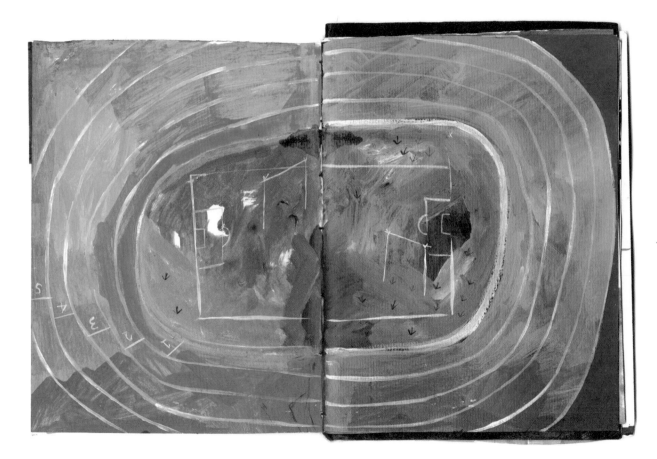

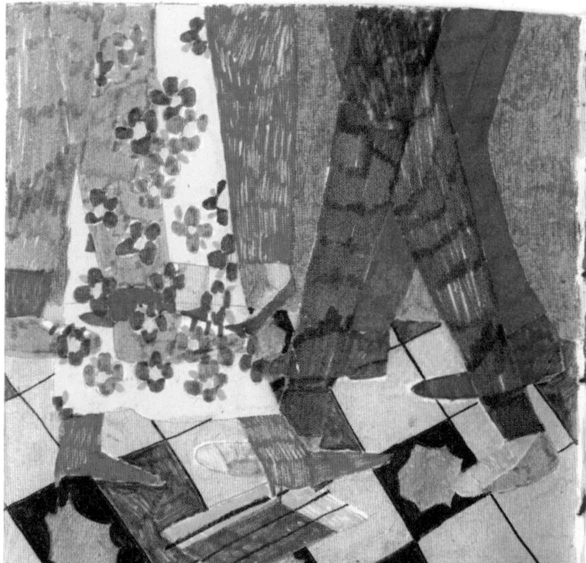

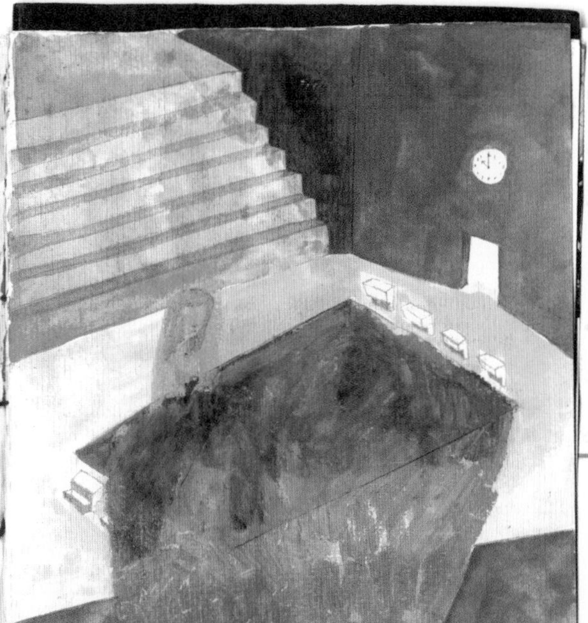

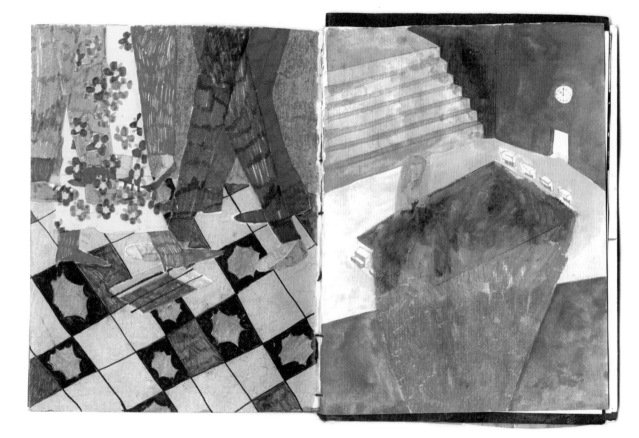

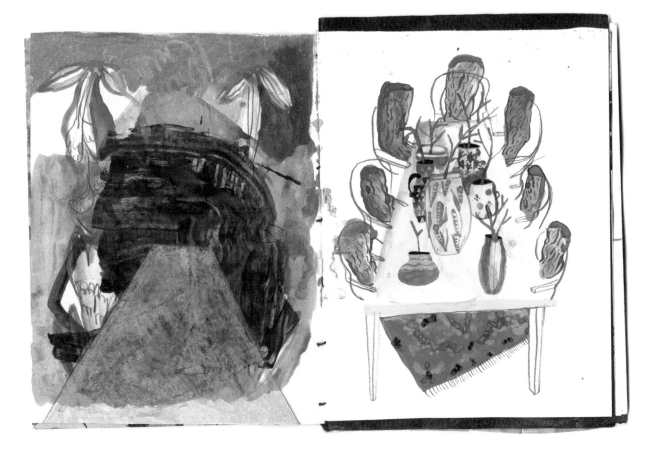

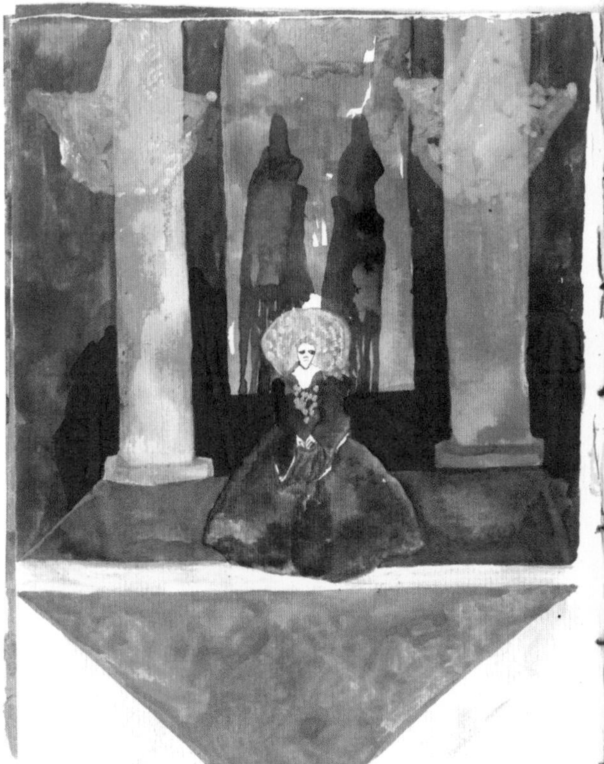

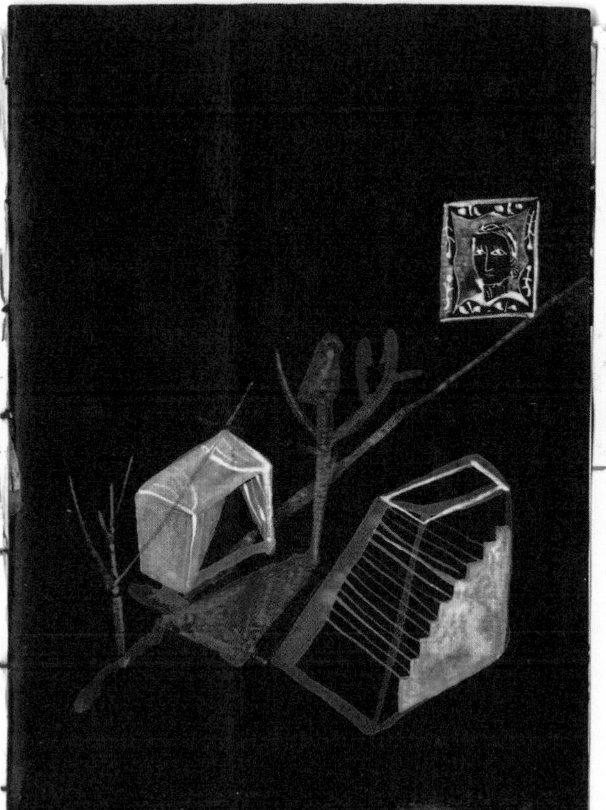

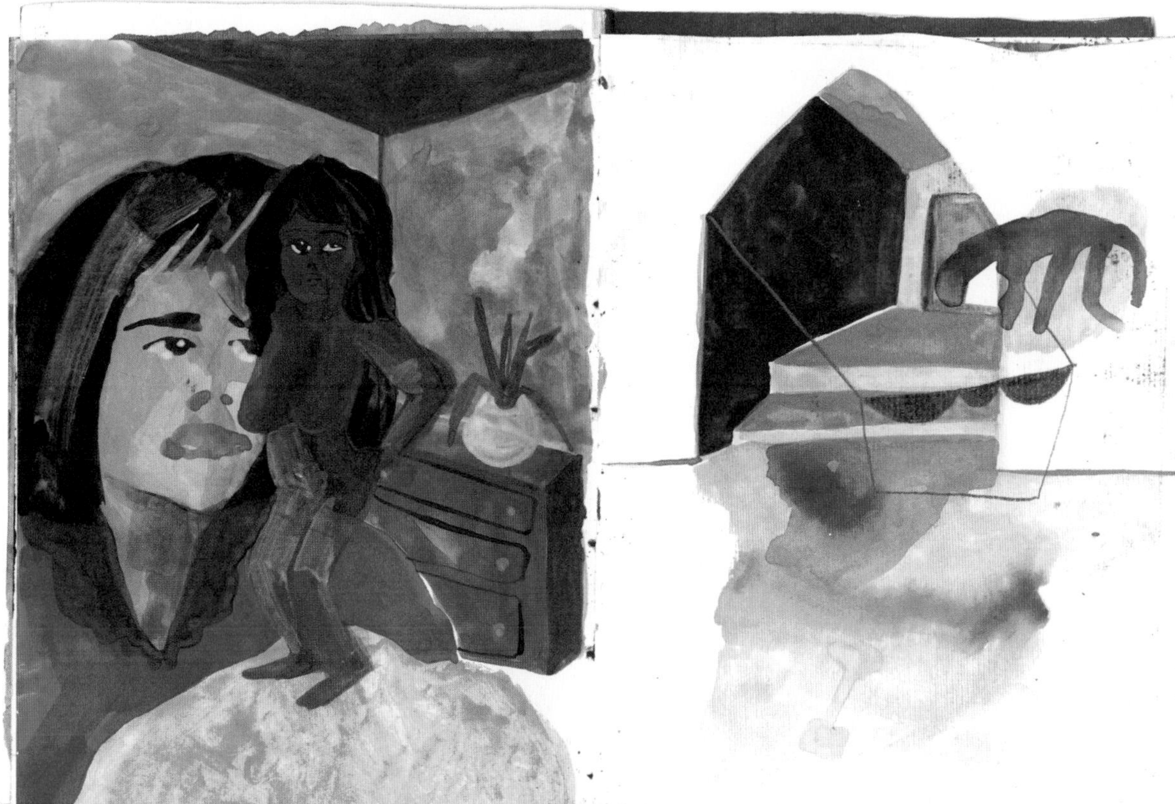

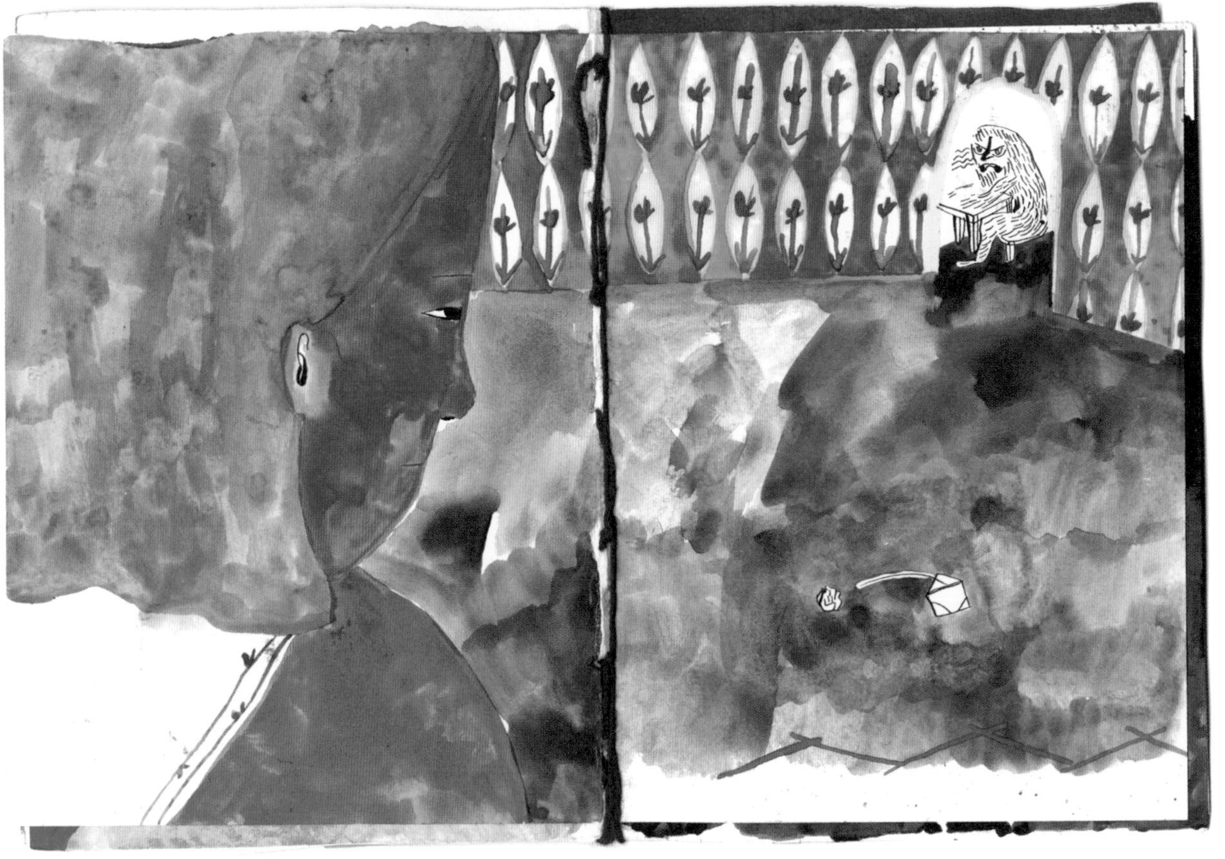

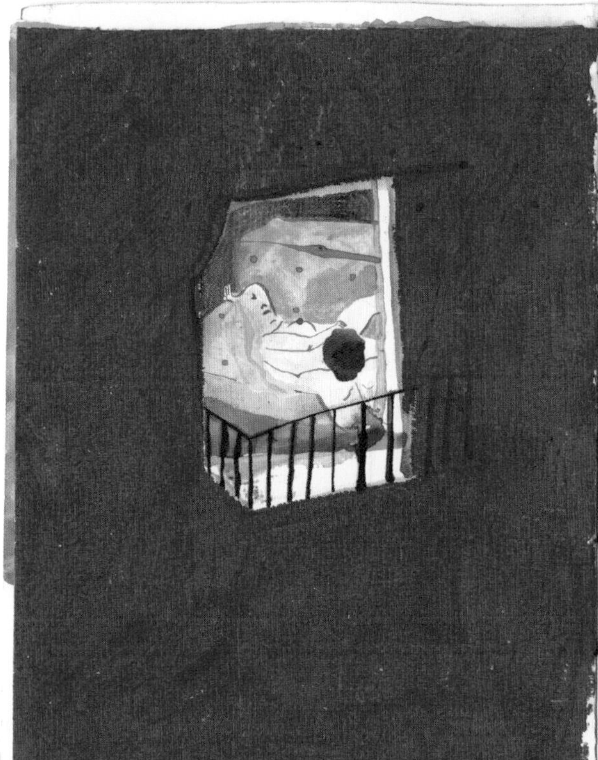

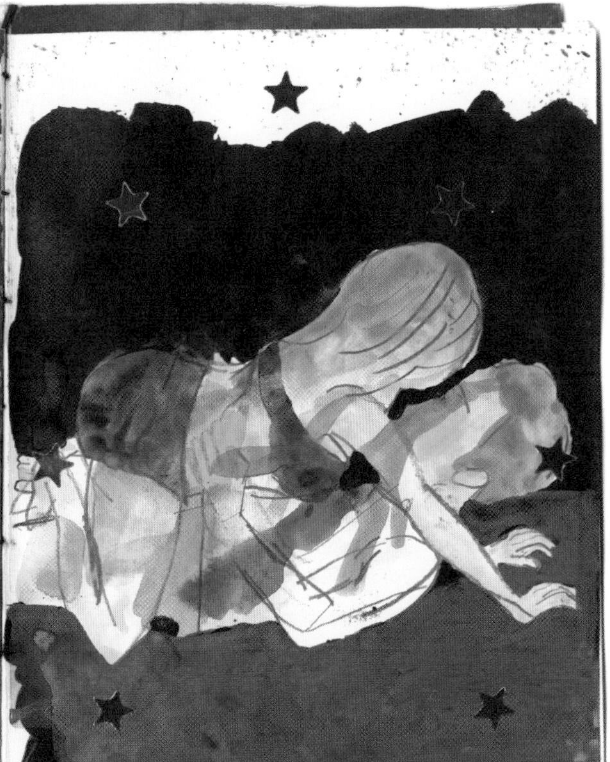

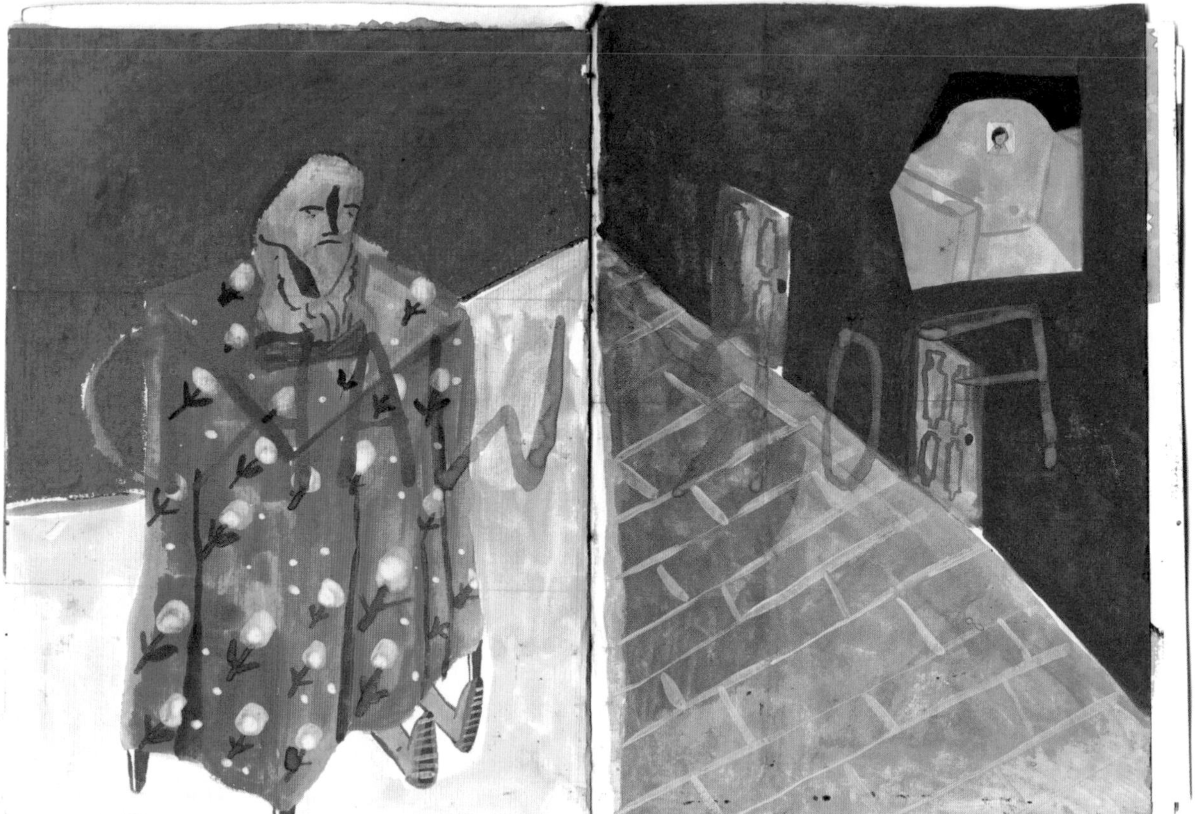

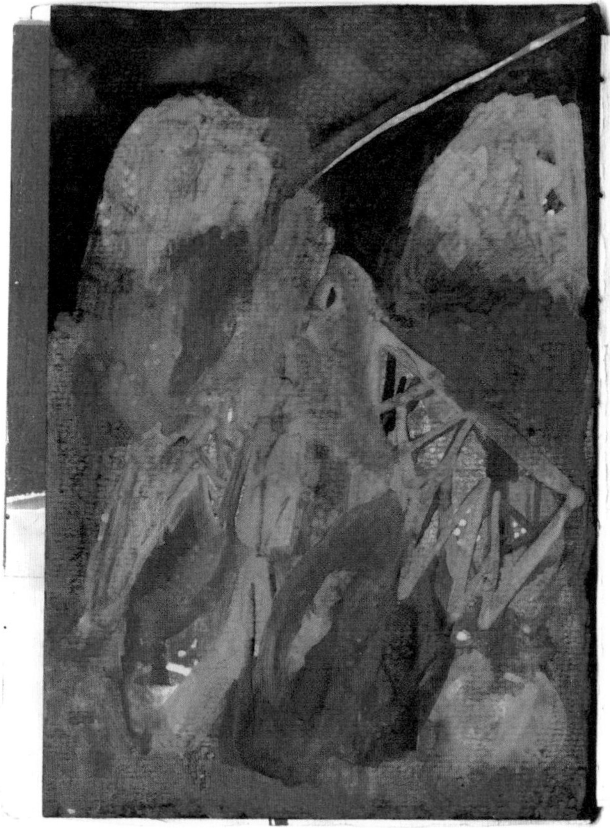

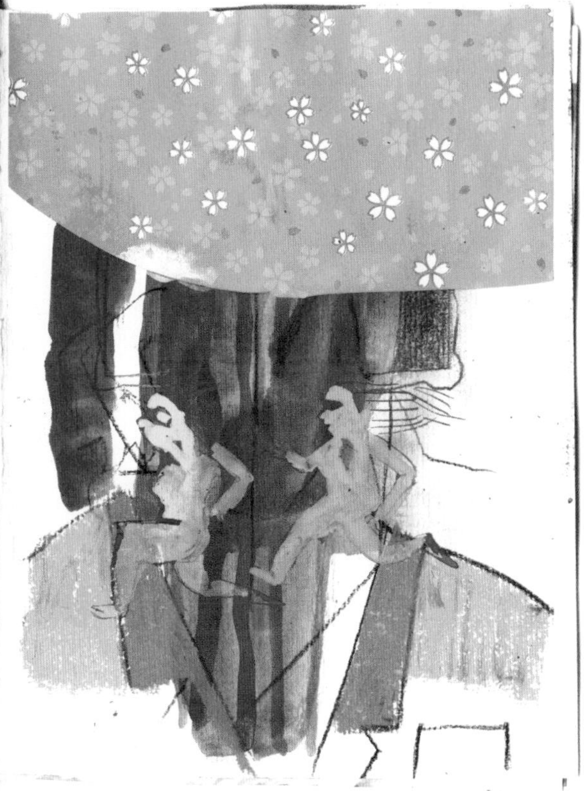

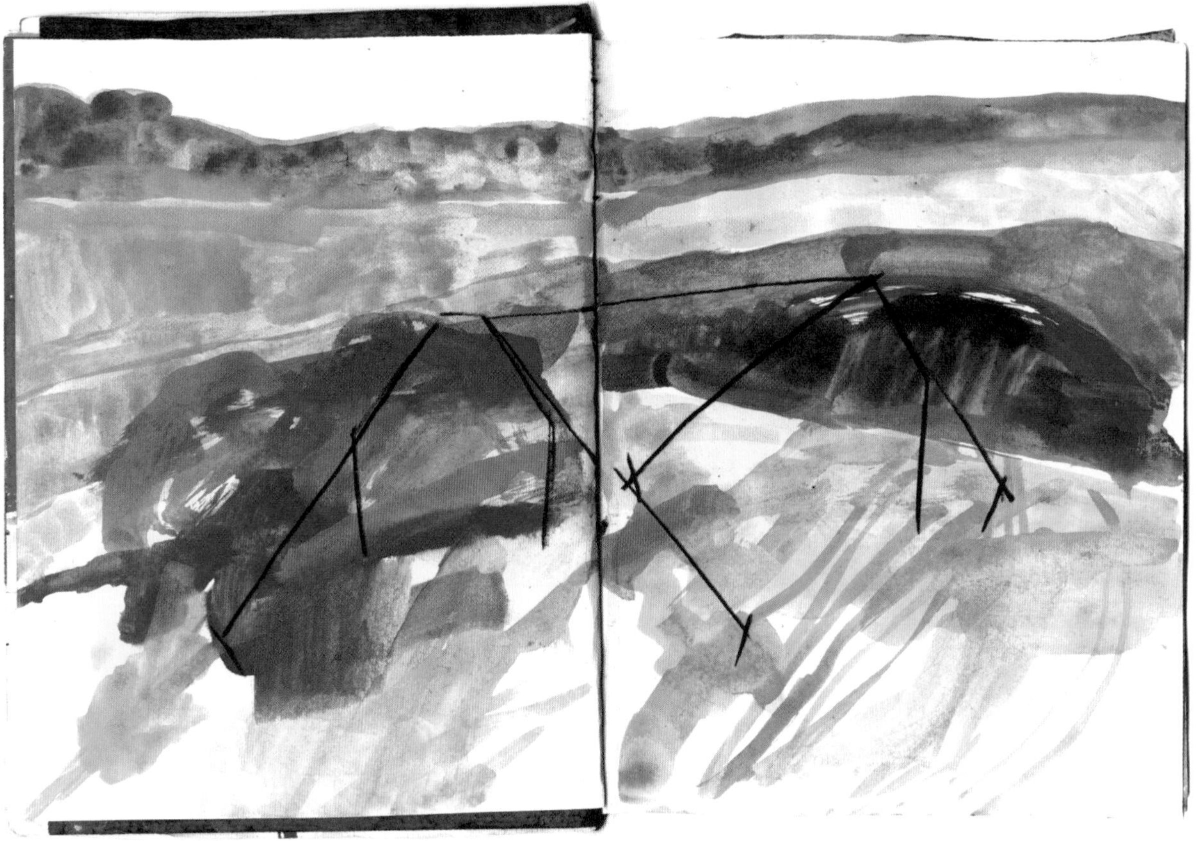

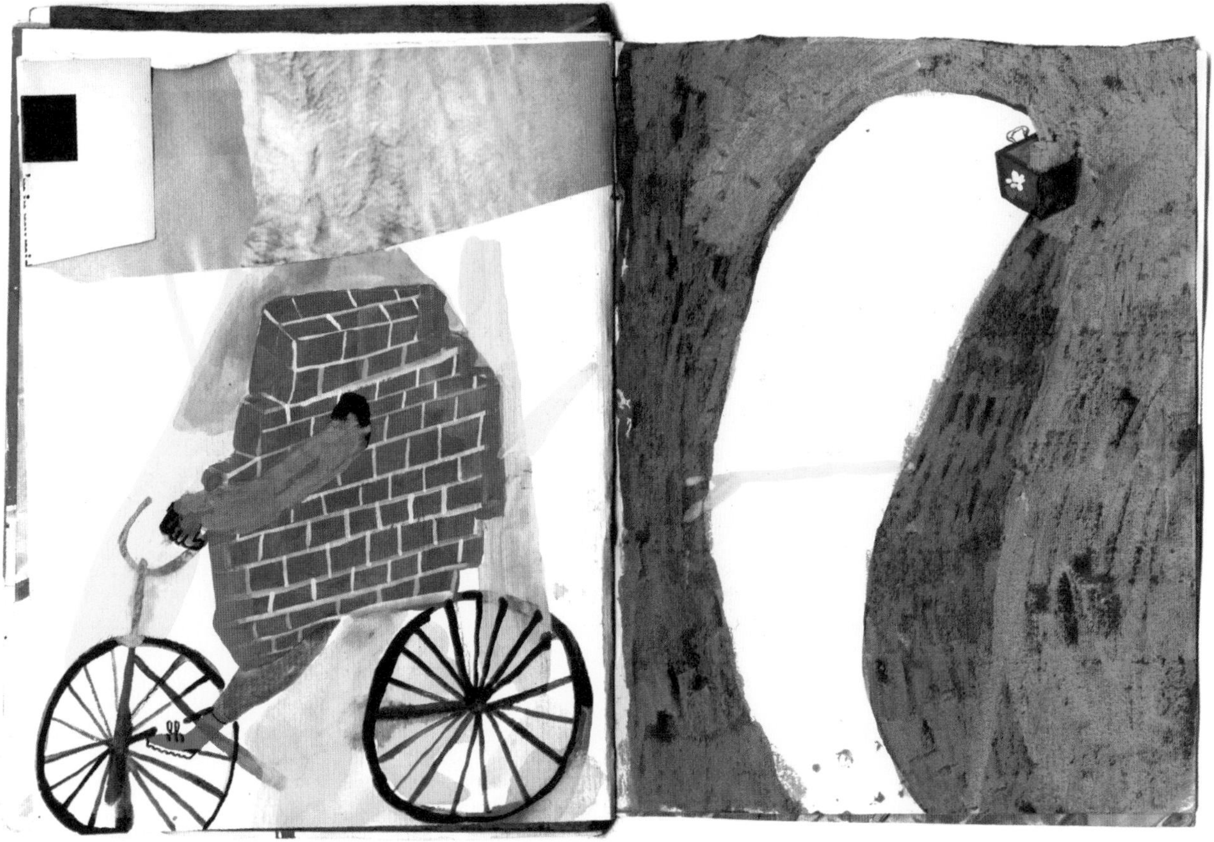

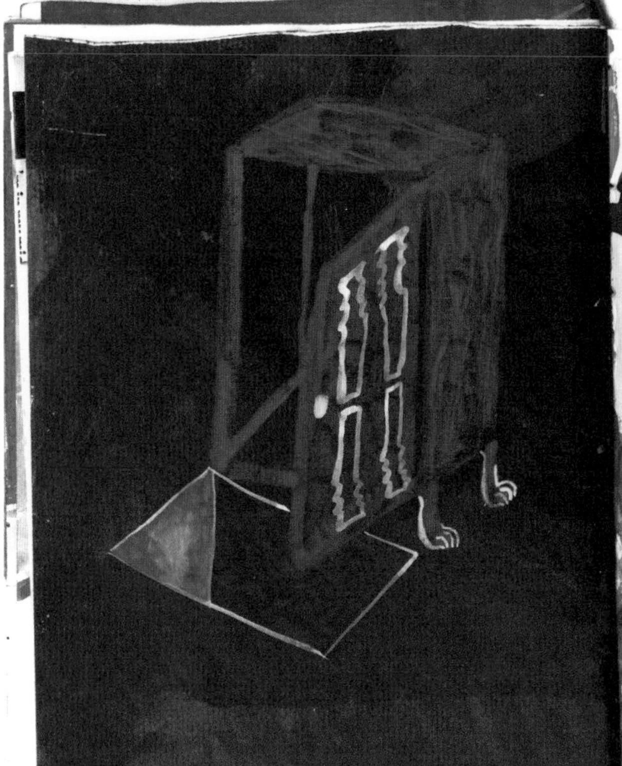

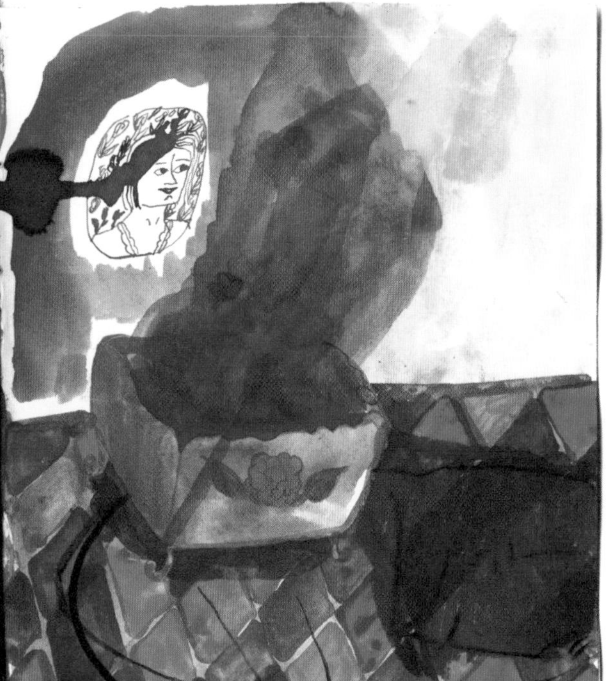

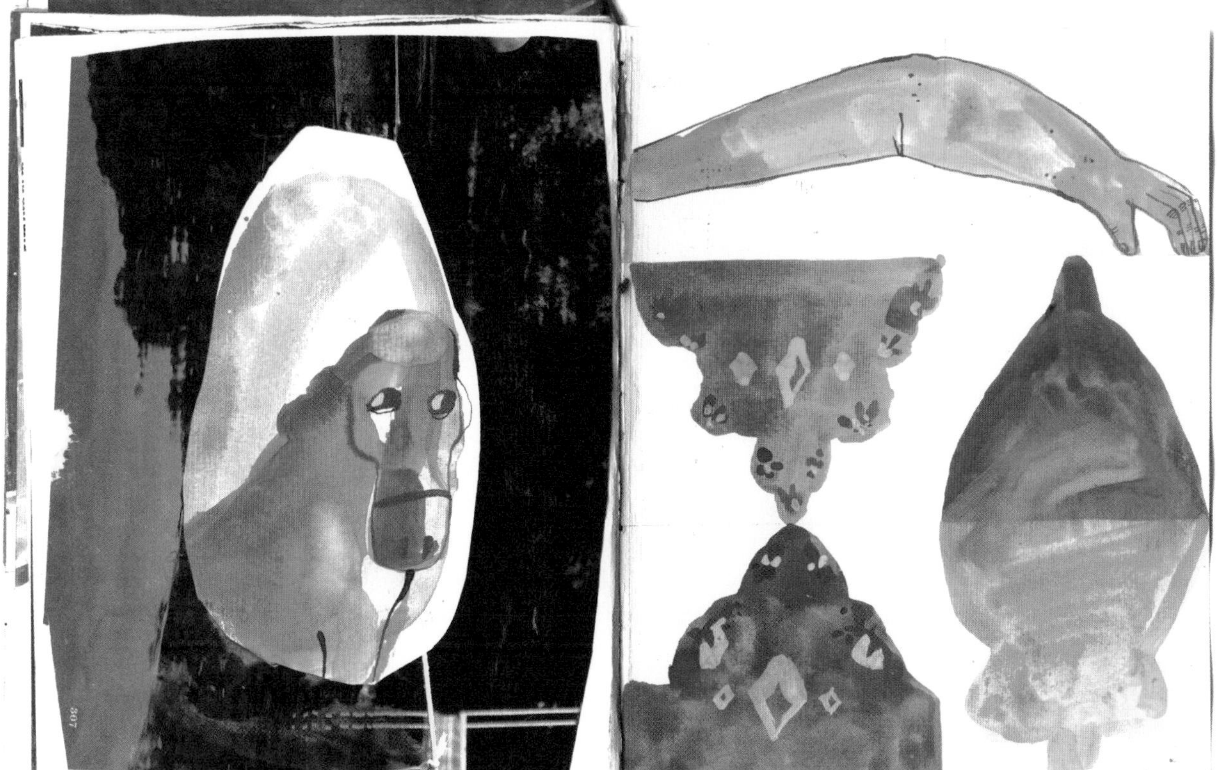
307

26 JUNE '13

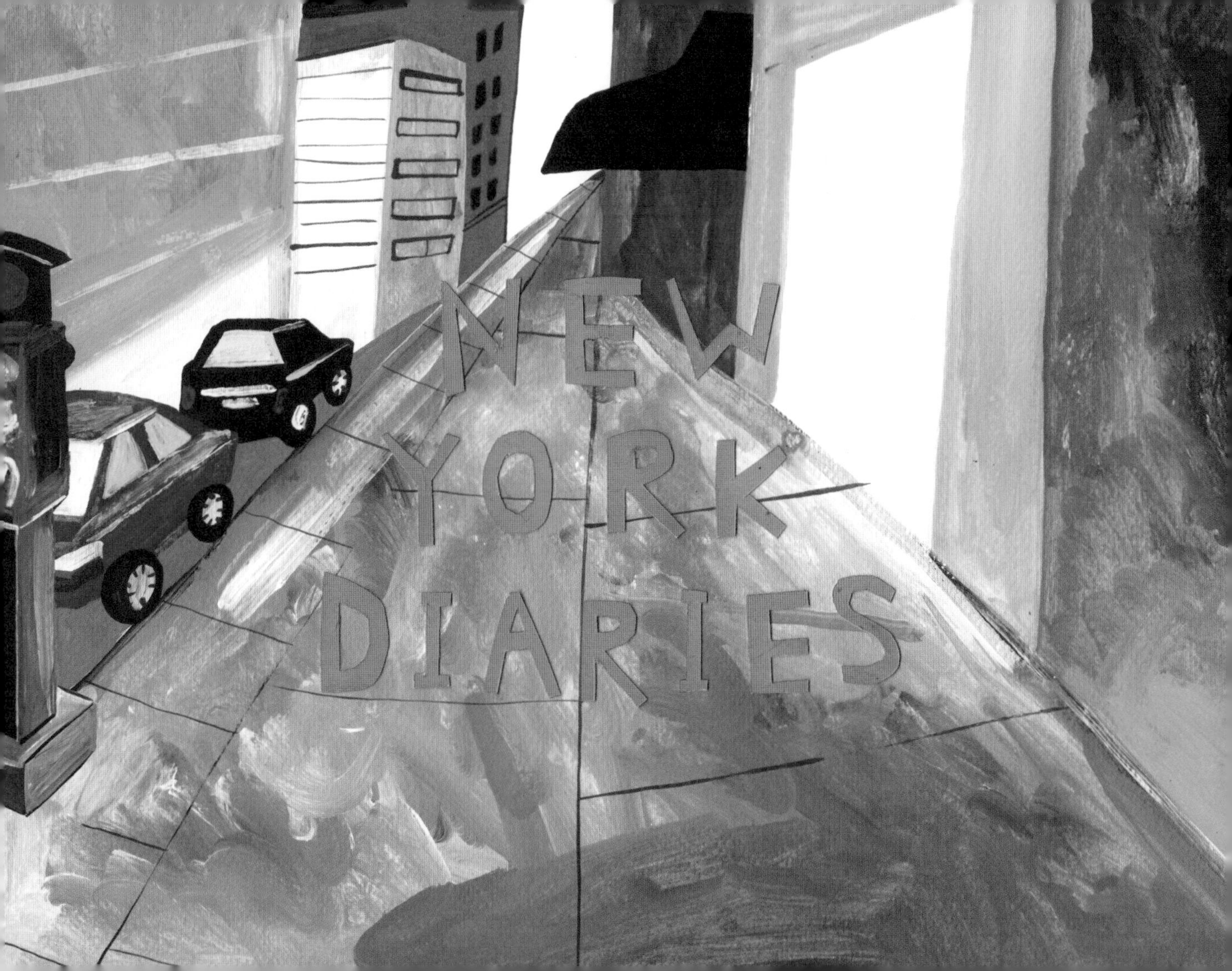
NEW
YORK
DIARIES

Vultures attacking a zebra at the National Museum of Natural History.

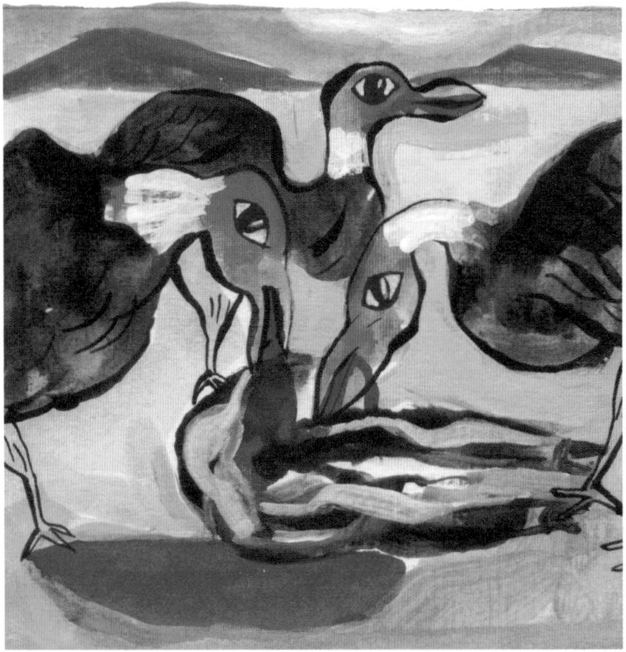

Hares hung like salami in a deli (museum of ~~nati~~ natural history)

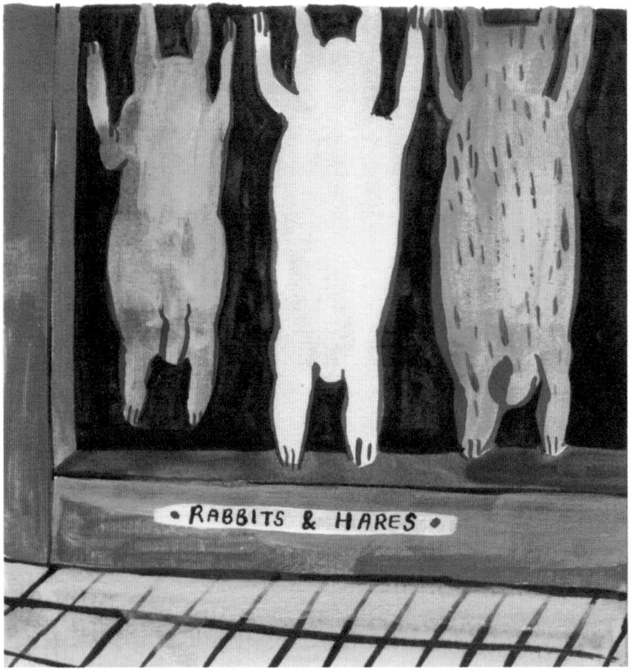
• RABBITS & HARES •

And the skeletons..!
Here's a monodont
Narwhal.

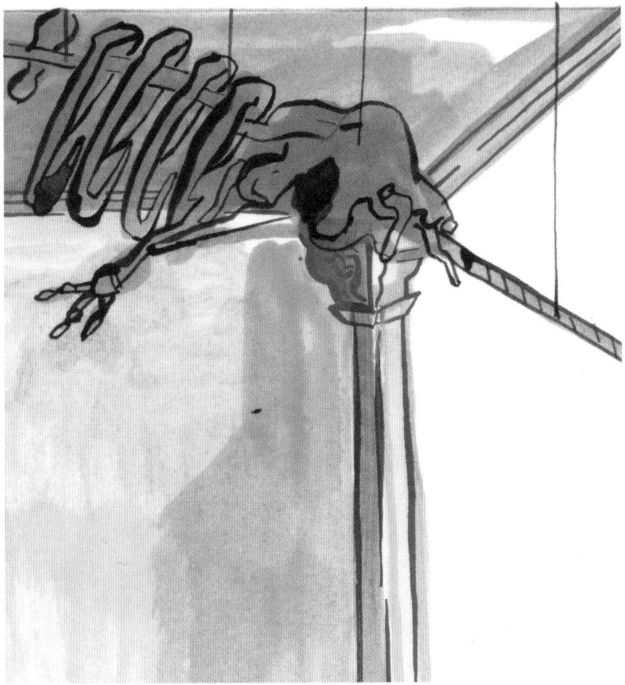

Saw a lady on the
subway, ~~with~~ who'd
very pink eyes.

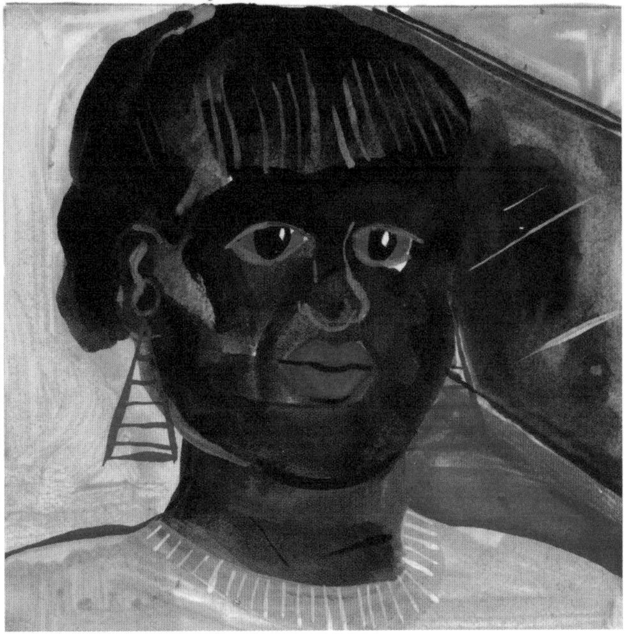

An old lady offering balloons for sale. One of them was out of air.

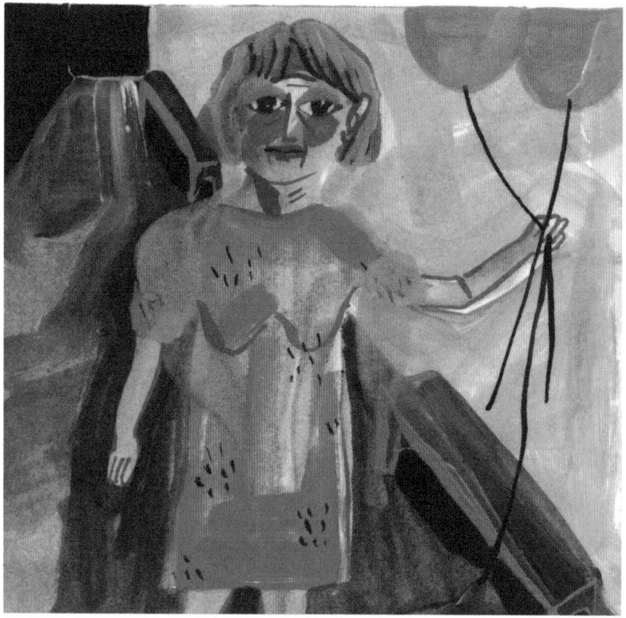

A family of Orthodox Jews in formal dresses and suits crossing the street.

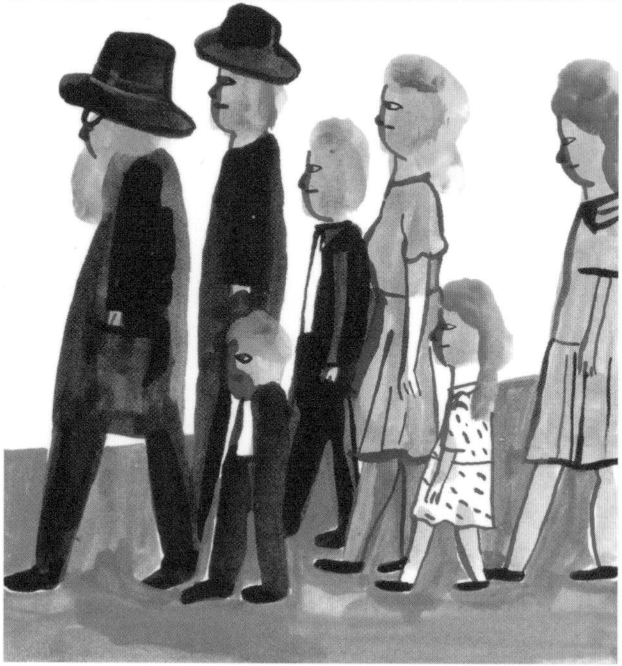

Lots of ~~shops~~ psychic reading shops offering to tell your future for ten bucks. Coincidentally, most of these shops use pink or purple for their shops' signages.

A man in white suit and pants wearing thick cologne waltzed into the room with Claude Monet's large water lilies painting, took a snap of it on his Ipad, and left.

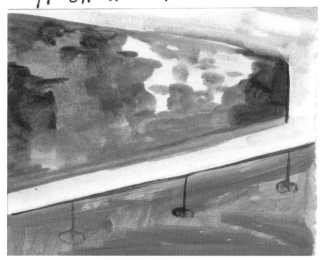

Visited Coney Island on a hot, Memorial Day. "Never again, on a holiday," we said.

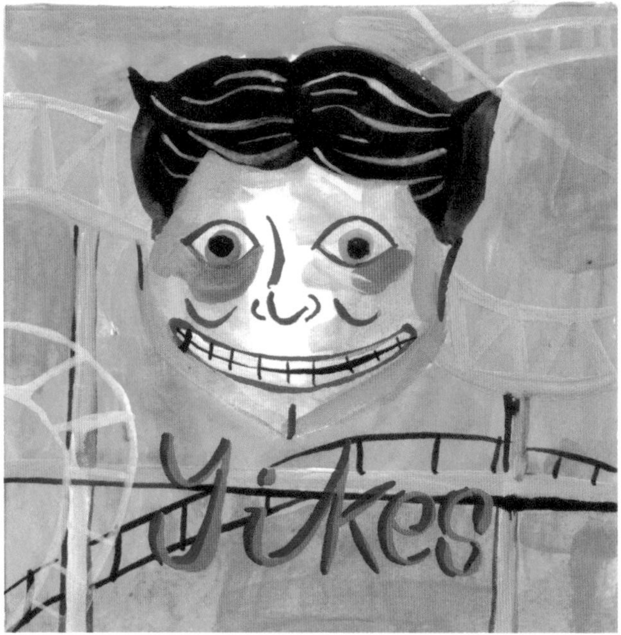
Yikes

A very public private life.

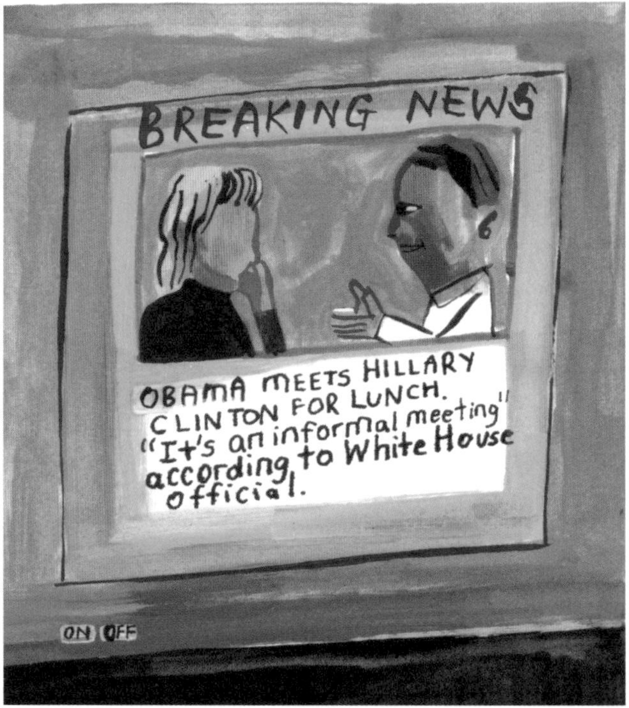
BREAKING NEWS
OBAMA MEETS HILLARY CLINTON FOR LUNCH. "It's an informal meeting" according to White House official.
ON OFF

Most of the time, people in NEW YORK talked real fast (for me at least).

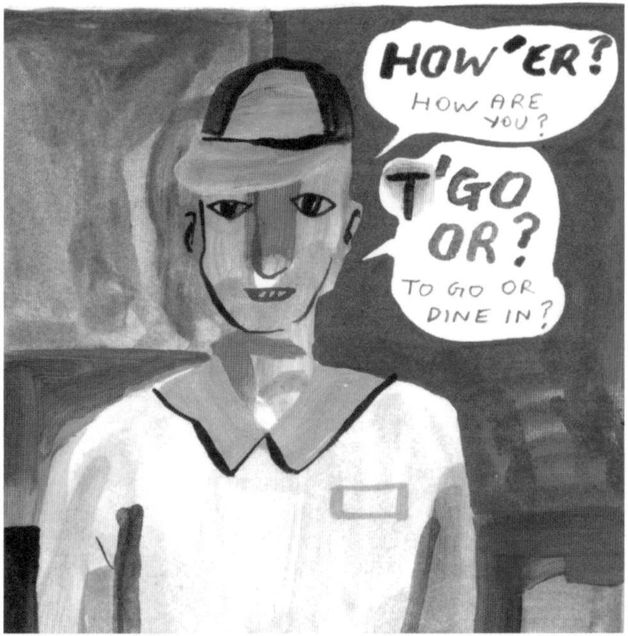
HOW'ER?
HOW ARE YOU?
T'GO OR?
TO GO OR DINE IN?

A man reads a text in Hebrew, while a woman (sitting beside him) prayed with her rosaries in one hand. She looked worried... and tired.

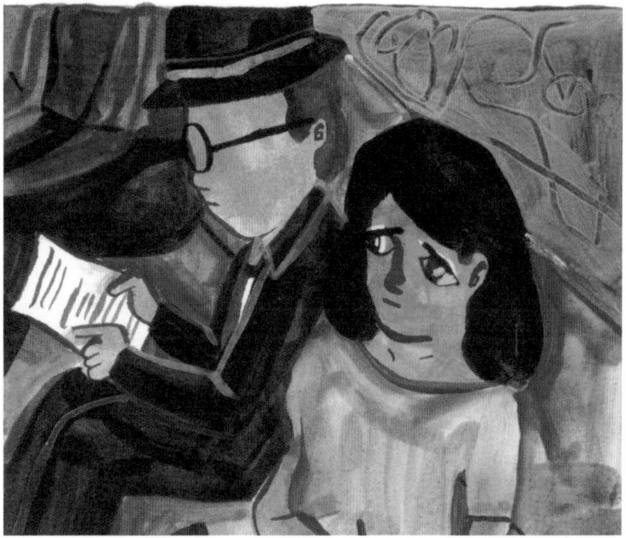

Witnessed a scuffle between 2 guys outside 14th STREET station. One guy egged the other on to fight him.

They darted and hopped around a lamp post, neither touching the other. A minute later, 2 cops arrived in a cop car.

10 minutes later, an ambulance, 4 cop cars, and 10 cops showed up. All gathering, trying to make sense of the disagreement between the two.

And while you are here...

Aristide Maillol's 'The River'.

We gathered to watch 'The Real L Word'. It made our troubles seemed .... less complicated.

Took a train from NY to Toronto. Along the way I saw: a house painted and strung with stars, tools and ··· a pentagram (?).

A brick building next to "Joe's food processing" which said "HORROR REALM" in bold, gothic red letters.

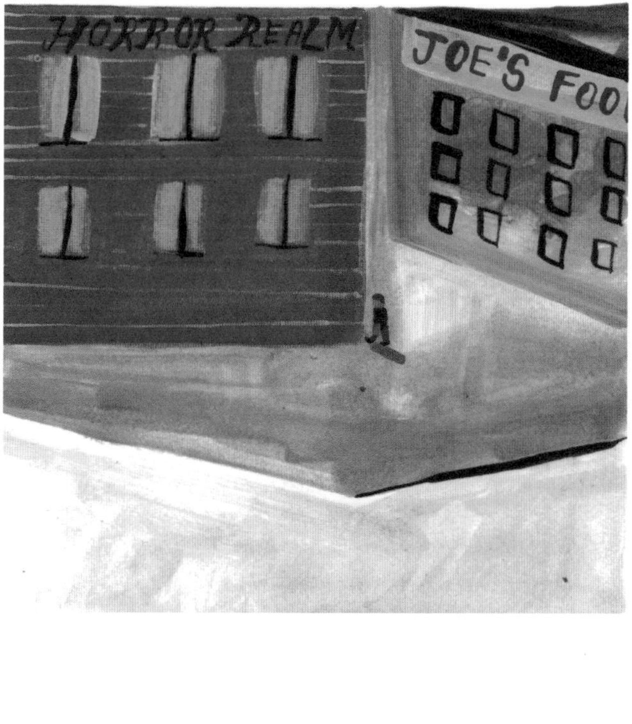
HORROR REALM
JOE'S FOO

A group of teenagers filming themselves doing skateboard stunts in a deserted dried field littered with rusty barrels and weeds.

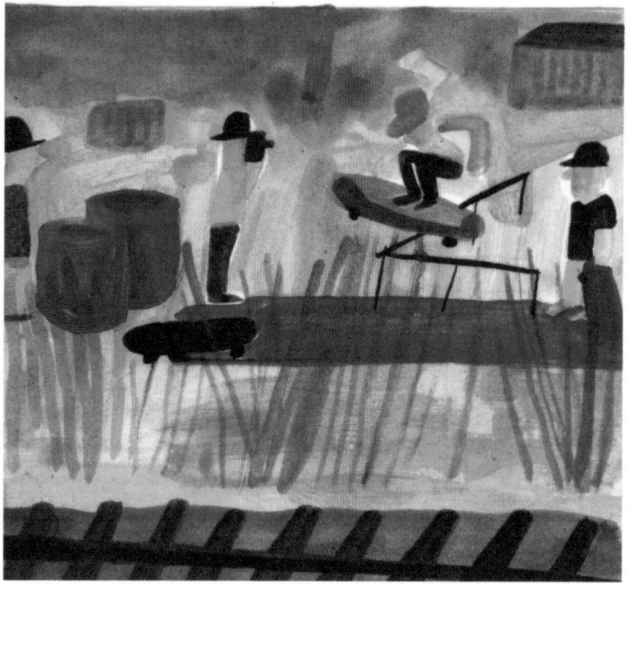

A pair of red stilettos dipped in a muddy creek.

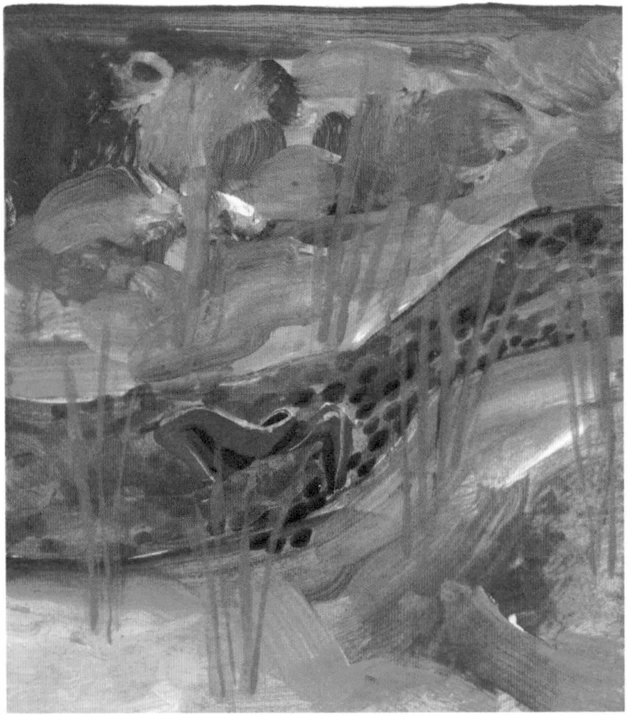

Glowing bluish-green waves of the Niagara Falls crashing through the steel pillars of the high bridge.

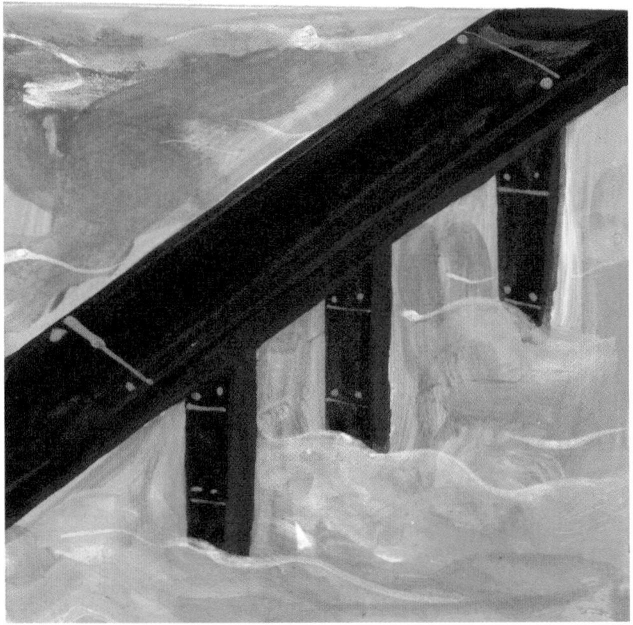

Realizing I'm in Canada when an exit sign reads "EXIT/SORTIE". Sortie. Sorted out? Never mind.

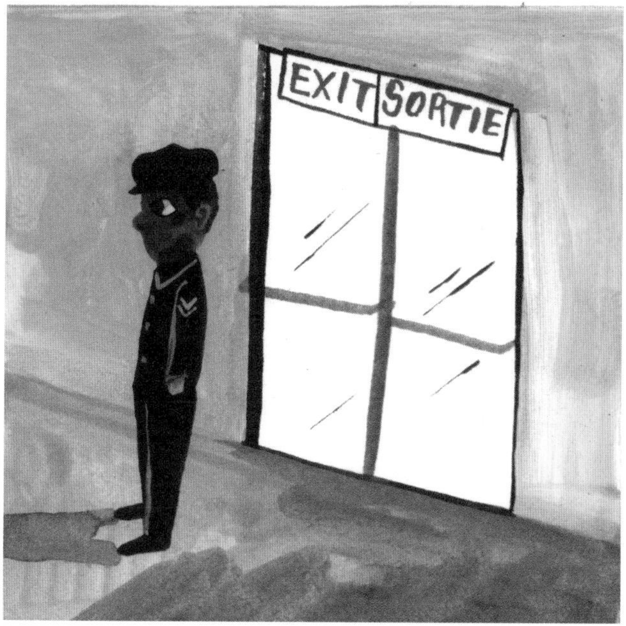
EXIT SORTIE

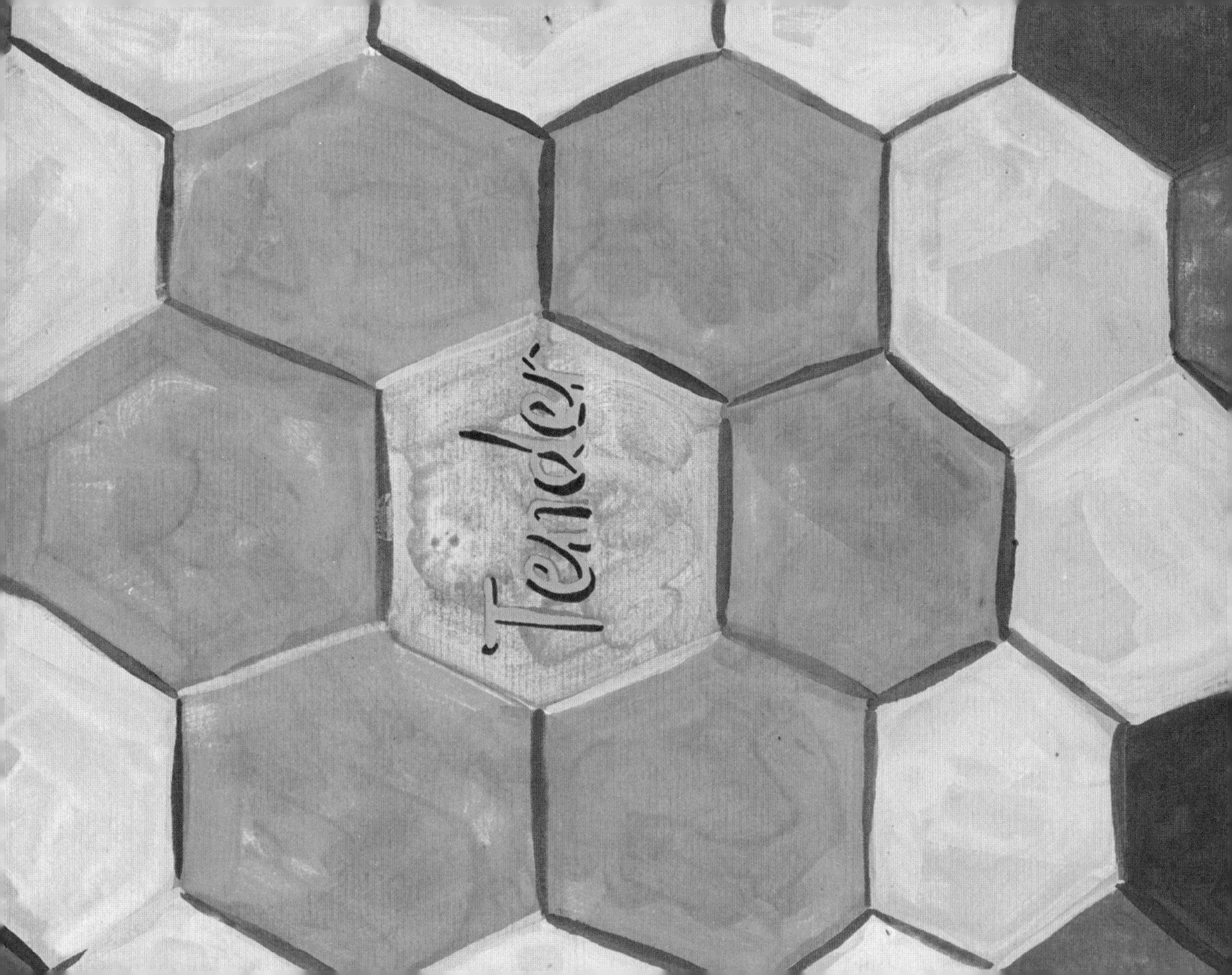
Tender

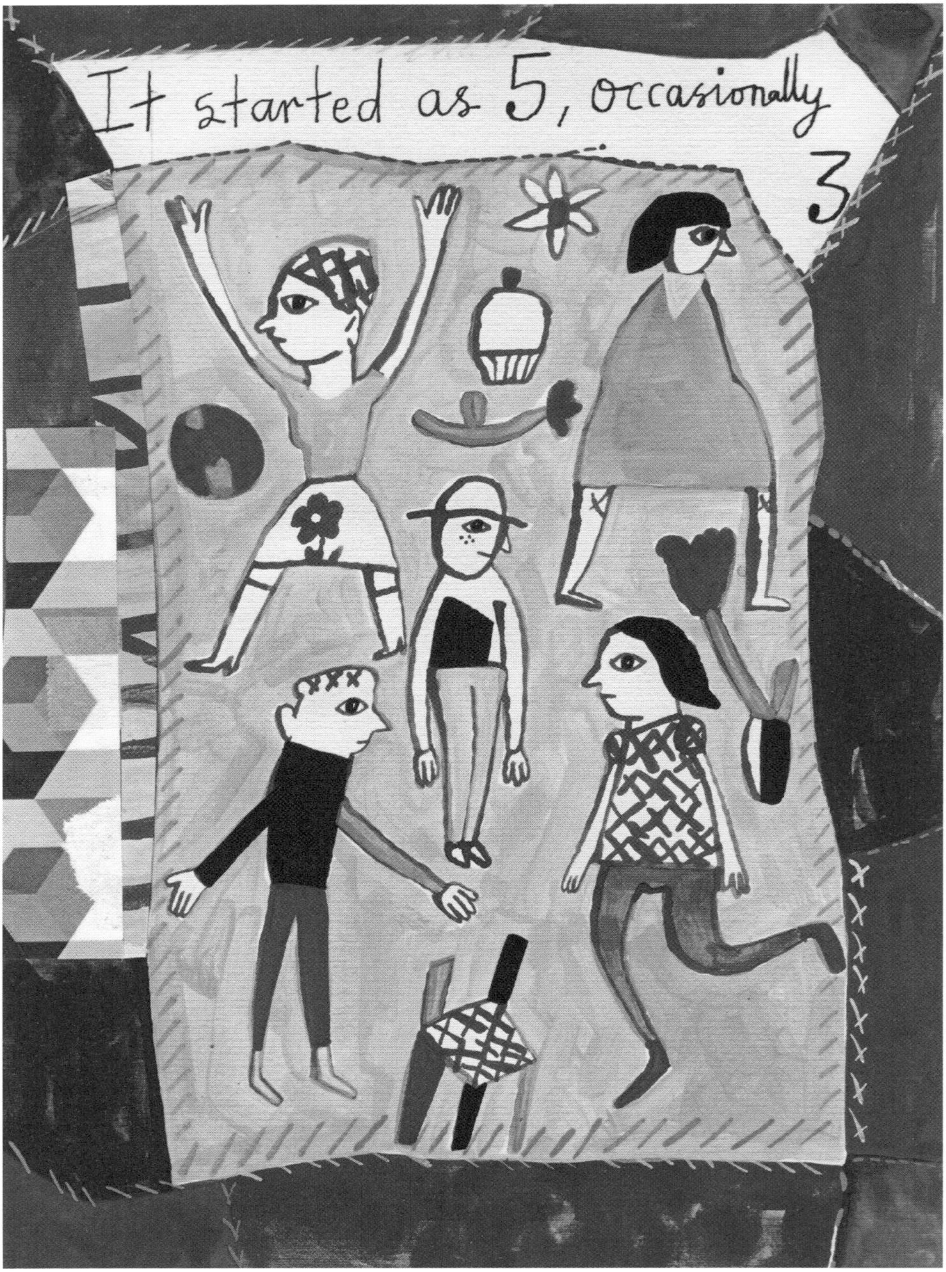
It started as 5, occasionally 3

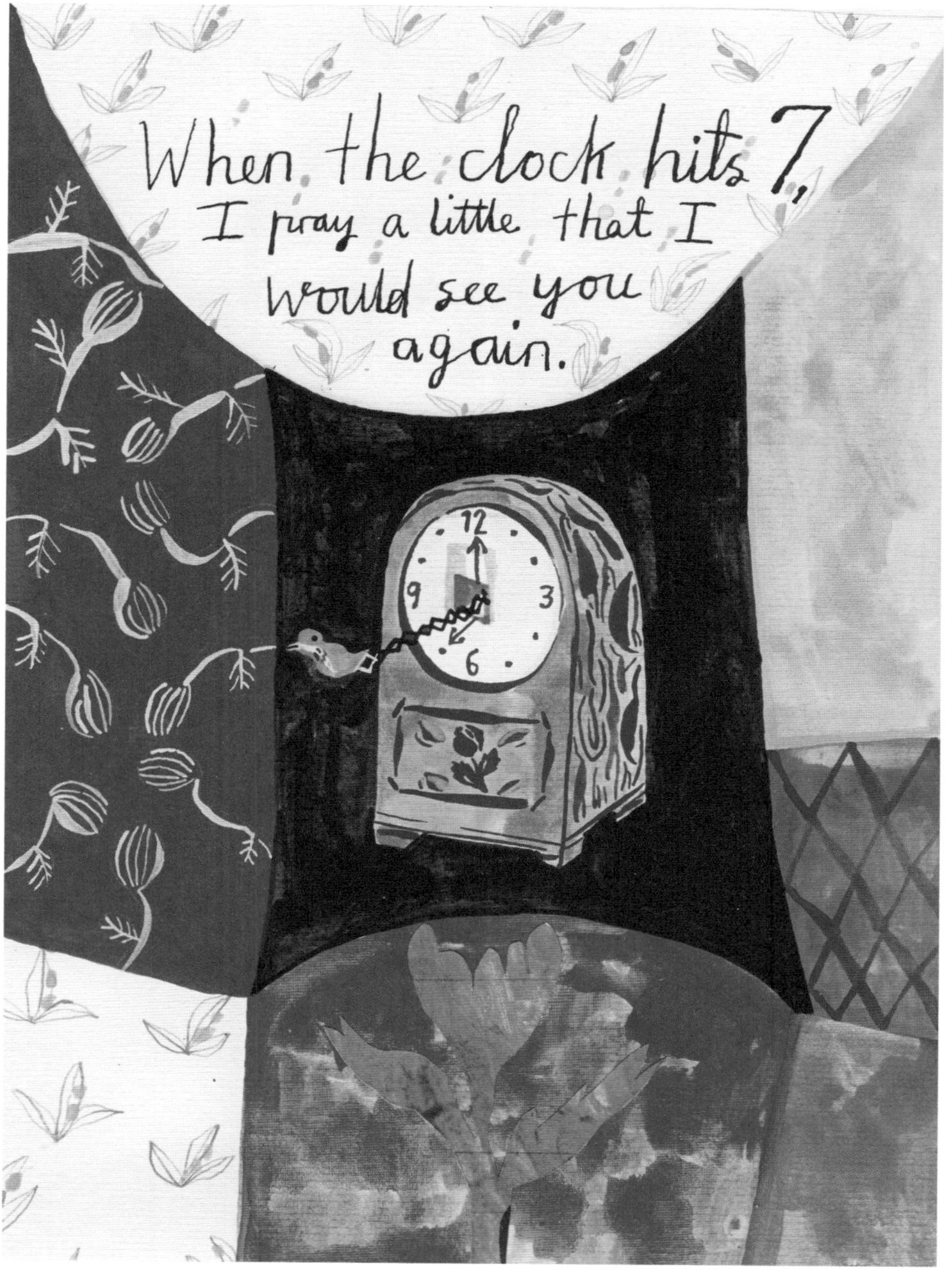
When the clock hits 7,
I pray a little that I
would see you
again.
9
12
3
6

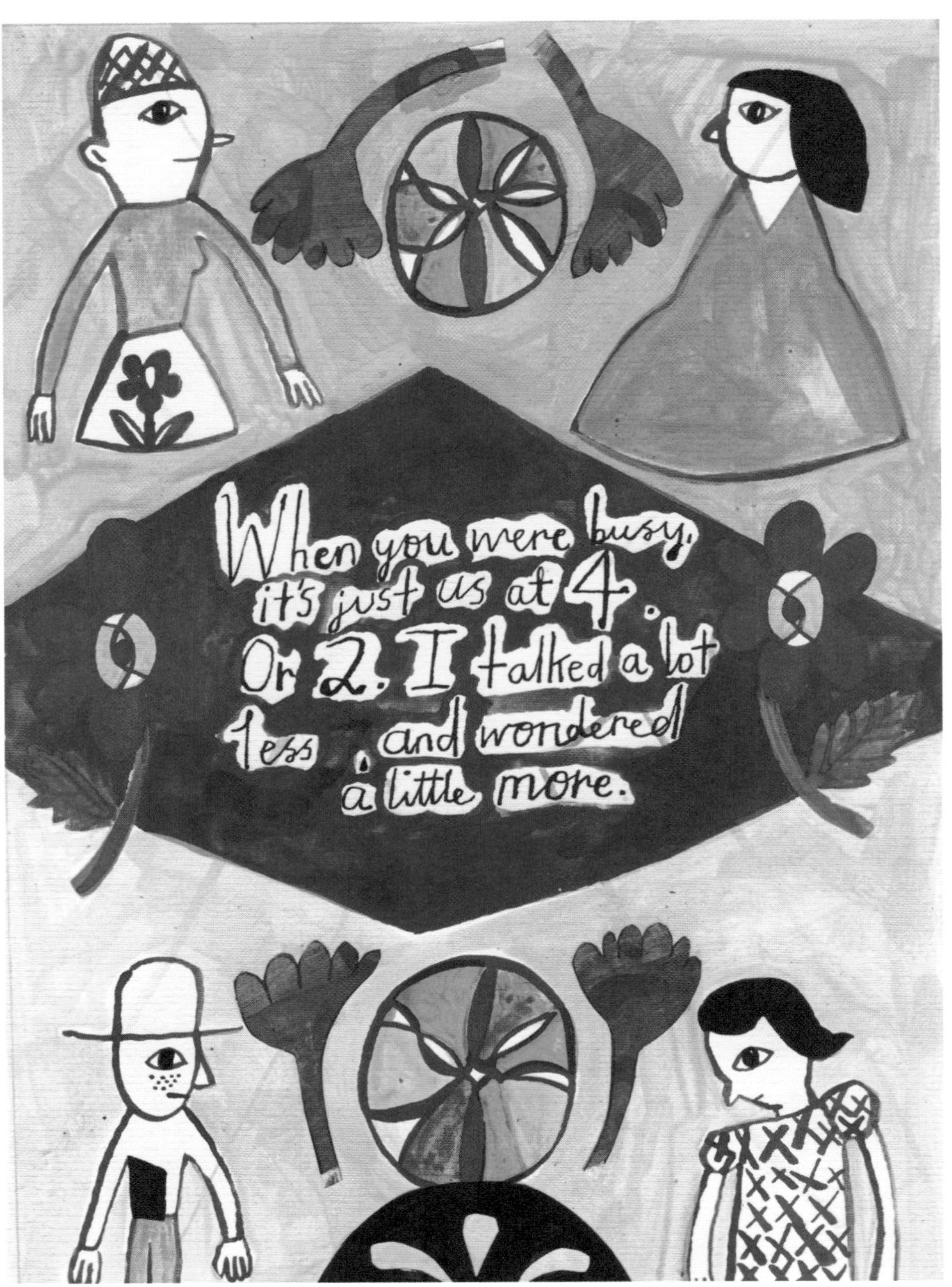
When you were busy,
it's just us at 4.
Or 2. I talked a lot
less and wondered
a little more.

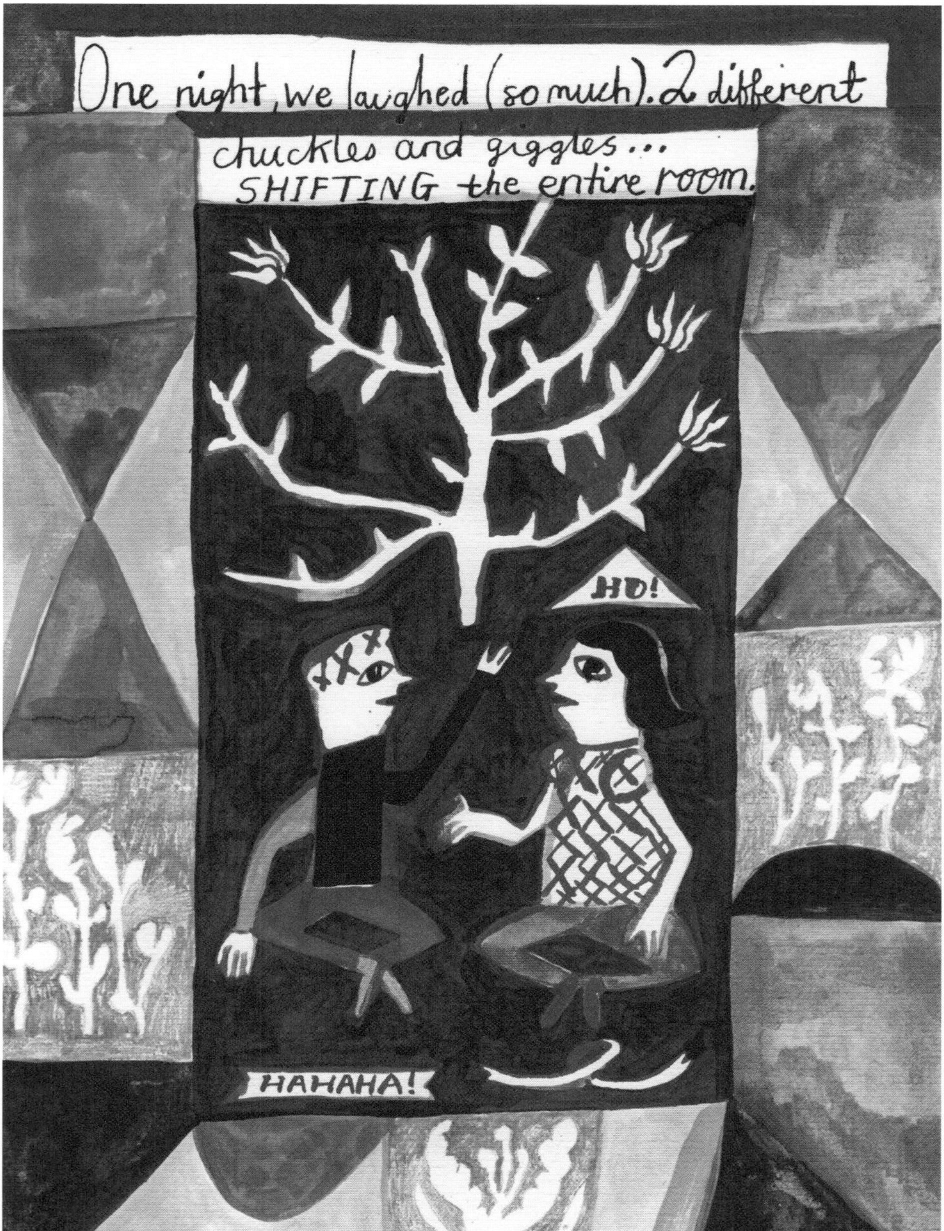
One night, we laughed (so much). 2 different
chuckles and giggles...
SHIFTING the entire room.
HO!
HAHAHA!

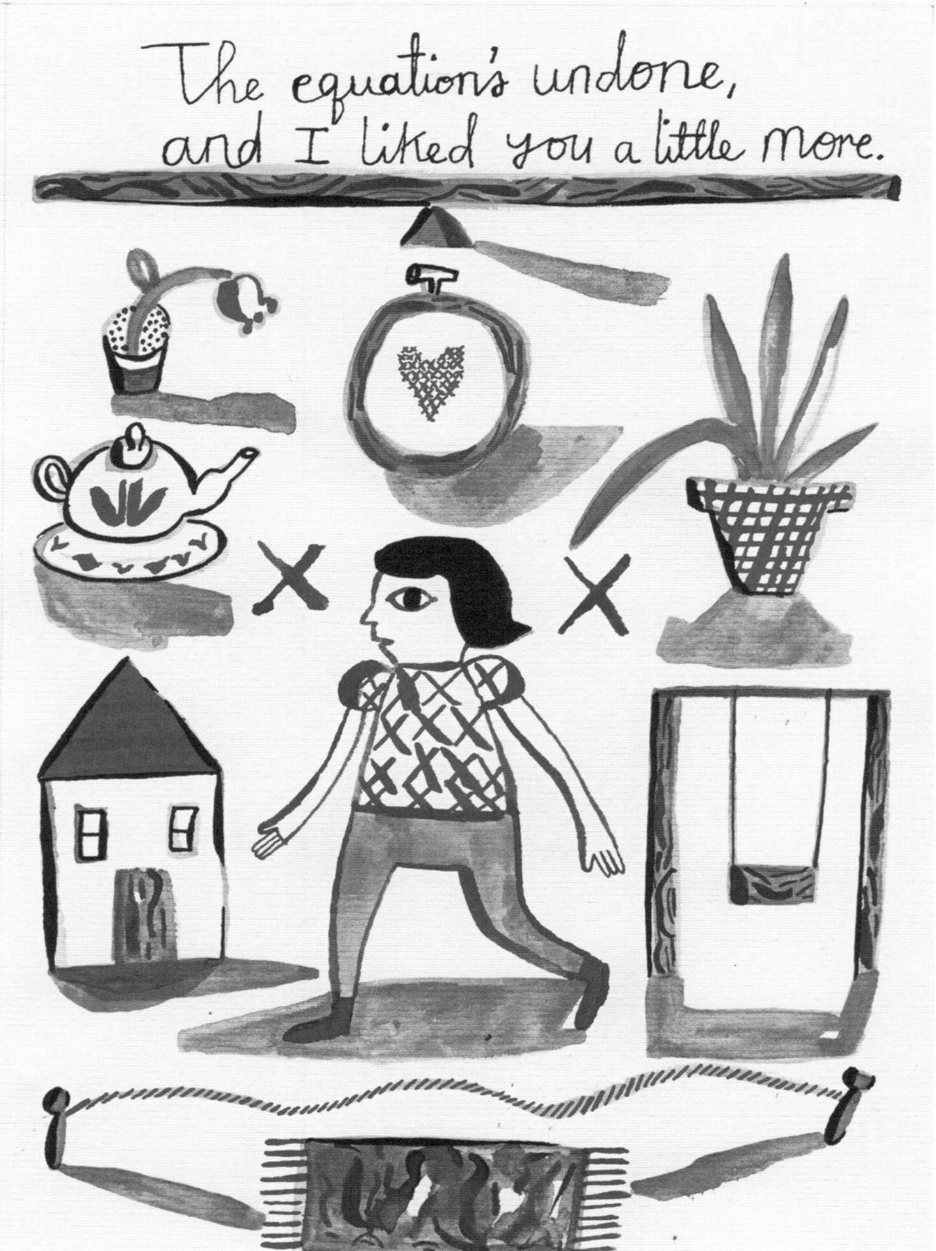
The equation's undone,
and I liked you a little more.

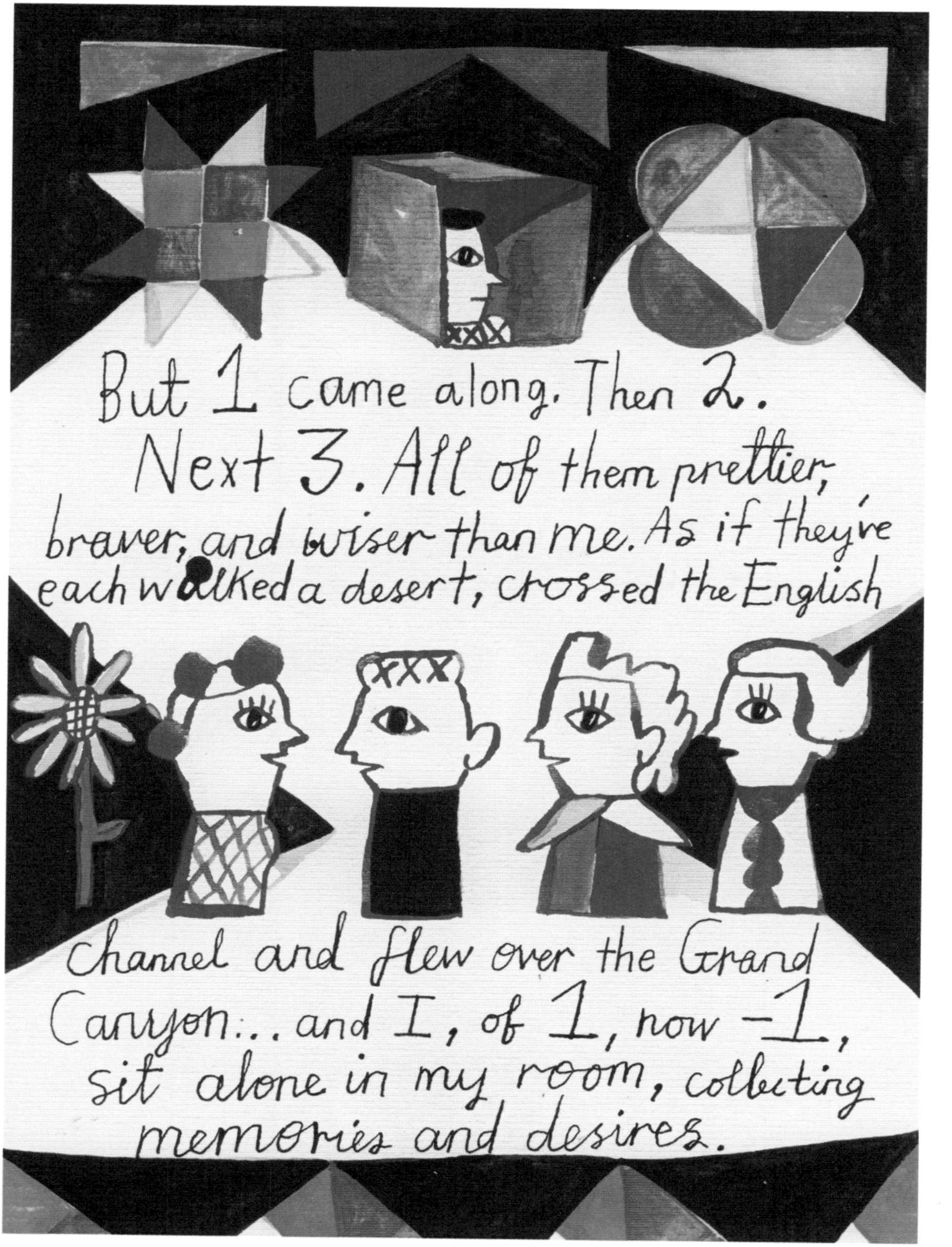
But 1 came along. Then 2.
Next 3. All of them prettier, braver, and wiser than me. As if they've each walked a desert, crossed the English
Channel and flew over the Grand Canyon... and I, of 1, now -1, sit alone in my room, collecting memories and desires.

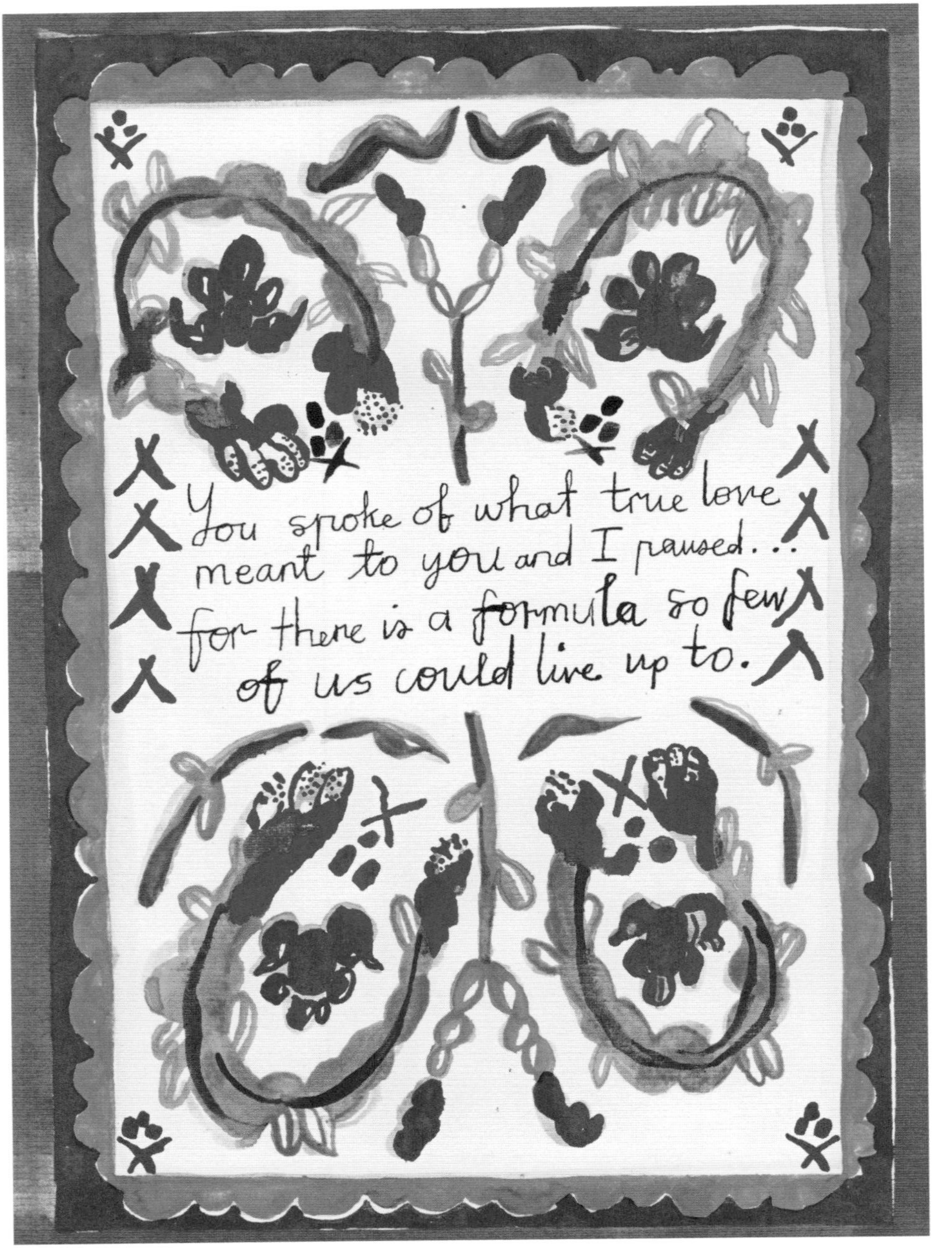
You spoke of what true love
meant to you and I paused...
for there is a formula so few
of us could live up to.

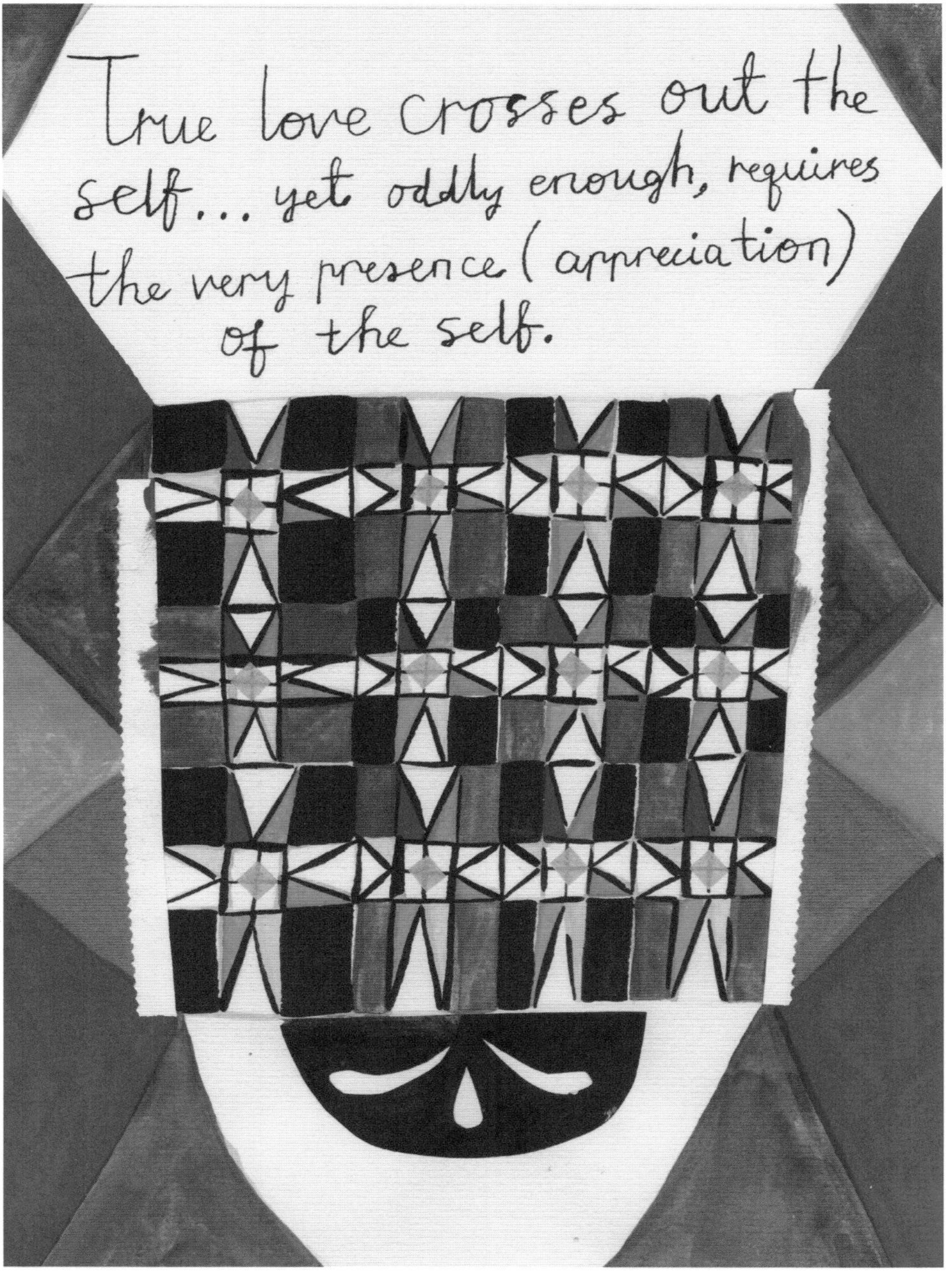
True love crosses out the
self... yet oddly enough, requires
the very presence (appreciation)
of the self.

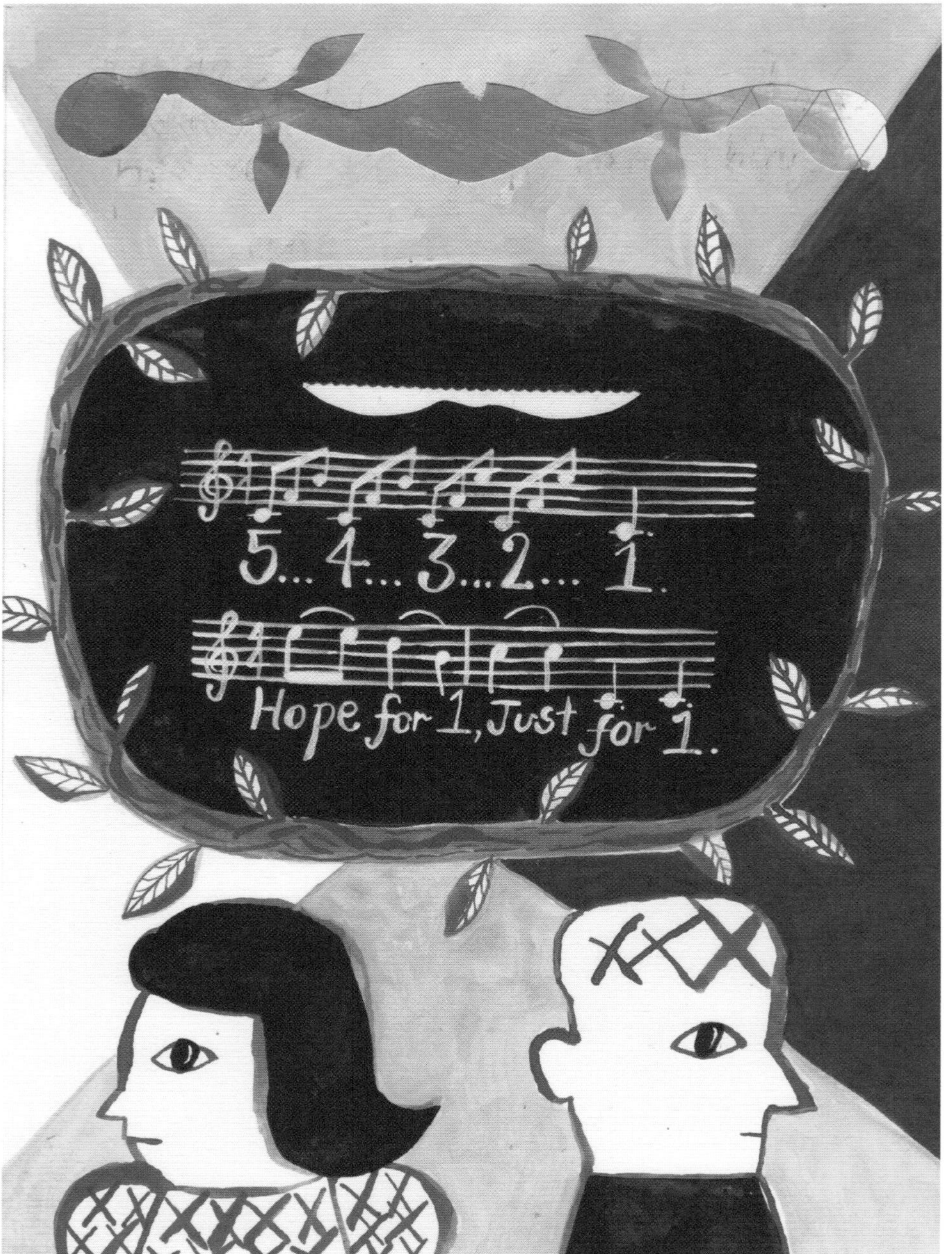
5... 4... 3... 2... 1.
Hope for 1, Just for 1.

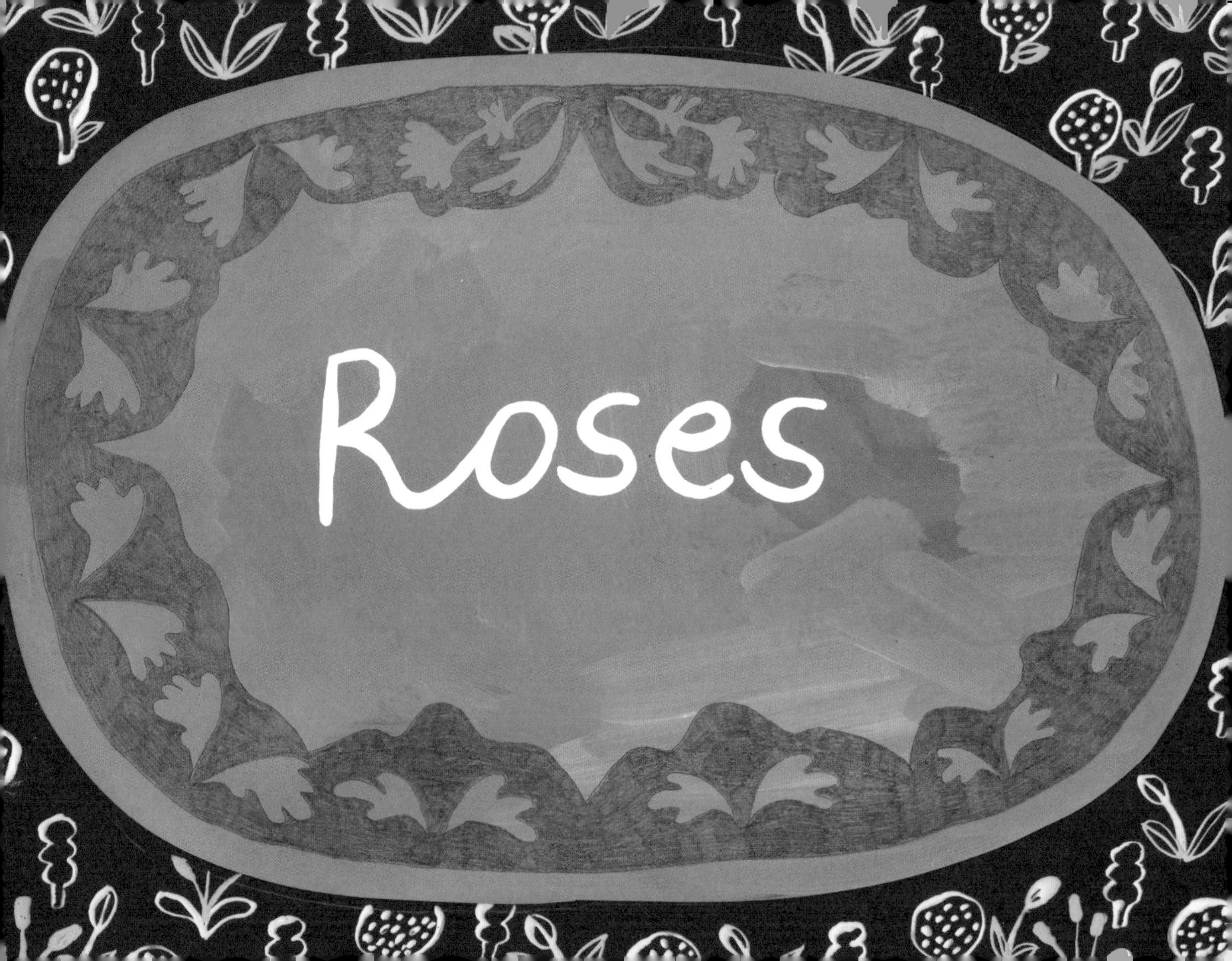
Roses

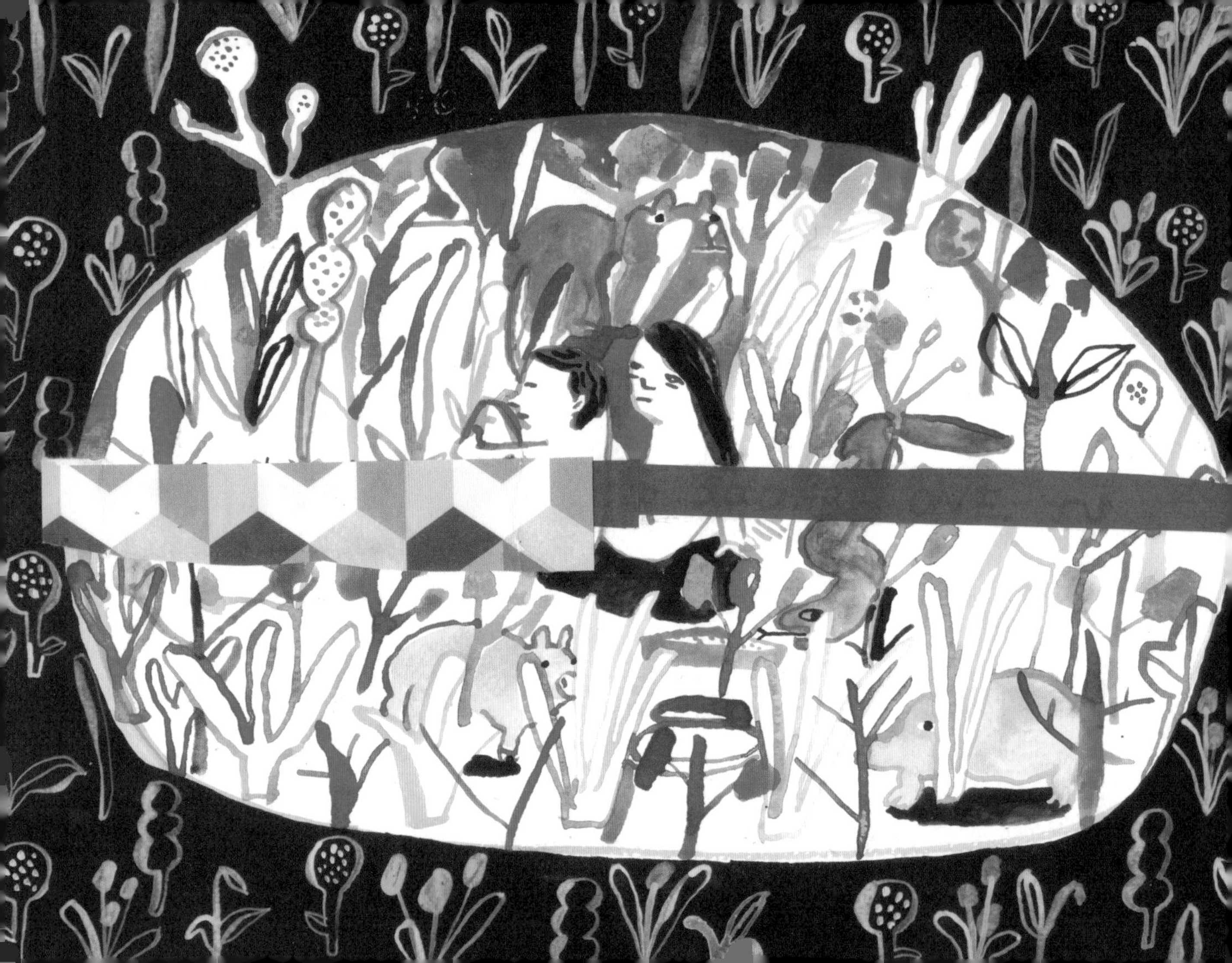

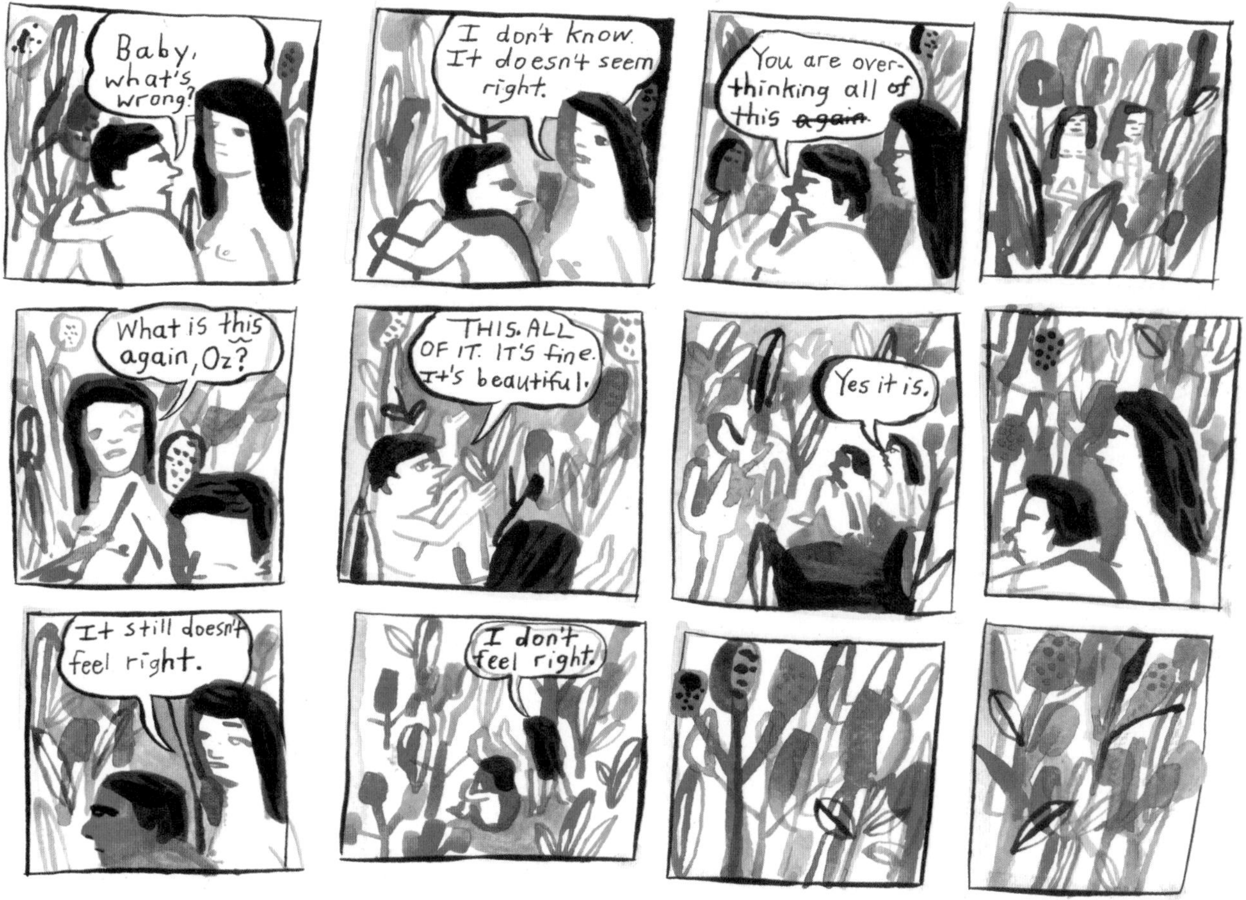
Baby, what's wrong?
I don't know. It doesn't seem right.
You are over-thinking all of this ~~again~~
What is this again, Oz?
THIS. ALL OF IT. IT'S fine. It's beautiful.
Yes it is.
It still doesn't feel right.
I don't feel right.

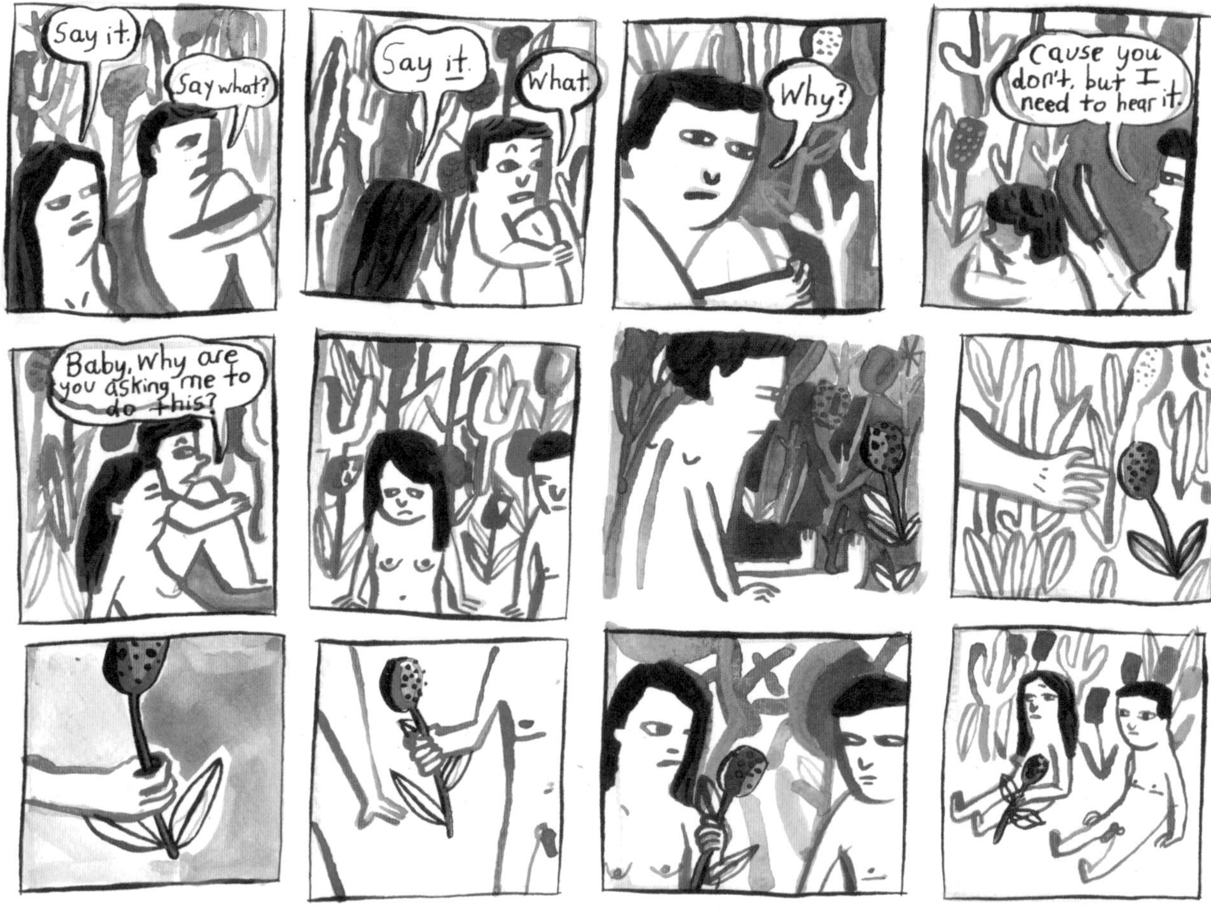
Say it.
Say what?
Say it.
What.
Why?
Cause you don't, but I need to hear it.
Baby, why are you asking me to do this?

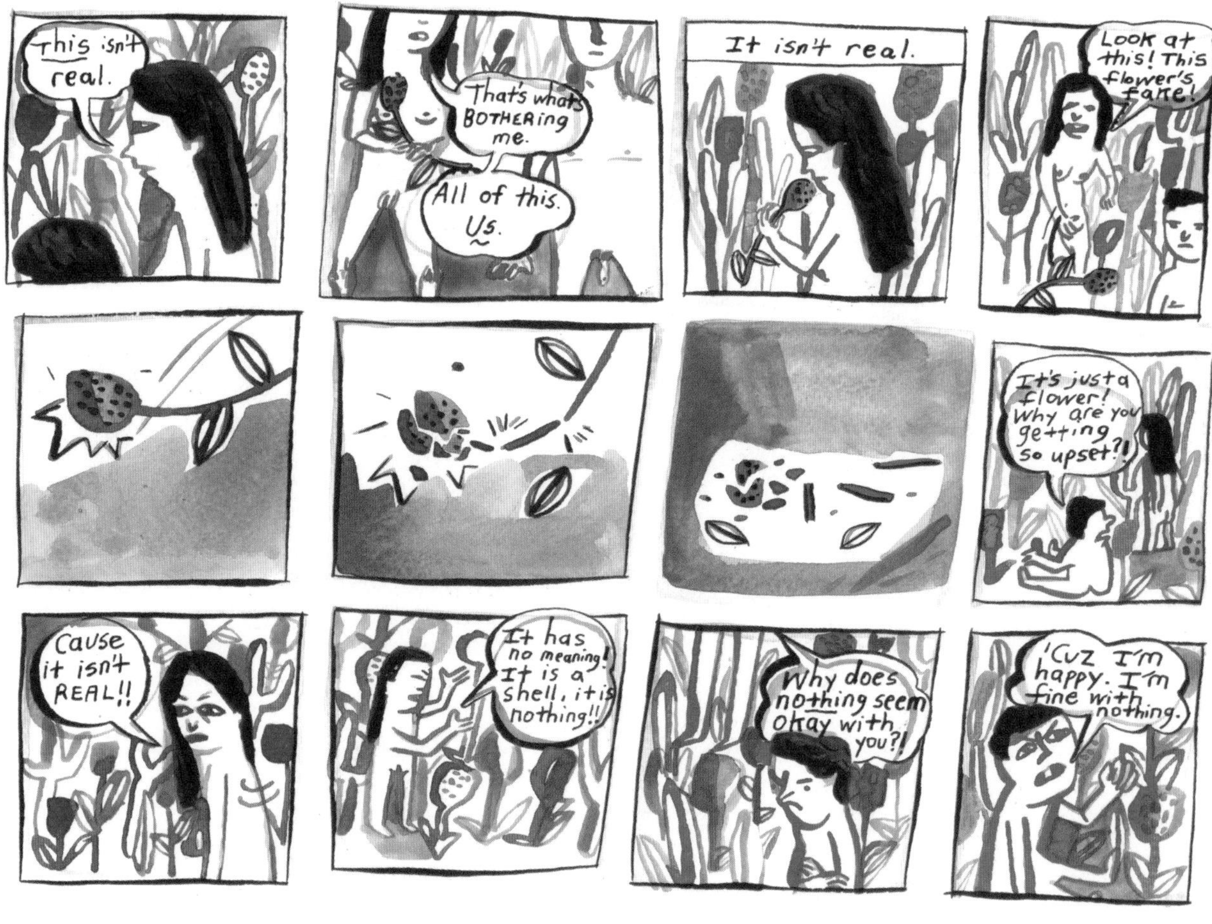
This isn't real.
That's what's BOTHERing me.
All of this. Us.
It isn't real.
Look at this! This flower's fake!
It's just a flower! Why are you getting so upset?!
Cause it isn't REAL!!
It has no meaning! It is a shell, it is nothing!!
Why does nothing seem okay with you?!
'Cuz I'm happy. I'm fine with nothing.

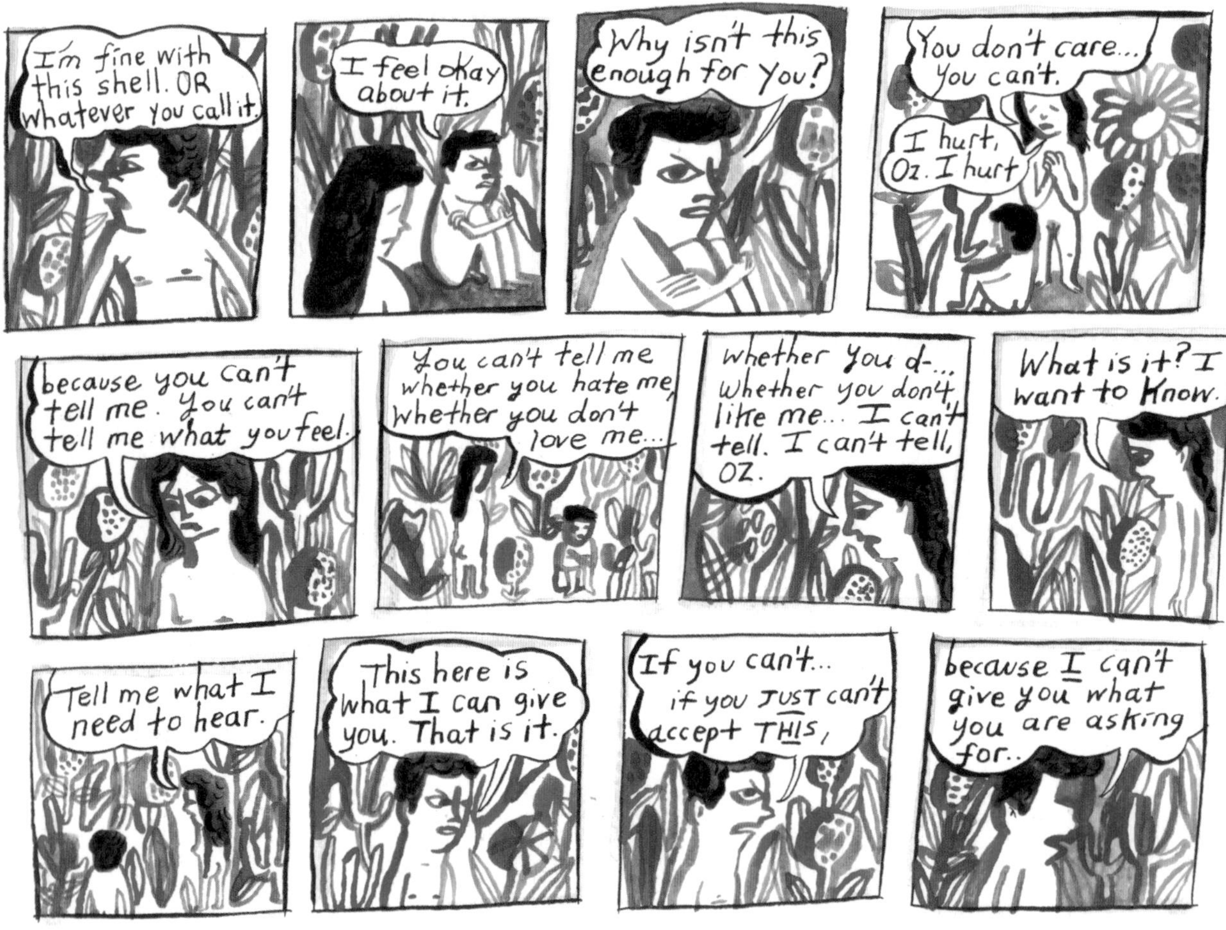

I'm fine with this shell. OR whatever you call it.
I feel okay about it.
Why isn't this enough for you?
You don't care... you can't.
I hurt, Oz. I hurt
because you can't tell me. You can't tell me what you feel.
You can't tell me whether you hate me, whether you don't love me...
whether you d-... whether you don't like me... I can't tell. I can't tell, OZ.
What is it? I want to know.
Tell me what I need to hear.
This here is what I can give you. That is it.
If you can't... if you JUST can't accept THIS,
because I can't give you what you are asking for..

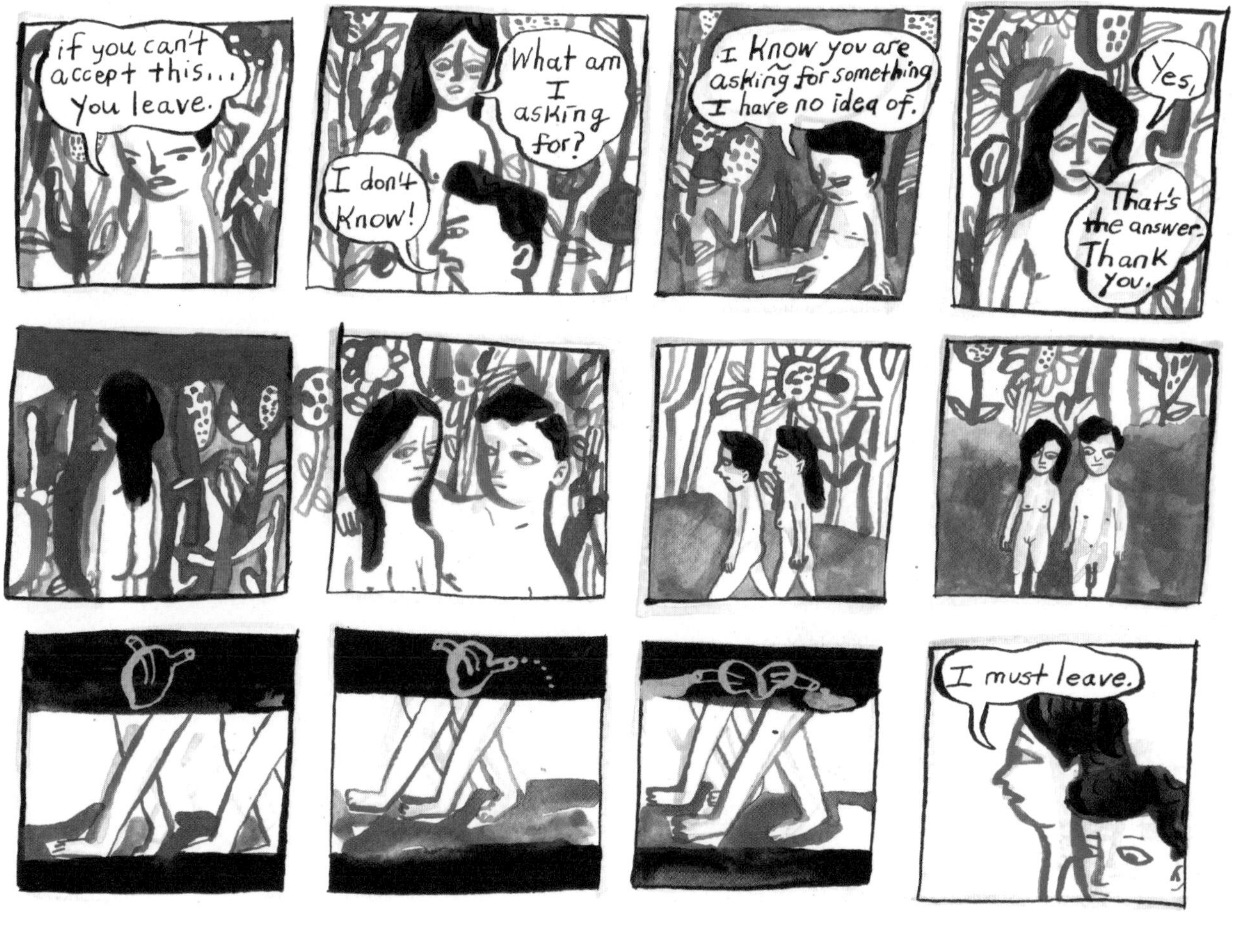
if you can't accept this... you leave.
What am I asking for?
I don't know!
I know you are asking for something I have no idea of.
Yes,
That's the answer. Thank you.
I must leave.

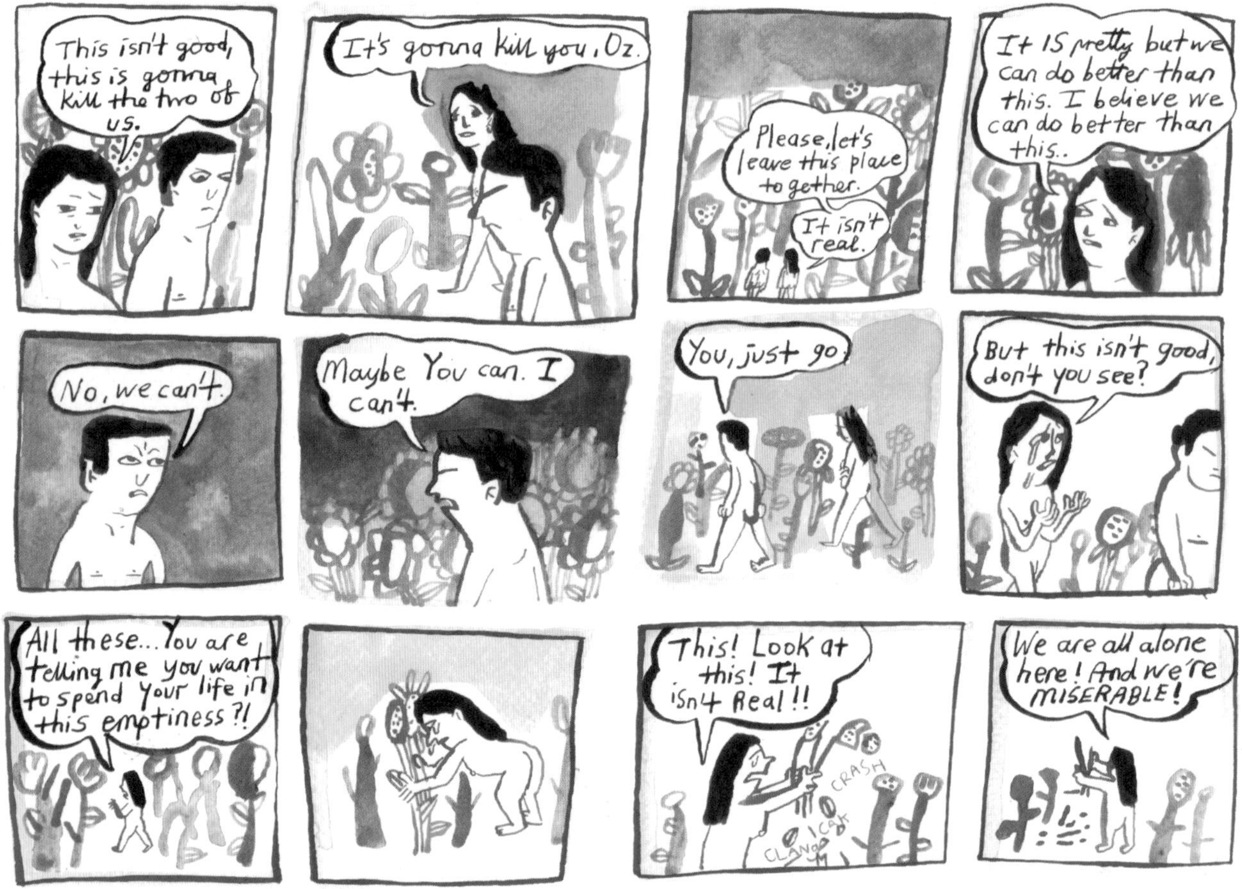
This isn't good, this is gonna kill the two of us.
It's gonna kill you, Oz.
Please, let's leave this place together.
It isn't real.
It IS pretty but we can do better than this. I believe we can do better than this..
No, we can't.
Maybe You can. I can't.
You, just go.
But this isn't good, don't you see?
All these... You are telling me you want to spend your life in this emptiness?!
This! Look at this! It isn't Real!!
CRASH
We are all alone here! And we're MISERABLE!

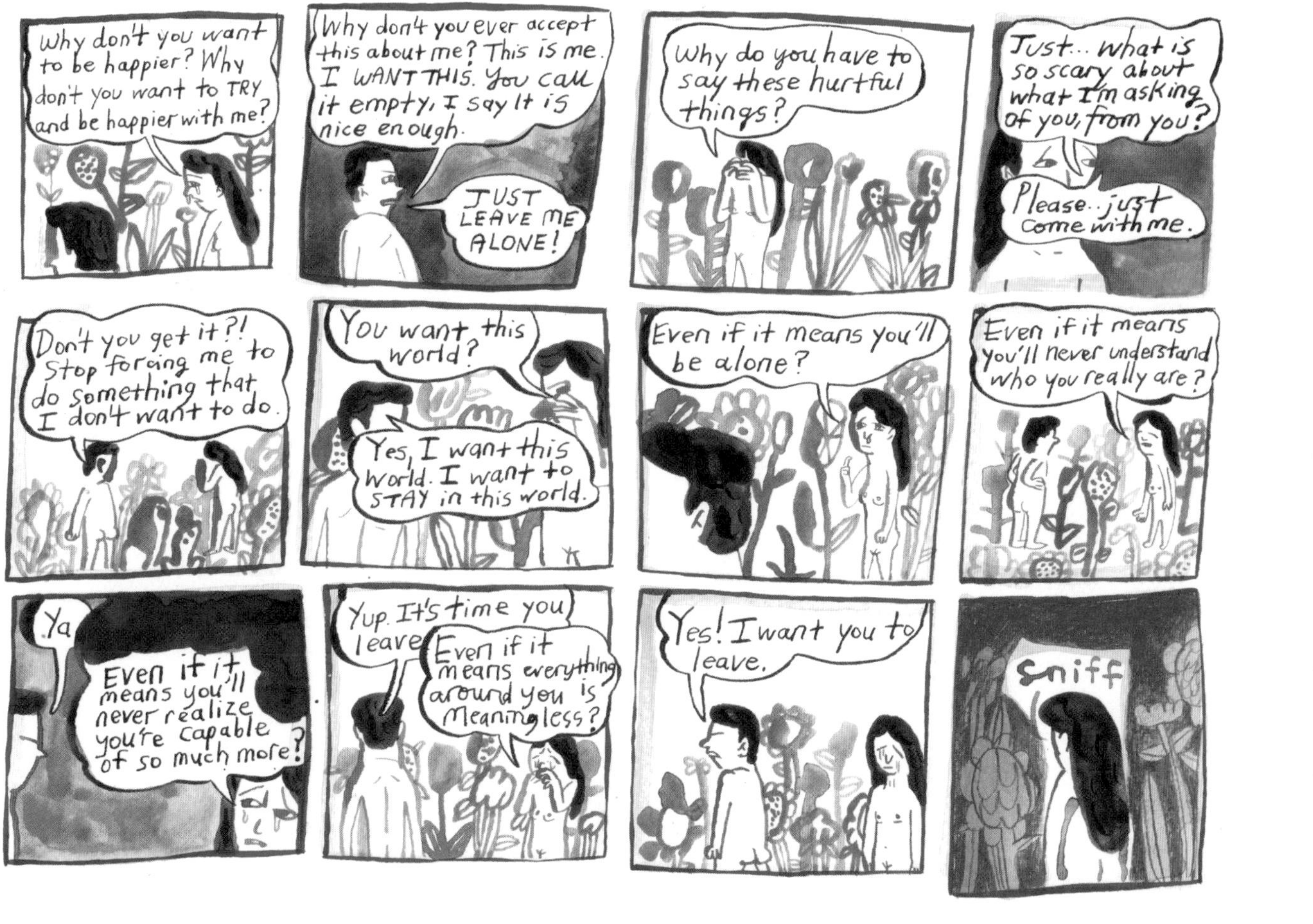
Why don't you want to be happier? Why don't you want to TRY and be happier with me?
Why don't you ever accept this about me? This is me. I WANT THIS. You call it empty, I say It is nice enough.
JUST LEAVE ME ALONE!
Why do you have to say these hurtful things?
Just... what is so scary about what I'm asking of you, from you?
Please.. just come with me.
Don't you get it?! Stop forcing me to do something that I don't want to do.
You want this world?
Yes, I want this world. I want to STAY in this world.
Even if it means you'll be alone?
Even if it means you'll never understand who you really are?
Ya
Even if it, means you'll never realize you're capable of so much more?
Yup. It's time you leave
Even if it means everything around you is Meaningless?
Yes! I want you to leave.
sniff

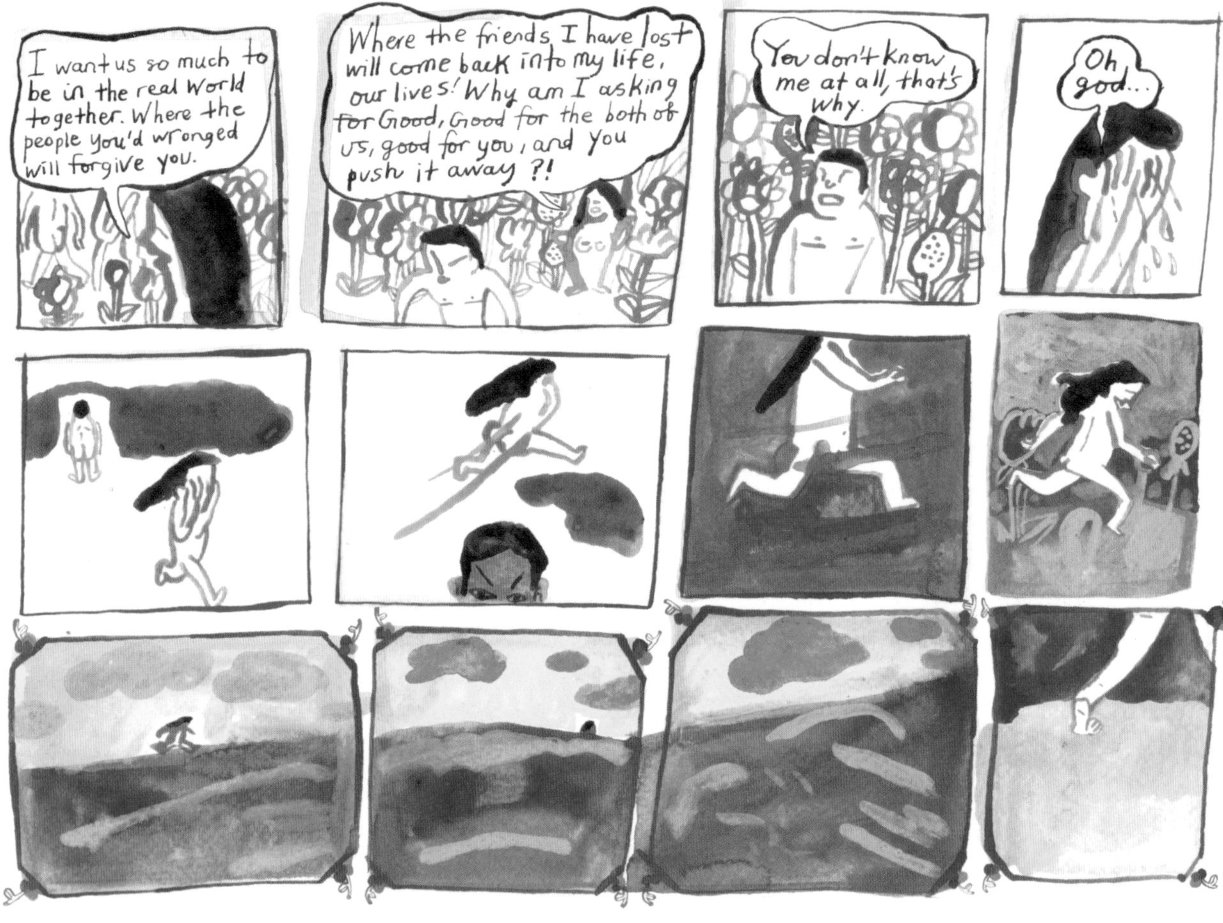
I want us so much to be in the real world together. Where the people you'd wronged will forgive you.
Where the friends I have lost will come back into my life, our lives! Why am I asking for Good, Good for the both of us, good for you, and you push it away?!
You don't know me at all, that's why.
Oh god...

[redacted] TO
WHERE

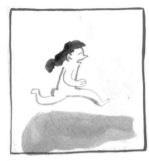

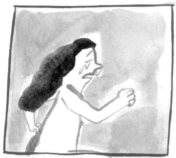

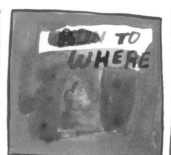

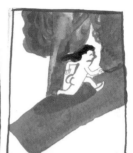

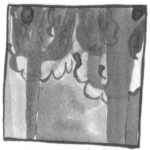

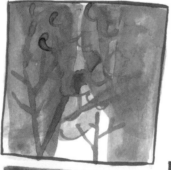

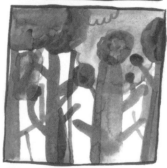

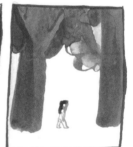

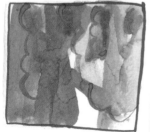

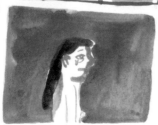

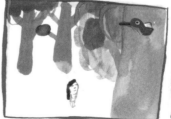

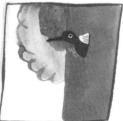

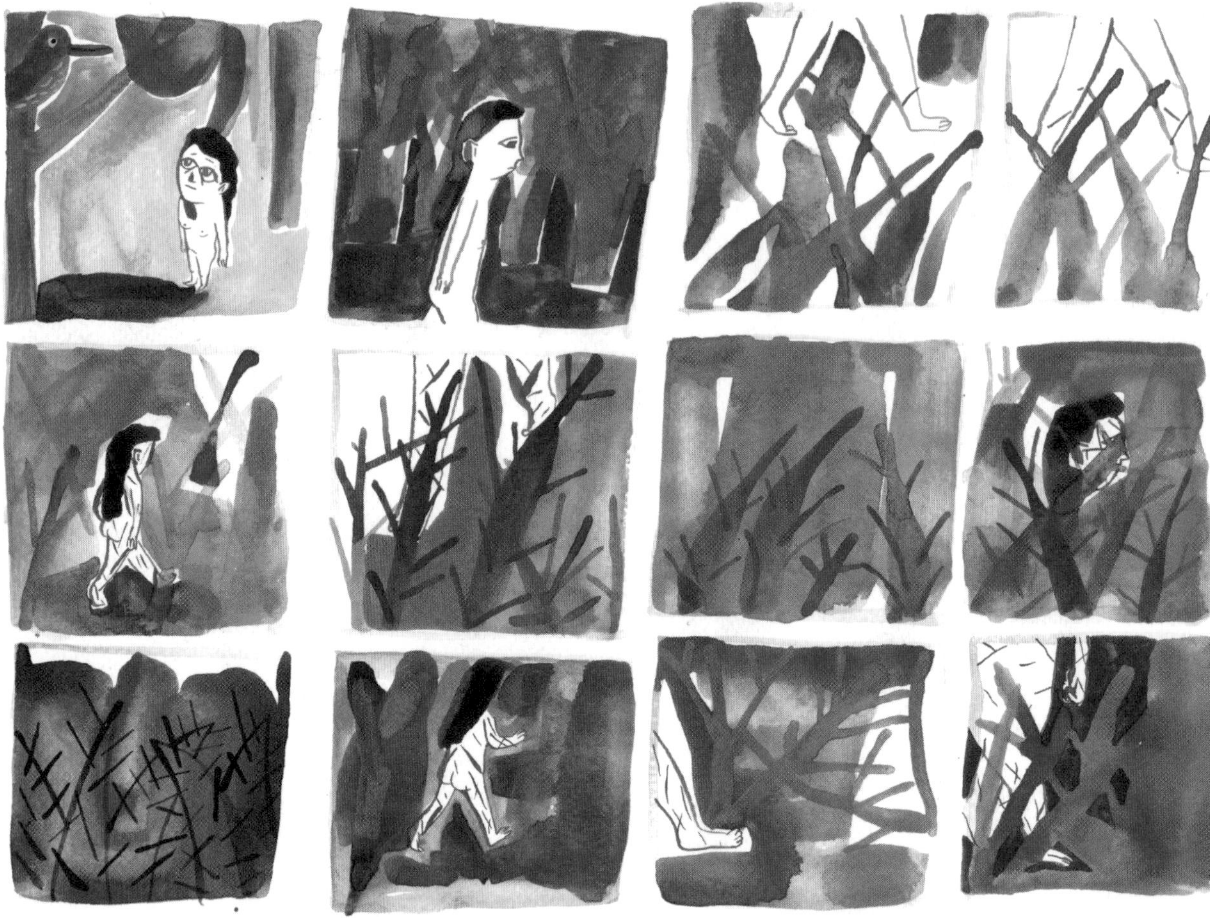

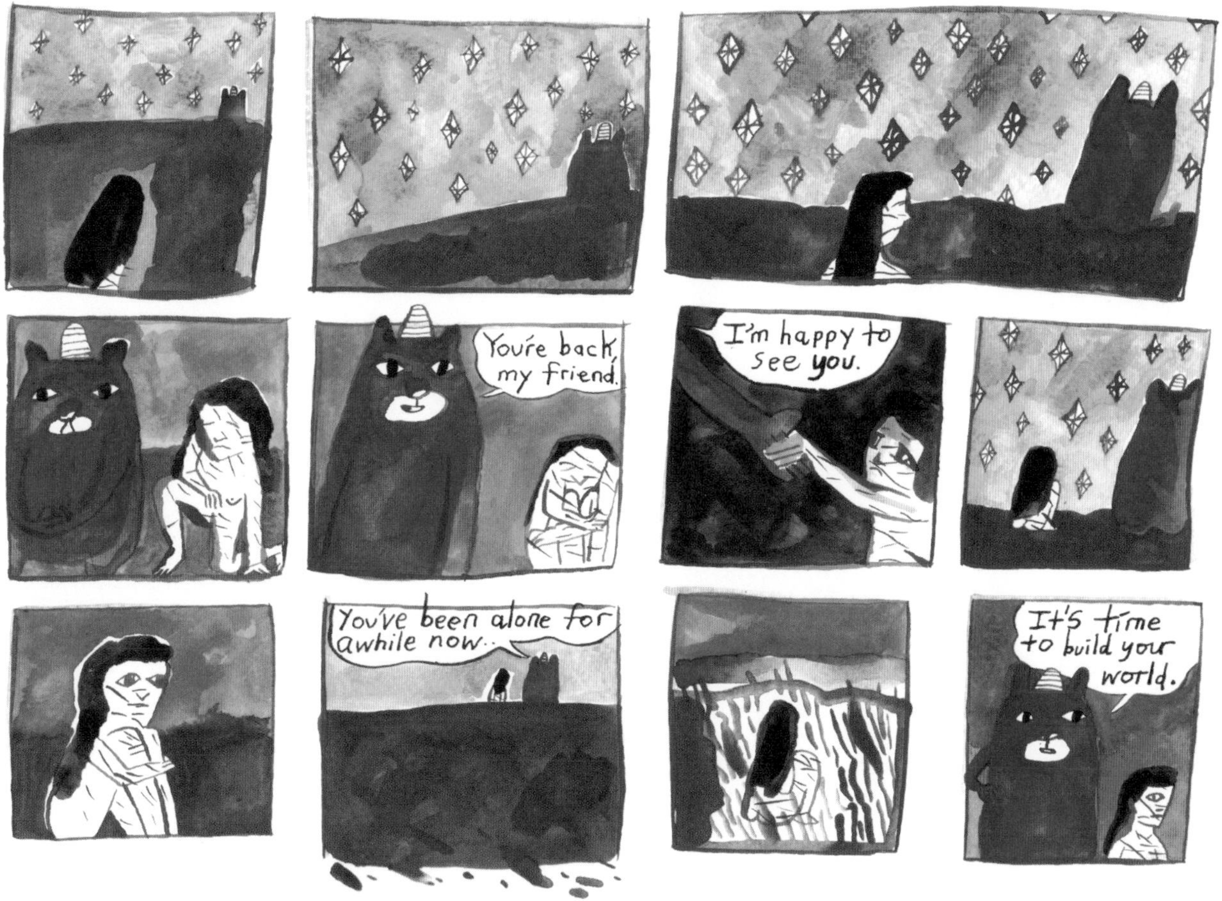
You're back, my friend.
I'm happy to see you.
You've been alone for awhile now..
It's time to build your world.

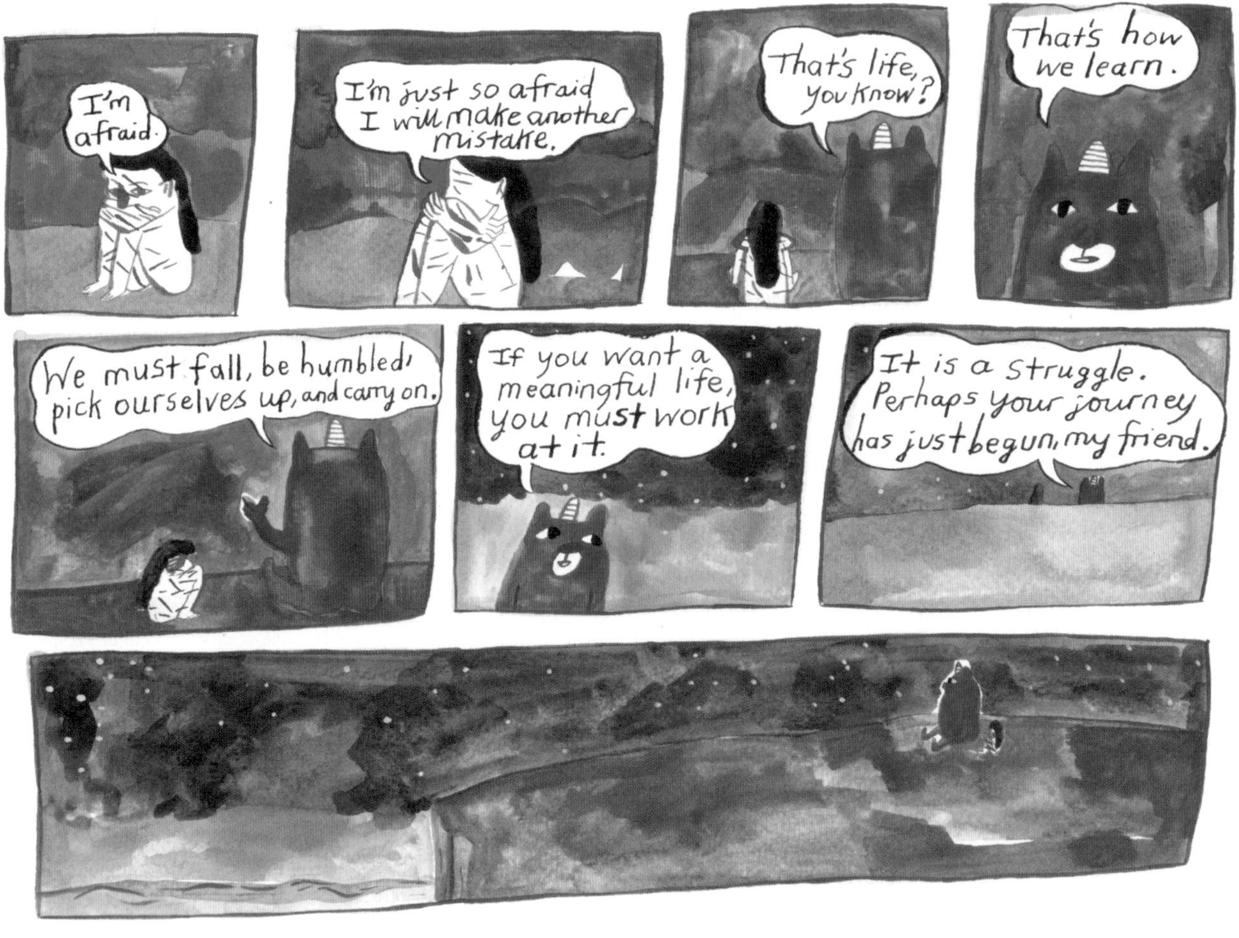
I'm afraid.
I'm just so afraid I will make another mistake.
That's life, you know?
That's how we learn.
We must fall, be humbled, pick ourselves up, and carry on.
If you want a meaningful life, you must work at it.
It is a struggle. Perhaps your journey has just begun, my friend.

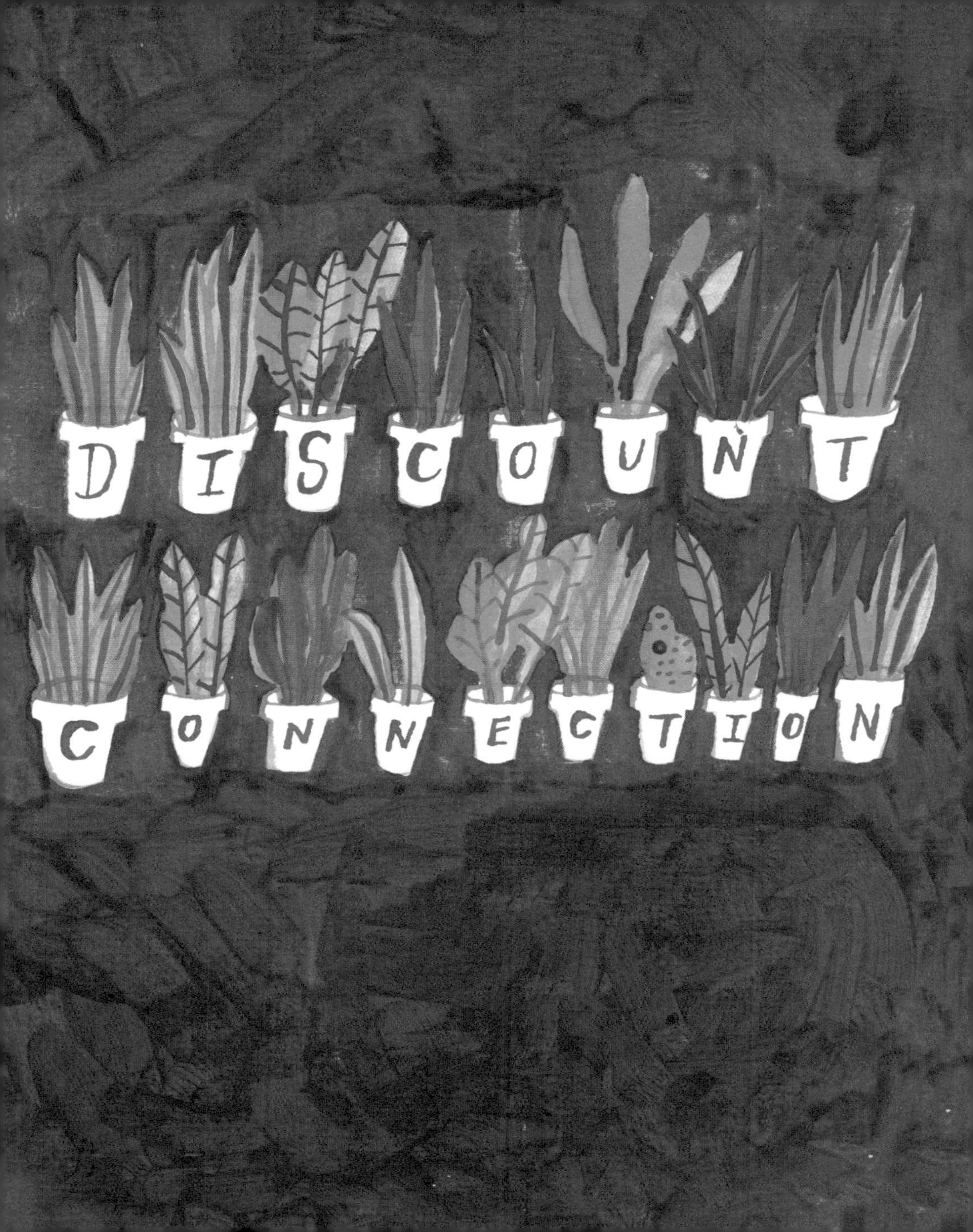
DISCOUNT
CONNECTION

I am stuck in the middle of a desert.

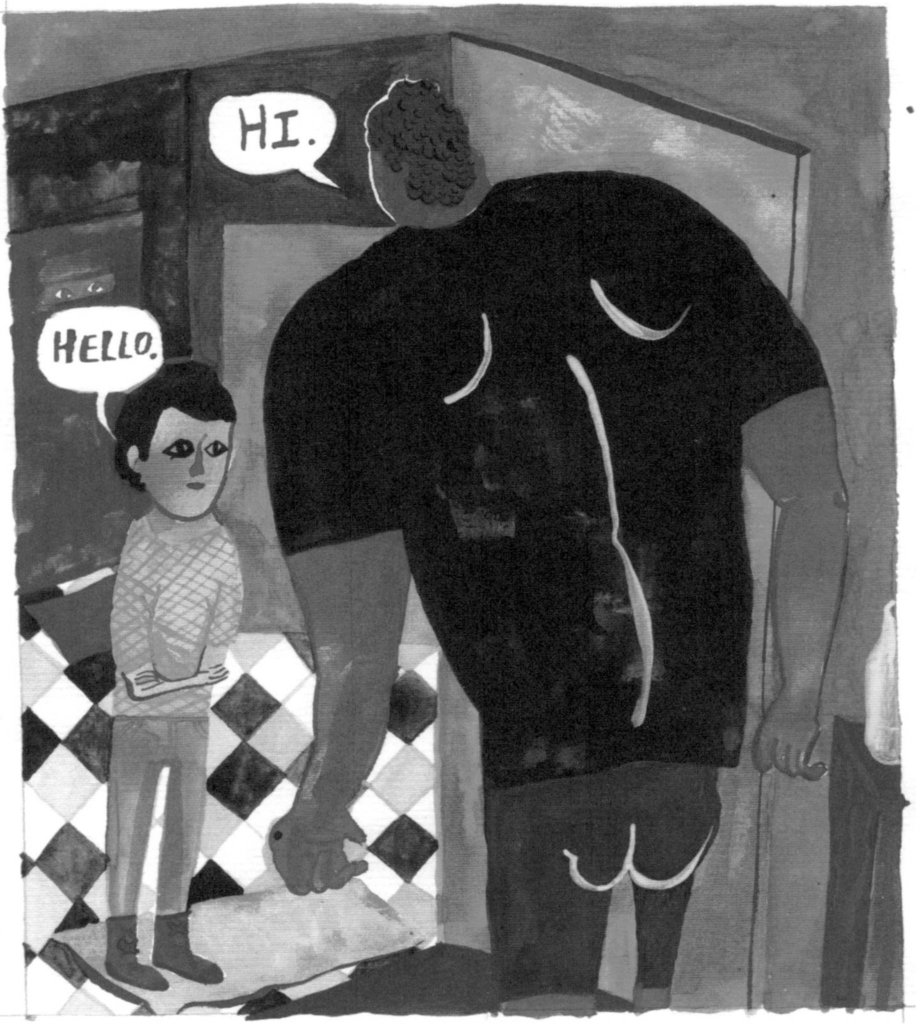
HI.
HELLO.

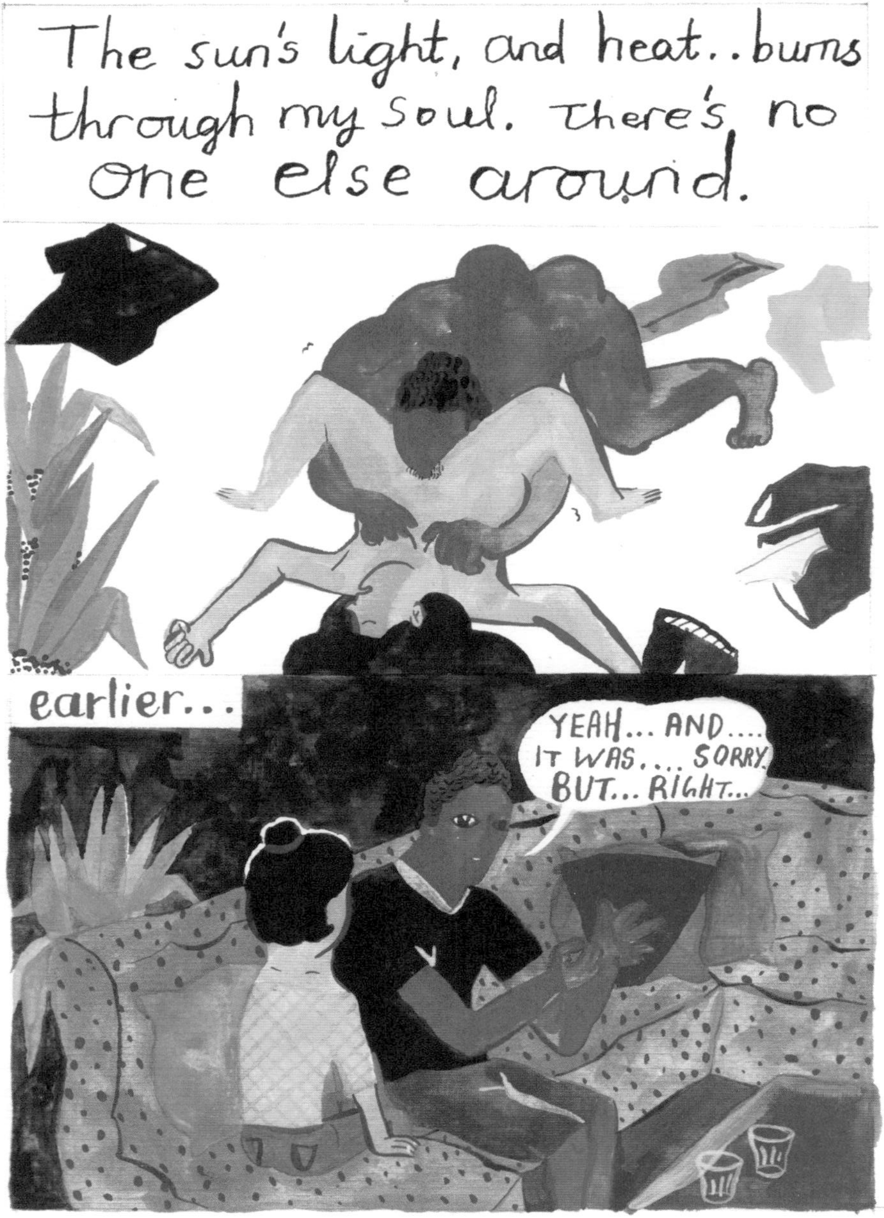
The sun's light, and heat..burns through my soul. There's no one else around.
earlier...
YEAH... AND.... IT WAS.... SORRY. BUT... RIGHT...

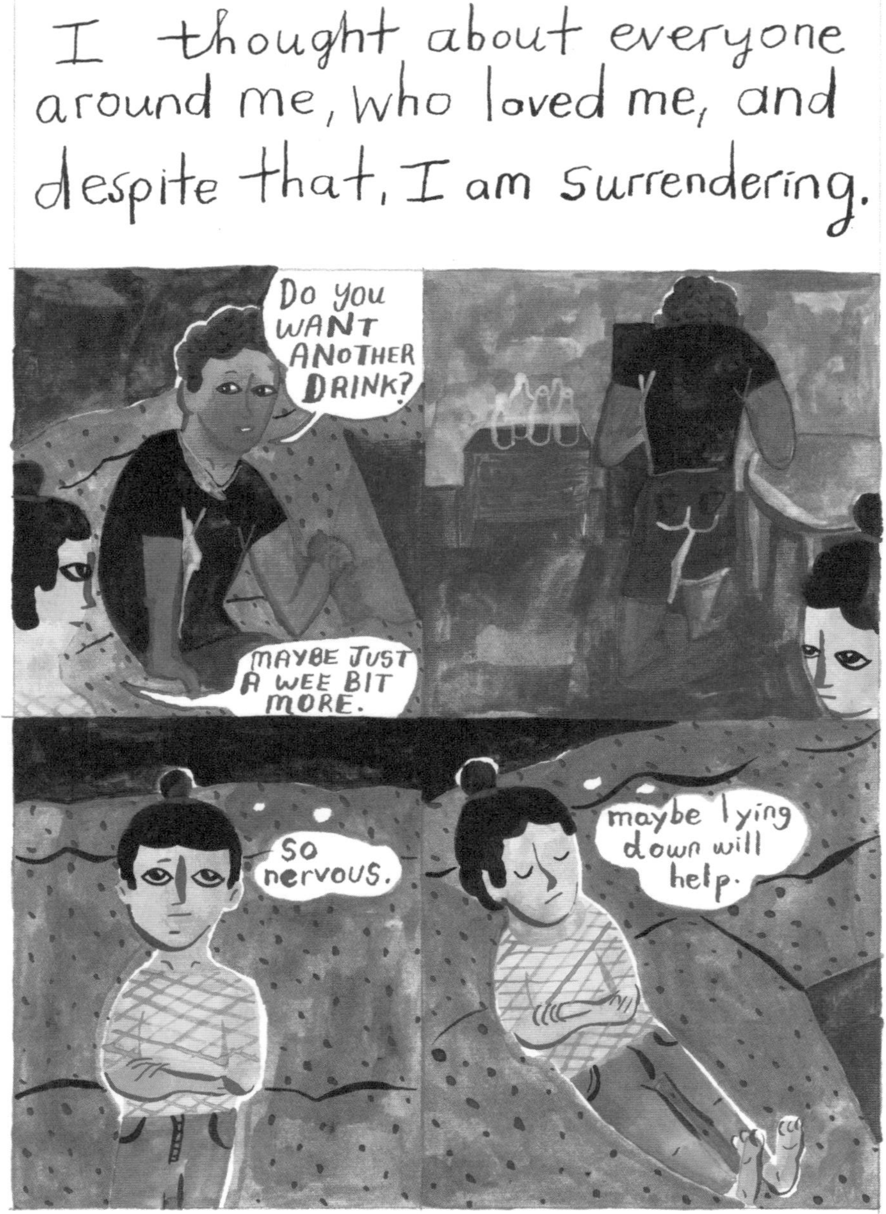
I thought about everyone around me, who loved me, and despite that, I am surrendering.
Do you WANT ANOTHER DRINK?
MAYBE JUST A WEE BIT MORE.
SO nervous.
maybe lying down will help.

I considered holding my breath, or lying down to just deplete, slowly but surely.

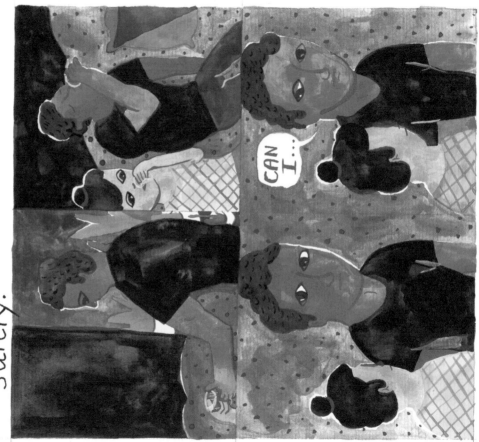

A mirage glistens in the distance; its false hope strikes my heart, already slowing its beat. Thump. Thump. Thump..... Thud.

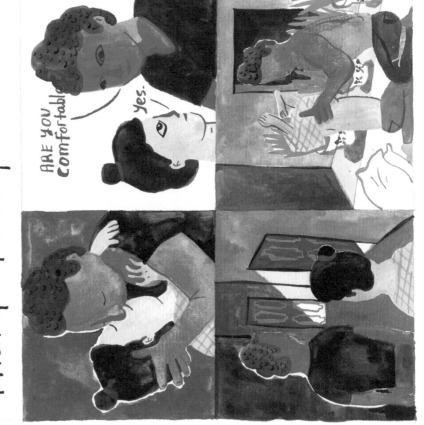

Darkness fell, yet I'm embraced... revived for a second by your words, thoughts, gestures, . . . , confessions.

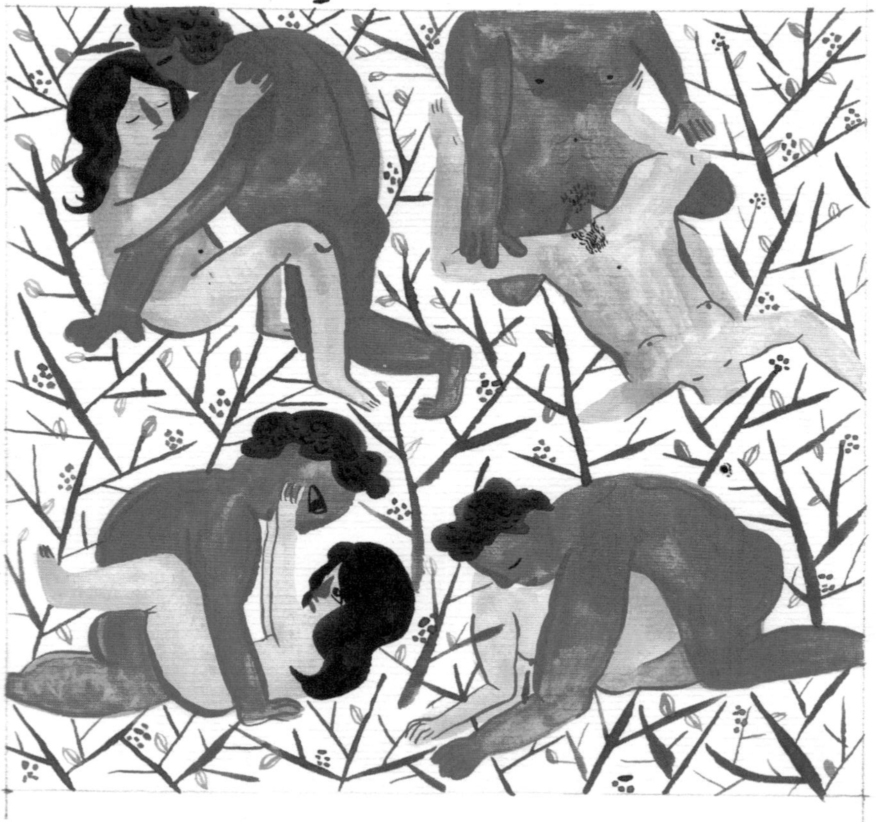

My heart starts beating again. It hurts like hell.

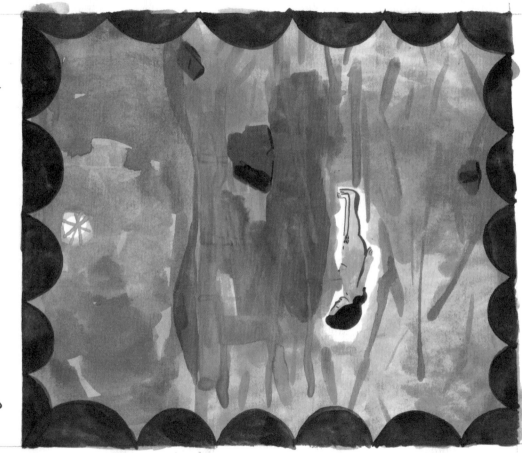

Lampung Diaries

I WAS in Lampung, Sumatra recently
and I regretted not bringing my camera.

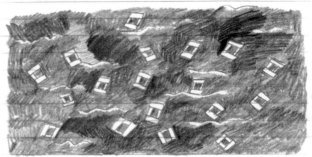

While the plane was ten minutes away
from Jakarta, I noticed strange floating
platforms on the surface of the sea.
That look ~~thi~~ like this (pictured above)
I wondered what they were used for.

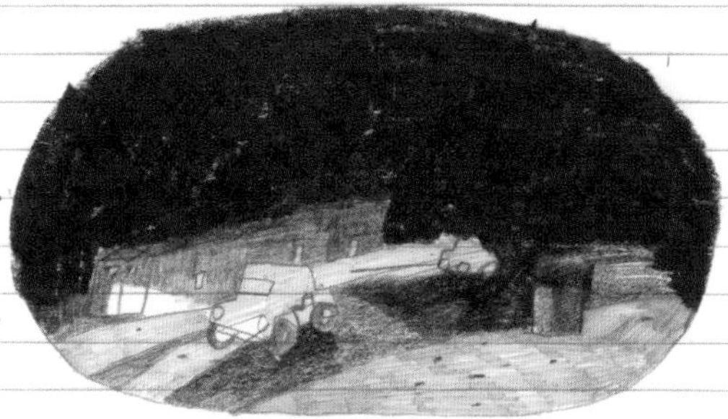

We arrived in Lampung at night. The streets were dark, lit only by the ~~occar~~ passing vehicles and shops that stayed opened. To this, my friend would turn to me and say "Welcome to Lampung!"

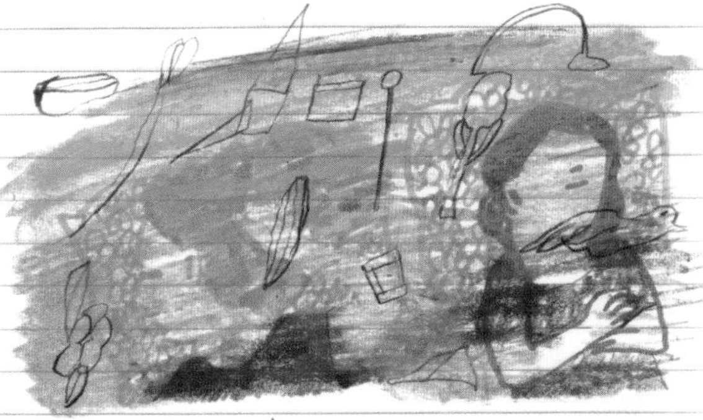

I fell into deep sleep on my first night in Lampung. with visions of it's dark-lit shops, streets, winding streets and bumpy roads swimming inside my mind . . . .

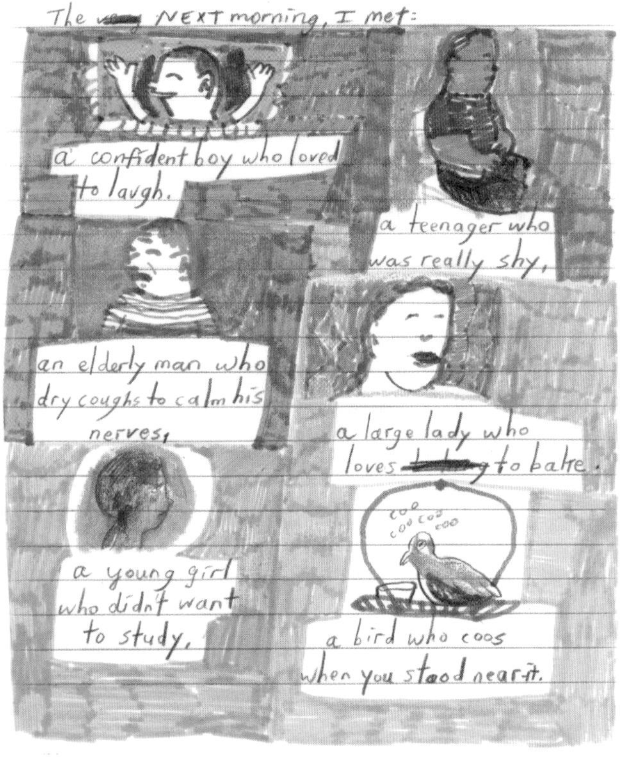
The NEXT morning, I met:
a confident boy who loved to laugh.
a teenager who was really shy,
an elderly man who dry coughs to calm his nerves,
a large lady who loves to bake.
a young girl who didn't want to study,
coo coo coo coo
a bird who coos when you stood near it.

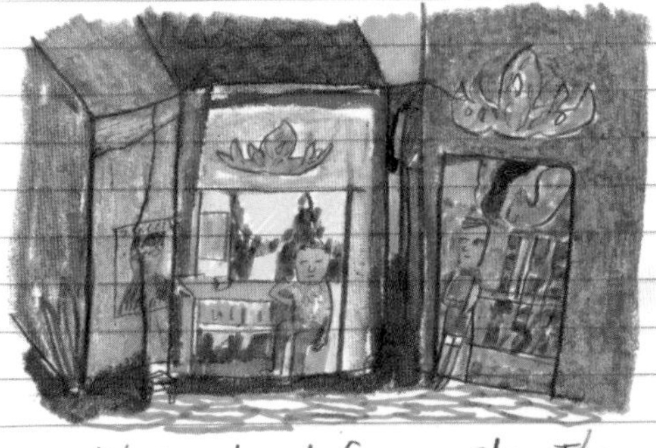

We went out for a ride.
I learnt, KELUAR means EXIT.

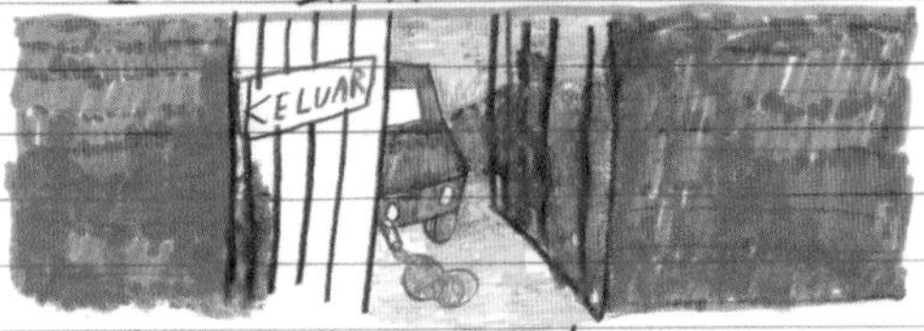
KELUAR

AND TOTOP means CLOSED.

OuR CAR passed by a bus terminal, my
FRiend's brother says So "Quite a number
of Kidnappings took place here-"

I saw a lady in a beautiful
batik dress, selling peanuts by
the road.

My friend says "Lampung means ...
vessel. Something to do with „ships."
Hence, a lot of ship motifs around
the town.

My Friend bought me this lovely
tapestry made by the locals. I
was very moved by her gesture.

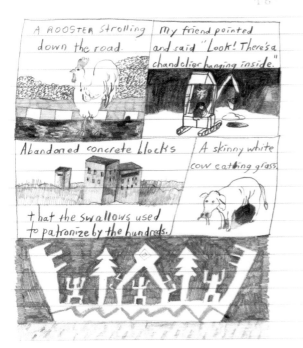

A ROOSTER strolling down the road.

My friend pointed and said "Look! There's a chandelier hanging inside."

Abandoned concrete blocks

A skinny white cow eating grass.

that the swallows used to patronize by the hundreds.

We were in the car, a little boy (6? 7?) holding newspapers knocked on the car's window.

I cannot forget his face.

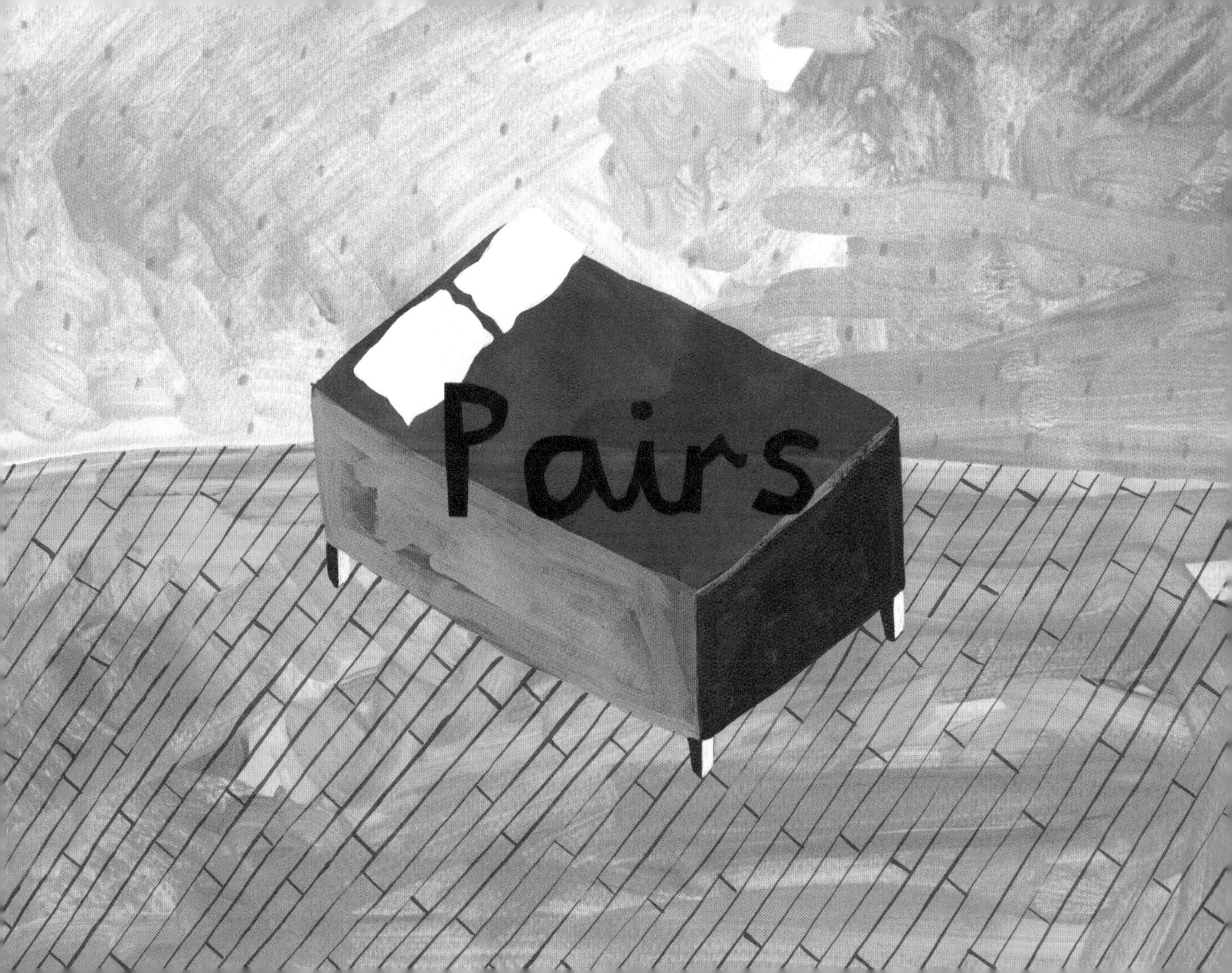
Pairs

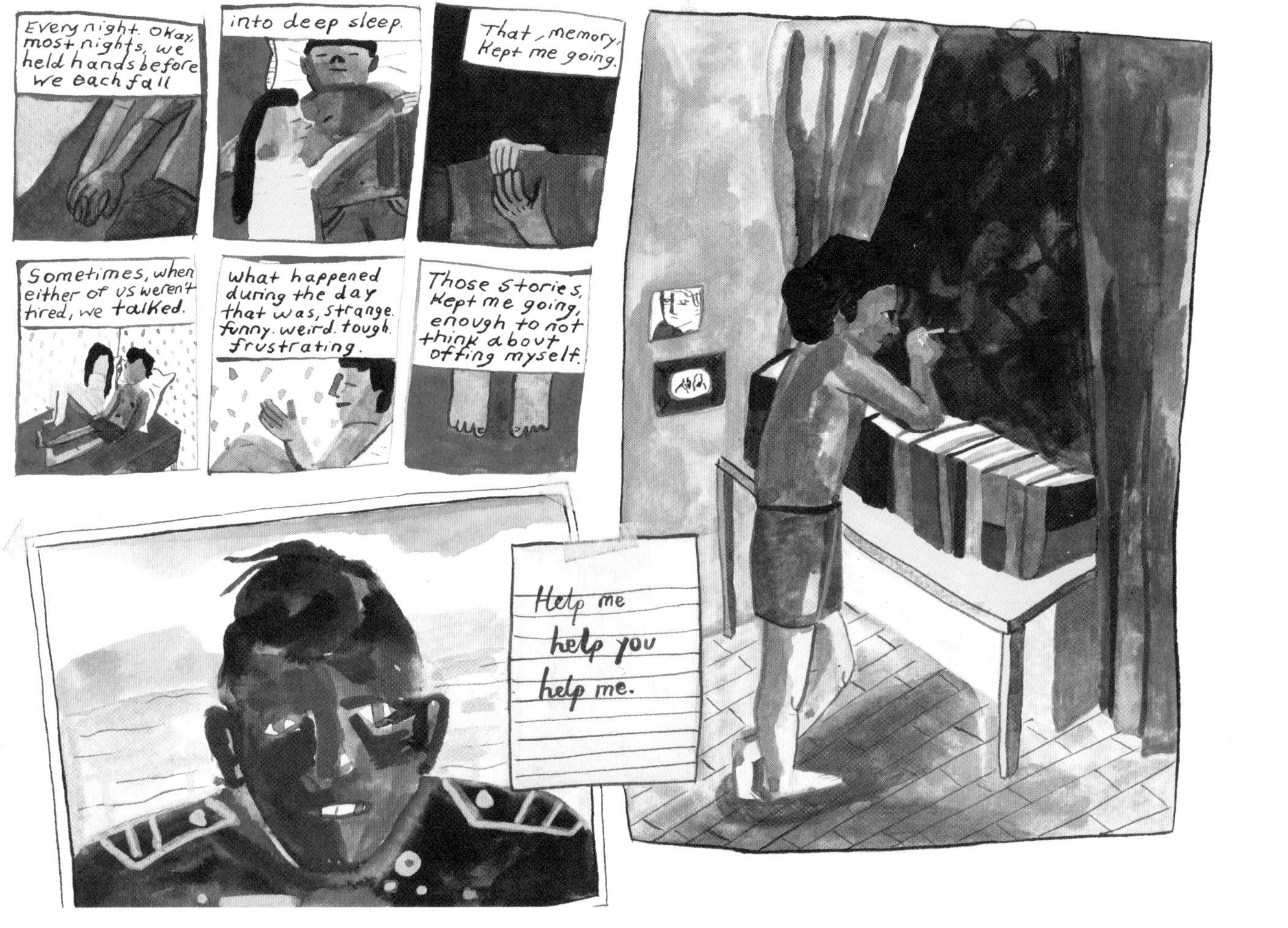
Every night. Okay, most nights, we held hands before we each fall
into deep sleep.
That, memory, kept me going.
Sometimes, when either of us weren't tired, we talked.
what happened during the day that was, strange. funny. weird. tough. frustrating.
Those stories, kept me going, enough to not think about offing myself.
Help me
help you
help me.

PAIRS

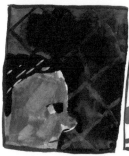

Please don't
do that.

He is dying from
cancer now.

The least you can do
is not smoke right now,
in front of me.

I could die right now
and you wouldn't shed a tear.

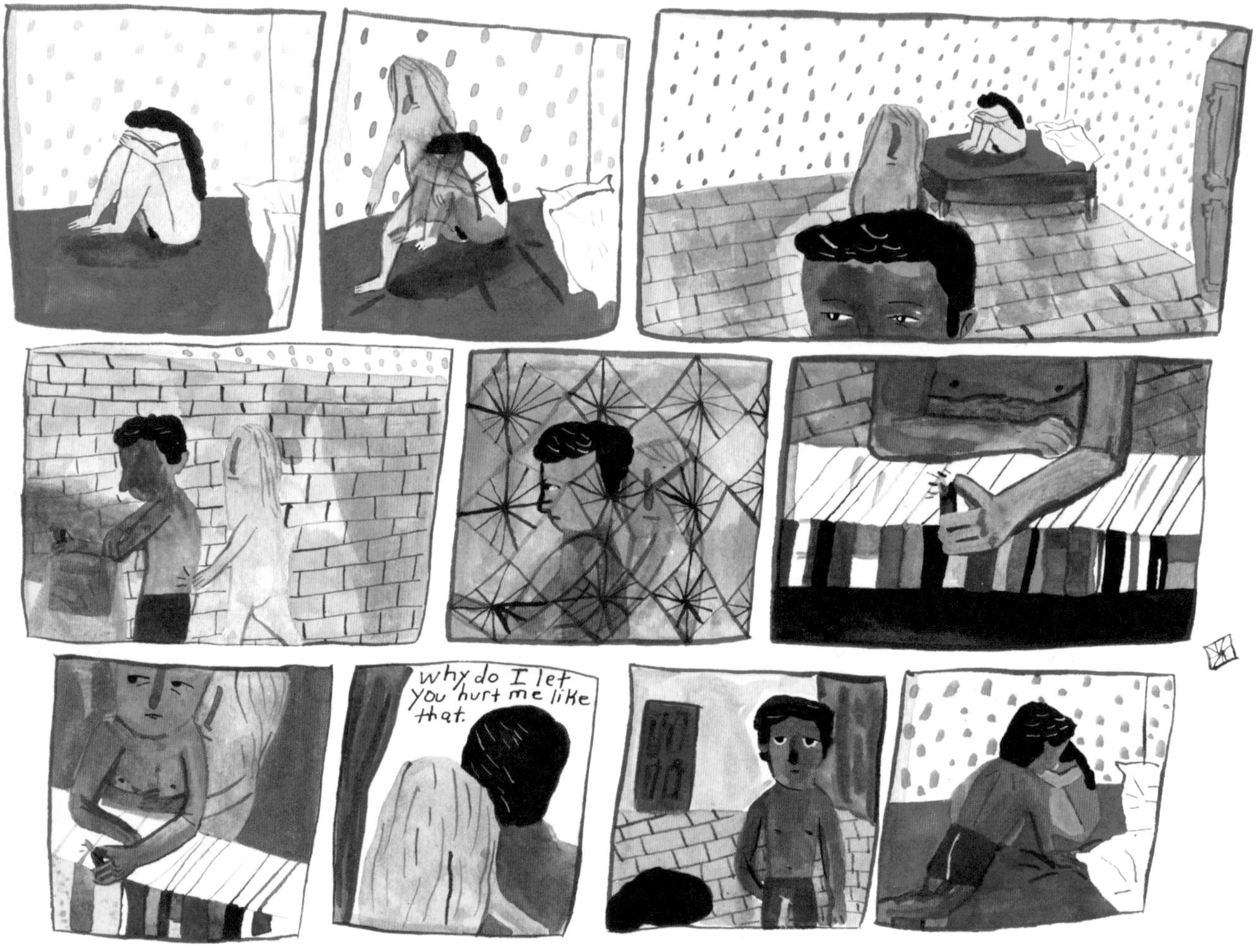
why do I let you hurt me like that.

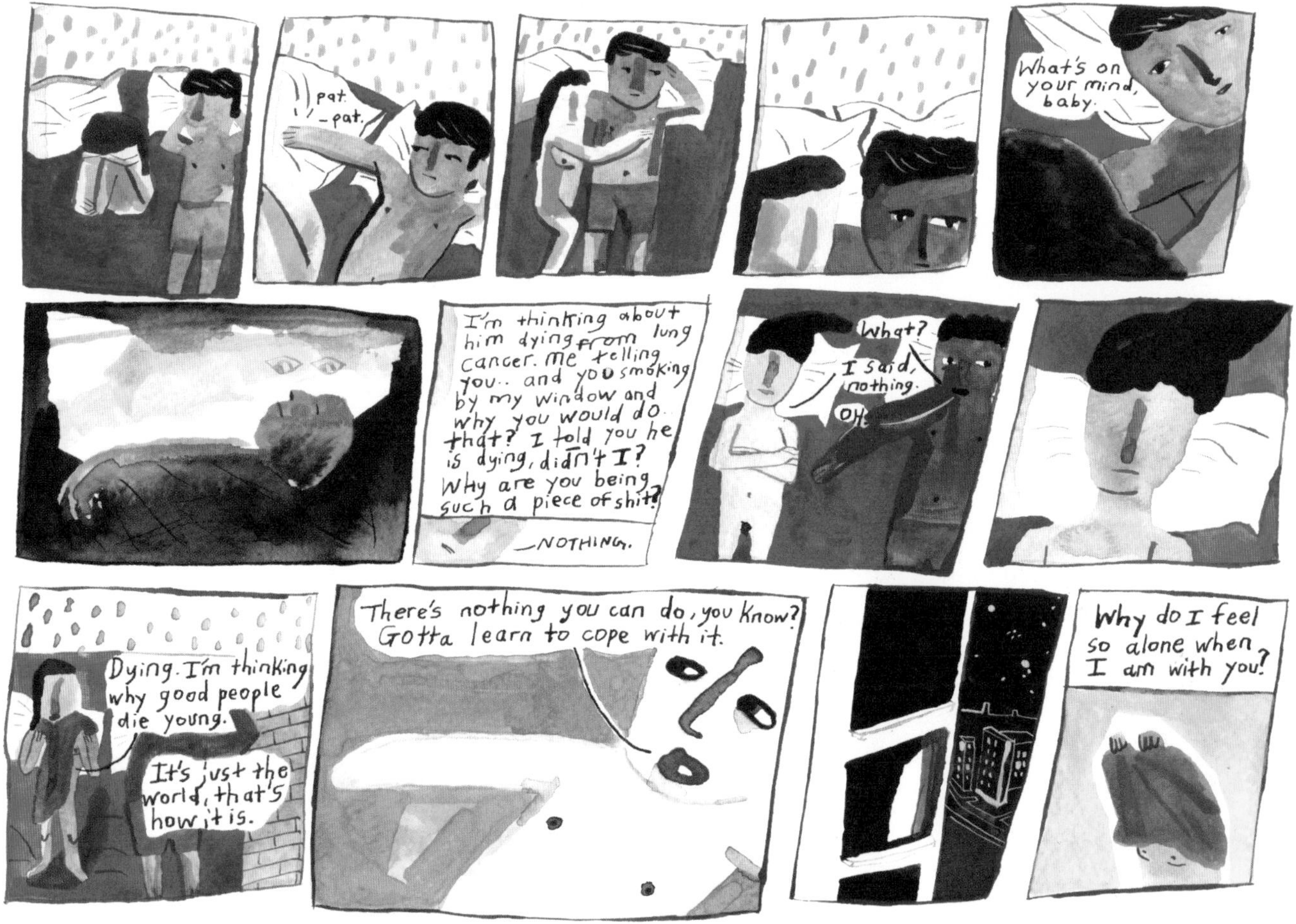
pat.
pat.
What's on your mind, baby.
I'm thinking about him dying from lung cancer. Me telling you... and you smoking by my window and why you would do that? I told you he is dying, didn't I? Why are you being such a piece of shit?
—NOTHING.
What?
I said, nothing.
OH.
Dying. I'm thinking why good people die young.
It's just the world, that's how it is.
There's nothing you can do, you know? Gotta learn to cope with it.
Why do I feel so alone when I am with you?

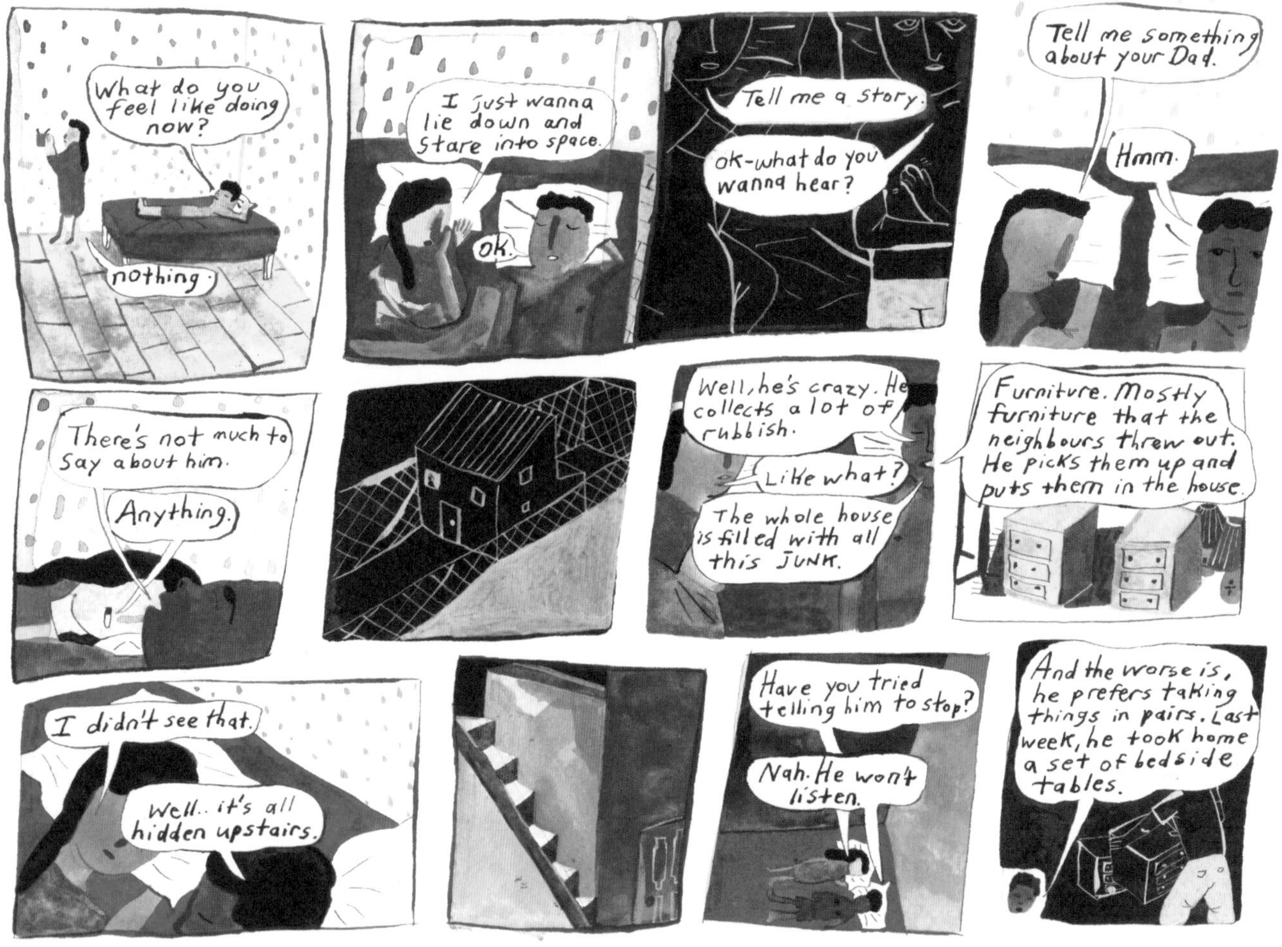
What do you feel like doing now?
nothing.
I just wanna lie down and stare into space.
ok.
Tell me a story.
ok-what do you wanna hear?
Tell me something about your Dad.
Hmm.
There's not much to say about him.
Anything.
Well, he's crazy. He collects a lot of rubbish.
Like what?
The whole house is filled with all this JUNK.
Furniture. Mostly furniture that the neighbours threw out. He picks them up and puts them in the house.
I didn't see that.
Well.. it's all hidden upstairs.
Have you tried telling him to stop?
Nah. He won't listen.
And the worse is, he prefers taking things in pairs. Last week, he took home a set of bedside tables.

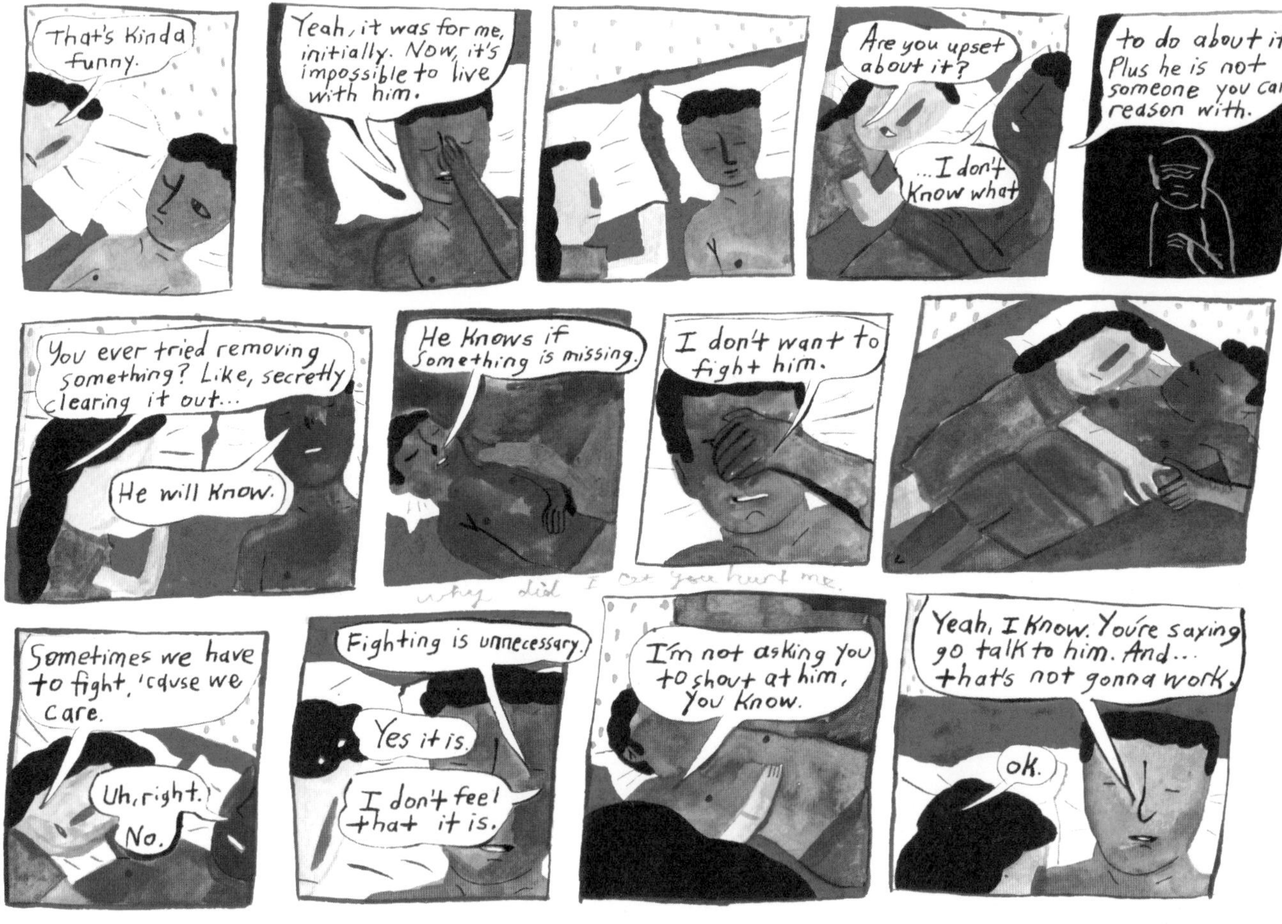
That's kinda funny.
Yeah, it was for me, initially. Now, it's impossible to live with him.
Are you upset about it?
...I don't know what
to do about it. Plus he is not someone you can reason with.
You ever tried removing something? Like, secretly clearing it out...
He will know.
He knows if something is missing.
I don't want to fight him.
why did I let you hurt me.
Sometimes we have to fight, 'cause we care.
Uh, right.
No.
Fighting is unnecessary.
Yes it is.
I don't feel that it is.
I'm not asking you to shout at him, you know.
Yeah, I know. You're saying go talk to him. And... that's not gonna work.
ok.

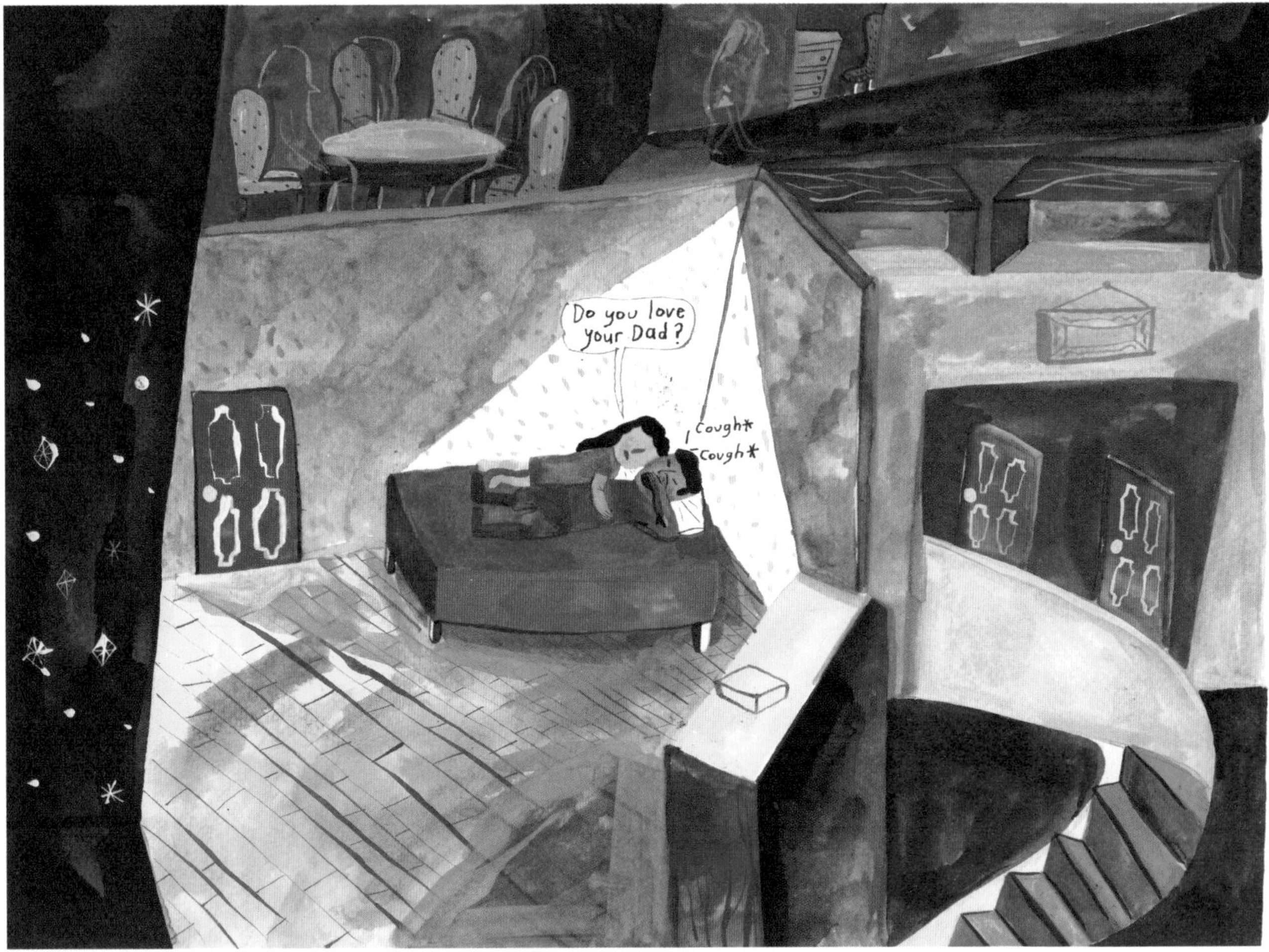
Do you love your Dad?
cough
cough

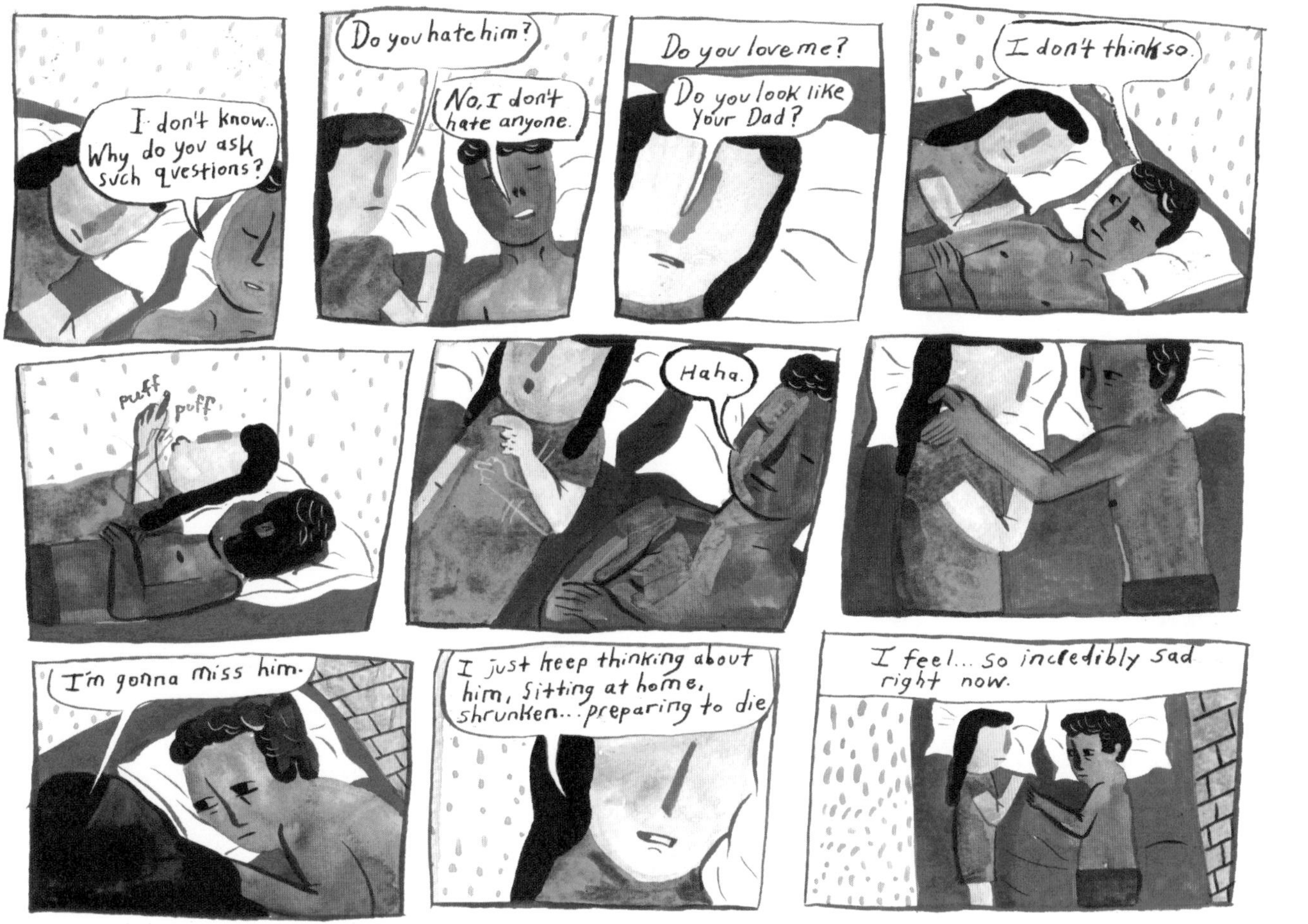
I don't know.. Why do you ask such questions?
Do you hate him?
No, I don't hate anyone.
Do you love me?
Do you look like your Dad?
I don't think so.
puff
puff
Haha.
I'm gonna miss him.
I just keep thinking about him, sitting at home, shrunken... preparing to die
I feel... so incredibly sad right now.

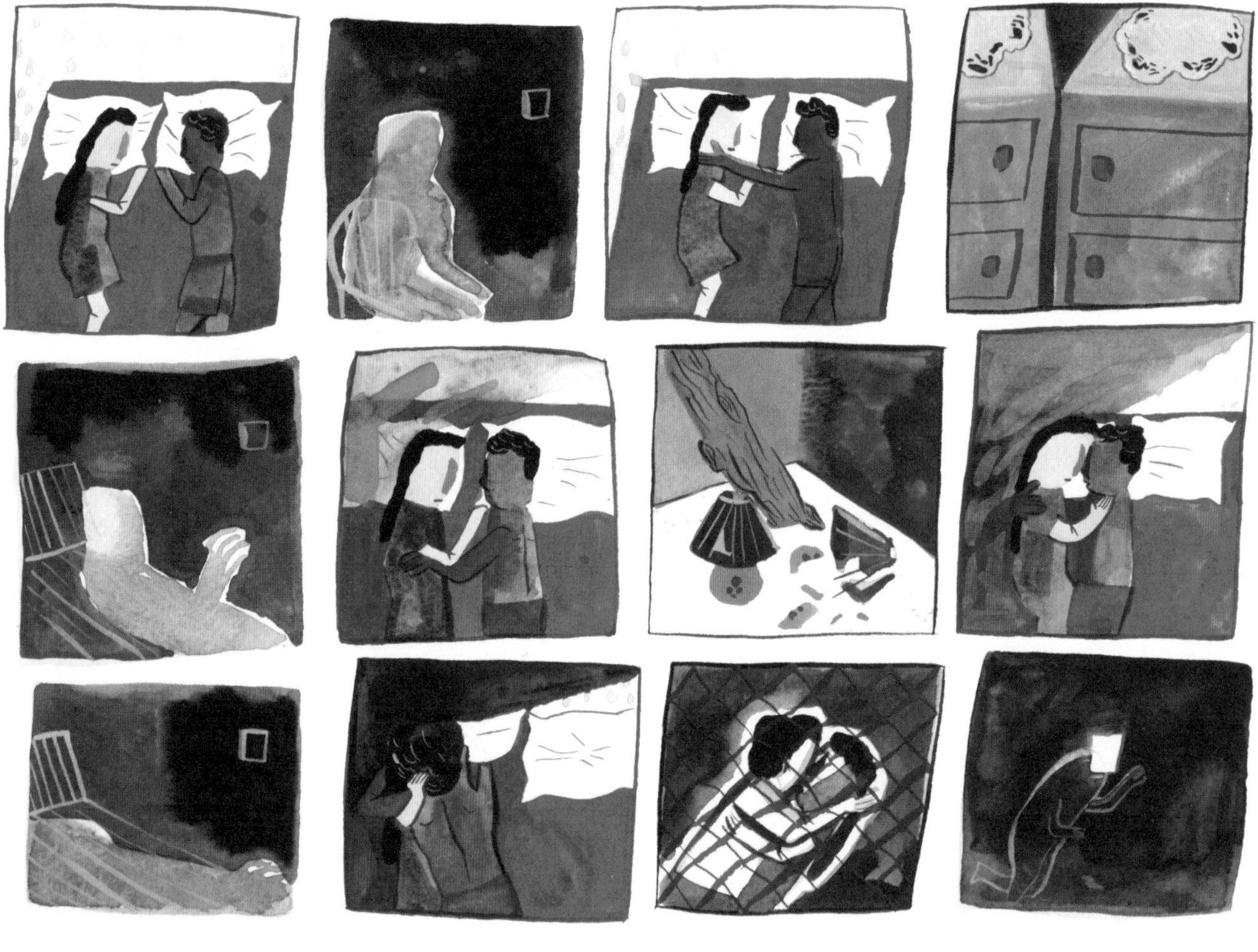

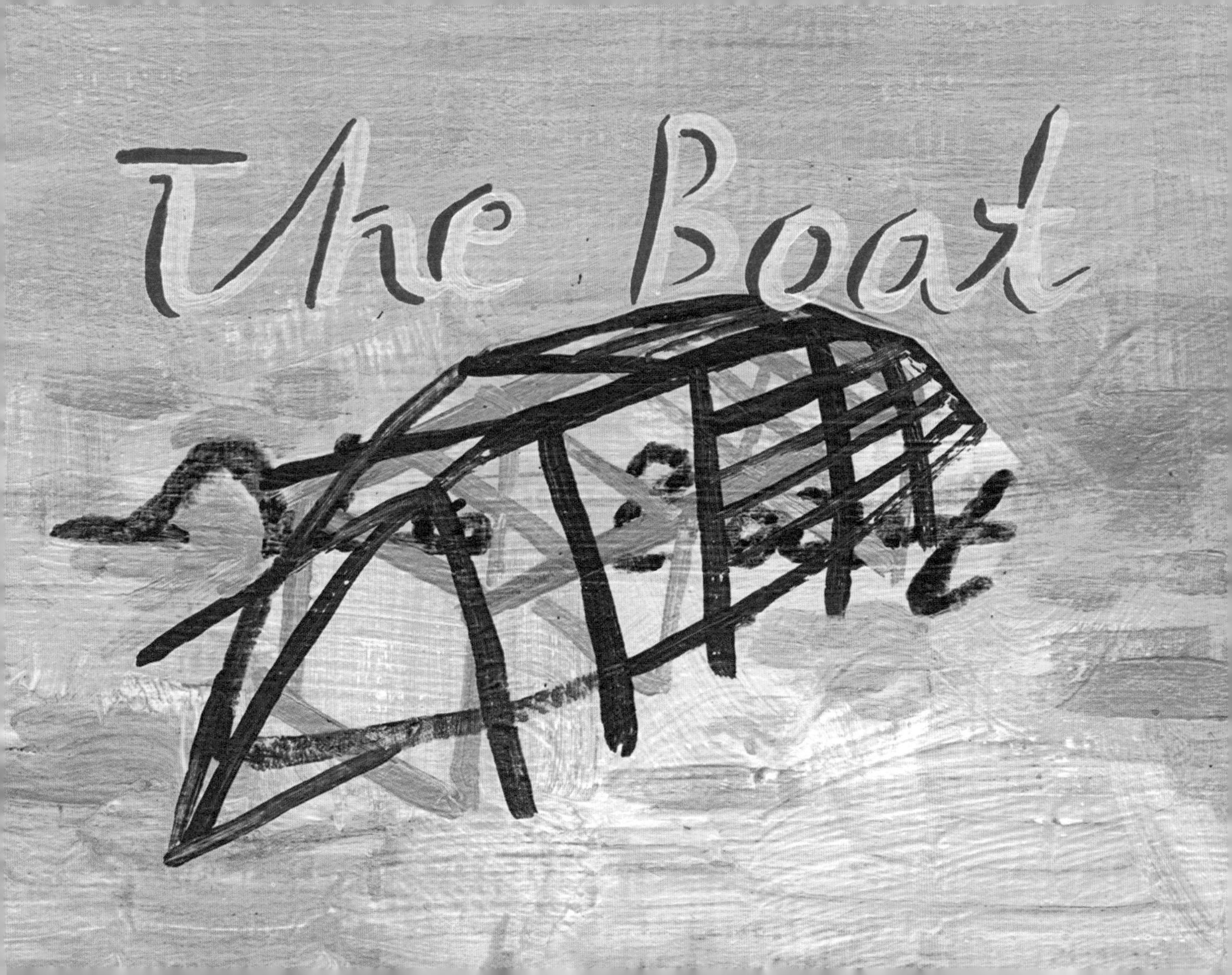
The Boat

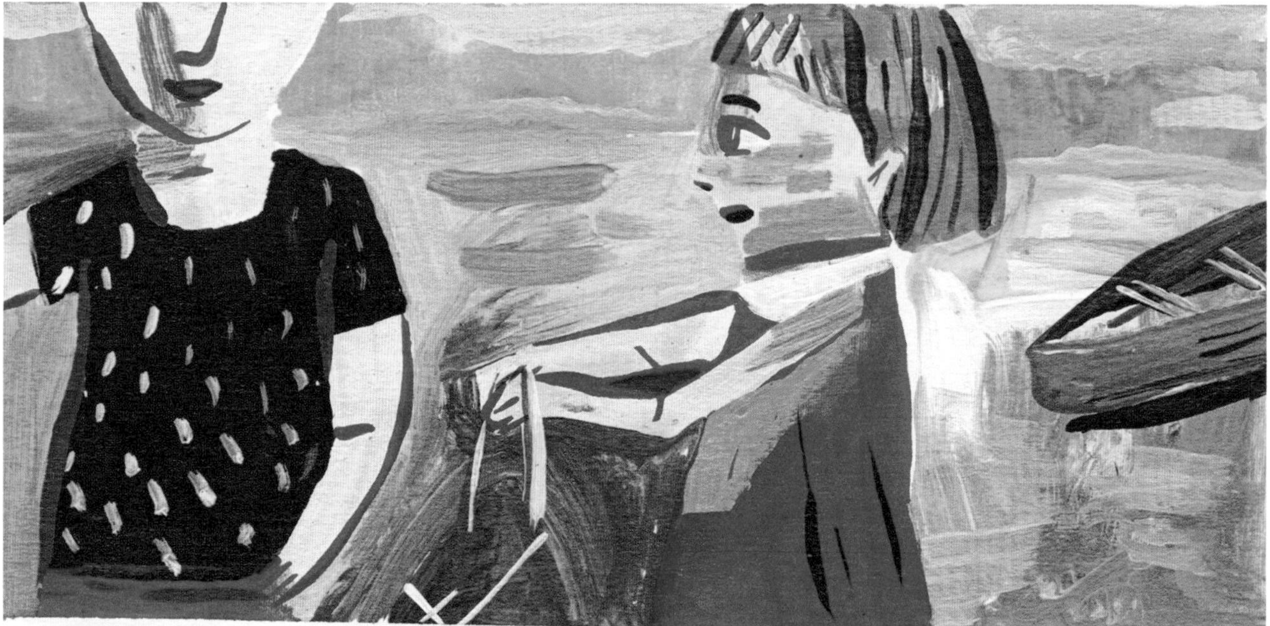

Boy: Grab that bag for me, please.

Girl: Okay, woah. That was unexpectedly.. very heavy.

Boy: Hold on, let me get that...
      are you okay?
Girl: Yeah, I'm good, thanks.

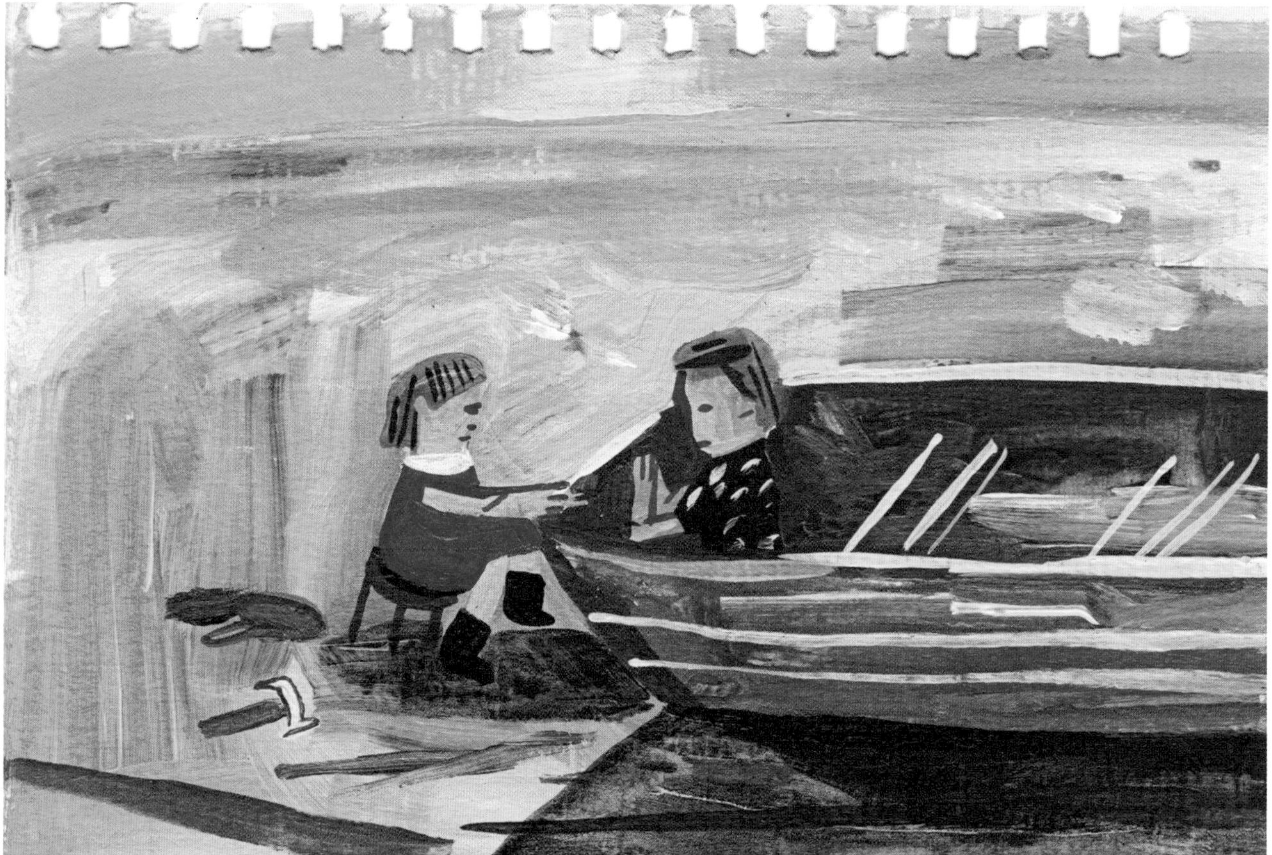

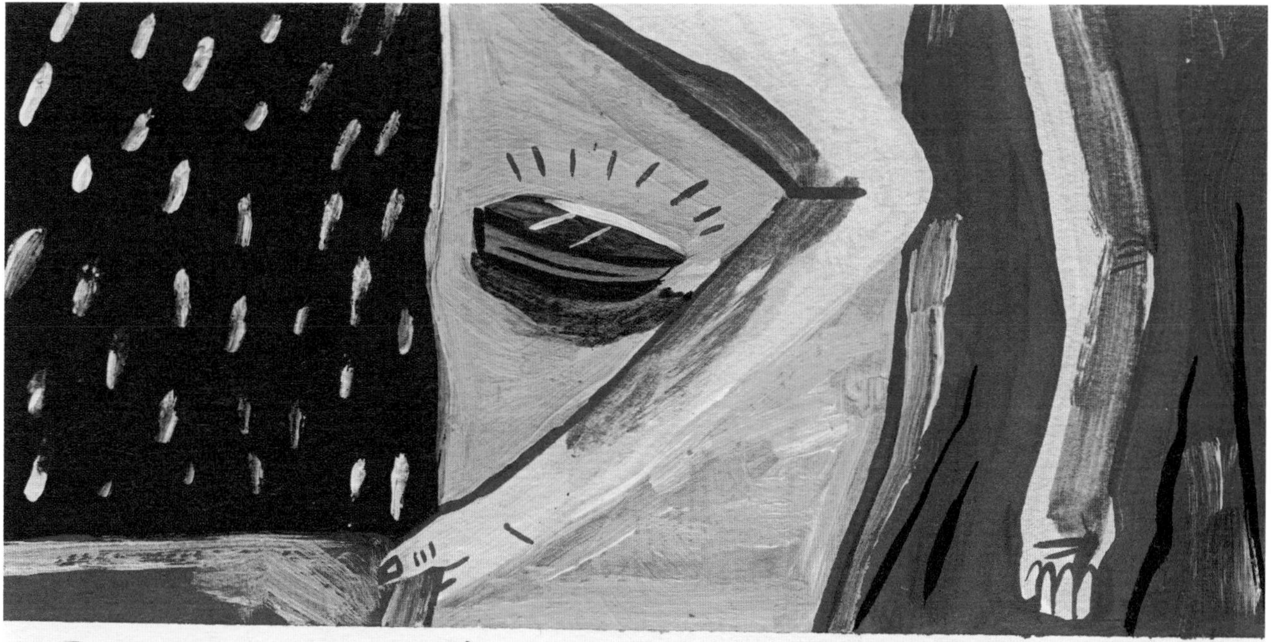

Girl: It looks amazing.

Boy: I cannot wait to take it out and see how it's gonna float on the lake.

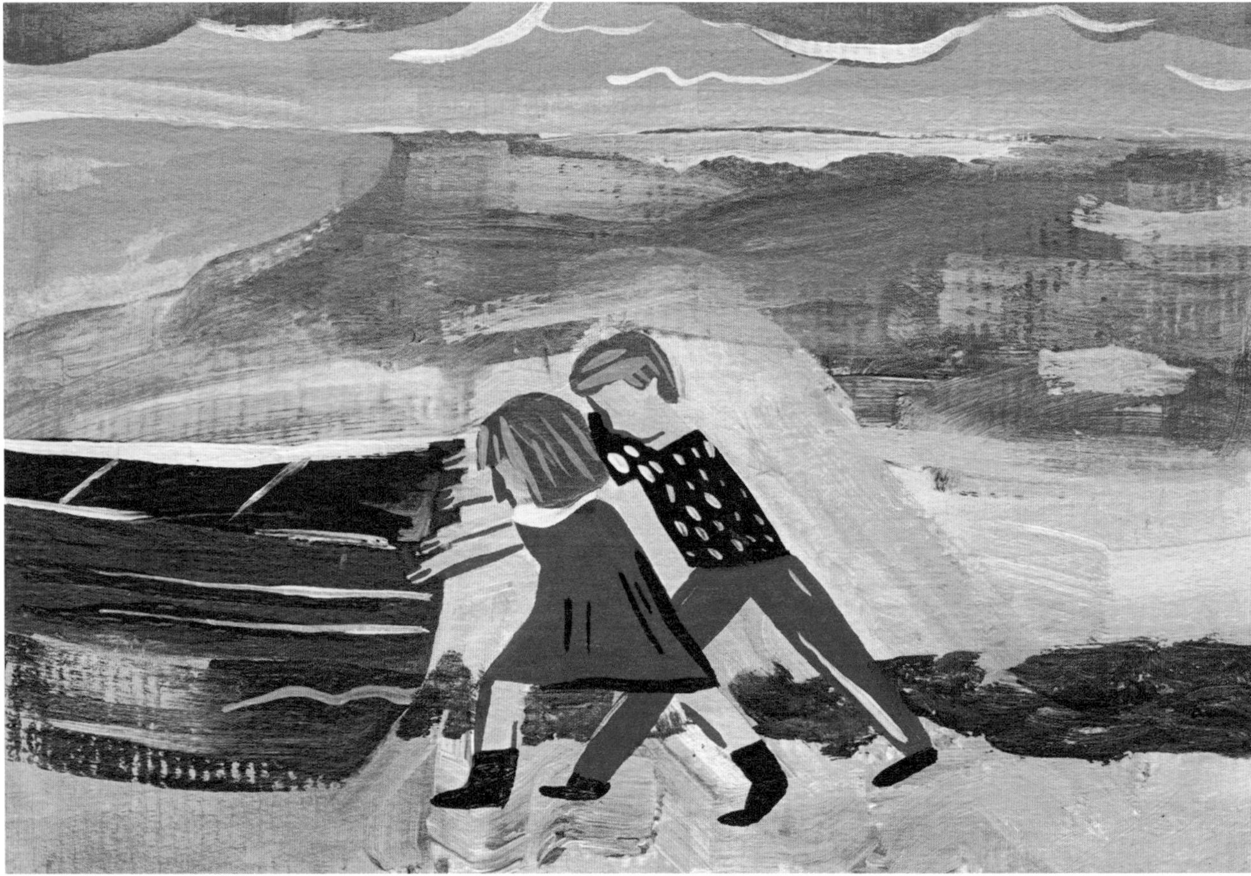

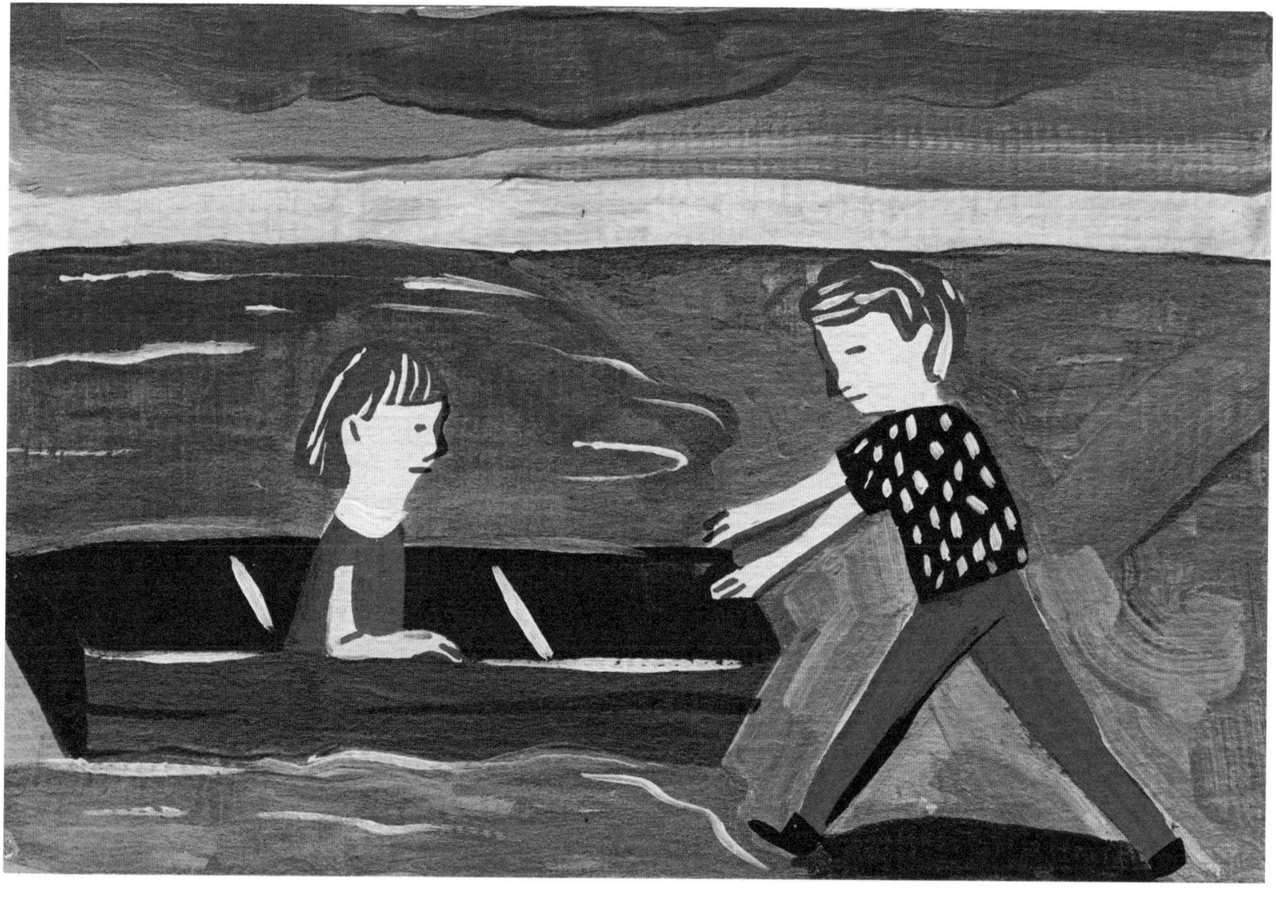

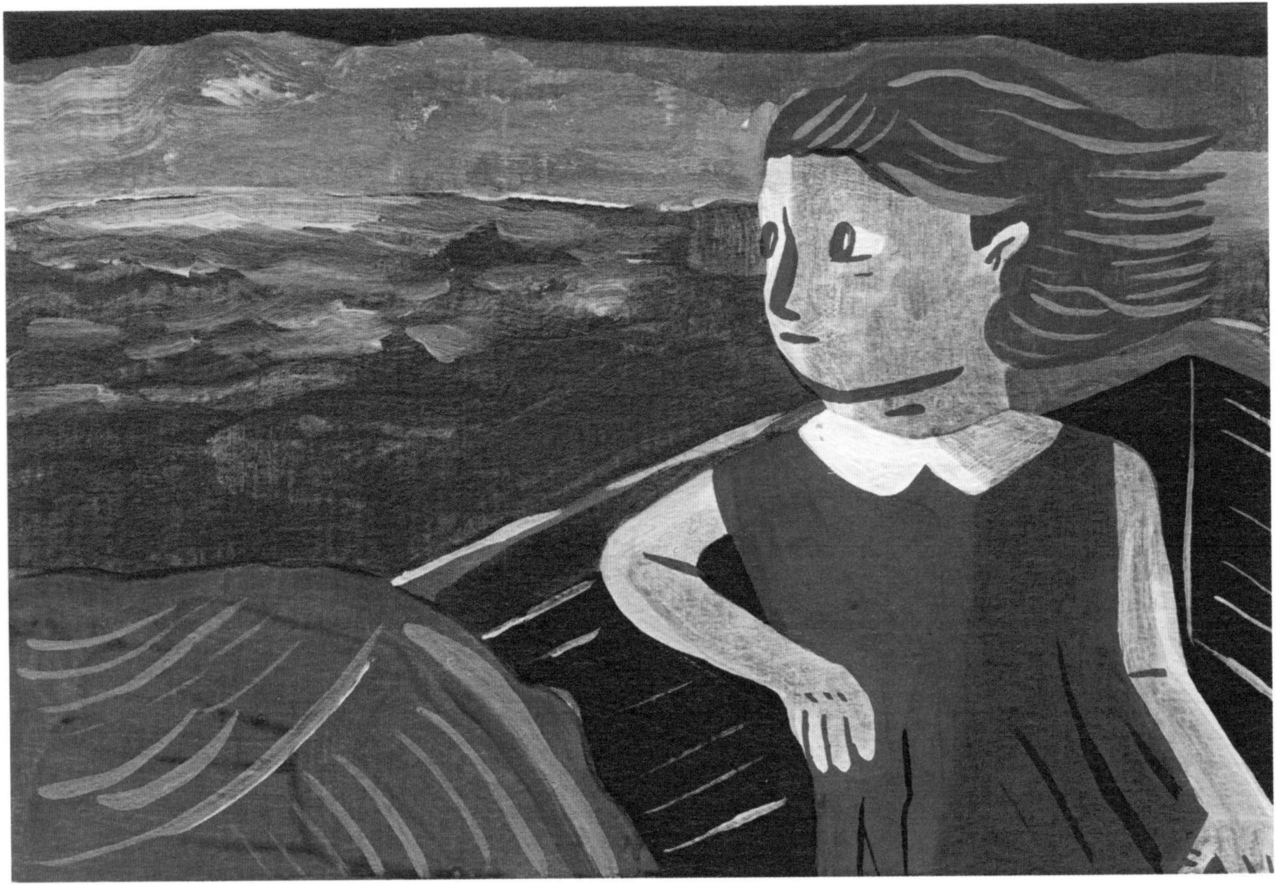

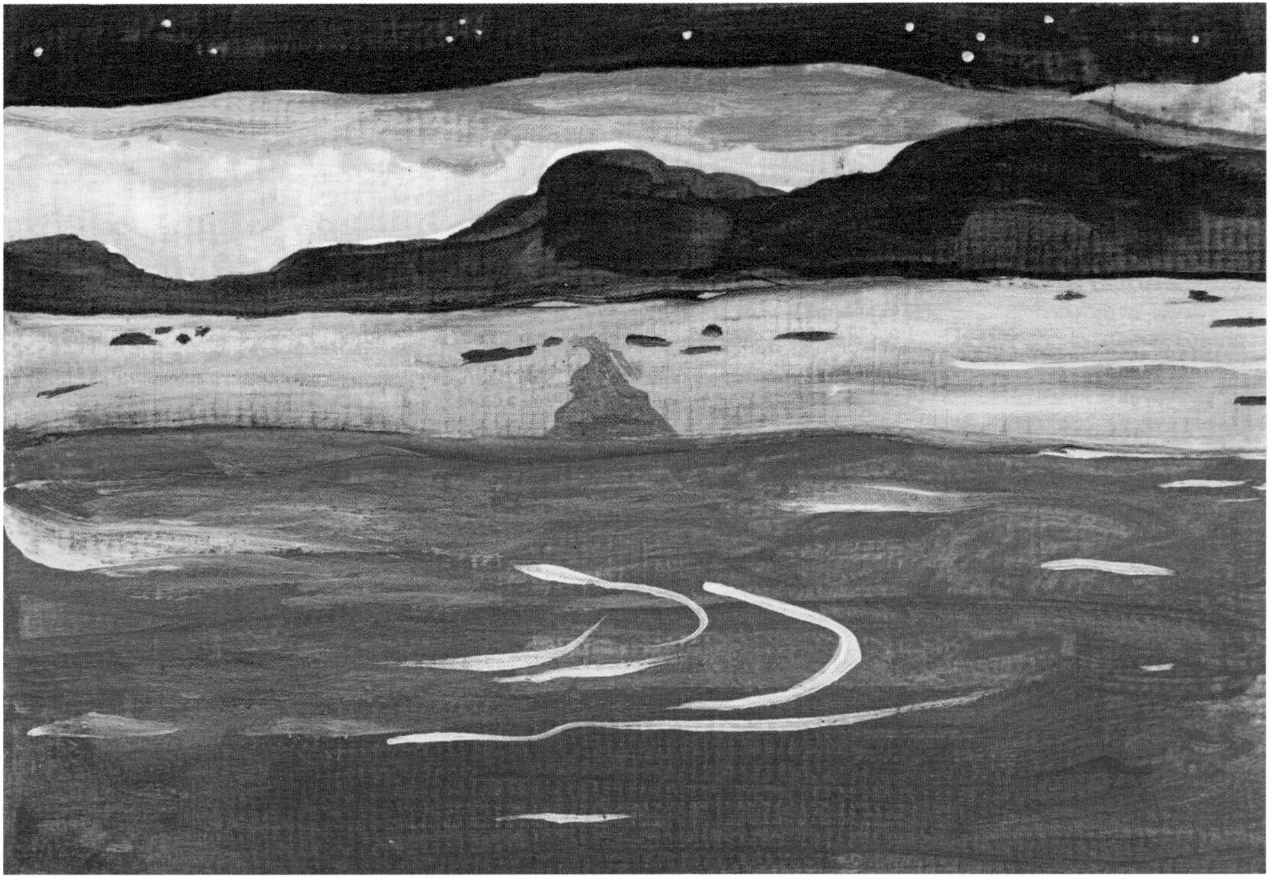

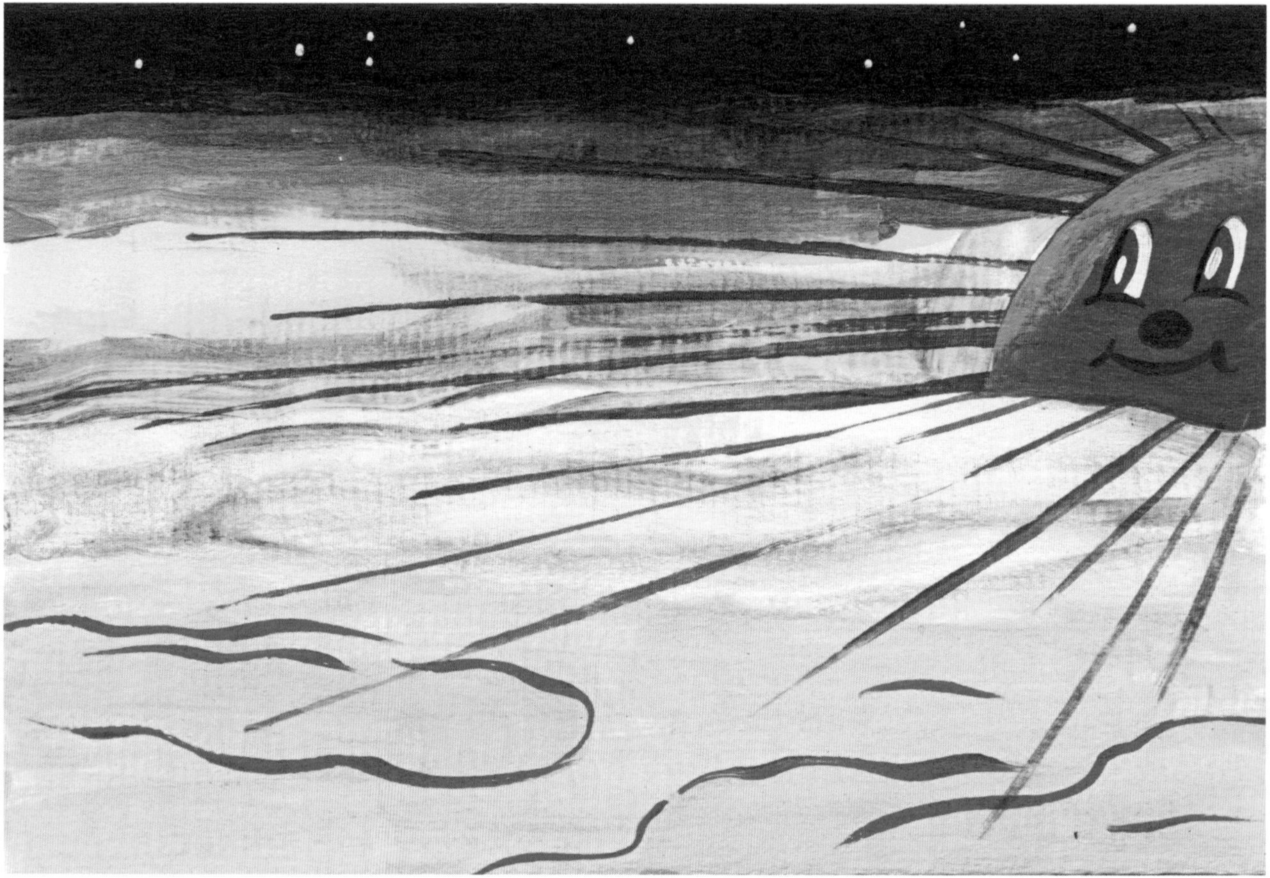

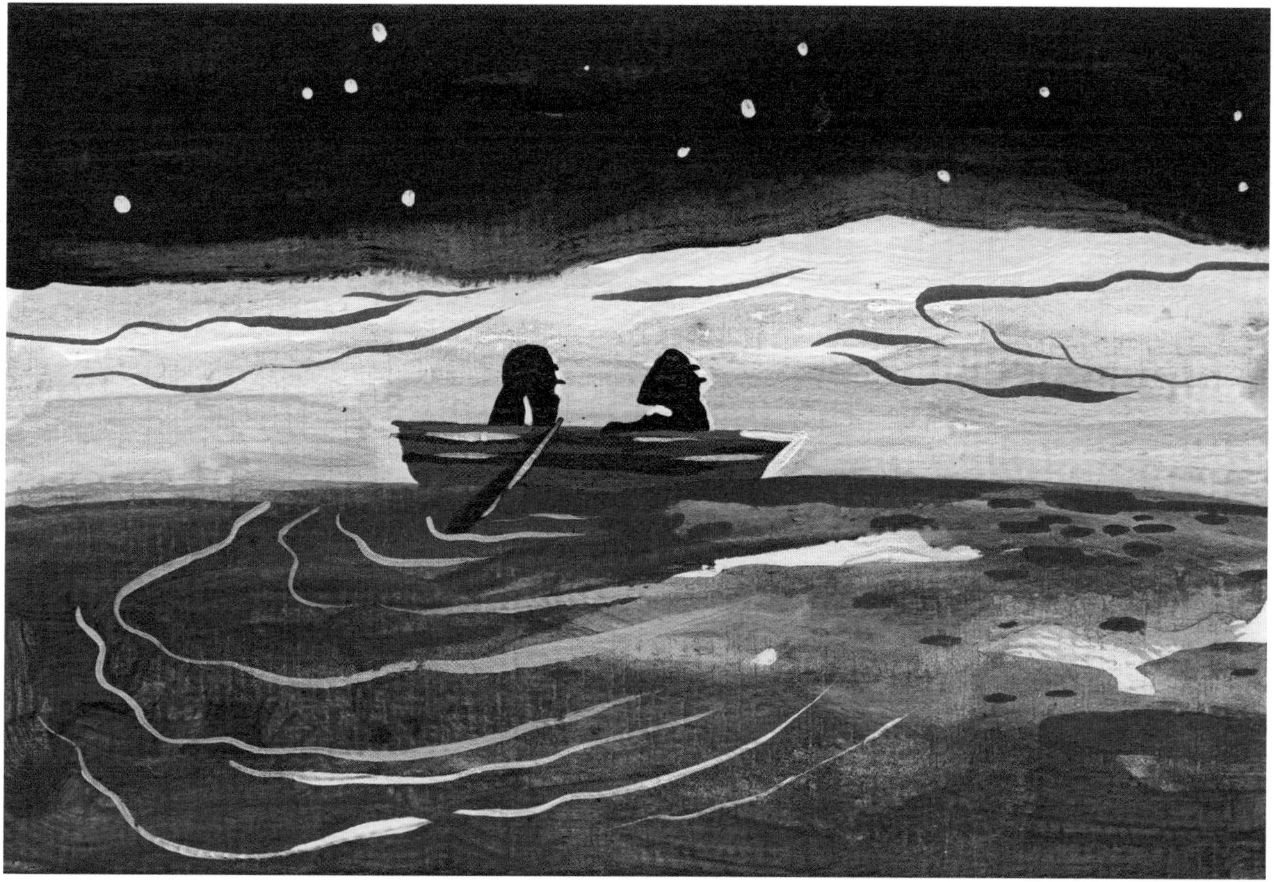

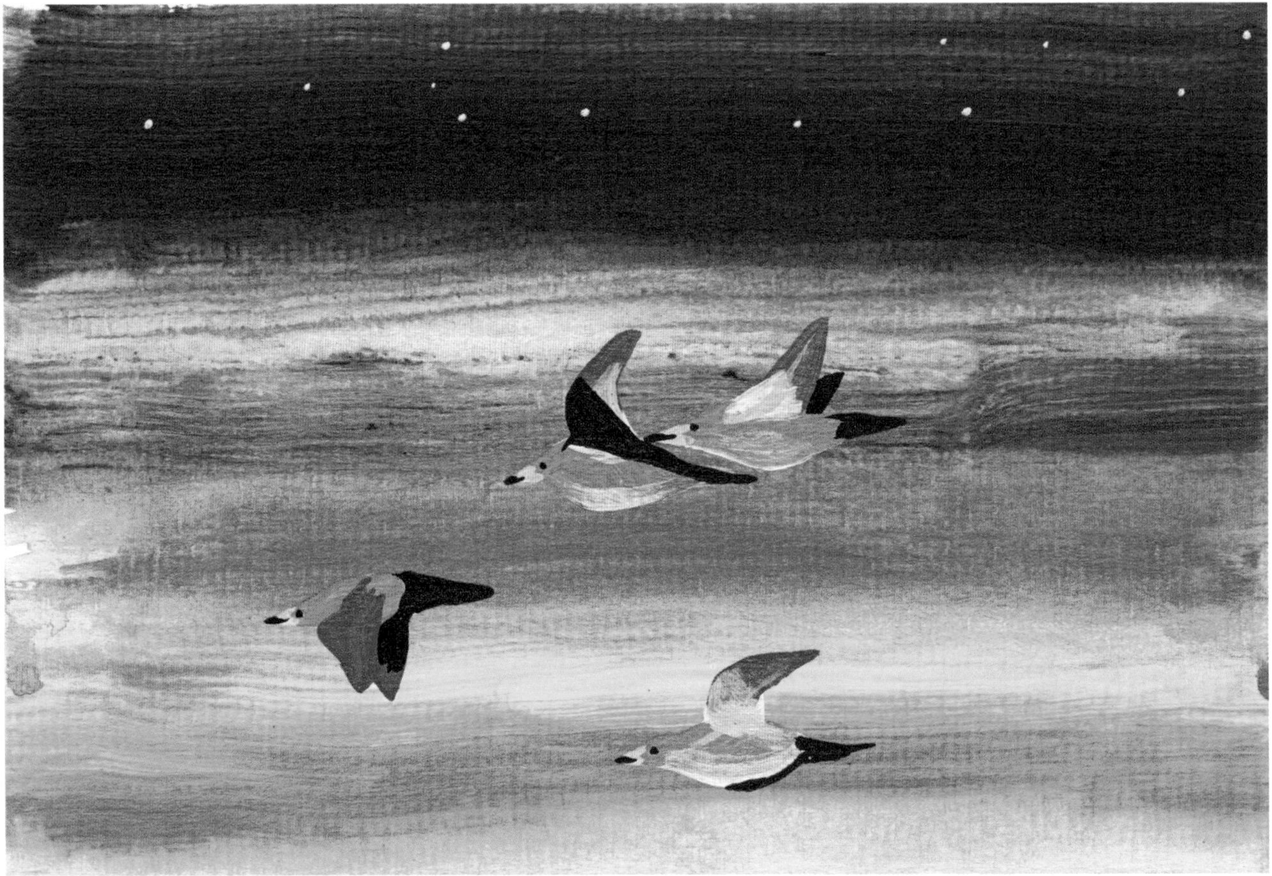

Girl: Really takes your breath away, doesn't it?
Boy: Mmm hmm.

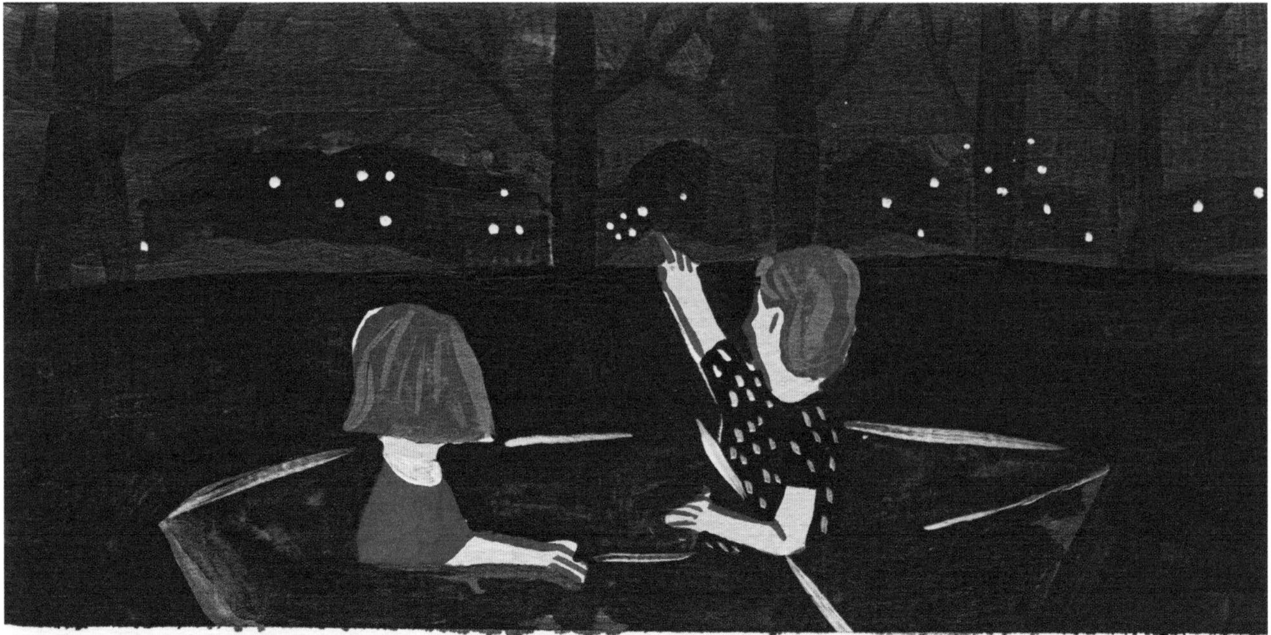

Boy: Look over there.

Girl: Wow....

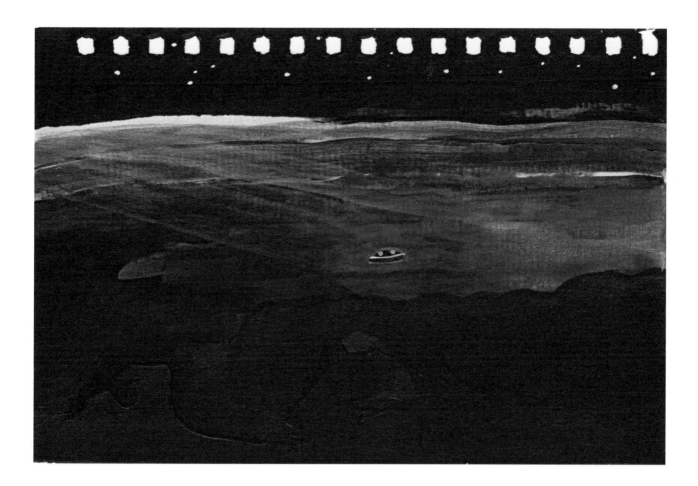

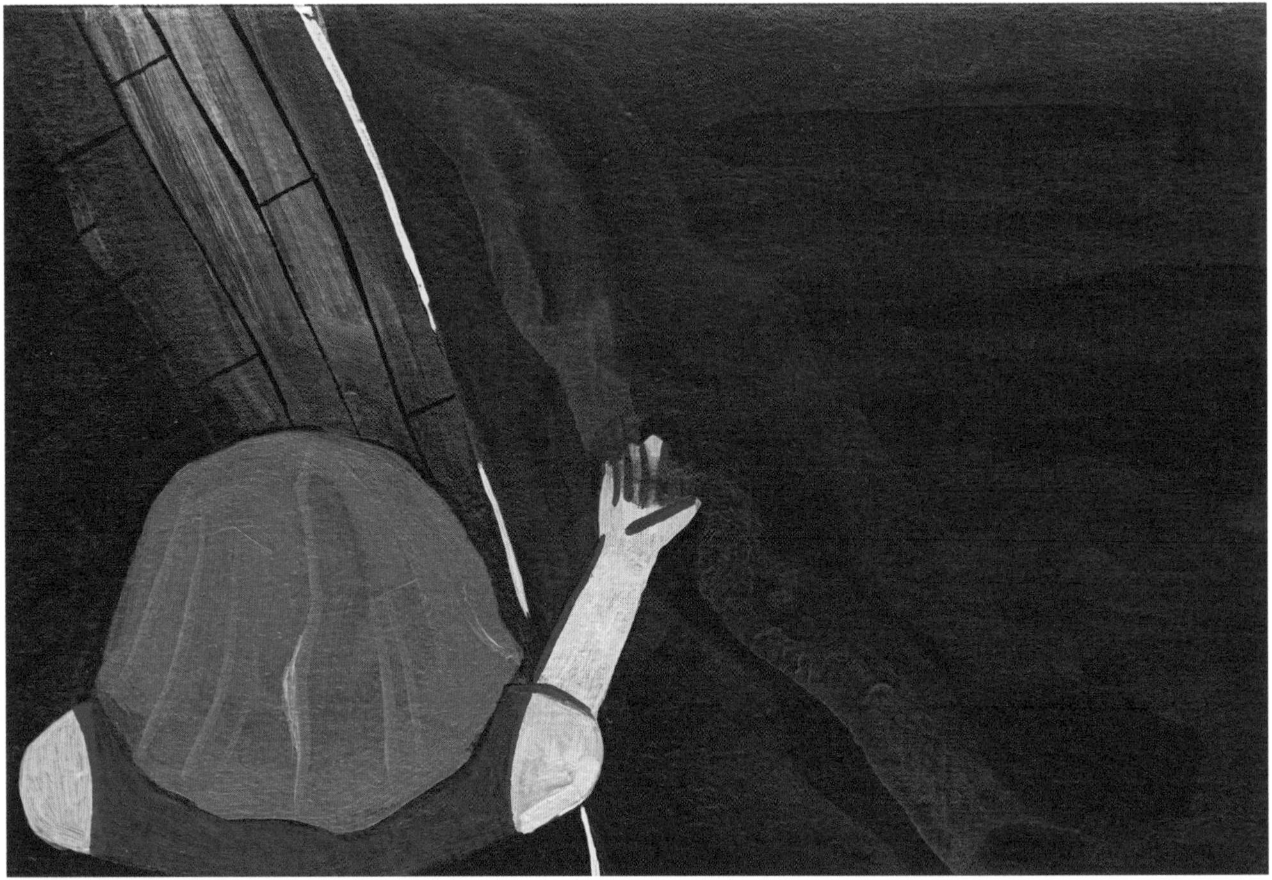

Boy: I could have missed all of this. If I hadn't changed my mind... if that switch

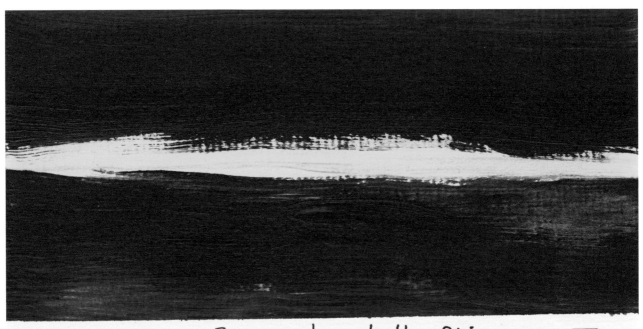

inside of me hadn't flipped, I
wouldn't be here, in this moment.

Girl: Just that change, that switch inside you.

Boy: Made all the difference.

Boy: Once the decision was made, I felt I could breathe, finally. But, it was finding that switch that was the crazy ride.

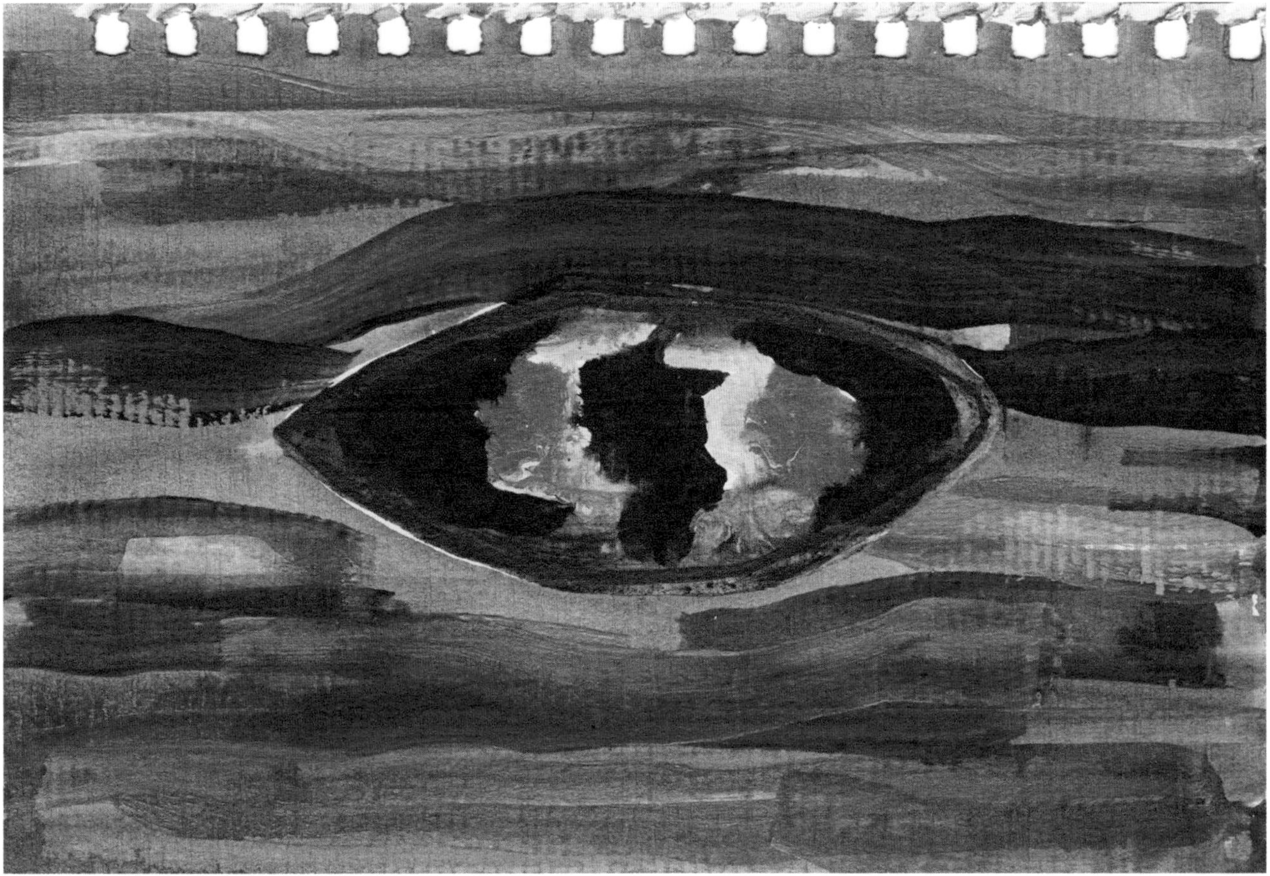

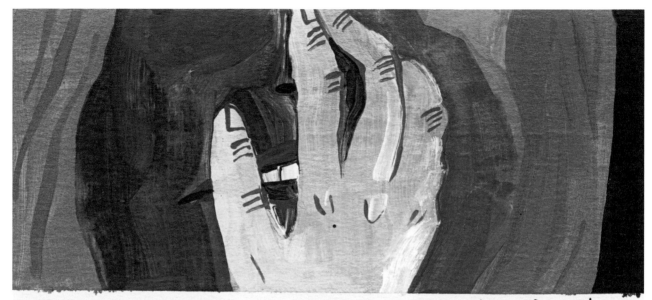

Girl: It sounds incredibly lonely to go through that.

Boy: Lonely, painful... and helpless.

Girl : What helped you get out of it?

Boy : A glimmer of realization that
I don't know everything... that I have

yet to know what can possibly
save me. That possibility helped.
The existence of a possibility helped.

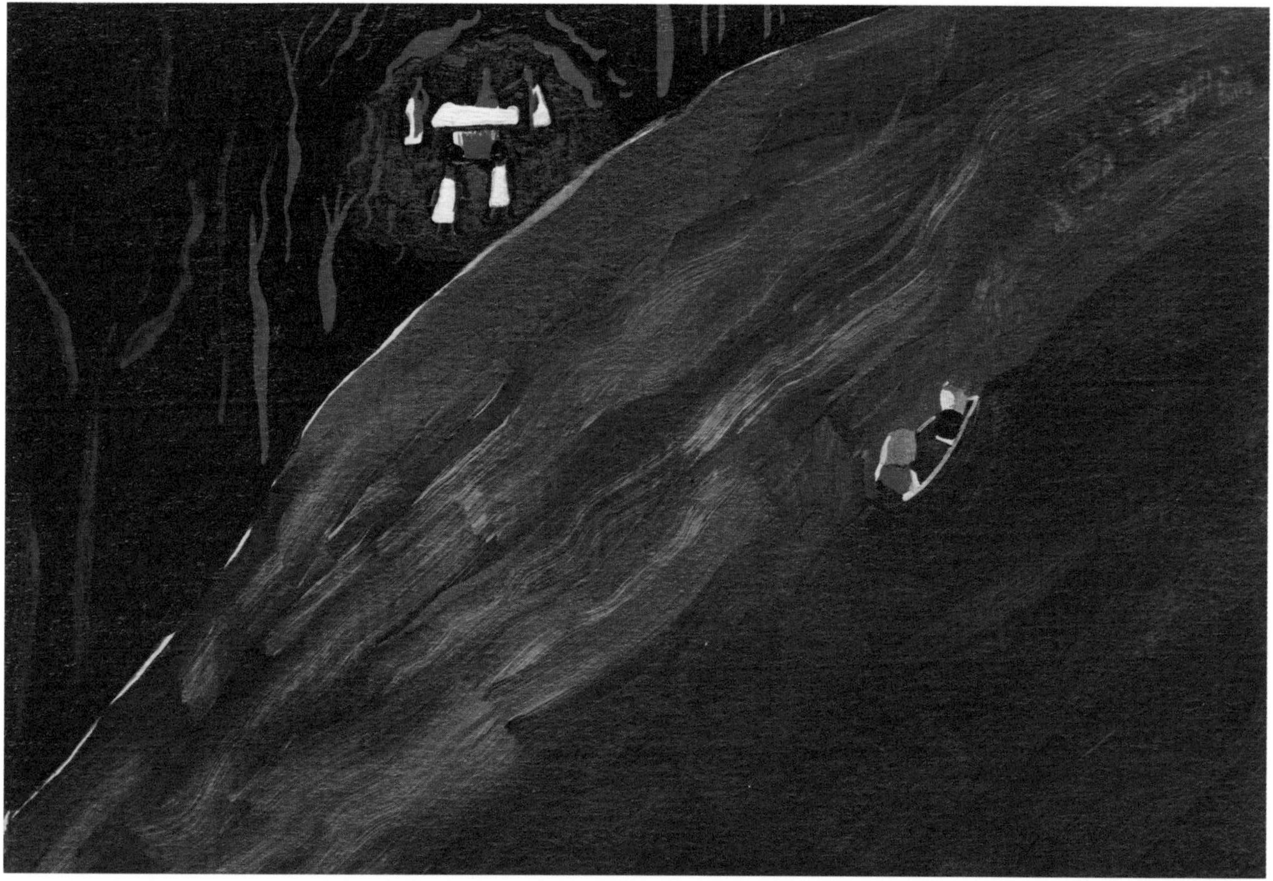

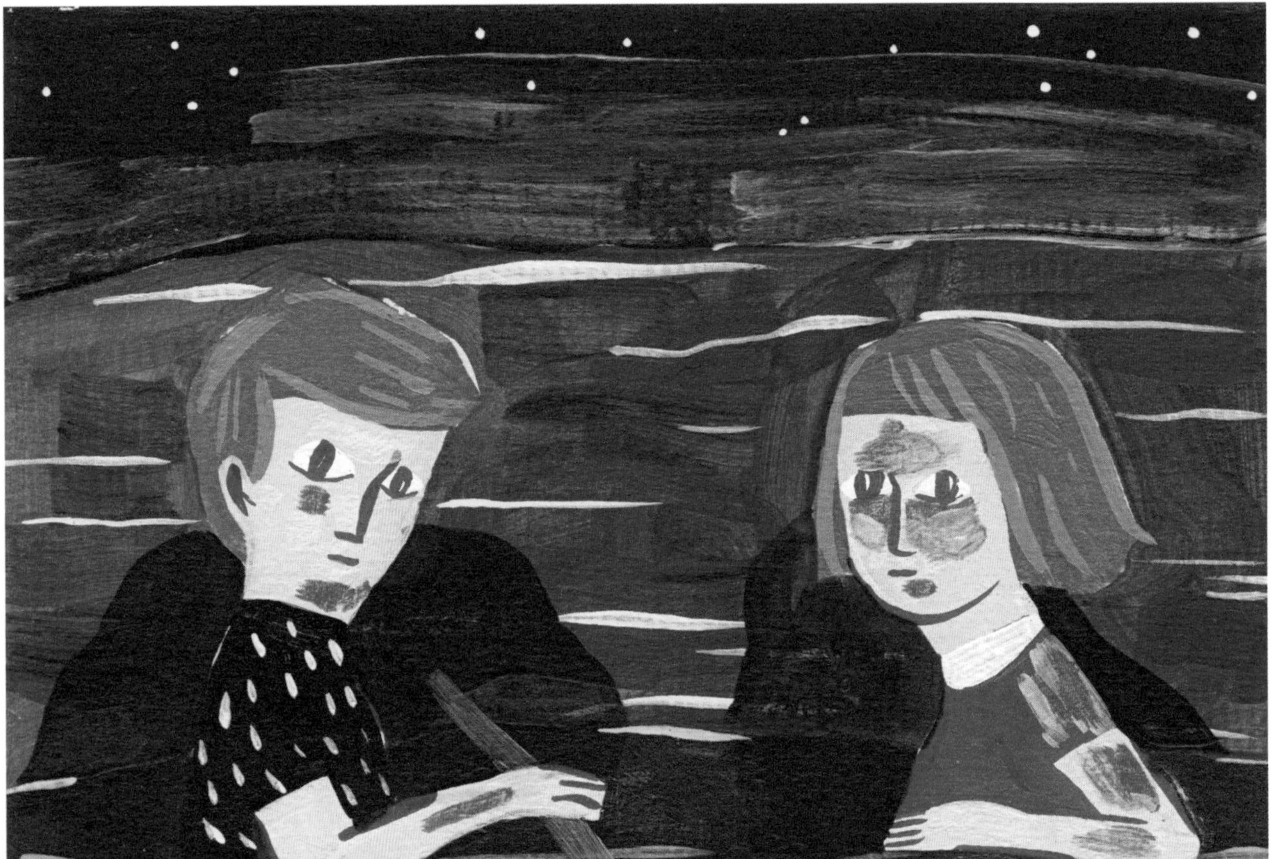

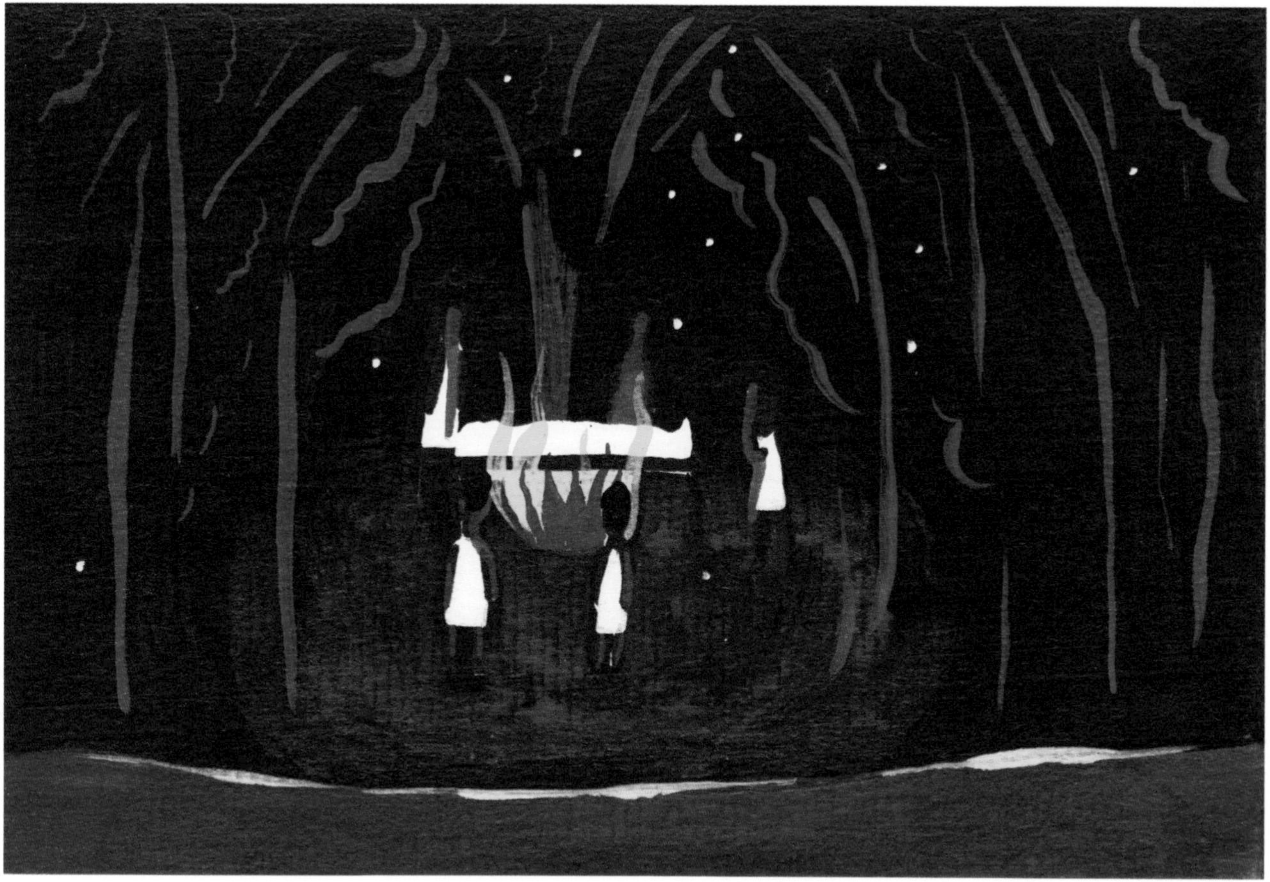

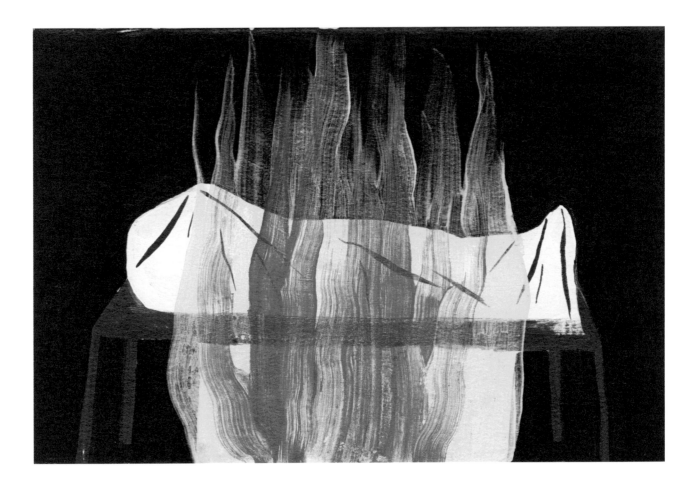

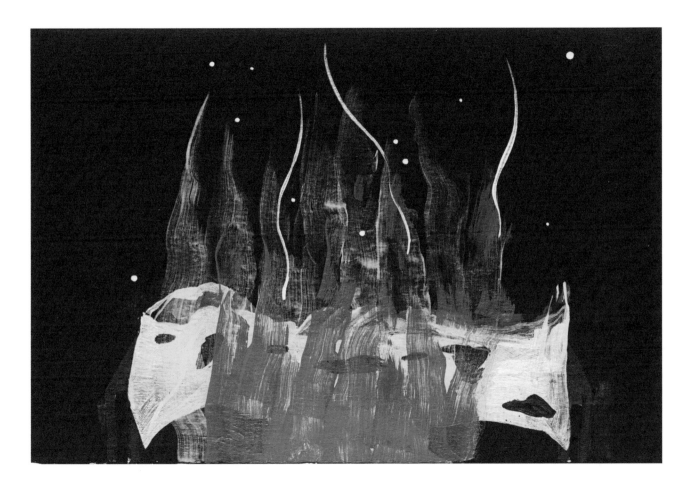

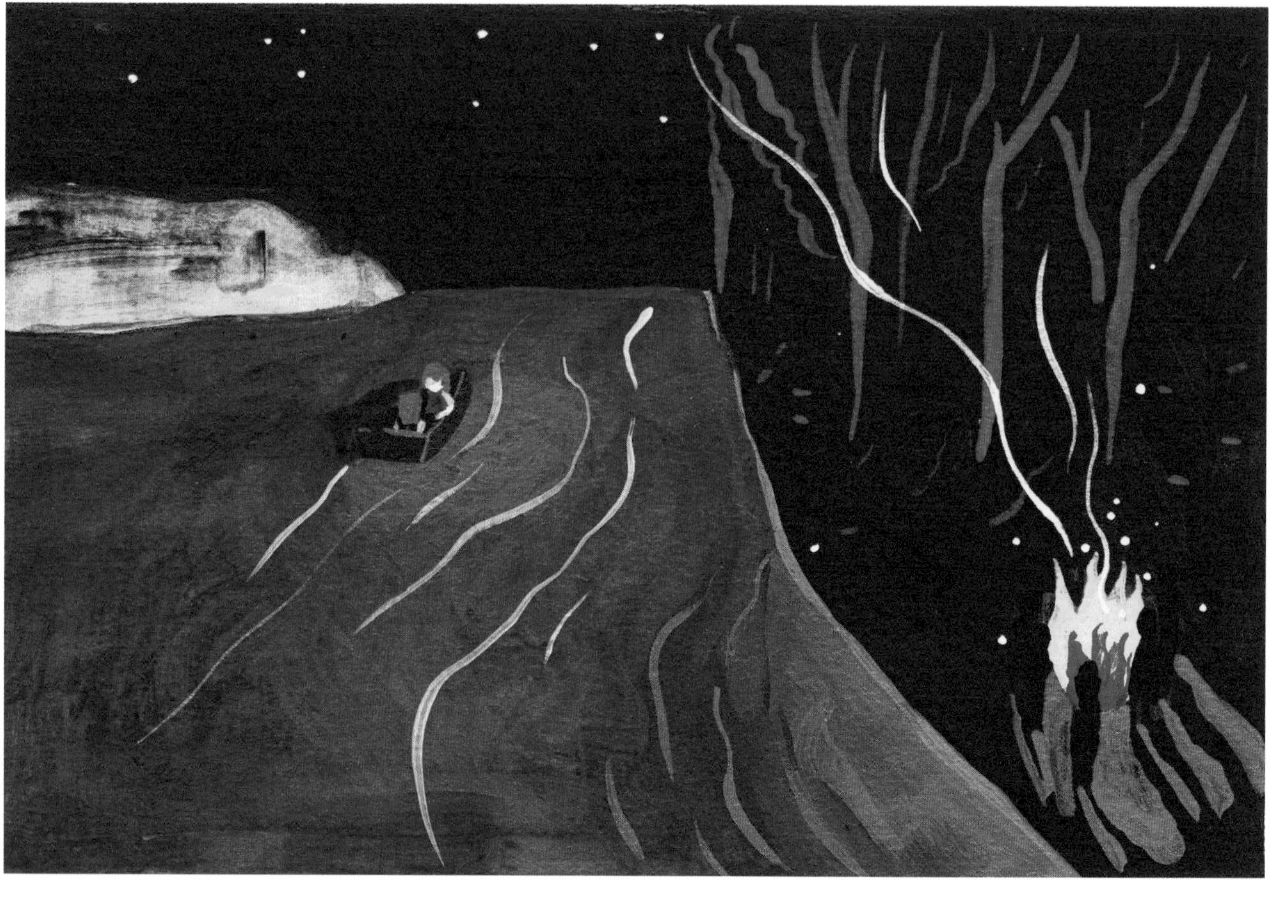

There is no full picture
of the future.

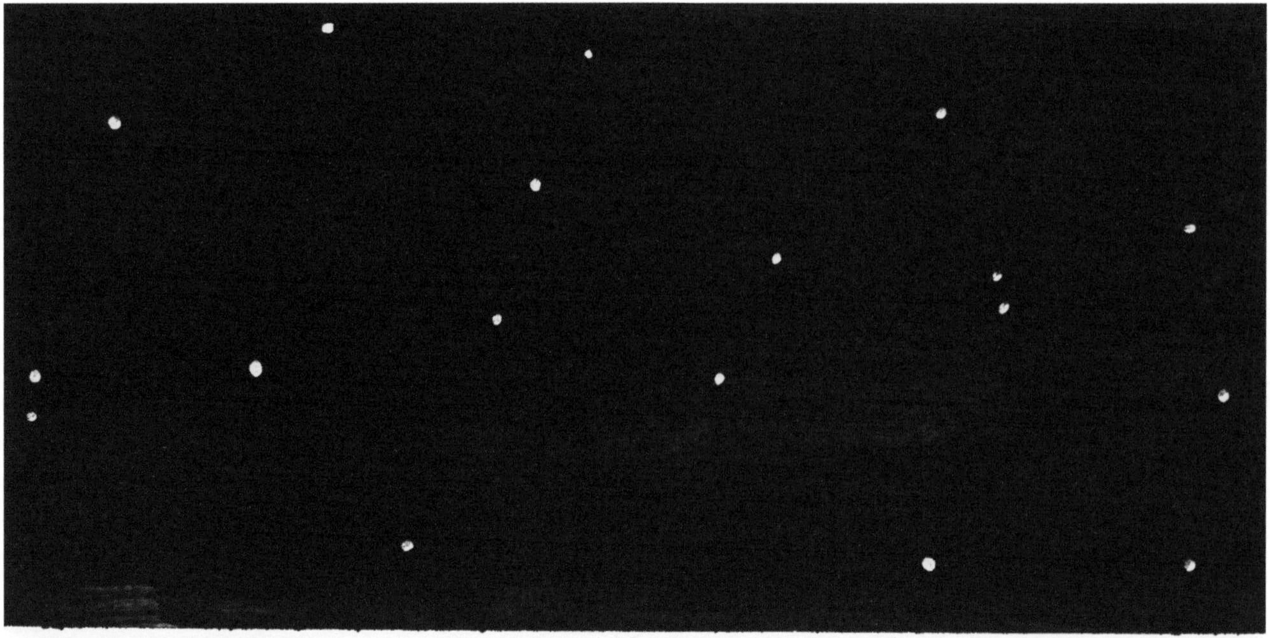

Just dots on paper.

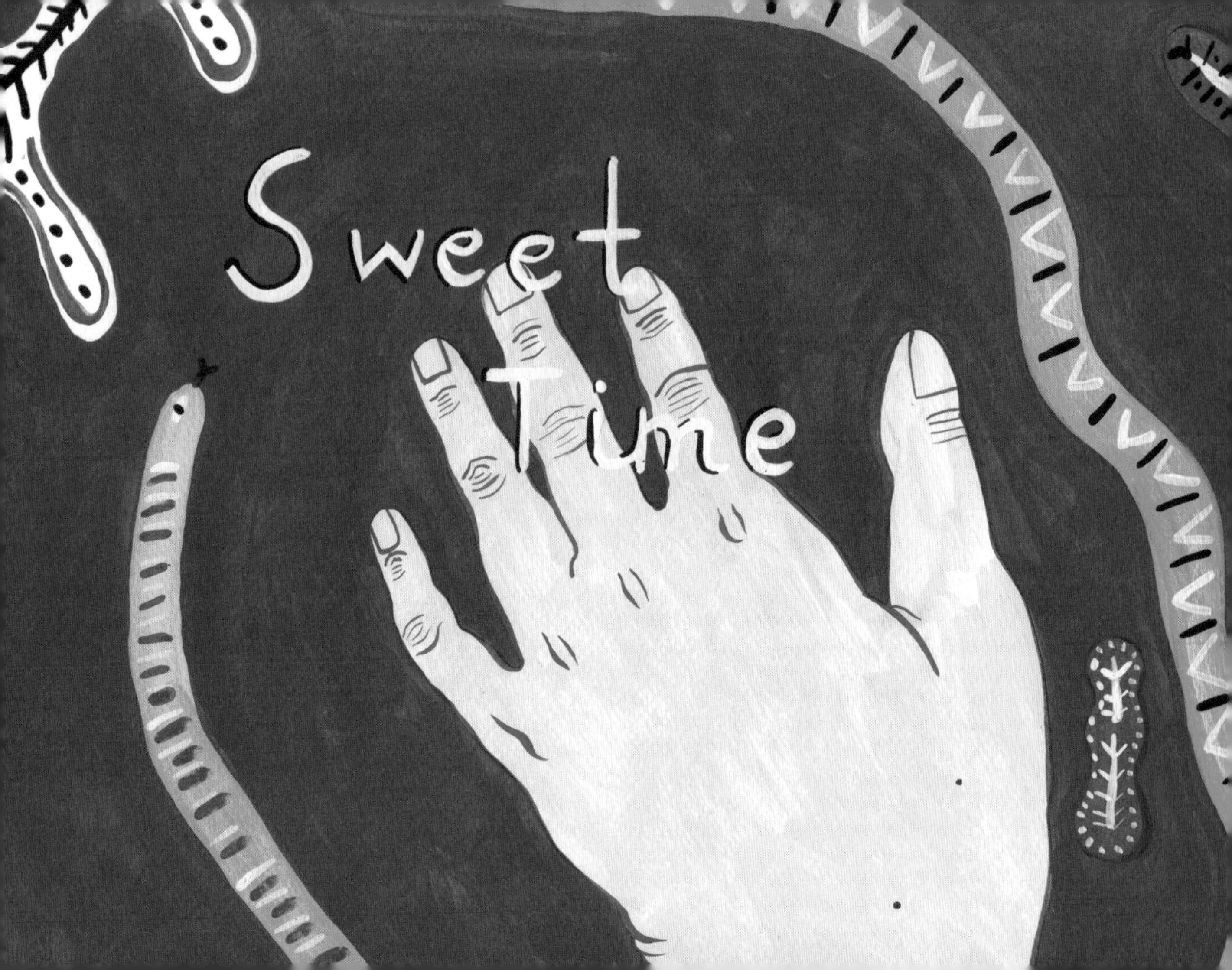
Sweet
Time

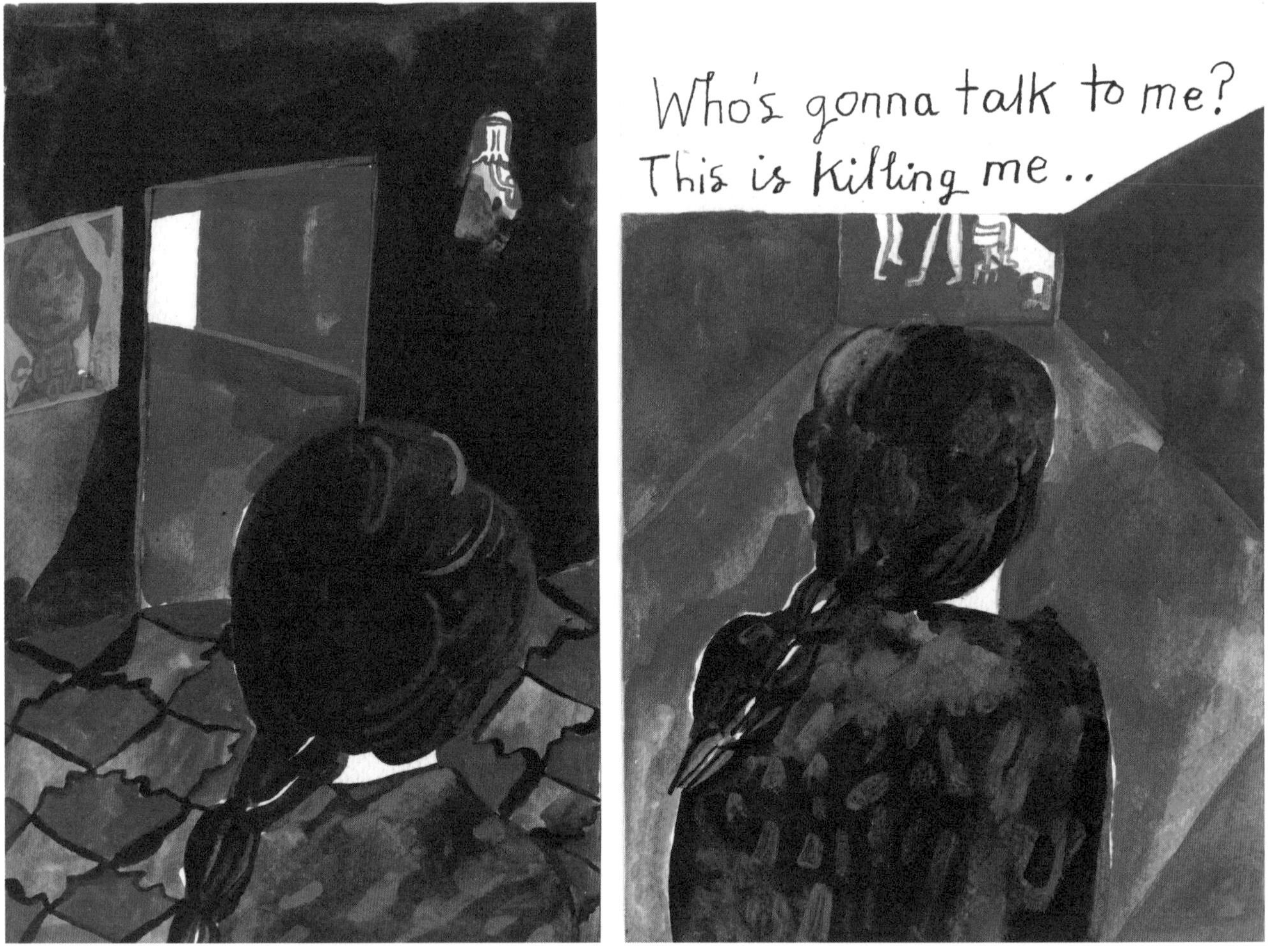
Who's gonna talk to me?
This is killing me..

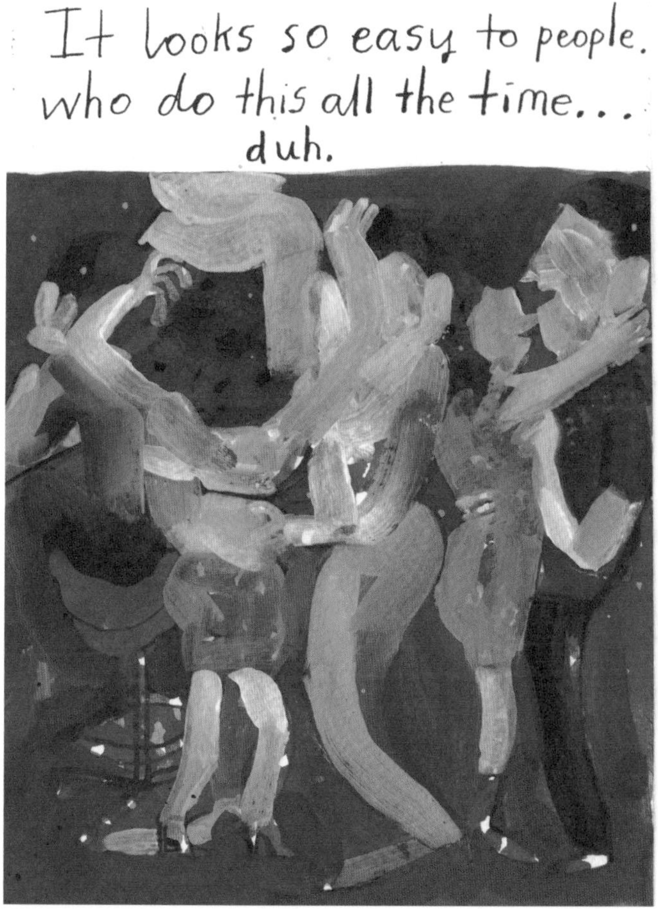
It looks so easy to people.
who do this all the time...
duh.

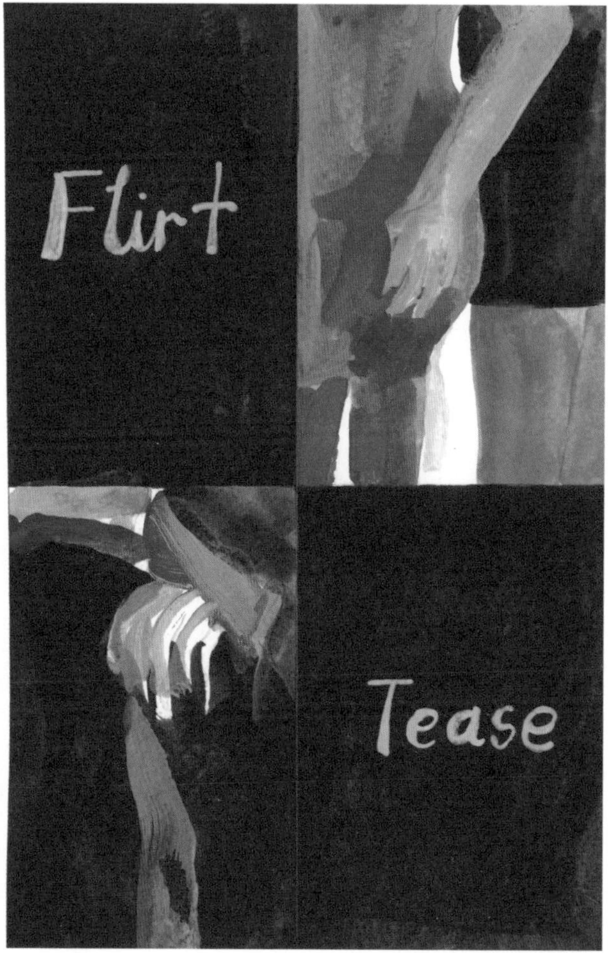
Flirt
Tease

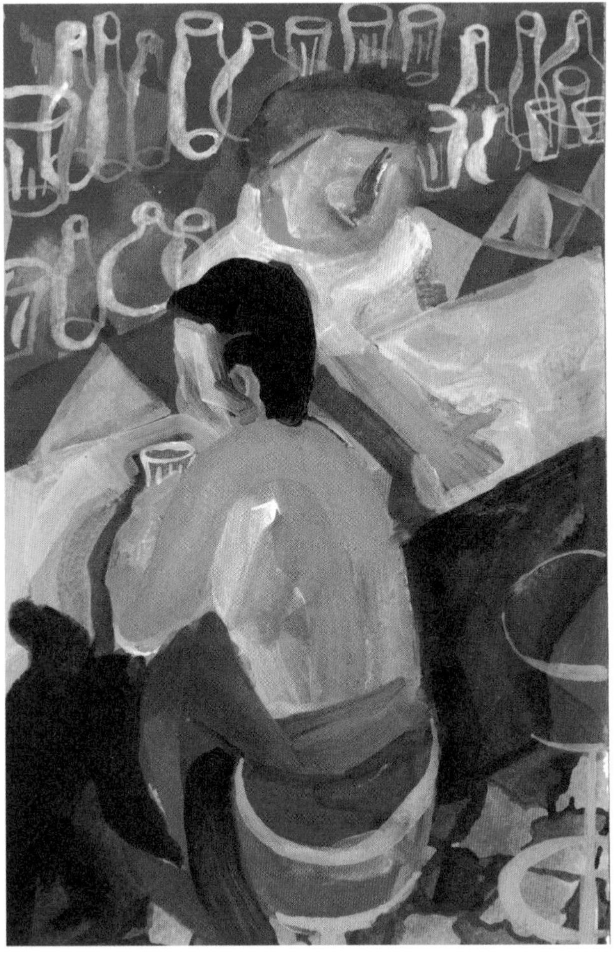

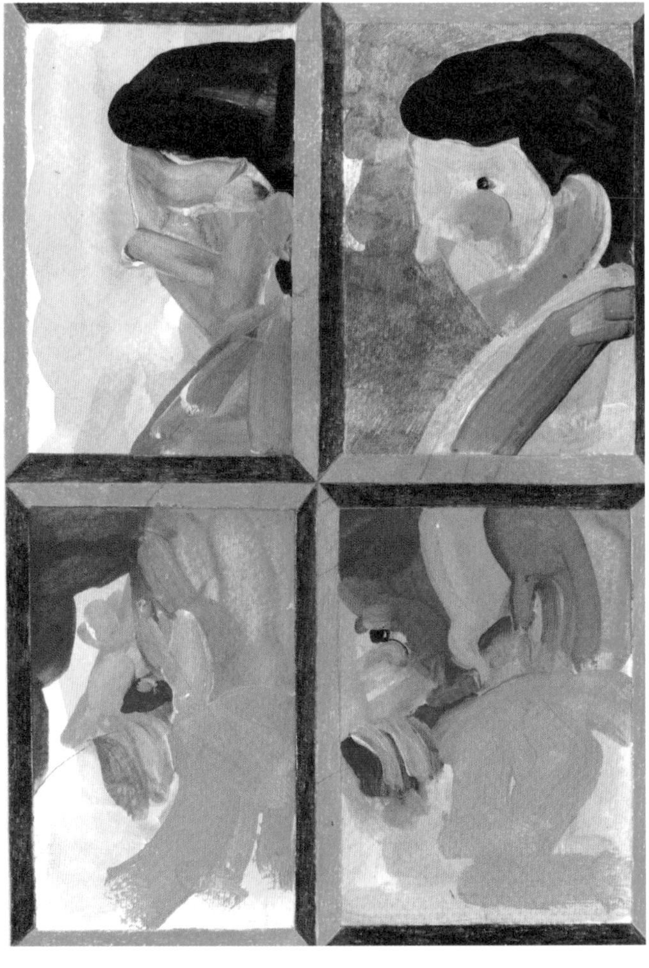

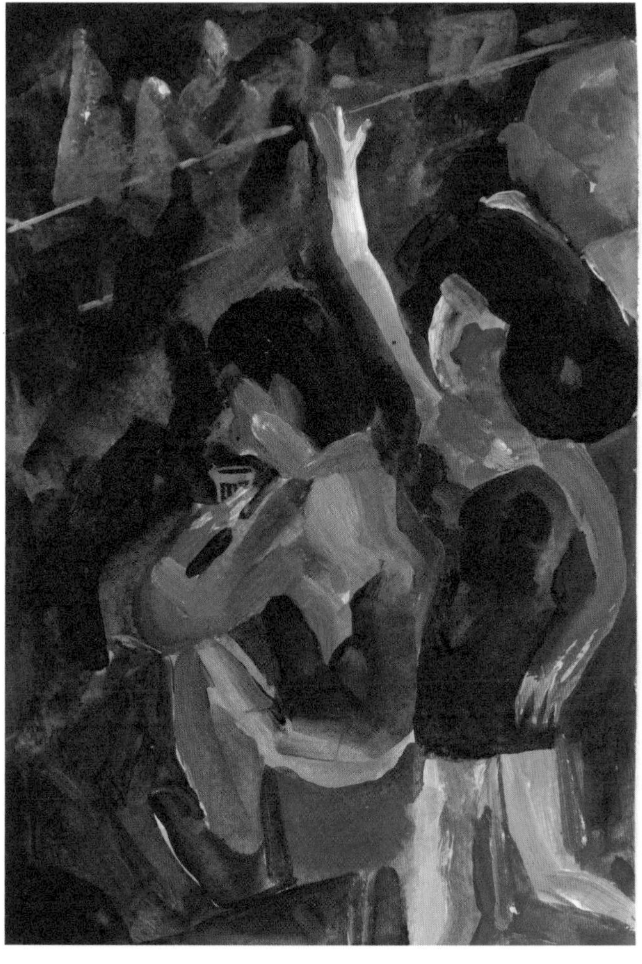

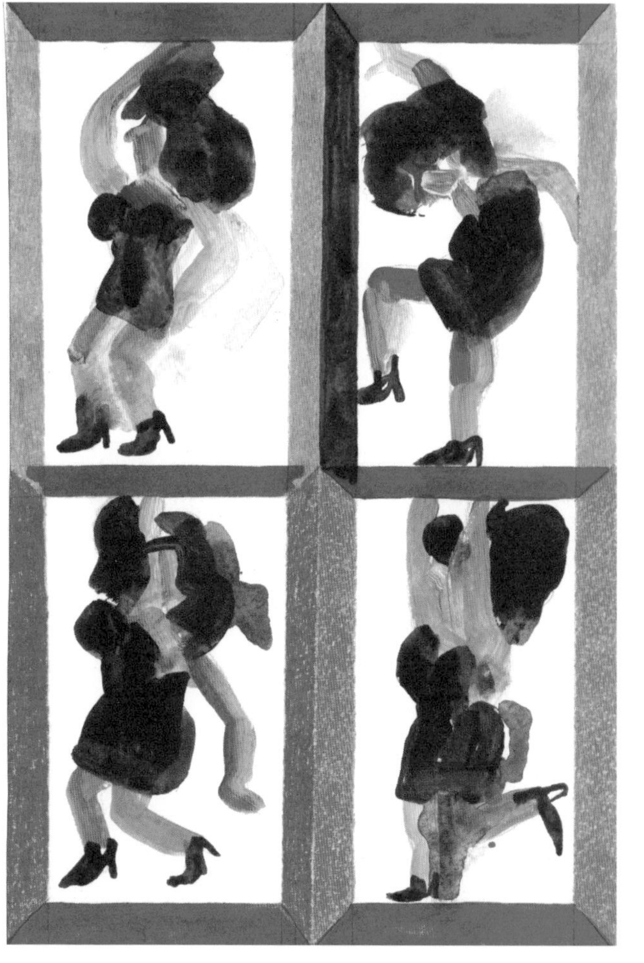

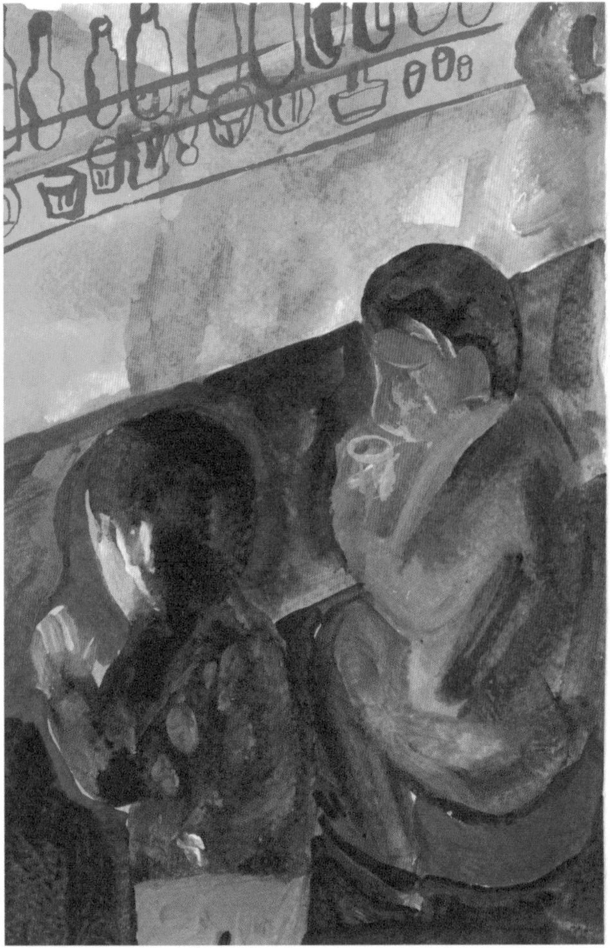
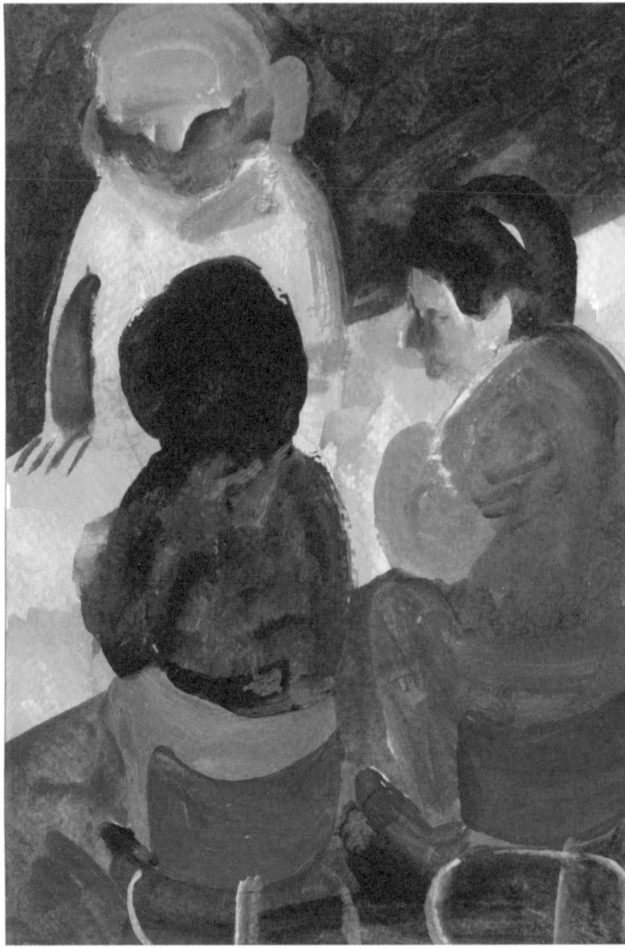

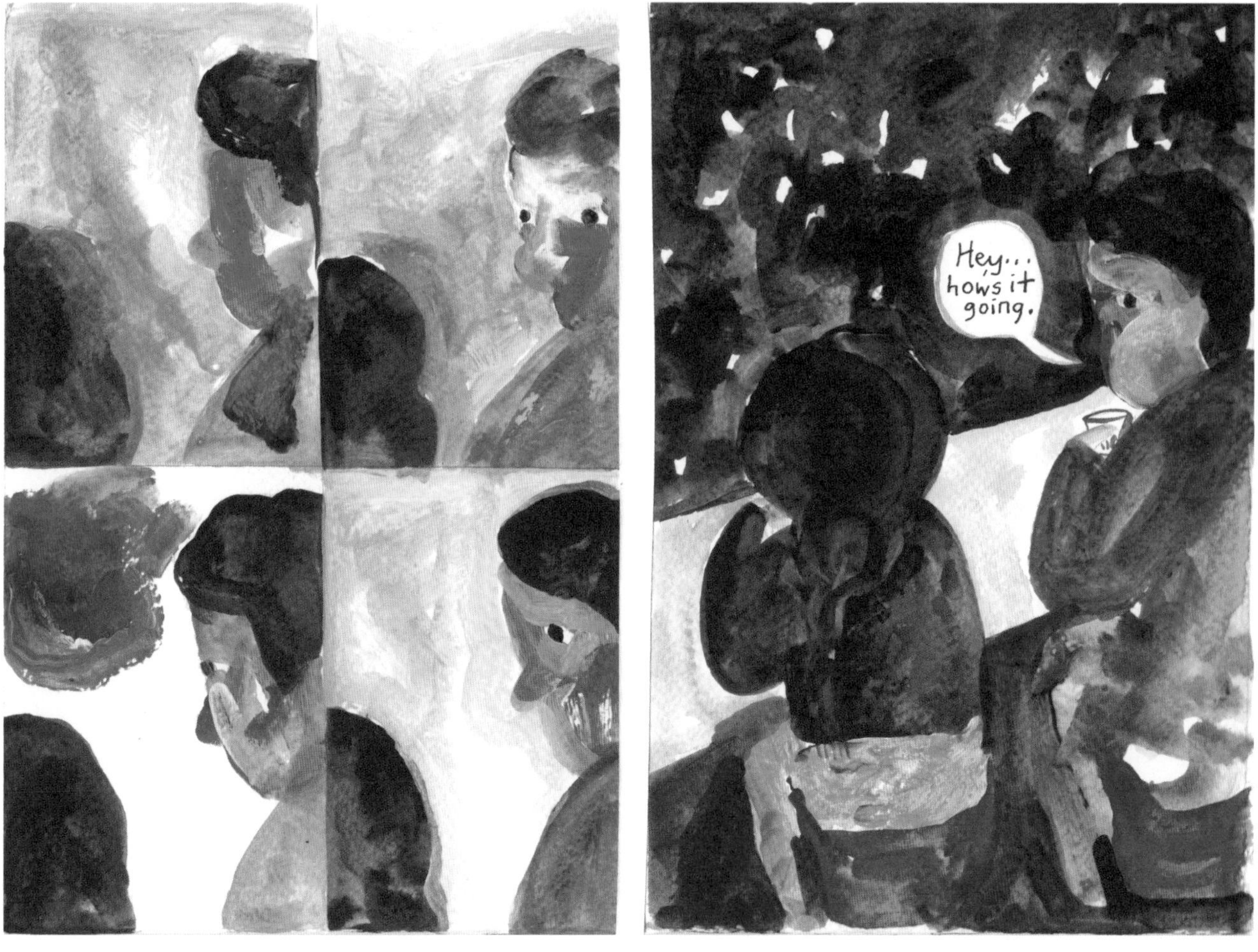
Hey... hows it going.

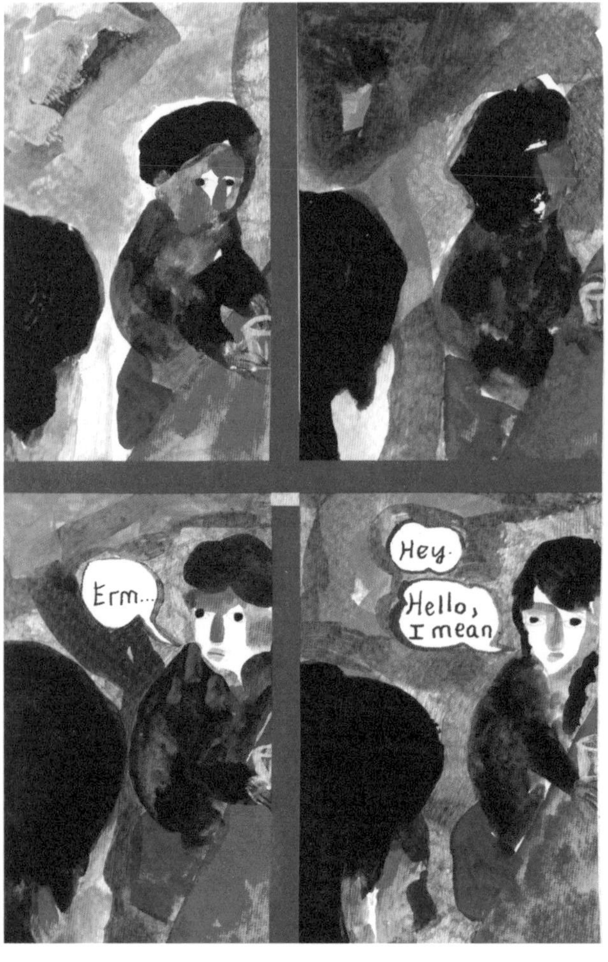
Erm...
Hey.
Hello, I mean

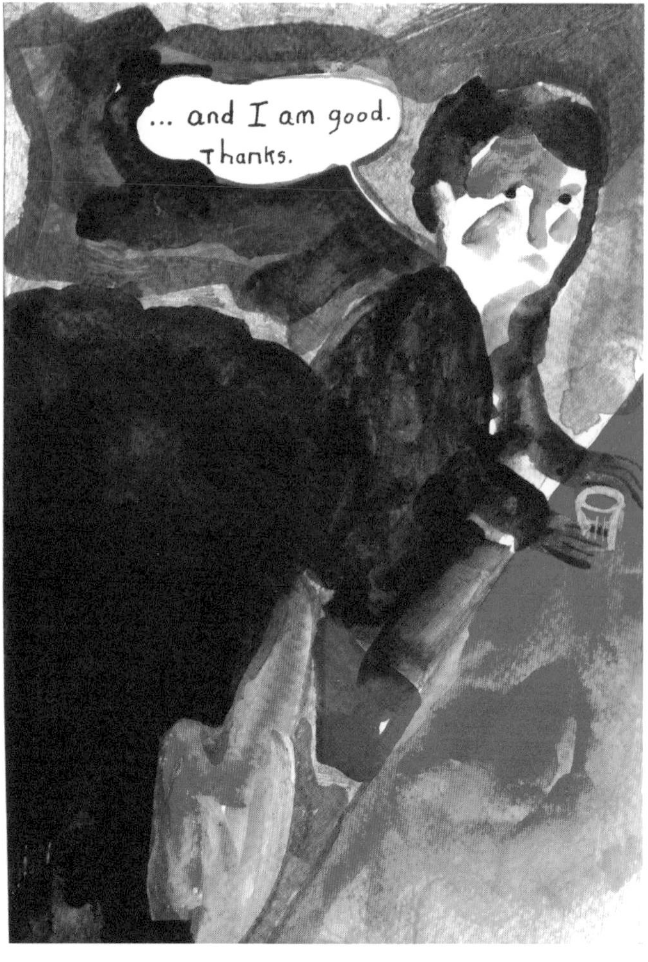
... and I am good. Thanks.

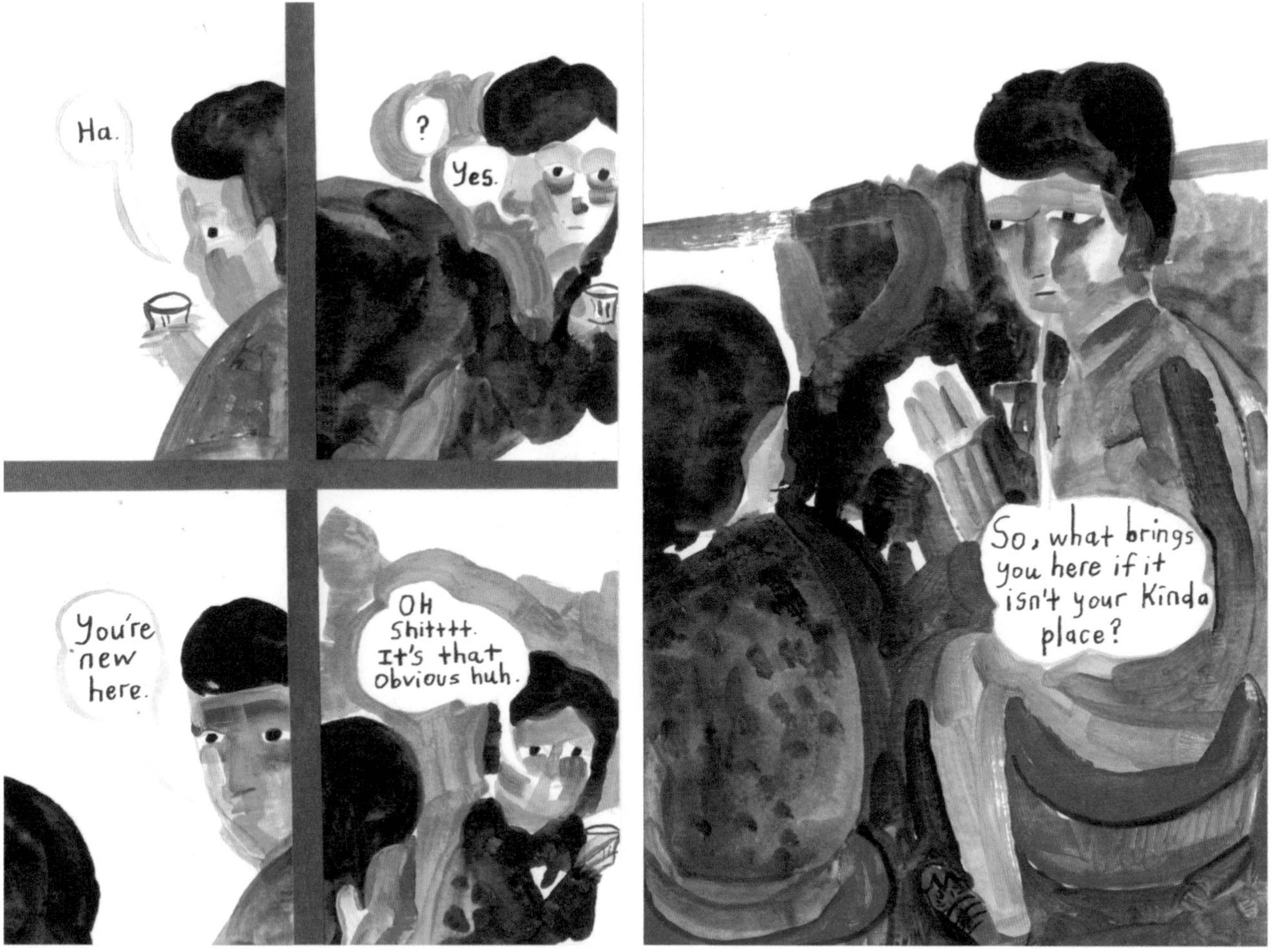
Ha.
?
Yes.
You're new here.
OH Shitttt. It's that obvious huh.
So, what brings you here if it isn't your Kinda place?

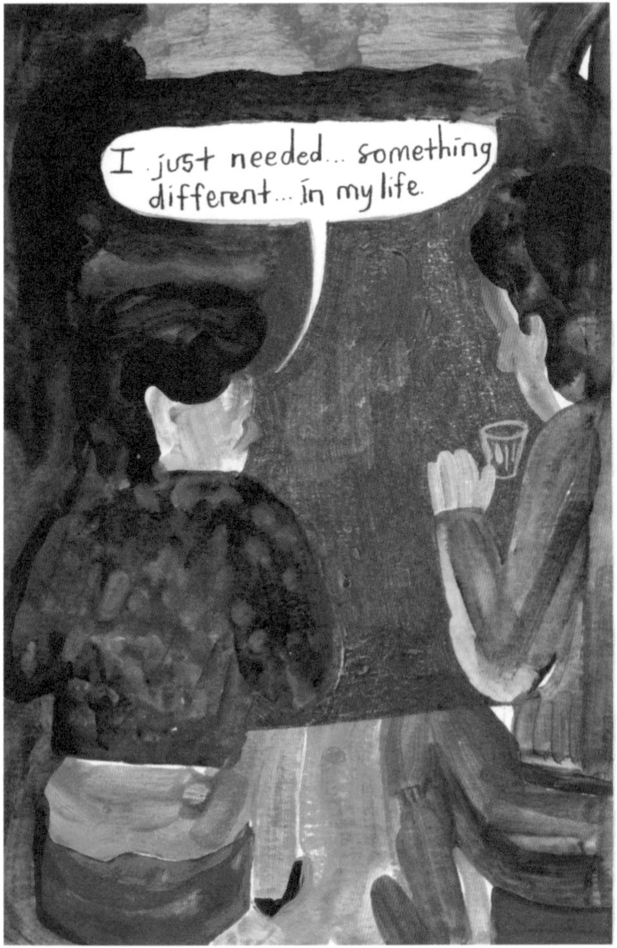
I just needed... something different... in my life.

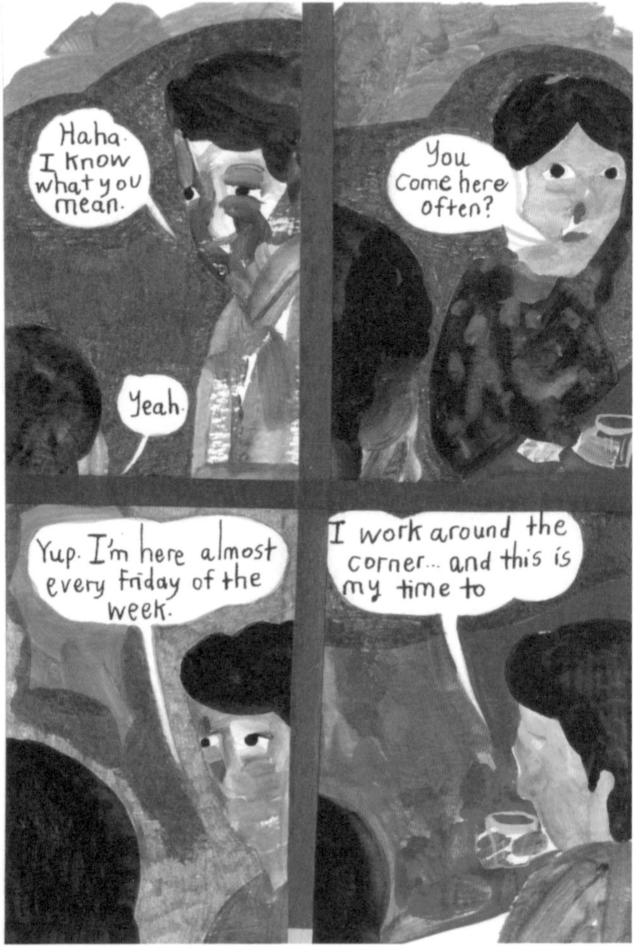
Haha. I know what you mean.
Yeah.
You come here often?
Yup. I'm here almost every friday of the week.
I work around the corner... and this is my time to

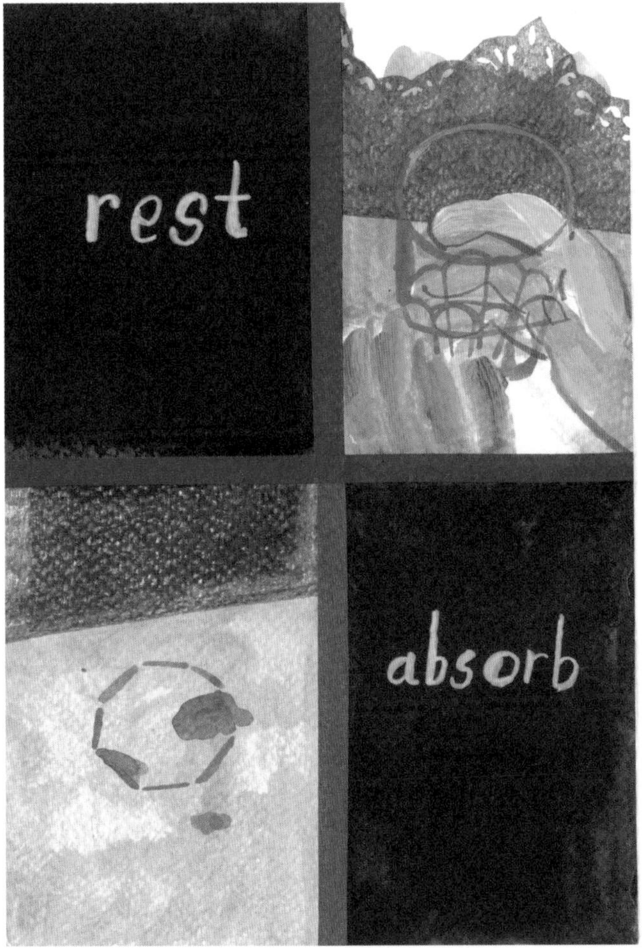
rest
absorb

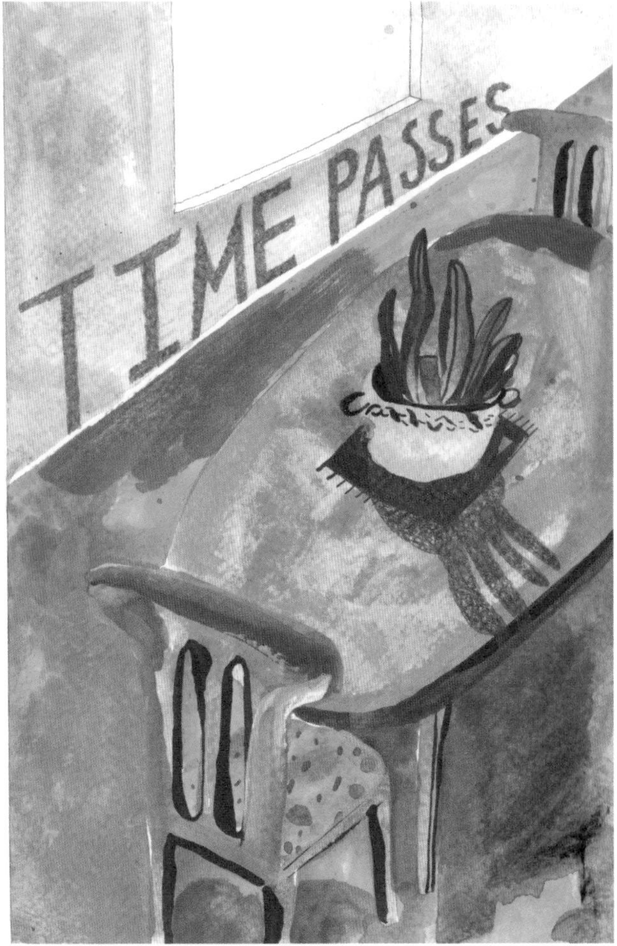
TIME PASSES

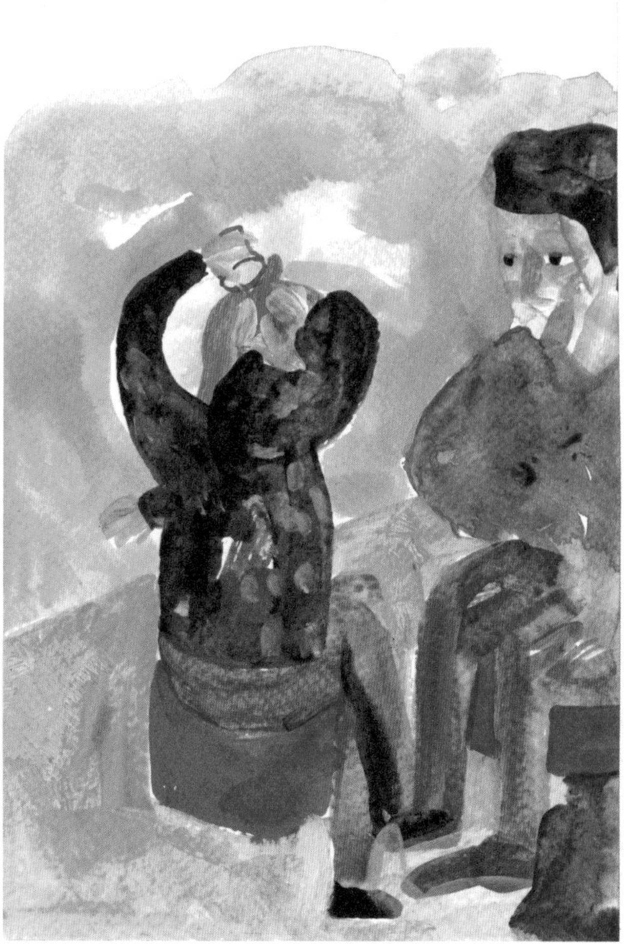

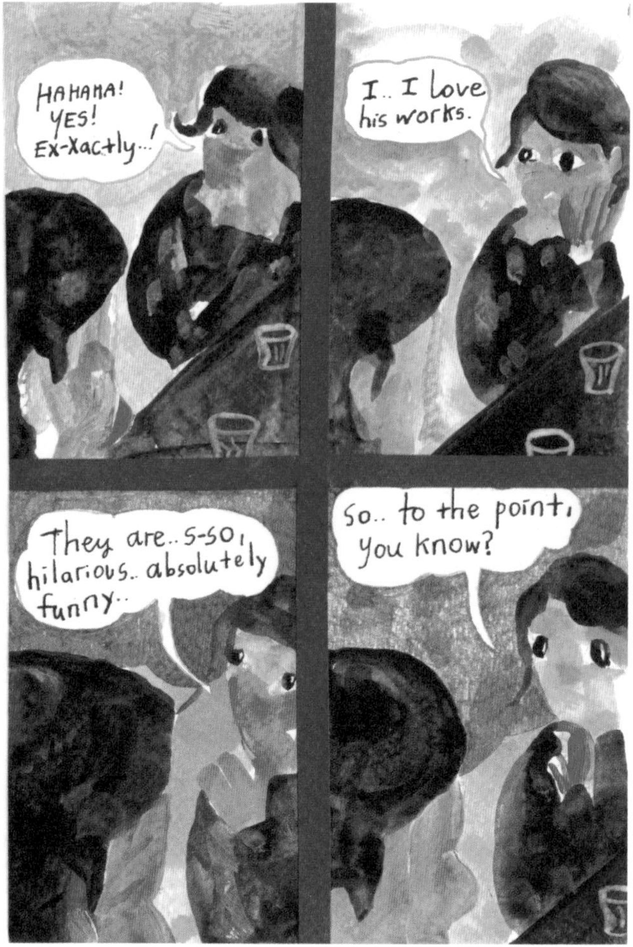
HAHAHA! YES! EX-XACTLY..!
I.. I love his works.
They are.. s-so, hilarious.. absolutely funny..
So.. to the point, you know?

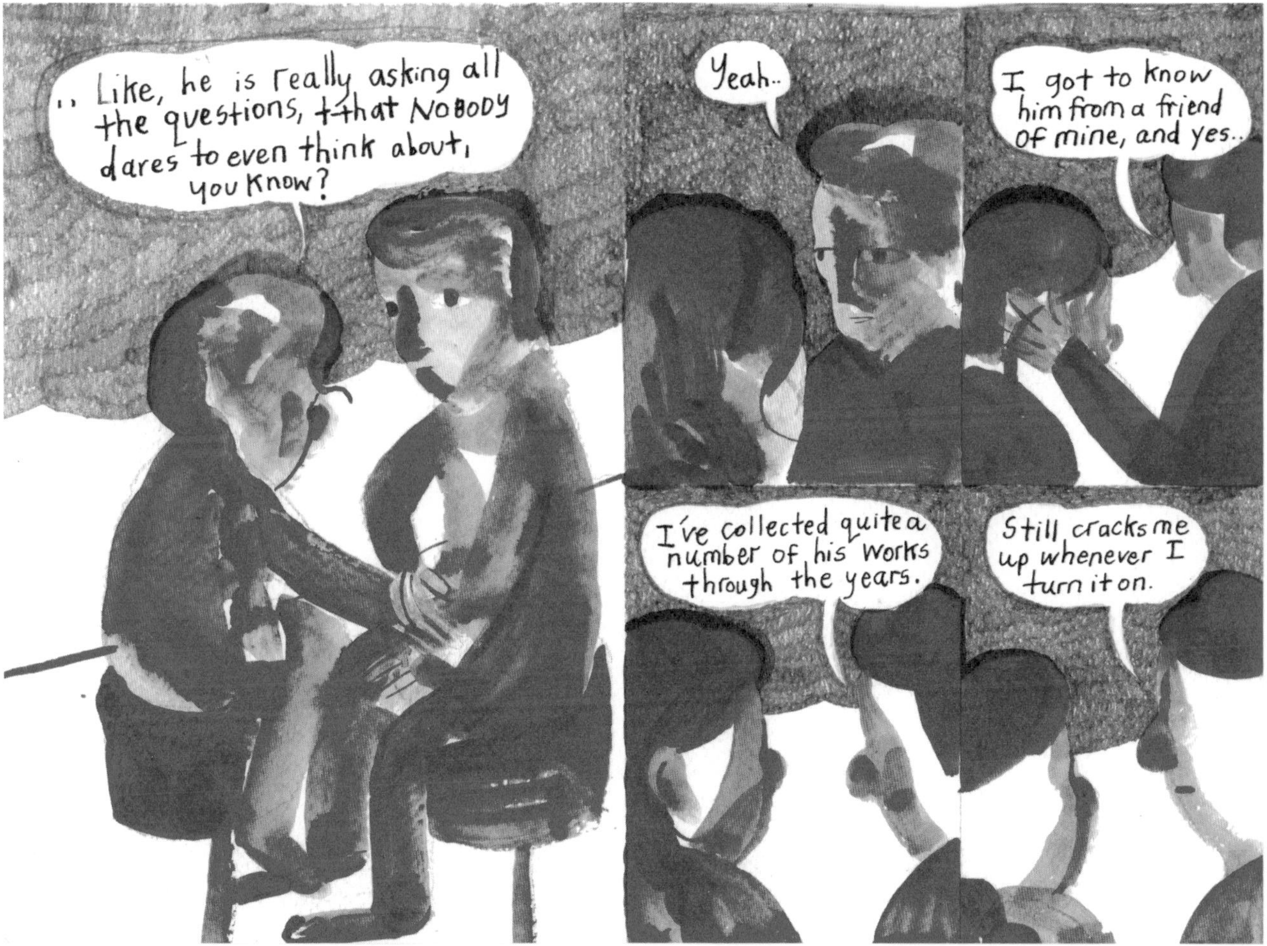
.. Like, he is really asking all the questions, t-that NOBODY dares to even think about, you know?
Yeah..
I got to know him from a friend of mine, and yes..
I've collected quite a number of his works through the years.
Still cracks me up whenever I turn it on.

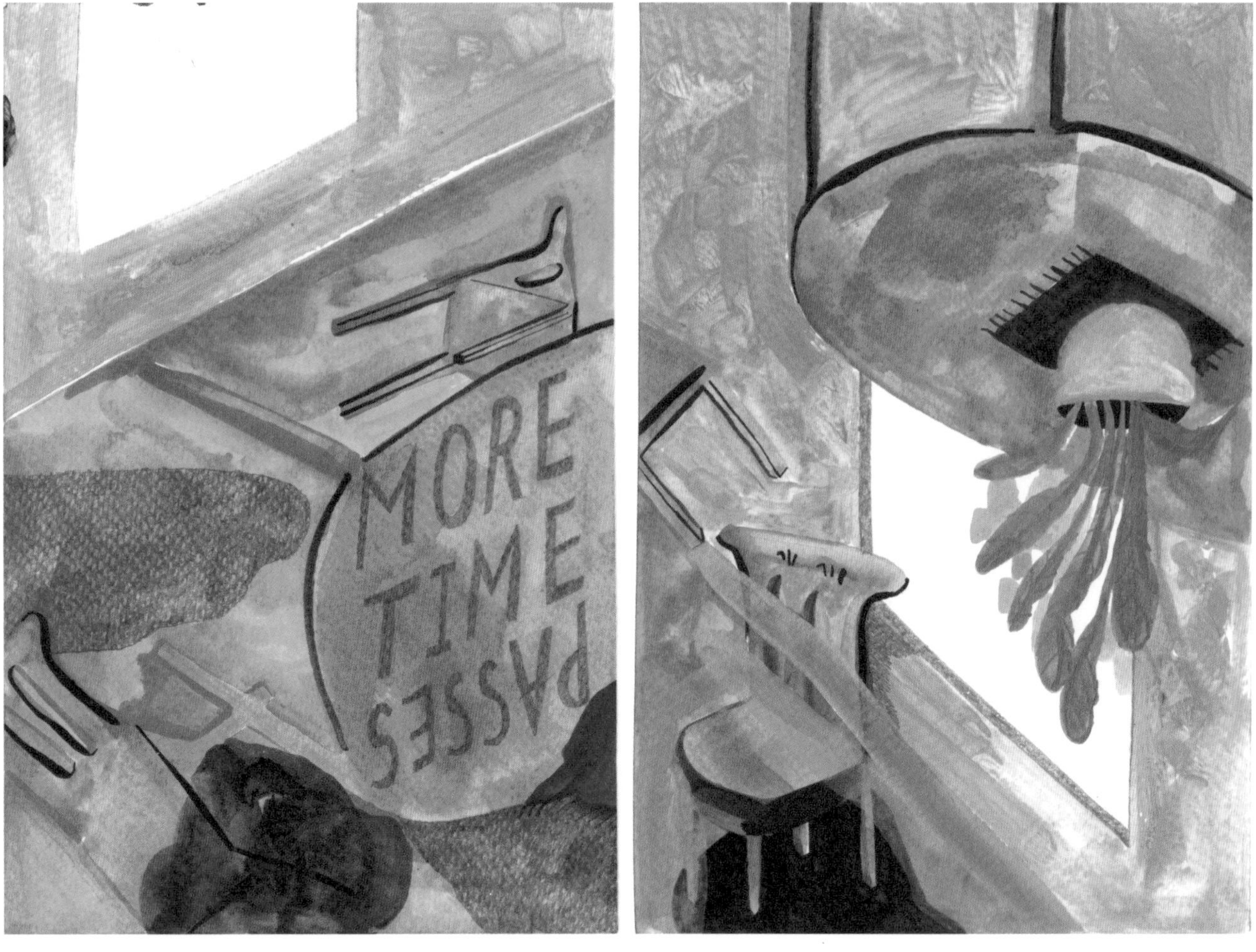
MORE TIME PASSES

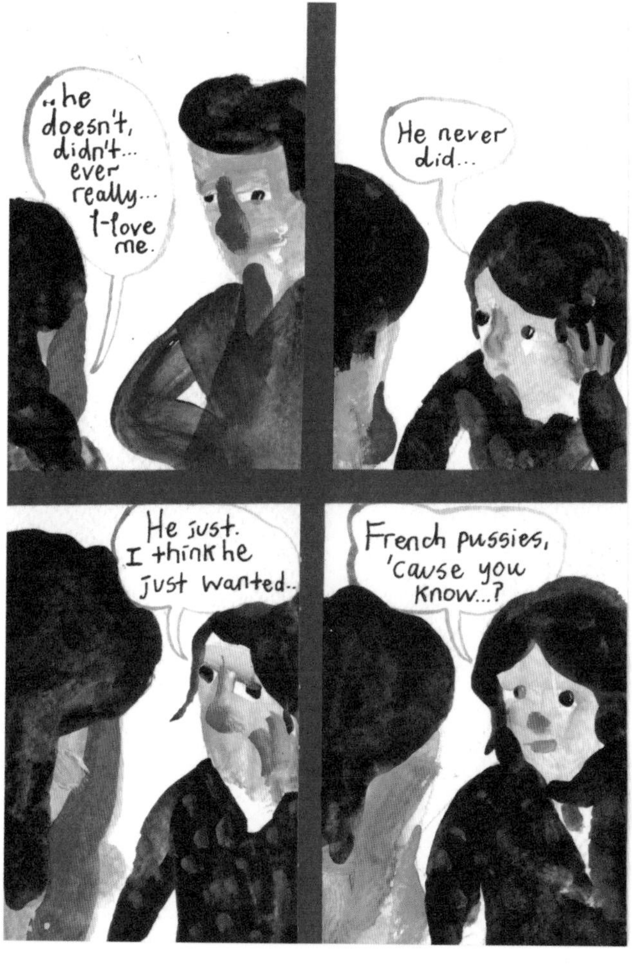
..he doesn't, didn't... ever really... l-love me.
He never did...
He just. I think he just wanted..
French pussies, 'cause you know...?

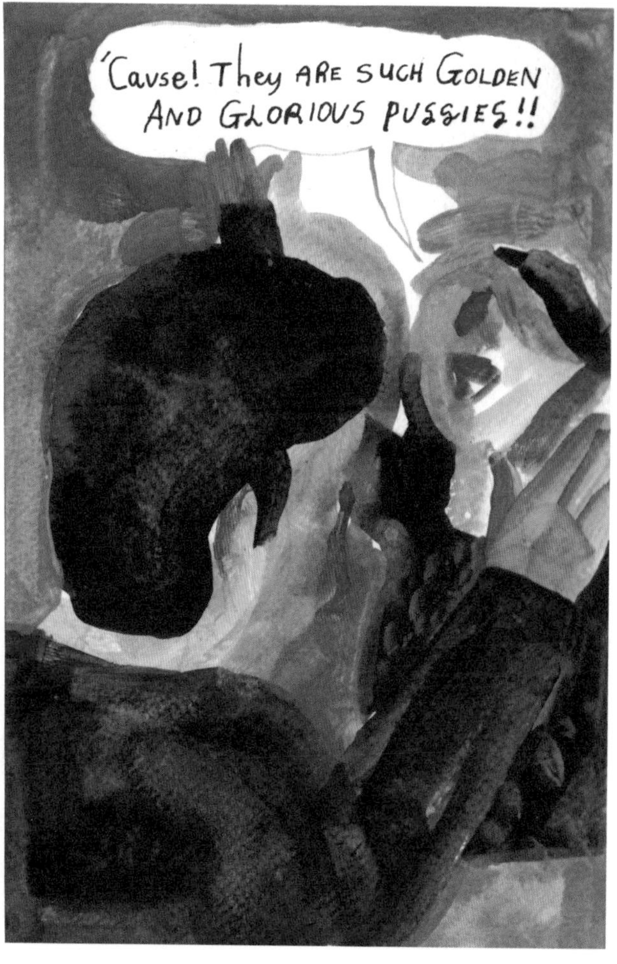
'Cause! They ARE SUCH GOLDEN AND GLORIOUS PUSSIES!!

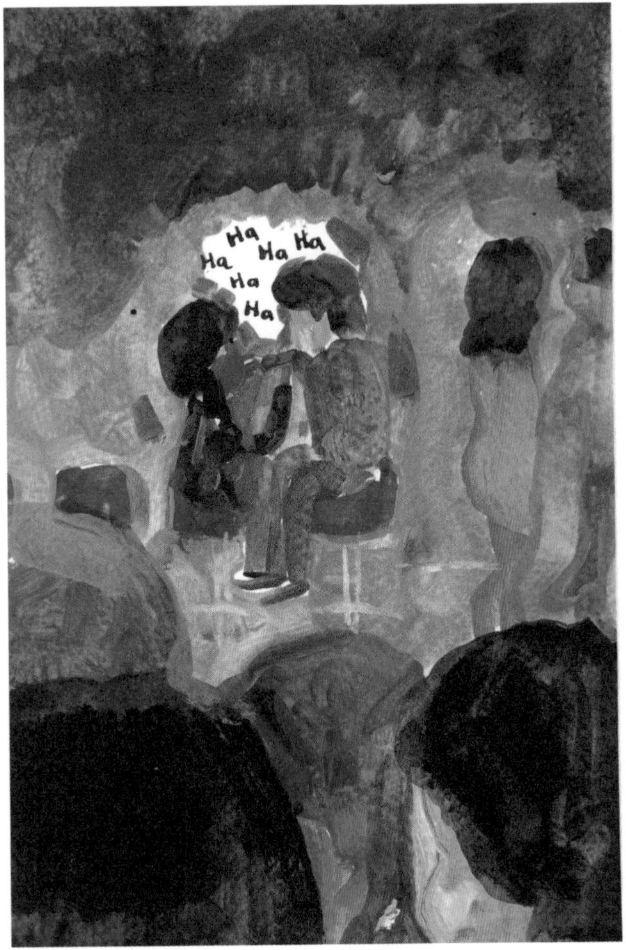
Ha Ha Ha Ha Ha Ha

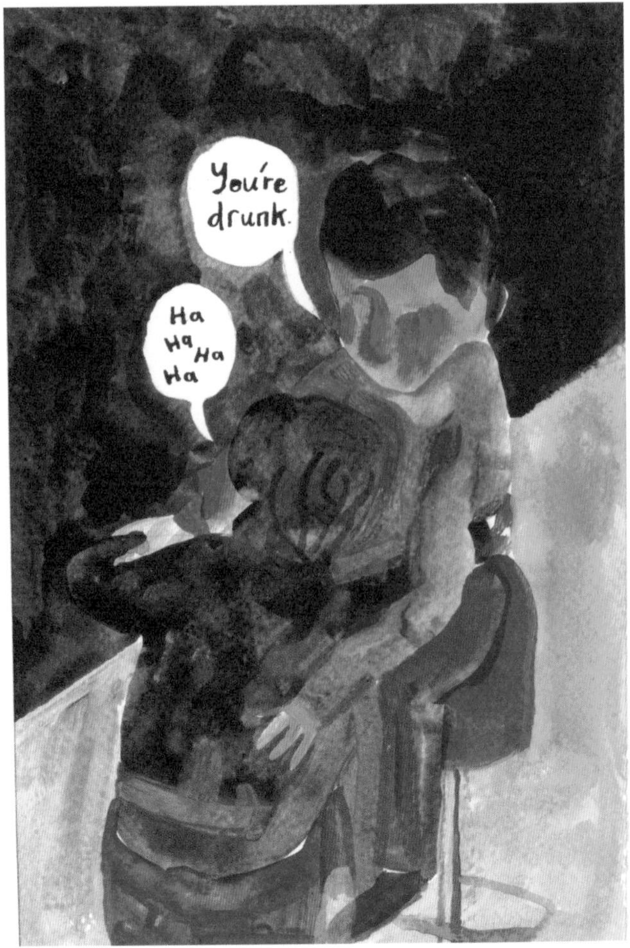
You're drunk.
Ha Ha Ha Ha

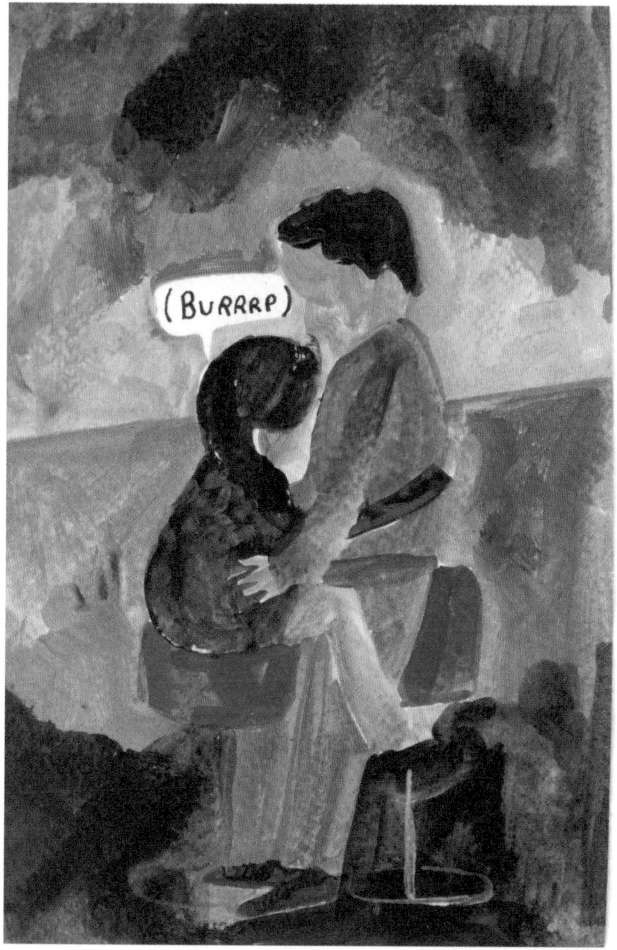
(BURRRP)

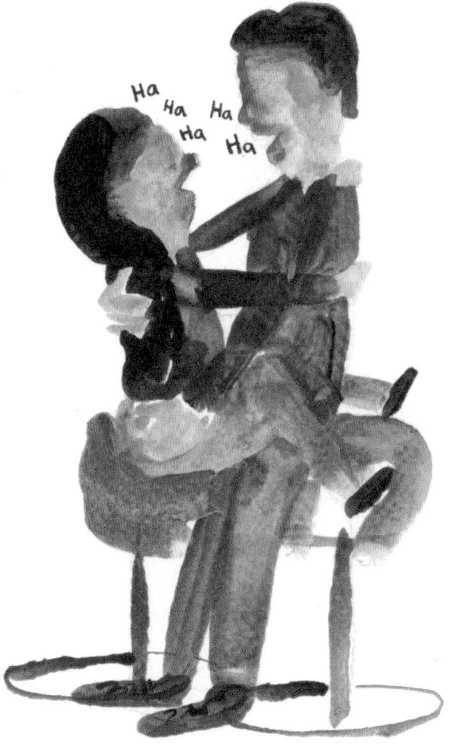
Ha Ha Ha Ha Ha Ha

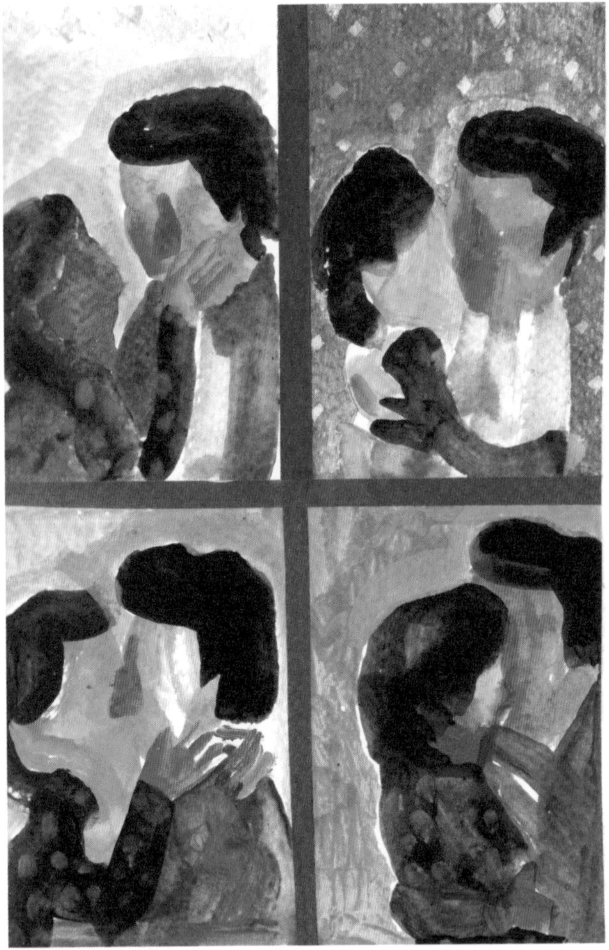

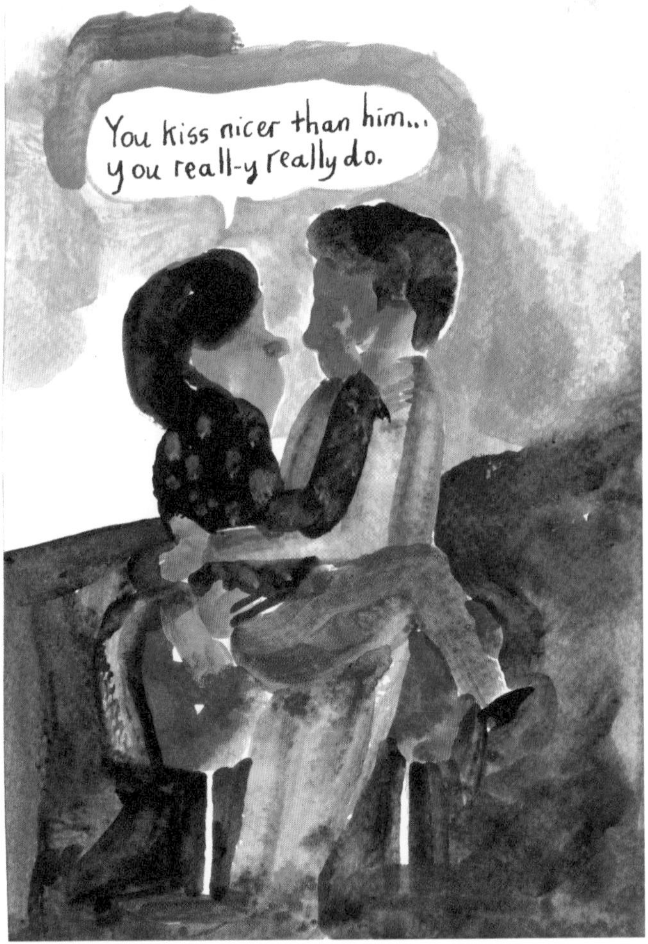
You kiss nicer than him... you reall-y really do.

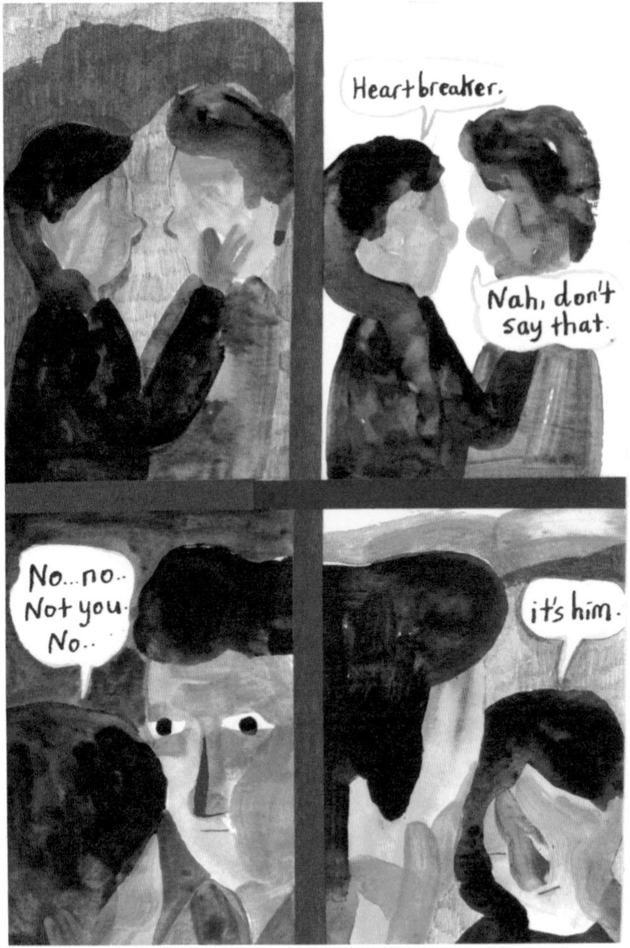
Heartbreaker.
Nah, don't say that.
No...no.. Not you. No..
it's him.
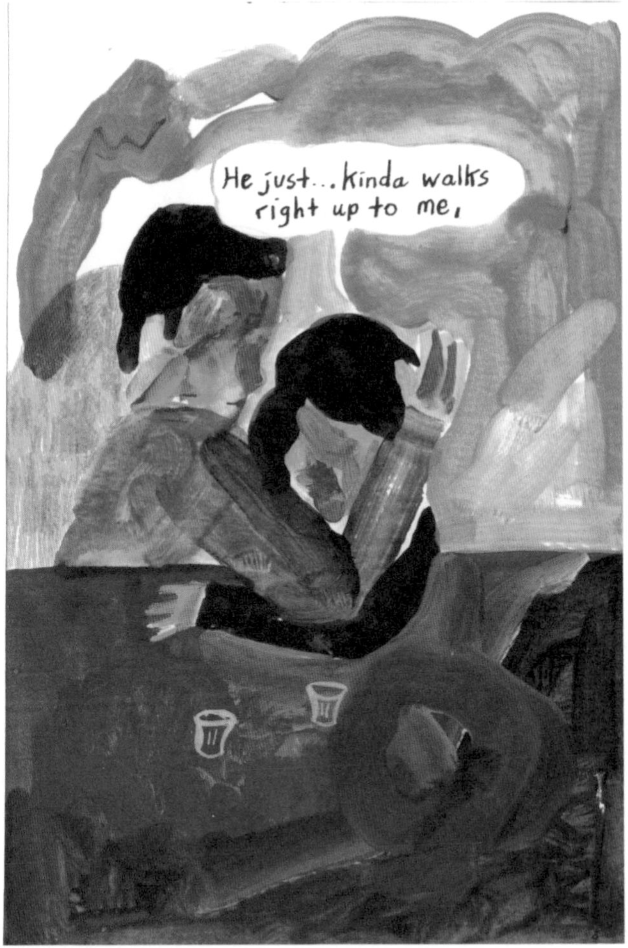
He just...kinda walks right up to me,

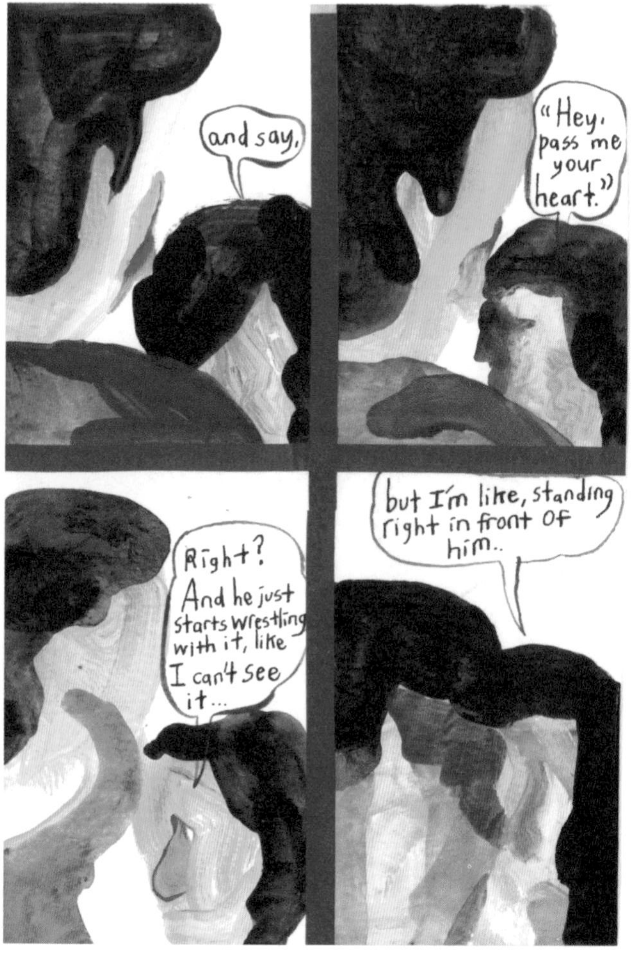
and say,
«Hey, pass me your heart.»
Right? And he just starts wrestling with it, like I can't see it...
but I'm like, standing right in front of him..

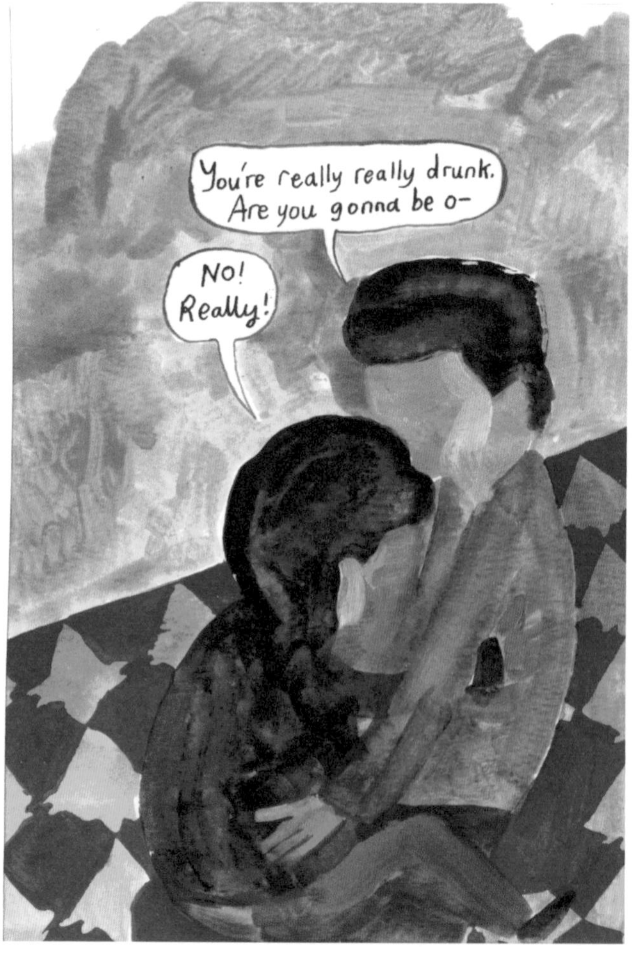
You're really really drunk. Are you gonna be o-
No! Really!

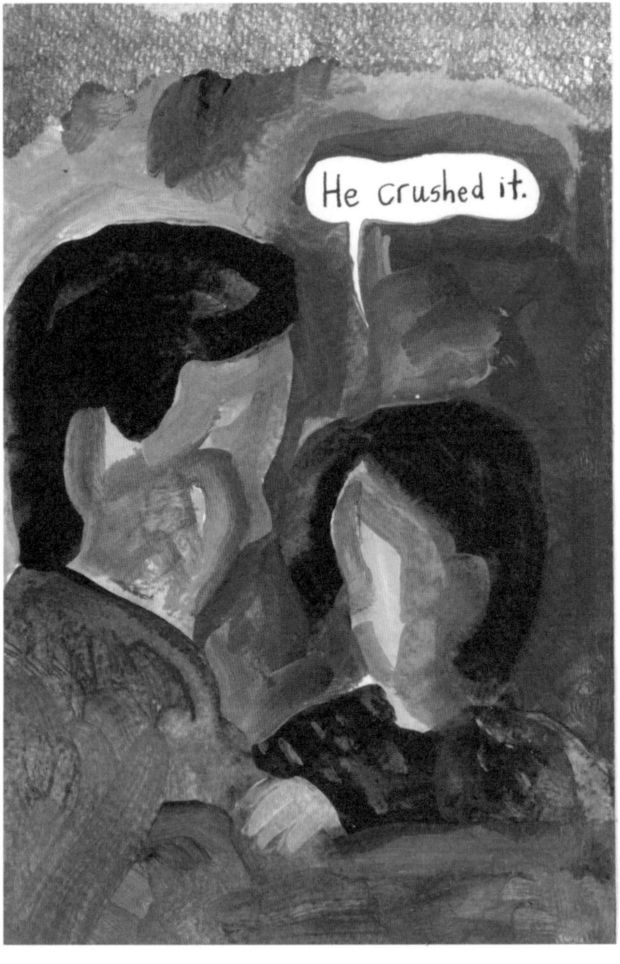
He crushed it.

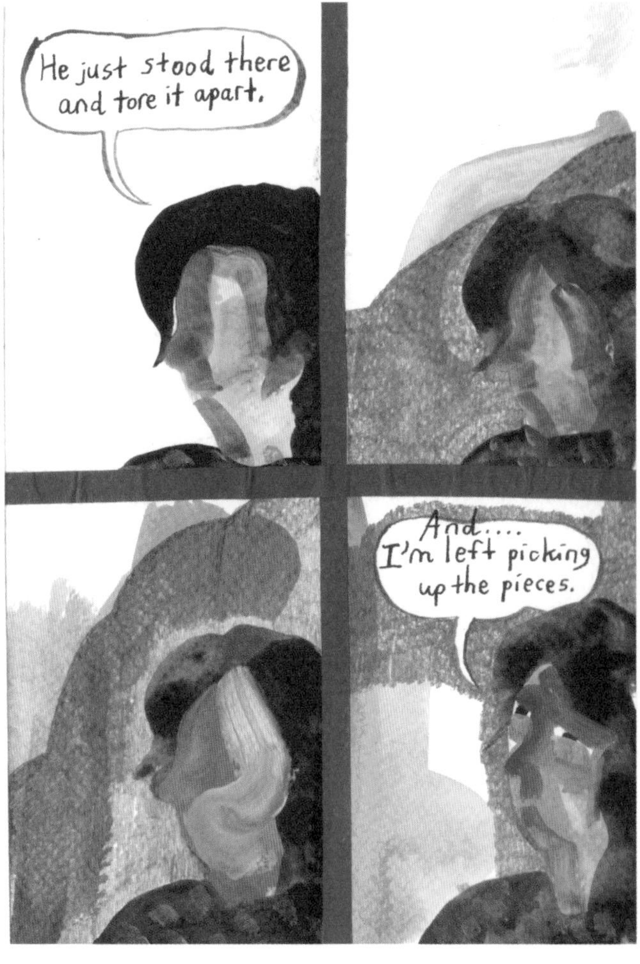
He just stood there and tore it apart.
And....
I'm left picking up the pieces.

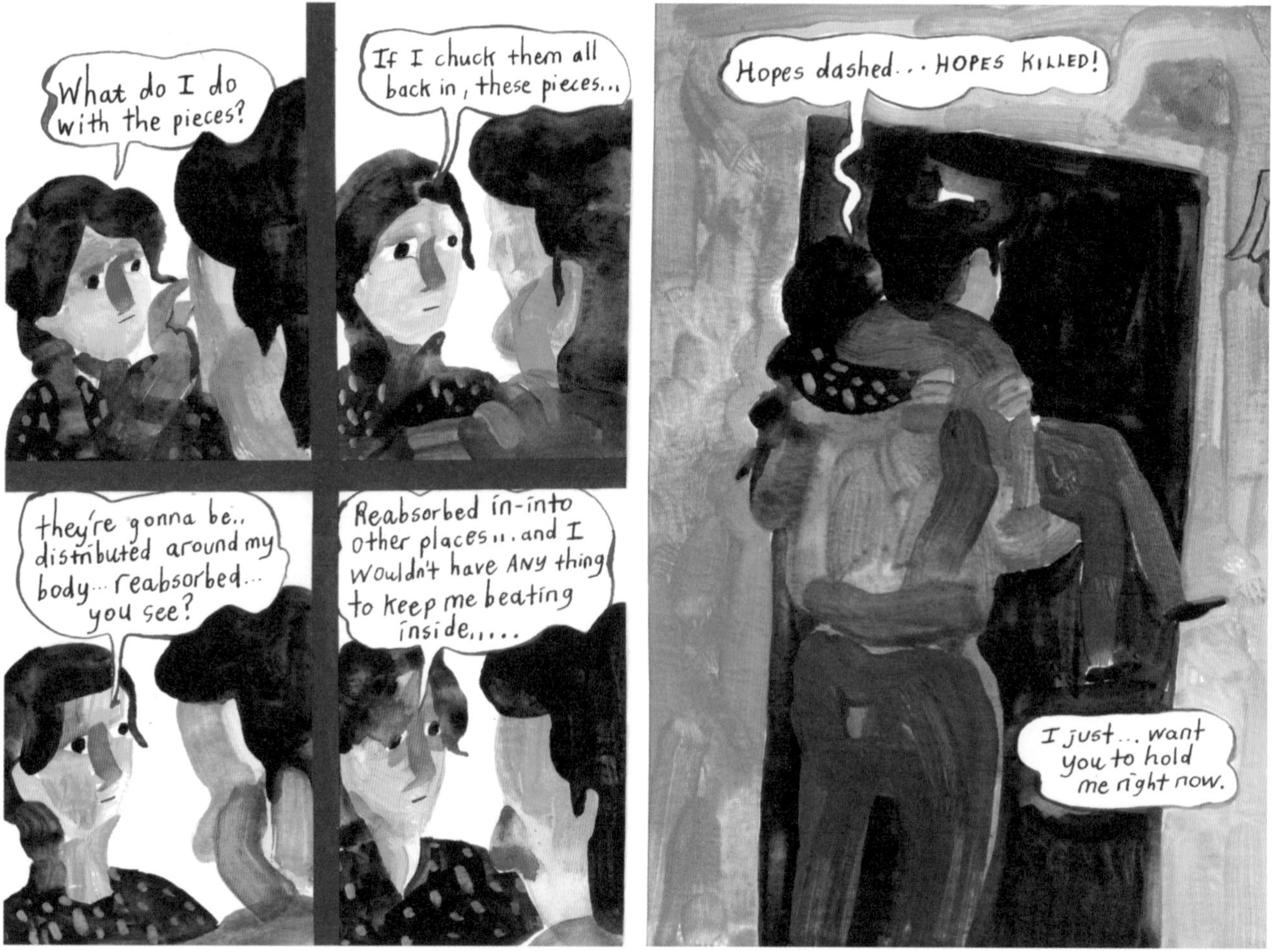
What do I do with the pieces?
If I chuck them all back in, these pieces...
they're gonna be.. distributed around my body... reabsorbed... you see?
Reabsorbed in-into other places.. . and I wouldn't have ANY thing to keep me beating inside.....
Hopes dashed... HOPES KILLED!
I just... want you to hold me right now.

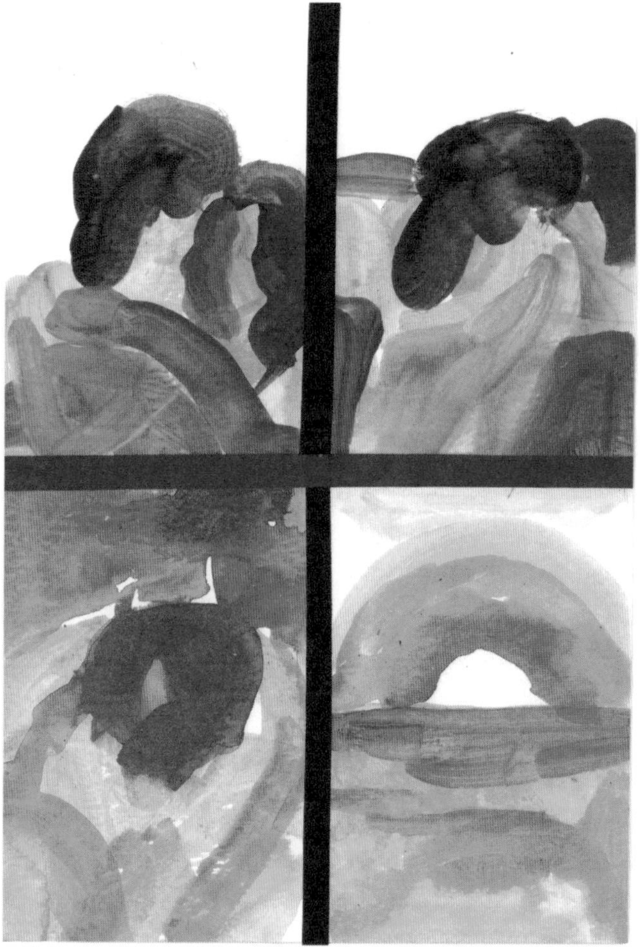
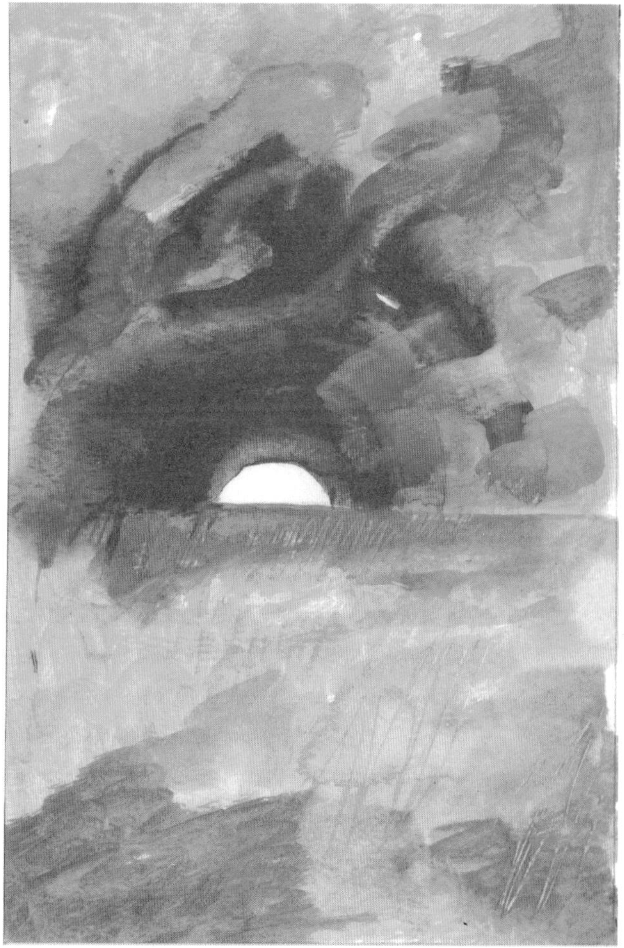

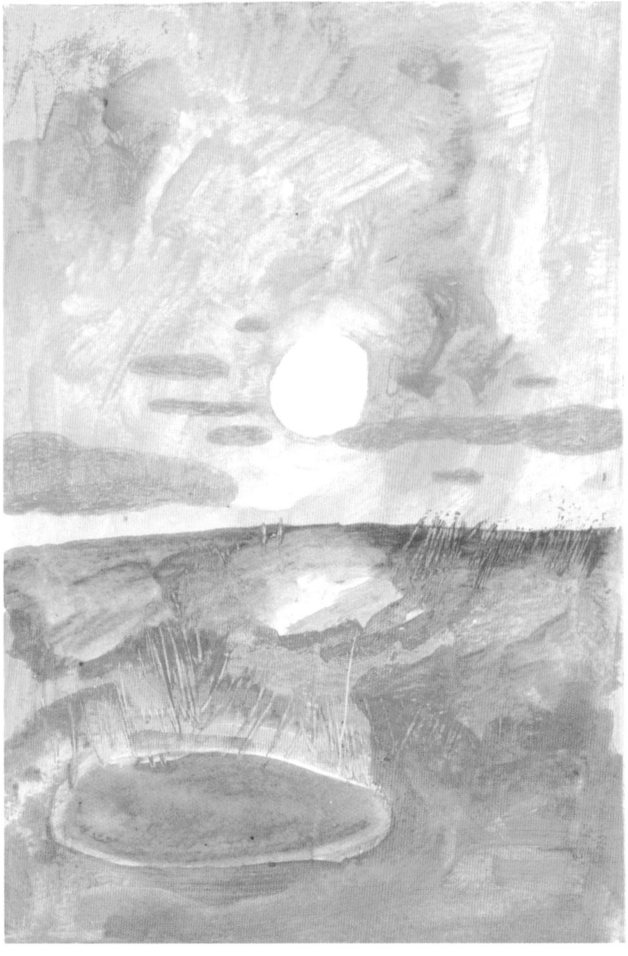

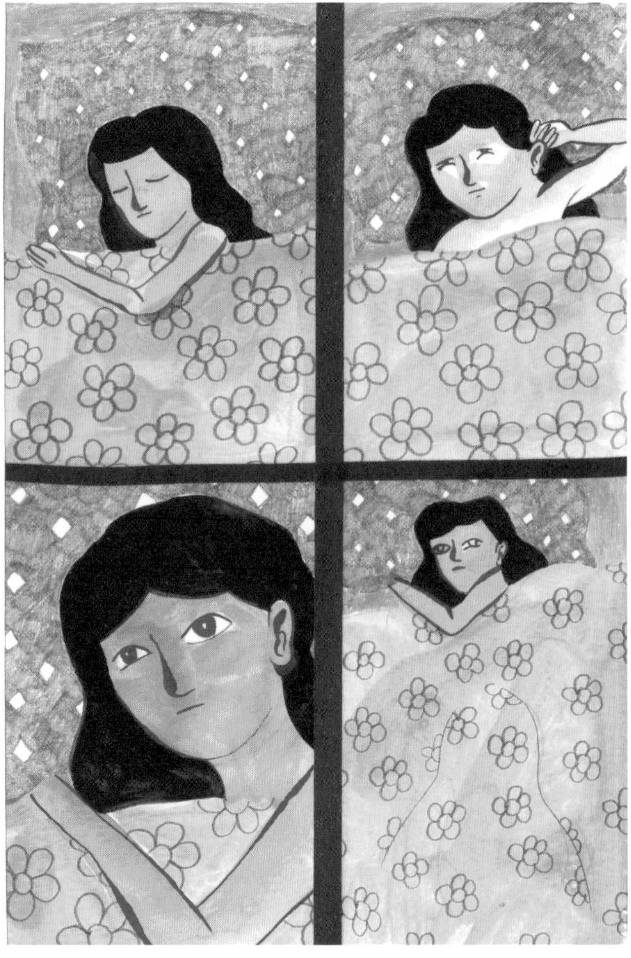

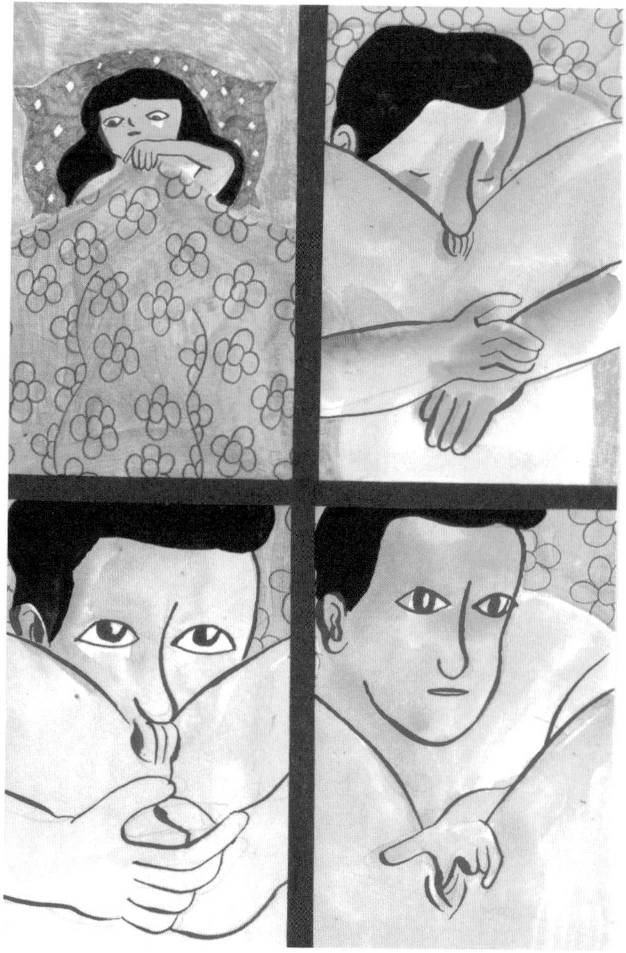

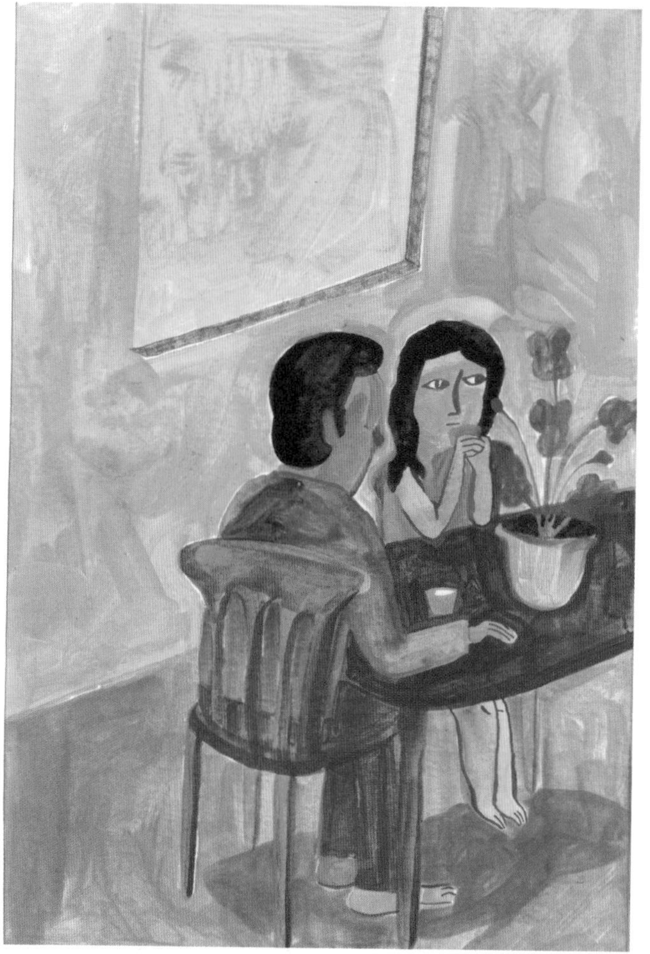